TRADITIONS OF INDEPENDENCE

British Cinema in the Thirties

Edited by Don Macpherson
In collaboration with Paul Willemen

BFI Publishing
1980

British Film Institute, 127 Charing Cross Road, London WC2H 0EA

This book is a tribute to the work of today's independent film makers and to all the members of the Independent Film Makers Association. It is their work and struggles in the Seventies which provided the impetus and the necessity for this critical return to the independent cinema of the Thirties.

Paul Willemen
Don Macpherson

Acknowledgments

The editor would like to express gratitude to the following people who have helped the book in their different ways:

For making unpublished research available: Trevor Ryan, Deke Dusinberre, Bert Hogenkamp, Victoria Wegg-Prosser, Claire Johnston, Annette Kuhn, Paul Marris, Terry Dennett, Jo Spence, Doug Allen, Anne Cottringer, Stuart Macintyre and Simon Hartog.

For discussion and encouragement: the London screenings group of the Independent Film Makers Association; members of The Other Cinema, The Berwick Street Collective, Cinema Action, Liberation Films; Paul Swann, John Ellis, Mark Nash, Francis Mulhern, Alan Fountain, Barry Salt, Ian Christie.

For facilities and aid: Jonathan Lewis and Elizabeth Taylor-Mead of Metropolis Films; Elaine Burrows; Jeremy Boulton; the National Film Archive; Gillian Hartnoll and staff of the BFI's Library Services; Stanley Forman of ETV; Nick Wetton of the Marx Memorial Library; Neville Higson of the Brynmor Jones Library, University of Hull; Lynda Myles of the Edinburgh Film Festival; H. J. Marshall of the Centre for Soviet and East European Studies, University of Southern Illinois.

For their collaboration and permission to use material: Ralph Bond, Ivor Montagu, Basil Wright, Thorold Dickinson, Jo Spence, *Sight and Sound, Film and TV Technician* (Roy Lockett), *Morning Star,* Frank Cass & Co. Ltd., Victor Gollancz Ltd., Mrs Grierson (Sparkman, Dale & Hood, Solicitors), Oswell Blakeston.

In some instances, regrettably, we were unable to trace the legal copyright owners of articles published in the Thirties in magazines now long defunct. We apologise in advance for any omissions in this respect and we undertake to make any reasonable adjustments in any revised edition of this collection.

Special thanks to Claire Johnston, Marc Karlin, Mick Eaton, Ian Potts, Peter Wyeth and Jill Pack.

The original essays in this book were written in 1978, and represent the views of their authors at that time.

Contents

Part IV: Avant-garde/Art/Criticism

Cover: Chamberlain as mannequin, from *Peace and Plenty* (1939)

Presentation

Paul Willemen

The notion of a critical return to the Thirties rather than a celebratory one, as most previous such returns have been, requires a few explanatory and cautionary remarks. Official film culture has enshrined the documentary movement as the highpoint of the British cinema. This movement has been identified with the name of Grierson and both have now achieved the status of holy cows. Moreover, post-war 'independents' and television documentarists have consistently invoked the glorious Grierson era in defence of their own aspirations and as an argument in favour of the setting up of state-funded film and TV practices which would shield individual artists from the grosser forms of market pressures. Consequently, criticism of the documentary movement and of the Griersonian ideology runs the risk of being regarded, not only as heresy, but as an attack on great artists and film makers who oppose the industry's monopolies. In fact, the basis for the critique proposed in this book is both less direct and more fundamental than such fears could suggest.

This critique has been made possible by the work of theorists and film makers since the late Sixties, a history of which the founding of the Independent Film Makers Association in 1974 and especially its first conference in May 1976 constitute the watershed. In its 1976 platform paper, the IFA Organising Committee proposed to define independence, not in terms of economic dependency, but in terms of a cinematic practice that would help bring about changes by opposing the dominant forms of production and the established circulation of films as luxury consumer goods with the types of marketing, publicity and journalistic promotion that such a system requires and imposes. Although it was a proposed BBC programme on independent cinema which, through its cavalier and autocratic treatment of the film makers involved (Aubrey Singer, Director of Programming for BBC-2: 'I'm not having that kind of film on *my* television'), sparked off the formation of the IFA, the impetus for the work within and by it derived from an involvement with cinematic practices.

Existing uses of the term independence, meaning either independence of state funding (as in 'Independent' TV) or independence of the duopoly controlling film exhibition (as in the Association of 'Independent' Producers), were criticised as being inadequate because solely founded on narrow economic considerations, or, worse, as misleading. The IFA proposed to define independence as an oppositional practice involving an opposition to the straitjacket imposed on film making by the profit motive and the

1

ideologies that justify, legitimate or simply fail to engage with the capitalist organisation of this cultural sector. As the Organising Committee's discussion paper, *Independent Film Making in the 70s,* adopted unanimously by the May 1976 conference, put it: 'What we are all averse to is artistic and political delimitation big capital invariably tends to impose. It imposes this control on two counts: the first is the short-term aim of making unchallenging films to attract large audiences immediately, thereby attracting large and swift profits. The second, closely connected, count is to contribute to the reproduction of this ideology that helps maintain the status quo—a status quo which of course includes the concentration of big capital in the same hands. Set against this ideology are the films of IFA members, many of whom see their work as aesthetically and politically innovatory in form and content. Thus we have become independent in the sense that we are "absent". We are absent because what we have made present in our work has been systematically censored by the established, productive and critical forces. Because our opposition to these forces stems from a sense of absence, it is an opposition which embraces many styles of film making. But these styles have one thing in common: they extend the language of film by confronting the established forces that so far have stifled all development in British film making. Our work together forms an aesthetic and political struggle in the field of cinema. (. . .) We have to remain independent of the need to make profits in order to have real artistic independence. Whilst constantly fighting for access to more funds and equipment for its members, the IFA must also defend and develop this political independence and aesthetic independence. For it is in this respect that the work of the IFA members is particularly important, and it is in this respect that we try to use the term "independent" meaningfully.'

By the same token, new sets of questions emerged more clearly and more urgently. The main one concerned the relation between independent cinema–TV and the state, at present and in the foreseeable future the single most important source of funds for such independent practices. These developments produced two reasons for 'returning' to the Thirties. First, as happens with any new movement, the IFA embarked on a search for its precursors and found them in the Thirties, the only time when film makers had presented an organised challenge to the dominant prejudices of the industry in directly political and ideological terms as well as in economic ones. Secondly, the Thirties provided a prime example of a state-funded sector of film making in the GPO and Empire Marketing Board Film Units. However, this renewed attention to the documentary movement, from a different perspective than had been adopted by established apologists for it, also produced some unexpected results. One of the consequences of the re-examination of the Grierson myth was that the GPO and EMB Film Units could best be understood as the—successful, as it turned out—attempt by a particularly reactionary state apparatus to integrate, use and thus defuse the considerable oppositional energy that had fuelled independent cinema in the wake of the General Strike and the acute economic and political crises that shook British capitalism in the inter-war period. As Francis Mulhern put it in his recent book *The Moment of Scrutiny*: 'The economic and social developments of the period led directly to the transformation, or effective creation, of modern Britain's most powerful cultural media, and, at the same time, undermined the habits and assumptions of the established humanistic culture, casting it into confusion and self-doubt.'

Griersonism can be seen as the state's answer to these developments, refurbishing the 'established humanistic culture' through a new, powerful medium under the benevolent but watchful eye of the civil service. The Griersonian brand of humanism fitted the bill extremely well with its appeal to all 'responsible citizens', reminding them of their 'civic duty' to inform themselves about 'their' society in order to play to the full their role as 'voters'. In the process, of course, any explicit notion of class conflict was abandoned and replaced by a demand that the state, presented as the democratically elected representatives of the people, be trusted to remedy social ills. However, one positive aspect of Griersonism is that it helped produce films that were useful in a different although somewhat marginal and ambivalent struggle: the fight to establish cinema as the Seventh Art. It is this aspect of the documentary movement which, although inextricably linked with its political-ideological function, has been singled out by official film culture and which has settled Griersonian cinema into the place of honour it still occupies today.

The complexity of this development is outlined in the articles by Claire Johnston and Annette Kuhn included in this book. However, the main focus of this book is on the many different practices which Griersonian cinema was called upon to block and contain. As Don Macpherson points out in his introduction, the reason for such a different focus is not to rescue exemplary masterpieces of independent cinema which official film culture somehow repressed, although now, with hindsight, it has become clear that the most productive examples of independent cinema were indeed achieved outside of Grierson's ambit (*Peace and Plenty* and *Hell Unlimited*). Moreover, as the IFA Organising Committee noted in its 1976 paper, the practice of film makers such as Ivor Montagu, Sidney Cole and Ralph Bond constituted 'an important beginning of a struggle for an independent cinema conceived not simply in economic terms but also in terms of the necessity for seeing it in relation to a broader social struggle; they challenged the static situation in which films were simply part of leisure and consumption in capitalist society by setting up different relationships between audiences and films as well as different production relationships, establishing film activity as part of a struggle in ideology' (even if the notions of ideology current in the 1930s were somewhat limited and at times even counterproductive).

So, although the Thirties offered examples of film making practices still relevant and productive in the Seventies (and which will no doubt continue to be so in the Eighties), the aim of this book is not to create a new pantheon, but to try to provide the material for an understanding of the dynamics of a complex situation. It is not a question of setting up two opposed camps: Grierson vs. the rest. On the contrary, the problem resides in the intimate links between the state-funded 'independent' sector promoted by Grierson and the civil servants on the one hand, and the intrinsic aspects of the oppositional cinema within and against which this cinema arose on the other. If Griersonism had been totally alien and opposed to all that independent film makers stood for in the Thirties, clearly no amount of state funding could have achieved the containment and defusing operations effected by the GPO and the EMB. The integrity and commitment of the film makers involved is beyond question in that respect. The reason for the success of the operation must be sought elsewhere. The book suggests, among other things, that the explanation can be found in the fact that both Grierson and the independent film makers shared a number of assumptions about the nature of the state as somehow beyond class conflict, as can be seen from the references to the Soviet Union as a fully-fledged Workers' State. Lenin's writings about the state (problematic in themselves, as Fernando Claudin lucidly explains in his book *The Communist Movement—From Comintern to Cominform*), if available at the time, appear not to have made any impact on the left intellectuals who participated in the cultural debates of the Thirties. This in turn raises the questions of Stalinism—not addressed at the time—and the effects of the Comintern on the positions taken up in Britain.

Finally, one point must be stressed. The critical perspective adopted here in no way implies a criticism of the genuine struggles and commitment of the independent film makers of the period. The editors of and contributors to this book are themselves too deeply involved in the independent cinema movement to underestimate the difficulties such an involvement entails. The aim of a critical return to the work and the situation of our predecessors is not to claim superior knowledge, but to examine in order to learn. Imitation or idolatry can serve no useful purpose in the present situation. On the contrary, that would be the most polite way possible of making the work of the likes of Ivor Montagu, Ralph Bond, Paul Rotha and many others politically irrelevant and thus relegating it to the dustbins of history. The realisation that the pioneers were imperfect does not make those who come after them any less imperfect. But by trying to understand the events and the social dynamic addressed by this book, and by trying to learn from that, the contemporary independent film makers' movement may be able to avoid repeating some mistakes (such as the undervaluing of a theory of ideology and of analyses of the state and of institutions) and contribute more effectively to the continuation and proliferation of the 'tradition of independent cinema' founded in the Thirties.

Introduction

Don Macpherson

In the context of an upsurge of independent film making in Britain since the late Sixties, debate has focused more on its American or European aesthetic and political traditions. Attention to British traditions has tended to be regarded as parochial or, worse, as unproductive. While much has been written, for example, on the importance of cultural debates and relations between film makers and the state in the Soviet Union, the only other state-sponsored 'experimental film unit' before the Second World War, John Grierson's GPO Film Unit, has been generally ignored by all but its apologists, with one notable exception: Hillier and Lovell's *Studies in Documentary*, which as the title indicates, avoids the problem of the interrelations between the aesthetics of realism, the state and notions of independence. This book therefore aims to introduce a critical perspective on this dominant British tradition of the 1930s, as well to open up a debate on a 'forgotten' tradition of independent political films from that period and to propose them for consideration in the context of contemporary independent cinema practices in Britain.

Grierson's tradition of documentary film making has until recently been allowed a privileged position in the history of progressive movements in British cinema out of all proportion to its conservative stance. It has constantly been represented as somehow 'essentially British' in a way which almost paralysed any thought of alternative developments. Drawing on the poetic realism of Flaherty and the concern for working people from contemporary Soviet film makers, Grierson forged a state-subsidised propaganda machine under a National Government urging a paternalistic social democratic view of non-conflictive politics under a 'strong' but 'benevolent' state. Combining reformist fervour with an interest in experimental aesthetics, and with a funding structure designed to inaugurate a new political era, the GPO Film Unit produced films 'portraying British life' which created a new realist mythology for a Britain struggling to represent itself to the world as a stable and contented nation.

Grierson's movement consistently held the middle ground of aesthetic innovation and political liberalism during the period, bringing together aesthetes, socially conscious but displaced intellectuals, and technicians, to produce hymns to a much vaunted British golden age of democracy. But Grierson's allegiance to the status quo has marginalised the alternative areas of political and avant-garde cinema in Britain. A key factor in this alternative

5

tradition was the politicisation of the struggle against censorship of Soviet films which had a major ideological impact in Britain as elsewhere in Western Europe. The films which were made in Britain during this time, and which were shown to audiences around the country, marked out an area of an independent cinema combining revolutionary notions of politics and avant-garde aesthetics and problematising realism as an aesthetic strategy. The tension between these and more traditional readings of the films as providing a working-class view of history can be roughly schematised as follows.

1. *A phase of experiment: 1925–29*
In which the London Film Society, founded by Ivor Montagu and others, stimulated interest among the progressive intelligentsia in film as a medium for expressing 'experimental' aesthetic and political views by showing imported and uncensored German and Soviet films to restricted audiences under club conditions.

2. *Crisis and militancy: 1929–33*
During a period of intensive anti-censorship struggles, economic depression and militant communist activity, Workers' Film Societies spread throughout the country, showing Soviet films and newsreels; counter-newsreels were produced by groups of workers and film makers (e.g., *Workers' Topical News*); a small number of films were produced from within the milieu of *Close Up*, the cosmopolitan avant-garde critical journal (e.g., Oswell Blakeston's abstract films, Kenneth Macpherson's *Borderline*) whose editors were also initially on the council of the Federation of Workers Film Societies (FOWFS).

3. *Recovery and transition: 1933–36*
A consolidation of practices led to the formation of small-scale production groups at a local and national level, eventually linked by a national distribution organisation, Kino. This was accompanied by, first, an increased coverage of demonstrations and public events in newsreel style (e.g., *Jubilee 1935*) and the making of agitational films around such issues as starvation and unemployment, including experimental montage films such as *Bread* by members of the Workers' Theatre Movement; secondly, the growth of theoretical work in magazines devoted to avant-garde cinema (*Film Art, New Cinema*), including work by European artists, accompanied by limited film production.

4. *Anti-Fascism: 1936–39*
Increased activity in counter-newsreel coverage of the Spanish Civil War; expanded distribution activities via the Left Book Club circuit; agitational films promoting a political understanding of the National Government's policies prior to war (e.g., Norman McLaren and Helen Biggar's *Hell Unltd.*, Ivor Montagu's *Peace and Plenty*). Avant-garde work diminished in the context of the international anti-fascist struggle, none of which was permissible subject matter for GPO films. When Norman McLaren joined the

6

GPO after making *Hell Unltd.* and a newsreel on the *Defence of Madrid*, he was to make nondescript documentaries on items such as the printing of the London telephone directory and the advantages of cooking by gas; his experimental animation film *Love on the Wing* (1938) was banned by the Minister of Posts as being too 'erotic' and too 'Freudian'.

The articles collected together in this book deal with different aspects of the conditions under which this alternative tradition developed during the 1930s. Annette Kuhn investigates the relationship between the institutional context of the state-sponsored GPO Film Unit and its realist aesthetics. Deke Dusinberre's article outlines an almost completely ignored tradition of avant-garde film making and theory in Britain which necessitates a rethinking of previous accounts of avant-garde activity in Britain. Paul Marris's article explores the uneasy relationship between film makers and left political groups during the 1930s. Trevor Ryan brings together previously unpublished research on the political organisations in the official and unofficial labour movement, their precarious economic position, their institutional conflicts and the struggle to cultivate and maintain their audience. A general overview of the period is given by Claire Johnston. In her wide-ranging article she contextualises the left cultural debates of the 1930s as well as providing a critique of the notion of 'alternative' histories.

The second main section is comprised of a collection of texts from magazines, newspapers, letters and advertisements, mostly unpublished since the 1930s. The texts, grouped in four main thematic areas (Censorship and the Law, Propaganda and Agitation, Avant-Garde and Art Criticism, and Amateur Films), provide a dossier of the legal, political and aesthetic discourses which established a certain conception of 'cinema' in Britain during the period. Ranging through critical reviews, melancholic commentaries, newspaper snippets, clerks' letters, conversation pieces, competition announcements, polemical arguments and 'handy hints', they form a tissue of strands which make up the period. Although the dossier mostly contains what could be described as key texts of the period, much has been included which would normally be described as ephemera. The rationale for inclusion is not only that such pieces are generally reliable indications of the spirit of the time, but also because the book has no pretensions to packaging another forgotten golden moment of cinema to be consumed at leisure. Rather the book attempts to introduce different elements into the present so as to stress the selective and constructed nature of what we call the past. It is not the intention to portray the period as one of subtle intellectual argument, bold aesthetic initiatives and unforgettable films: to have done so would at best have been poetic licence and at worst a falsification of history. But the crucial question is how this alternative tradition has been forgotten—or repressed—while Grierson's tradition occupies pride of place in several history books, and its anniversaries are celebrated as official great moments in cinema. It does of course suit some writers to represent histories as smooth lines of continuity and inevitable successions of events, erasing divergences or opposition from memory. So this book tries to reconstruct the history of cinema in Britain as a terrain of possibilities, whose outcome is not foreclosed.

However, it would be misleading to present a book which claims to have achieved a coherence of the past, or to have remembered events which had somehow been forgotten. Most importantly, the book refuses the kind of recollection which is possible and highly pleasurable when one no longer has the power to make things happen. Instead the book attempts to survey the objective conditions which permitted a so-called movement and the ideologies which nourished it to flourish. It is therefore a problem of seeing the 1930s critically and historically; of finding what transformations those ideologies have *for us*.

There remain only some comments on the history of the book itself. Originally conceived as an accompaniment to debates and films in a season of British cinema at The Other Cinema in London in Spring 1978, the idea of the book changed with the events which led directly up to the closure of The Other Cinema (Exhibition) in December 1977. The irony of editing a book on the strengths and weaknesses of independent cinema during that period was not lost. Several of the issues at stake in the book—conceptions of 'independence', the relationship between 'professionalism' and 'amateurs', the problems of developing a new audience for new kinds of films, and the social and political function of cinema and TV—were being enacted before our eyes and without the benefit of hindsight or editorial distance. Fittingly, in one of the last series of discussions to be held at the cinema, Ivor Montagu and Edgar Anstey, two of the 1930s generation of film makers, debated with an audience the problems of film making and censorship. While many of the audience had previously little knowledge of Montagu's or Anstey's work in the 1930s, there was a response of surprise at the similarity of many of their concerns. Later in the same series, the first open public discussion of the role of the 'professional' film maker in Northern Ireland took place under the same roof. In this way, the book, always somewhere between a journalistic enterprise and a scholarly thesis, has emerged as a kind of historical novel written by many hands, and to be completed by others.

PART I

'Independence' and the Thirties*

Ideologies in History: An Introduction

Claire Johnston

> 'The loss of confidence in traditional historiographical procedures . . .
> has produced a severe hiatus in the study of the cinema. No one now
> accepts (simplistic) accounts of film history . . . and yet no one knows
> how to do much better, except at the cost of a sceptical unwillingness to
> do anything.'
> Geoffrey Nowell-Smith, 'On The Writing of the History of the Cinema: Some Problems'
> in *Edinburgh '77 Magazine*.

The work that has been produced in recent years on oppositional film
practices in the 1930s (see e.g. Bert Hogenkamp's study of film in the labour
movement[1]) marks an attempt to examine for the first time an area of social
practice in the cinema of the Thirties which has been repressed by orthodox
film histories of the 'documentary movement' of the period. As such it has
performed an important and progressive function. Nevertheless, as Trevor
Ryan suggests in his essay in this collection, such historical work lays itself
open to the production of new myths which ultimately obscure the 'lessons of
history'. The point, however, is not to demystify such work but to question its
underlying assumptions in order to elaborate more fully the determinate relations in operation in the ideological formation known as 'independent' film
practice during this period; that is to say, through a conjunctural analysis
which can provide the conditions of production of such a history.

Hogenkamp's work draws its rationale from traditions of labour history
developed in the early 1960s by such radical historians as E. P. Thompson.
His book *The Making of the English Working Class* marked a turning point in
labour history out of which the writing of feminist historians such as Sheila
Rowbotham (e.g. *Hidden from History*) and the work of the *History Workshop*
group have developed. This re-writing of a new kind of history, of popular
movements ignored by orthodox historians and of women ignored by male-
dominated writing of history, has undoubtedly performed a progressive

*This essay is a revised version of a paper given at the History/Production/Memory—Special Event held at the
Edinburgh Film Festival in 1977. I would like to thank Don Macpherson, Paul Willemen, Peter Wollen and
Keith Tribe for discussing the paper with me.

function at the present time in that it has provided particular political groups with a sense of the historicity of their action. But as Keith Tribe suggests in his article 'History and the Production of Memories',[2] it is 'often forgotten that this "history" is itself only constituted as a response to the histories that it opposes. While it is important to reveal the existence of past struggles, such revelation provides no effects in itself . . . The "lessons of history" are not inscribed in the simple existence of a past; they are the product of the construction of a history which can be deployed in contemporary arguments.'

In much of this tradition, the theoretical assumptions underlying the concept of class imply a rejection of the notion of classes as functions of the process of production as a whole. Instead, class is posed in terms of the raw material of experience: as transcendent consciousness. Such assumptions are evident, for instance, in Hogenkamp's work on film and the labour movement in that he fails to account for the relative autonomy of the ideological and the marginality of the 'independent' film movement from labour in organisational and class terms, leaving the way open for voluntarist assumptions in his analysis of the use of film in the labour movement during this period.

As Rosalind Coward has pointed out in her analysis of the journal *Working Papers in Cultural Studies*,[3] the left-Leavisite legacy of Hoggart in cultural studies has posed an analogous epistemological notion of culture as an expressive form given by groups to social and material conditions. Culture is seen as the product of a free human consciousness which in its turn is a fixed reflection of the social order. Such a conception of culture fails to confront, as she suggests, the question of how systems of representation operate their own levels of effectivity, and the question of the non-unitary subject in history opened up by the work of Freud and Lacan. Within such a conception of culture history is posed as a collection of past events and individuals, and the political importance of memory consists essentially of a work of recovery of these events and individual contributions. As Keith Tribe argues, such assumptions conspire to show that: 'the past informs and underwrites the validity of the present, and the writings on the past are guaranteed by their very involvement with the past. The past is history, and the writing of history is thus endowed with an autonomous effectivity. History not only exists, it is truth . . . To learn lessons from the past, it is necessary only to unlock this truth.'

The question of memory for political and cultural struggles in the present is of fundamental importance, but precisely as a process of re-constitution rather than of mythical recovery. Freud posed the question of memory as a production rather than as a recovery of the past for the history of the subject, rather than mythical recovery. In his work on hysterical repression he developed the concept of *Nachträglichkeit* (deferred action) in which experiences and memory-traces in the past are revised at a later date to fit with fresh experiences, and are endowed with not only new meaning, but physical effectivity. Such a concept refuses a reduction of the subject's history to a linear determinism in which the past is seen to act directly on the present. Indeed, it is precisely the subject's process of revision of the

10

past which produces effectivity and significance for the present. For Freud, deferred action facilitates access to a new level of meaning for the subject, thus opening up the possibility of the re-working of his/her earlier experiences which in the first instance has been impossible to integrate fully into any meaningful context. Human sexuality, with its unevenness of temporal development, was seen by Freud to be the most typical field for the operation of deferred action.

Seen in these terms, memory as a point of articulation between psychoanalysis and historical materialism has an important role to play for political and cultural struggle, but one which has yet to be explored fully. The real danger in posing a memory of the past for struggles within oppositional film practice at the present time is to found it on a notion of mythical recovery based on oral histories of the major protagonists of the period, as in the book *Journey to a Legend and Back: The British Realist Film* by Eva Orbanz. Such a recovery of the past can be mobilised as a 'truth' to justify a particular aesthetic position—in this case, the realist documentary—in the face of developments which have posed the importance of struggles on the terrain of representation itself for political cinema at the present time. Psychoanalysis points to the importance of memory precisely as a reconstitution of the past for the history of the subject, posed by and for the political and cultural struggles of the present. In such a reconstitution of the past, as Keith Tribe writes, history's principles of validation have necessarily become disconnected from the existence of any prior chronology. In this sense the past cannot be seen as an object of study, a point made most forcefully in the final chapter of Hindess and Hirst's *Pre-Capitalist Modes of Production*. Stripped of its crass if dazzling polemics—which could be seen potentially to perpetuate the 'severe hiatus' in the study of the cinema referred to by G. Nowell-Smith, rather than 'to alleviate' it—their anti-historicism opens up the possibility of a radical reassessment of the political objectives of historical investigation. The conditions of production of history can therefore be seen as determinate relations in a given conjuncture.

It is in the context of such an anti-historicist reformulation of memory for political and cultural struggle that Michel Foucault's work on the archive, developed in *The Archaeology of Knowledge*, becomes important. For Foucault, history is a discursive institution, an institution of power. As an order of discourse, history is thus essentially a work of representations, a heterogeneity of discourses in struggle; the past is constructed from such a set of discourses thrown up by history and accumulated in the archive. What his work emphasises for political and cultural struggle is the notion of transformation and struggle within discourses, within the 'system of enunciability' which the archive comprises in any given conjuncture. Thus struggles around access to the archive and the repression of 'alternative' discourses within history as an institution of power governed in socially determinate ways (Foucault's emphasis being on the state apparatus) assume a crucial role. Ideological struggles around different articulations of historical representations produced in and for the present thus constitute a radical reformulation

11

of the idea of memory in relation to history. What such a reformulation dispenses with is precisely any possibility of 'origin' or 'truth', and what it stresses is the non-unitary nature of the subject, history and memory.

The following analysis of the discourses of 'independence' in the Thirties places itself within such an anti-historicist reformulation of the articulation between memory and historical materialism. Through a conjunctural analysis the reconstitution of the heterogeneity of discourses identified with 'independence' during the period serves to problematise both orthodox histories of the 'documentary movement', such as Alan Lovell and Jim Hillier's *Studies in Documentary* and Forsyth Hardy's *Grierson on Documentary,* and histories deriving from the more progressive approaches of the labour historian, such as Bert Hogenkamp's study. Such a reconstruction of the discourses of 'independence' opens the way for a displacement of current critical discourses of 'film history' and the cultural and educational institutions which support them. At the same time, while it should be stressed that such an intervention cannot be immediately productive for political and ideological struggles within the 'independent' movement at the present time—the aim of such an analysis being precisely to emphasise the differences between past and present conjunctures—it nevertheless produces concepts which have political implications for current 'independent' practice and thus for future strategy. In this sense, the emphasis placed on cinema as a social practice within the discourses of 'independence' in the Thirties and today, suggests that a certain notion of historicity returns, and is important to preserve, if the transformation of the space of cinema as an institution (involving radically different articulations of production/distribution/exhibition/criticism) is to be carried further.

THE THIRTIES

As yet no serious analysis of the Thirties has been undertaken which could function to undermine the mythologies surrounding the period. The only study which attempts to examine the role of culture on the left in relation to the social formation, *Britain in the Nineteen Thirties* by Noreen Branson and Margot Heinemann, offers little more than a simple reflection theory, ignoring the materiality of artistic production and the relative autonomy of the ideological in relation to the political and the economic.

For British intellectuals the economic catastrophe of 1929 undermined the dominant assumptions of liberalism on the left. The 'Red Decade' which was to follow marked a turning point in the sense that Marxism did penetrate the national culture for the first time. At the same time it mirrored the insularity and backwardness of that culture and failed fundamentally to challenge it for two reasons: the nature of the British intelligentsia itself and the inherent defects of British Marxism founded on Soviet orthodoxy which proved inadequate to transform underlying cultural assumptions. The struggle between communism and fascism which characterised the 'Red Decade' found the intelligentsia unprepared. The lack of a 'real creative school of British Marxism', as argued in *Russian Economic Development Since the Revolution* by Maurice Dobb, meant that the 'Red Decade' left little appreciable impact on the intelligentsia as a whole.

Tom Nairn, in *The Twilight of the British State*,[4] characterises the British intelligentsia as playing a uniquely central and political role in promoting social integration within civil society in the absence of a 'second bourgeois revolution' in Britain: 'The more habitual use of the term indicates an intellectual stratum distanced from society and state: thinkers and writers distanced from and critical of the status quo. In the English social world, however, almost the reverse is the case . . . From the outside judgement has been impeded by the developmental singularity of the thing: an intellectual class of great power and functionality, yet not either created by or in critical opposition to the state—neither a state-fostered technocracy (on the French model) nor an "alienated" intelligentsia (on the Russian model) . . .

'The nucleus of the English intellectual class was formed by civil society itself, not the state. From the mid-nineteenth century up to the present day, this civil armature has been created by a small number of private elite educational institutions: the "Public Schools" and the old universities . . . Originally patrician liberalism depended upon a supposedly "natural" governing elite; a land-based stratum with certain characteristics of caste. The functional intelligentsia formed from the 1830s onwards was in essence a still more artificial perpetuation of this, where civil institutions gradually replaced landowning as the foundation of hegemony.

'. . . the British state is (. . .) distinct: it is a case, and really the only case, where oligarchy engendered democracy through an organic social strategy that preserved its own nature (and deeply marked and infirmed the "democracy" which emerged). In this case, elitism was neither fossil survival nor aberration, it has remained the enduring truth of the state. British Labourism is the story of how working-class politics made its own compact with that truth. The bourgeoisie made an alliance with the English form of landlordism, and this was expressed by the formation of the liberal intelligentsia; in turn, that stratum took charge of the emergent political force of the proletariat in the first quarter of the twentieth century. In the archetypal person of J. M. Keynes it conceived the new, most general formula for this second alliance, which has lasted from the Great Depression to the present and seen the Labour Party become the main support of the declining state.'

Within such an analysis, the unique character of the English intelligentsia rests on a belief in the concrete nature of the constitution, an unfailing ability to adapt to new pressures from below and the development of strategies of compromise and concession epitomised in the Fabian tradition on the left. Nevertheless, the 'Red Decade' marked a potential challenge to such a liberal intelligentsia, and interest in the theory and practice of Marxism grew rapidly during this period. As Francis Mulhern has observed in his essay 'Caudwell's Literary Theory'[5]: 'For the first time and so far the last time in their history, large numbers of British intellectuals found themselves compelled to pay serious attention to Marxism'.

Faced with the realities of national and international crisis, a Marxist culture developed which began to impinge on the national culture as a whole: books such as Strachey's *The Coming Struggle for Power,* Laski's *Communism,* journals such as *New Writing, Left Review* and the activities of the Left Book Club indicate this widespread growth in interest in Marxism within the intelligentsia during the period.

However, little is known of the specificity of Marxist culture during this period and the form of British Marxism which fed into it. The only detailed analysis of British Marxism which throws some light on the question is as yet unpublished: *Marxism in Britain: 1917-33* by Stuart MacIntyre.[6] MacIntyre's study is important in that it to some extent undermines the 'stunted stereotype', as he puts it, of British Marxism and provides considerable insight into the formation of the Marxist intelligentsia of the 'Red Decade'. Essentially, British Marxism could be characterised as an incomplete and derivative version of Soviet Marxism: untheoretical in nature, with no indigenous creative school (although Maurice Dobb's contribution to British Marxism should not be underestimated). Until the late 1920s, British Marxism was largely a working-class phenomenon. During this period Marxists were active in the British Labour Movement and they had exerted an influence out of proportion to their numbers. The emphasis placed by Marxists on education prior to the 'Red Decade' through the Plebs League and the Labour Colleges can be seen as decisive in accounting for this impact on the Labour Movement. The Communist Party's increasing emphasis on political activism at the expense of its educational strategy towards the end of the Twenties proved to be a severe miscalculation. The leading Marxists of the Twenties were self-educated workers; by the end of the decade the Communist Party, faced by a rapidly dwindling membership, began to recruit from the middle-class intelligentsia, now increasingly predisposed to Marxism, but nevertheless formed by the ideology of British Labourism. This failure to develop its educational policy of the Twenties, together with a marked absence of Marxist debate within academic circles, meant that the Labour Movement largely continued to derive its ideas from bourgeois sources.

Basically it was to a Leninist version of Marxism that British Marxists had access, but a Leninism which was ill-understood. An incomplete but nevertheless substantial selection of Marx and Engels was available, together with Lenin's *Collected Works* and the work of Bukharin, Plekhanov, Trotsky, Bogdanov and Stalin. There was, however, a marked neglect of continental writings, particularly the work of Korsch, Gramsci and Lukacs, accounting, to a large extent, for British Marxism's failure to adapt Soviet orthodoxies to the British situation. The limitations of British Marxism during this period can be seen most clearly in its conception of ideology and class consciousness. What dominated the indigenous Marxist writing of the period, particularly evident in Strachey's writings, was an essentially economic understanding of historical materialism. At the beginning of the Thirties a belated recognition of the superstructure as an active set of processes began to develop and with it some notion of the relative autonomy of the ideological. However, this redefinition of the role of ideology remained marginal to British Marxism and a cruder position continued to dominate in which ideology was seen as 'dope', false ideas inculcated by the capitalist class to deceive and manipulate the workers. Such a conception of ideology as empty and superficial led to a widespread attack by the Communist Party and the Labour Movement on the capitalist-controlled press. A conspiratorial theory about the ruling class's control of the organs of public opinion and the educational apparatus became a means by which Marxists could explain the absence of class consciousness within the working class. In general, attitudes to art, education and popular entertainment as a whole displayed a certain contempt for the British working class. In this phenomenon it is possible to discern the way in which the inadequacies of British Marxism became entangled in the dominant assumptions of the liberal intelligentsia. In the same way the Marxist conception of the state proved to be a major stumbling block for the new left intelligentsia. While it undoubtedly had an impact on the writings of some of the leading intellectuals such as G. D. H. Cole and Harold Laski, forced to radically revise their positions after the fall of the second Labour Government in 1931, they nevertheless drew back from the full implications of the Marxist conception of the state, in favour of a conspiratorial notion of 'the city', maintaining an unshakeable belief in constitutionalism and social democracy. With the publication of Lenin's *What Is To Be Done?* in the late Twenties the Communist Party itself shifted its emphasis on these questions to an attack on the 'social fascist' Labour Party and trade union leadership, and a new analysis of class consciousness began to develop with a greater concentration on the analysis of concrete issues rather than abstract revolutionary demands. But this re-examination by British Marxists had come too late; membership of the party had by this time slumped drastically and strategies deriving from such a reassessment became impossible to put into practice.

Within such a context it is possible to see how the artistic production of the period became enmeshed in these contradictions. The left intelligentsia was essentially a literary left. Francis Mulhern in his essay on the Marxist literary critic Christopher Caudwell describes the literary movement in the following terms: 'The new generation of social critics was formed in the image of its predecessors; it was, above all, a *literary* left. Its intellectual preoccupations were pre-selected by the very culture against which it pitted itself. Thus, while the decade produced no important political or sociological analysis of the British crisis, its output of "revolutionary poetry" and literary criticism was truly prodigious. These Marxist literary essays varied greatly in quality, scope and emphasis, but they were united in their insistence that literature could be understood and evaluated only in relation to the social conditions in which it was produced. Hence literary criticism came to be regarded as the elucidation of the social determinations of a text, as the identification of the "social equivalent" of a given character, sentiment or situation. There was also a common limitation: although this criticism was newly sociological and political, no profound re-definition of literature was implied. Literature was datum; only interpretation and judgment was controversial.'

Apart from the work of Caudwell, the influence of the established literary tradition in the left intelligentsia, with its refusal of a notion of art as practice in favour of notions of reflection, expression and 'reality', remained intact. It is in this period that it becomes possible to discern the beginnings of a specific inflection of literary ideology later to be depoliticised and codified by Leavis and placed within the academic institution, which Terry Eagleton in his book *Criticism and Ideology* has characterised as 'left-Leavisism'. Such a literary ideology was to have an important function in relation to the development of 'independent' film practice.

'INDEPENDENT' FILM PRACTICE

If we examine the elements at play in the ideological formation which has come to be known as 'independent' film practice in the Thirties, there would seem at first sight to have been a radical redefinition of practice on the left. With the campaigns around anti-fascism, poverty and peace, film could no longer be seen as an object for consumption. Art in general could only be understood and evaluated in terms of the social conditions in which it was produced: it was imbued with a new social and political content. As far as film was concerned this was determined by a different mode of insertion into production, distribution and exhibition and a different conception of the reception of film (use of films for discussions, etc) brought about by the political requirements of the day. Because films made for the state had to be shown outside established networks and were free, they too were inserted into these networks to a limited extent. If we analyse the components of the practices which developed during the period it becomes clear that the term 'independent' film practice was both a broad and specific definition in operation in the conjuncture. In order to understand the content of the term 'independence' it is necessary to look more closely at the cultural field in which it functioned; the terms by which it acquired its particular meaning.

An important component of the term 'independence' rested on the rejection of Hollywood both as an economic system and as the dominant mode of representation. In 1931 Ralph Bond, a communist and one of the major figures in the workers' film movement, wrote in *Plebs*: 'We can and must fight capitalist influences in the cinema by exposing, in a Marxist manner, how it is used as an ideological force to dope the workers. That can be done by exhibiting the films of the only country where the workers are the ruling class, and by making our own films, not to initiate "new spirits" and "new religions", but to aid and encourage the workers in their fight against capitalism.' The magazine of the 'independent' movement, *Cinema Quarterly* (1932-35), edited by Norman Wilson with Forsyth Hardy and Basil Wright as contributing editors, was published in Edinburgh. It mounted a massive attack on Hollywood as a dominant mode, denouncing the 'artificiality' and 'psychopathology' of the spectacle, acting styles and narrative structures. 'Creativity' and 'freedom' were seen to be impossible within the Hollywood system. Such a position was determined to an extent by the state of British film production at the time. The British film industry had been driven almost to extinction in

16

the 1920s by Hollywood, with American distribution, and its practices of block booking and blind booking, effectively keeping British films off the screen. The Cinematograph Act of 1927 sought to protect the industry by introducing quotas, so that finance capital began to invest in the industry, but this proved ineffective as distribution remained in the hands of the big American companies and films were made which satisfied quota requirements (the 'quota quickie') largely depending on foreign technicians. In fact, this was an important factor leading to the formation of the union, the ACT, in 1933.[7]

In its first editorial, *Cinema Quarterly* pointed to the new audience for 'independent' cinema which was developing: the film society movement had only touched the 'tip of the iceberg'. The editorial of the magazine itself was entitled 'The Spectator' and its function was conceived as setting up a forum for 'independent' film-makers to discuss their problems. As such it saw its role as a 'complete periodical' for the 'thoughtful spectator and the intellectual film-maker' and was directed at 'all those interested in documentary, experimental, propaganda and educational work'. An important feature of this conception of film-maker and audience rested with the need to demystify the film-making process itself. *Cinema Quarterly* became the official organ of the Independent Film-Makers' Association which was founded in the autumn of 1933 and based in Edinburgh; its board of advisors were Anthony Asquith, John Grierson, Andrew Buchanan, Stuart Legg, Paul Rotha and Basil Wright. In August 1934 the IFMA held its first summer school which aimed at such a demystification: Asquith, Buchanan, Grierson, Legg and Rotha giving talks on various aspects of production accompanied by practical film-making activities and screenings and discussions of films. Such work, however, was spasmodic and short-lived and the IFMA was dissolved.

Another important component of 'independence' lay in developments in amateur film-making in the late 1920s and the technological developments around sub-standard equipment and stocks. Essentially the 'independent' movement saw itself as the vanguard of the amateur movement. The First National Convention of Amateur Cinematographic Societies was held in London in October 1929 with the aim of developing the amateur movement, establishing a central body to which amateur societies could affiliate. At the conference it was decided to establish a film library of amateur films, a technical bureau and the magazine *Amateur Films*. In an article in *Close Up* in December 1929, Ralph Bond complained of the lack of direction of the movement and the danger that amateur film-makers would simply ape the dominant modes of Hollywood. He called for the necessity to develop a 'theory and practice' of the amateur movement around the documentary idea and the importance of social and political content. *Cinema Quarterly* saw its task as precisely to provide such a direction to the amateur movement and mounted a systematic attack on the technicist and philistine orientation of most amateur cinema clubs. In the autumn issue of 1933 the amateur section of the magazine became the 'independent' section and was directed at all film-makers working on sub-standard stock with an interest in developing their work along 'documentary', 'experimental', 'propaganda' or 'educational' lines. It set up a scenario service to which writers could submit scripts for amateur film-makers to draw on. The importance of the scenario was a constant emphasis in the 'independent' section of the magazine, which also contained information about new developments in sub-standard equipment, stocks and new sound equipment. The Independent Film-Makers' Association saw its aims as (a) putting members in touch with each other with the aim of working together on joint projects; (b) giving professional advice; (c) constructive criticism of other members' films; (d) the setting up of a catalogue and distribution network; (e) the setting up of a scenario service and an information sheet giving the themes required by commercial companies and educational organisations; (f) the publication of a regular information bulletin, and summer schools. What is particularly interesting in this connection is the attitude to 'propaganda' and advertising. 'Independent' film-makers saw no contradiction in regarding their work in these terms. Advertising films displaying the 'new attitude' of the documentaries were applauded in the pages of *Cinema Quarterly* and the idea of documentary itself was intimately bound up with a notion of propaganda.

A striking feature of the 'independent' movement of this period is that there appears to have been virtually no ideological gap between film critics and film-makers; indeed most of the film-makers saw their role within the movement as intimately bound up with not only propagandising for the new documentary form, developing audiences and articulating a political commitment, but also engaging in the current debates about the films of the time. To an extent this was the legacy of the work of the London Film Society which Ivor Montagu played a large part in founding in 1925, and the movement which developed out of it.

A communist, Montagu was one of the leading figures in the Workers' Film Movement as co-founder of the Progressive Film Institute and its 16mm distribution outlet Kino. It was initially through the work of the London Film Society that Soviet films reached an audience, and were often shown in the context of lectures on the montage theory of the Russian School. Later, as 16mm films were exempt from censorship, Soviet films were distributed and exhibited widely in the Workers' Movement on 16mm. The particular appropriation of montage theory by Montagu was in terms of a notion of 'film grammar' based on Pudovkin's writings. In such an appropriation montage was seen in terms of 'style' and articulated within the documentary ideal of 'creative' interpretation of events, thus losing the real advances made by montage theory. At the same time, within such a notion of 'artistic creativity', Soviet film-makers became the subject of a personality cult and the idea of cinema as a social practice in Russia in the 1920s was lost. Montagu's notion of the Soviet cinema had a widespread influence, not only within the film society movement but also within 'independent' film practice, hints for amateurs in the film magazines reflecting the above notions of 'style'.

Grierson's ideas about documentary as the 'creative interpretation of reality' seen within the context of 'responsible propaganda' were widely

18

disseminated within the 'independent' film movement, and he combined his role of backing 'independent' film-makers within the state institutions with writing and lecturing within the movement.[8] An important feature of Grierson's belief in the 'freer and saner' relations of production within the state institutions as opposed to the industry was a notion of professionalism as a craft deriving from the liberal socialist tradition. Professionalism in film-making was emphasised in the movement but it represented an opposition to a depersonalised division of labour characteristic of the dominant mode.

With the formation in 1935 of the Workers' Film and Photo League, the socialist wing of the amateur cine movement, and Kino, a Communist Party cadre-oriented amateur association, the 'independent' movement acquired a space for its activities and ideas. As distribution networks they could draw on the exhibition possibilities opened up by the fact that 16mm safety stock escaped censorship and films were shown widely on the left in Co-operative halls, Labour Party branches, trade unions and through the Left Book Club. The anti-fascist front provided the basis for the viability of these networks, and 'independent' films reached a wide political and social spectrum.

* * *

How then are we to understand the coincidence of these components within a practice self-consciously defined as 'independent'? It is important that the structural coherence of these components should be analysed in terms of the internal dynamic of ideological practices rather than as a simple reflection of the political and economic determinations (as with Hogenkamp) or as the representation in the ideological of the different socio-intellectual histories of the major protagonists (as with Lovell and Hillier). At the same time, as Annette Kuhn has shown, ideologies thrown up by institutions do not provide sufficient determination to explain the film practices involved.

In fact, the terms of the coherence of these determinations can be found in the dominance of literary ideology as suggested by Mulhern. Fundamental to that ideology is the notion of the full, expressive subject present to itself. In his critique of the privileging in linguistics of the spoken word as opposed to writing, Derrida proposes in his book *On Grammatology* the term logocentrism to describe this effacing of the materiality of language, the search for the perfect transparency of meaning, and posits the voice as the prototype of a signifying practice which allows the subject to imagine itself as unique source of meaning. In this way the signifier is effaced and becomes no more than a temporary representation granting access to the signified. In cinema this notion of the voice as the most transparent form of the presence of the speaking subject acquires a particular modality. The image is even more transparent than the voice, although the voice is still required to guarantee it and to fix its meaning. This notion of the full, expressive subject, present in the literary ideology of the time, when transposed into the field of cinema produced the possibility of two seemingly different conceptions: the full subject as creative individual requiring artistic freedom, etc. (see Grierson's definition of documentary), and the collective subject of a class, conceived as a monolith speaking with its own voice. The potential contradiction in this double notion of

19

subject revolves round the relation between the subject and its discourse. In the first case the subject is endowed with the right to state its subjective view, while in the second the subject becomes the neutral passage through which the collective voice speaks. The role of the film-maker, in this last instance, is both to act as vehicle and as testifying witness (a pure presence—'I was here'), and visual discourse organised round this pure statement of presence is thus presented as the untrammelled passage of the collective subject—the working class.

The profound rejection of Hollywood as an economic system and as a dominant fictional mode combined with the transcription of logocentrism into the cinematic institution dialectically determining each other have to be seen in terms of the following series in the ideological formation (this listing does not claim to be exhaustive):

(a) cultural isolationism which prevented critical assimilation of the way this combination of determining factors had been articulated in other ideological formations (e.g., the Surrealist movement in France, Russian Formalism, the debate on realism in the German Communist Party);
(b) the artisanal/craft system of production as opposed to the relations of production of big industry;
(c) the redefinition of notions of realism brought about by photo-journalism;
(d) the emergence of the mass audience bringing about the need for technological innovation.

What constituted the terms of coherence of the wide spectrum of 'independent' film-making at this time can be seen as precisely the conjuncture produced by a cinematic practice under the two dominant determinations (i.e. anti-Hollywood/logocentrism) within a field delimited by the subsidiary determinants outlined above. It must be stressed that none of these series is autonomous but interrelated in a complex manner with other ideological, economic and political series. To give an example: the need to propagandise for political platforms had effects on the development of technology and the scientific series, which, in their turn, had ramifications on the terrain of ideological practices. It must also be stressed that each series has a different, but not unconnected historical development.

THE FILMS
The general determinants at work in the ideological field outlined above produced within these common assumptions different types of films:

(a) the 'poetic' realist documentary associated with the name of Grierson (*Industrial Britain, BBC – The Voice of Britain*, etc);
(b) the documentary as journalistic witness to events (*Challenge to Fascism, Workers' Topical News, Defence of Madrid*, etc);
(c) fictional representations of the history/experience of the working class (*Voice of the People, Advance Democracy*, etc);
(d) visual discourses illustrating speeches (*Peace and Plenty*, etc);
(e) experimental films (*Hell Unltd, Rainbow Dance*, etc).

Each of these categories of film is a product of a cinematic practice within a

20

terrain determined and circumscribed by the series outlined above and under the dominance of the anti-Hollywood/logocentrism couple. The explanation for the difference between the categories can be located in the different sets of boundaries set up by institutions (such as the state, the Progressive Film Institute, the Workers' Film and Photo League) and the distribution/exhibition networks (Workers' Film and Photo League, Kino, the Left Book Club) within which they were situated. For example, the dominance of the ideology of creative subjectivity and artistic freedom had most play within the state institutions, whereas the ideology of the subject as witness representing the voice of the working class found more space within the workers' movement and its organisations.

Over and above these primary determinations on the production of films, no 'independent' film practice would have been possible without an institutional space through which it could operate, i.e. the distribution and exhibition networks and organisations such as the Independent Film-Makers' Association. Ironically, the space for distribution/exhibition was opened up by a loophole in the 1909 Cinematograph Act, which still legislated for cinema as a commodity according to whether or not it was inflammable. In this way 16mm safety stock was exempt from censorship as well as fire regulations and this meant that films could be exhibited by any group anywhere, allowing the existing organisations of the labour movement to function as an exhibition network so that the distribution networks had the possibility of finding an audience.

CONCLUSION

This outline of the terrain which constituted 'independent' film practice in the Thirties would suggest that we have to examine the notion of the conjuncture concretely. It is pointless to approach the subject in terms that are too general. As far as cinema is concerned, it becomes necessary to address a specific, localised conjunctural formation. 'Independent' film practice is governed, in this analysis, by a set of terms mutually defining each other, changes in one term producing a restructuring of the field in question, producing a process of historical change.

It is particularly important in such an analysis, however, that specific components of the formation are not treated in isolation and formalistically designated 'reactionary' or 'progressive' per se. The 'progressive' or 'reactionary' character of specific components will depend on their function within the complexity of the conjuncture. For instance, notions of the full subject function differently in the cinematic institution and in the literary field. As is demonstrated in this analysis, it allowed different types of textual practice—Drifters as well as Hell Unltd., perhaps the most interesting film of the movement. At the same time, notions of artistic freedom helped to make space for experimentation with cinematic specificity (e.g., Peace and Plenty). The ethos of amateurism current during this period, although implicated in myths of neutrality and a notion of class as monolithic subject, helped to make the space for a different social practice of cinema possible.

Such a conjunctural analysis, therefore, points to the need to locate each of the practices involved more precisely in terms of the mode of subjectivity in operation. As we have seen, the dominance of literary ideology in the conjuncture in its two aspects (i.e., subject and voice) cannot be accounted for in culturalist terms, that is to say, in terms of the political backwardness of the British left. A conjunctural analysis would provide a way in which subjectivity and the dominance of literary ideology would be seen to be produced and determined within an articulation of practices. In this sense literary ideology, when seen in combination with the effects of a negative definition of Hollywood, becomes a product of over-determination. In addition the particular form and effectivity of logocentrism within 'independent' film practice during this period requires some analysis of the articulation of the ideological instances with the political (i.e., the political platforms which situated the films) and the economic ones (i.e., Hollywood's domination of the market). Any analysis of class struggle in relation to cinema, therefore, must abandon any notion of the autonomy of practices in favour of the analysis of the conditions of existence of each practice, their relation to each other, and the forms they take which cannot be specified in any but conjunctural terms. Within the heterogeneity of discourses comprising 'independent' film practice during this period there are specific regulations of address across particular practices, institutions and audiences, each producing different orders of subjectivity which are important to analyse in their specificity if we are to assess their effectivity in terms of class struggle. As Colin MacCabe has suggested, 'a class is not a subject, an identity, but rather the ever-changing configuration produced by the forces and relations of production. A set of economic, political and ideological forces constantly constitutes classes in struggle and classes can find no definition outside those struggles'.

To date, work on subjectivity in the text, drawing as it has done from psychoanalysis, has concentrated on the individual as subject rather than the more complex question of class identity. Such work has tended, as Paul Willemen suggests,[10] to lead to 'an essentialist dogma, a strategy of attack against all forms of imaginary unity as such, ignoring historical and social determinations altogether'. A conjunctural analysis of the kind I have proposed would call for a redefinition of the problem of subjectivity and the text away from such an 'essentialism'. The issue of class and identity is always a conjunctural question. The problem is to produce a theory of subjectivity which, while accounting for psychic relations, at the same time offers an analysis of discourse which includes the ideological representations of the political and the economic instances of the social formation. Clearly the effectivity of 'independent' film practices in the Thirties can only be understood in such terms, and it is in precisely such a redefinition of cinema as social practice that strategies for 'independent' film practice today can be identified and developed.

22

NOTES

1 *Skrien*, July/August 1975; shortened version in *Sight and Sound*, Spring 1976.
2 *Screen*, vol. 18, no. 3, Winter '77/78.
3 *Screen*, vol. 18, no. 1, Spring '77.
4 *New Left Review*, nos. 101/102.
5 *New Left Review*, no. 85.
6 Ph.D. thesis, Cambridge. A version of this thesis will be published under the title *A Proletarian Science: Marxism in Britain* 1917–1933.
7 See Michael Chanan's *Labour Power in the British Film Industry*, BFI, London, 1976.
8 For an analysis of the term 'independence' in relation to Grierson's work in the state institutions, see Annette Kuhn, ' "Independent" Film Making and the State in the 1930s', in *Edinburgh '77 Magazine*.
9 Ibid.
10 'Notes on Subjectivity', in *Screen*, vol. 19, no. 1, Spring 1978.

British Documentary in the 1930s and 'Independence': Recontextualising a Film Movement*

Annette Kuhn

Anyone with the slightest knowledge of the history of cinema in Britain will no doubt be aware of a tradition of 'British documentary', commonly understood as both a film 'movement' associated with the name of John Grierson and also as a set of films made largely during the 1930s and 1940s within specific institutional contexts. The 'British documentary movement', so defined, is massively documented and commented upon, although in fact the history it has constructed for itself, or had constructed for it, is undoubtedly a partial one, both in terms of the representation of the movement itself (precisely as a 'movement') and of the type of evidence marshalled to produce that history.

The dominant representation of British documentary constitutes it first of all as a set of texts whose qualities mark them as 'art' films. Secondly, and related to this, the films are commonly seen to have emerged in a glorious but isolated moment in the history of British cinema: roughly the 1930s and the Second World War. One of the consequences of this view is that the possibility of there being a relation between the forms of cinematic representation associated with the documentary movement and those prevailing in other historical moments or institutions remains generally unacknowledged. This is especially evident in assertions that the movement came to an end at a certain identifiable point in time. This view makes it possible to argue, for example, that 'By the time the Crown Film Unit was abolished [1952] . . . there is fairly general agreement that British documentary had gone into a decline'.[1]

Where the possibility of the above mentioned relation is acknowledged, all the films concerned tend to be appropriated for a somewhat unproblematic notion of 'realism', which is also held to be characteristic of certain products of the commercial cinema in Britain in the 1940s and 1950s and/or of television documentary forms in more recent years. The tendency results partly from the difficulty of defining realism and the looseness with which the term is deployed, and partly—and perhaps more significantly—from the actual nature of the films which have been put forward as constitutive of the documentary movement. So-called poetic documentaries such as Robert Flaherty's *Industrial Britain* (1932), Basil Wright's *Song of Ceylon* (1934), Harry Watt's *Night Mail* (1936) and Humphrey Jennings' *Listen to Britain* (1942) are much more commonly seen as representative of that movement than are, for in-

---

*This paper is based on a presentation given at the Edinburgh Film Festival in August 1977 in relation to an article by the author, 'Independent' Film Making and the State in the 1930s, *Edinburgh '77 Magazine*.

24

stance, films such as Cavalcanti's *Pett and Pott* (1934), William Coldstream's *Fairy of the Phone* (1936) and Norman McLaren's *Love on the Wing* (1937), although all of them were produced in exactly the same institutional setting: the state-sponsored film units associated with the name of John Grierson, who is invariably hailed as the instigator of, and dominant influence on, the British documentary movement.

The question as to the precise criteria which have presided over the construction of the history of the British documentary movement therefore relates not only to the films themselves but also to the ways in which the authorship and production of those films have been conceived. Because the point of origin of the films has been placed in individual film-makers, it is considered sufficient to construct the history of a 'movement' solely from the accounts of participants, of the 'authors'. It is no doubt for this reason that the existing history of documentary film-making in Britain consists very largely of anecdote and memoir.[2] The 'movement' is then conceptualised as the sum total of a select set of texts whose points of origin are individual film-makers, so that on another level these individuals collectively constitute the movement. This is simultaneously the determining factor and the outcome of the set of methods adopted, and of the nature of the evidence called upon in the construction of the movement's history.

In the present context, the assembly of different kinds of evidence for the writing of a/the history of the British documentary movement is, however, not intended to produce a 'better' history of that movement, but to *recontextualise* it. Indeed, in this process of recontextualisation the very notion of an autonomous British documentary movement vanishes merely through placing the cinematic practices involved in the relatively unfamiliar context of 'independent' film practices. To ask questions relevant to the notion of 'independence' is to demand information which, in this case at least, cannot be answered by recourse to existing evidence: 'It is evident that for the history which already exists, certain questions are irrelevant, are simply not raised: on what bases were film makers financed?—how were production decisions made?—what relationship subsisted between film makers and sponsors?—how could film makers organize their work?—what kinds of films could they produce?'[3]

However, in relation to the terms that preside over the production of history as a discipline, that is as a discourse of academic institutions, there is the risk that the use of 'official' evidence, as opposed to personal memory or anecdote, will just focus attention on the 'quality' of the evidence at hand. But the questions at issue here do not turn on the production of 'better' evidence for the purpose of closing gaps or filling in the details in a history whose orientation is already fixed. The point is rather to assemble new evidence as a means of *displacing* what we know as the documentary movement, indeed to subvert the category itself—firstly, by re-placing the set of practices constituted in it within a broader conceptualisation of 'independence' in the cinema in the 1930s, and secondly by looking at the specific notion of independence in operation at this time. This may be achieved through an

25

examination of the characteristics of the conjuncture which provided the conditions of existence for this particular film practice.

'INDEPENDENCE'

Such a programme inevitably means that the documentary movement will be regarded as in certain respects occupying the same terrain as other film practices, such as those centred on Kino and the Film and Photo League, more readily understood as 'independent'.[4] The 'independence' of these latter practices is perhaps most easily seen in terms of the political positions they inscribe and the institutional operation of those positions with regard to sources of sponsorship, relations of production and modes of distribution. That their 'independence' is definable on a number of levels raises the question of how the notion of 'independence' is in fact to be understood in relation to film-making. 'Independence' cannot usefully be considered in a universal manner; it is more appropriately regarded in terms of the characteristics of its historical conjuncture. The 'independent' film movements of the 1930s existed as a set of institutional practices defined in terms of particular modes of organisation for the production of films, inscribing a series of at times contradictory positions with regard to their own practice.

Among these positions is the tendency, particularly evident in the orthodoxy of the state-sponsored documentary movement, to reject cinematic fictions in favour of 'actuality'.[5] Alan Lovell remarks, for instance, on the moralistic approach to fiction films underlying Grierson's frequent references to their 'meretriciousness'. The implication is that the creation of filmic fictions inevitably involves illusion or mystification, which makes it morally indefensible. Such a view, and the positions implied in it with regard to truth, ideology and the relation between film and spectator, as well as 'art' and entertainment, is indicative of a certain hostility towards the commercial film industry. This is much in evidence, for example, in the pages of *Cinema Quarterly*, a journal produced from Edinburgh between 1932 and 1935, and very much associated with the documentary movement. In the first paragraph of the journal's first editorial, the shortsightedness of the film trade's attitude to 'intelligent' films is condemned.[6] Accompanying this antipathy towards fictional forms of representation there is a conviction that to work in the industry is to suffer an inhibition of artistic freedom and to have one's integrity curbed according to box-office requirements. Grierson himself often expressed this view, particularly when arguing the advantages of sponsorship by institutions not motivated by a demand for immediate return, financial or otherwise. In this instance, the rejection of the fictional film as an area of intervention is thus related to a rejection of the characteristic system of production of that type of film: studio-based production financed by private capital. However, this is not to suggest that there was a unified position on this issue shared by all the 'independent' groups. The reasons for wishing to develop non-fictional forms of representation might range from the equations fiction = entertainment and actuality = art on the one extreme, to equating fiction with crude commercialism because of its dominantly capitalist system of production on the other. Even the apparently unitary movement towards the cinematic representation of 'the real', therefore, could have its basis in contradictory impulses, as is argued in Claire Johnston's essay in this book.

PRODUCTION AND 'AUTHORSHIP'

This antipathy towards the commercial film industry was associated with a particular 'realist' aesthetic, although unspecified at the time. But it also produced the advocacy or adoption of alternative ways of organising film production itself. Industrialised systems of film production particularly common during the 1930s and 1940s, with studio production still in its ascendency and the attempted application of the principles of 'scientific' management to the labour process in film production, were rejected on the grounds that they were an inevitable and alienating concomitant of the profit motive. In the left film groups of the 1930s, this rejection was accompanied by the adoption of models of collective work in film production which operated in such a way that in the body of texts constituting that particular movement individual authorship is abolished; if an authorial voice exists, it is a collective one.

Within the state-sponsored independent sector, however, a model of collaborative work was adopted which embodied characteristically 'pre-capitalist' or early capitalist artisanal relations of production. Emphasis was laid repeatedly on the ideal of craft-type manufacture with its associated implications of apprenticeship and training. The existence of the film units for which Grierson was responsible was quite overtly defended on the grounds that they provided a training ground for people new to film-making. Cavalcanti has described the situation at the GPO Film Unit when he was there in the following terms: 'The working conditions were similar to mediaeval artisanship; the work was collective, the films of each one were discussed.'[7] While Henri Langlois described it as a film school which worked in much the same way as the Renaissance studio.[8]

The system of recruitment and promotion developed by the units certainly institutionalised this particular model of production relations: potential 'creative' talent could, for example, be employed at initially very low rates of pay, or even without pay, on the assumption that training would be given.[9] The distinction implied here between collaborative and collective production for the work of the film units and the workers' film-making groups respectively is important to the extent that in the film units authorship remained a slightly problematic issue both for those immediately concerned and for that history of the documentary movement which seeks to create *auteurs*: accounts of the production of certain films suggest that screen credits do not necessarily reflect the 'true authorship' of those films, particularly since much actual production work was done collaboratively. On the other hand, the very retention of credits for the contributions of individuals indicates some residual—or emergent—concern with individual authorship. To this day there still exists controversy over credits on certain films produced within the state-sponsored units.

27

A final point to be made with regard to the positions inscribed by 'independent' film practice turns on the *total* character of that practice: the tendency to locate the act of film production within a series of related practices and then to view these as a whole. Alongside 'independent' film production, partly of necessity because of its place 'outside' the industry, systems of 'independent' distribution were developed in clubs, trade unions, political parties, schools, film societies, and so on. The 'Imperial Six'[10] notwithstanding, commercial distributors were not keen to handle even the government-sponsored films, and Grierson's system of non-theatrical distribution was a way of bringing films produced in the units to what he saw as a potentially very large audience outside the established cinemas. This concern to create and to educate an audience for 'independent' films was evident also in the continuous critical work surrounding the productions of the film units in particular. The journal *Cinema Quarterly* had close links with the work of the film units and those working in them, as did its successor *World Film News*, which was published monthly between 1936 and 1938. What is perhaps most remarkable about the work of these and other film journals of the period, such as *Close Up* (1927-1933) and *Film Art* (1933-1937), is the broad sweep of their criticism, which included the products of the American and British studios as well as European and Soviet cinema, covering experimental, documentary and fiction film, while simultaneously promoting the exhibition and amateur film production activities of the film societies.

In addition, *Cinema Quarterly* was the organ of the Independent Film-Makers' Association, founded late in 1933 'to co-ordinate the efforts of those who are seriously engaged in the production of experimental, documentary and educational films.'[11] The IFMA news sheet, 'The Independent Film Maker', was included in each of its issues between Winter 1933 and Winter 1934, and in Summer 1934 the association held its own Summer School. All this serves merely as an indication of the extent to which activity in one area of 'independent' film production had reverberations in other areas. It was, for example, possible for people working in the units to engage in 'independent' film-making outside them, and in this sense the existence of the units and their training function may have provided some of the conditions of existence of other practices. It is clear then that 'independent' film production was not only regarded ideally as a totality which embraced distribution, education, criticism and the creation of audiences, along with film-making itself, but also that in these respects the separate 'independent' film practices were inter-related to varying degrees. This was certainly true in the sense that a number of the film-makers involved moved from one sphere to another, and also that the principal critical journals promoted various kinds of 'independent' film-making. That this should be the case is perhaps surprising in view of the political, organisational and aesthetic differences which, at least from a contemporary perspective, fairly clearly distinguish the different sets of practices, notwithstanding their common 'independence'. The fact that a shared rejection of fictional forms of cinematic representation, an abandonment of industrial relations of film production in favour of models of collaborative or collective production, and an adoption of a 'totalistic' position with regard to 'independent' film practice could nonetheless encompass a variety of political and aesthetic positions, is to be explained in terms of the precise character of the different practices concerned.

PROPAGANDA, EDUCATION AND THE STATE

The set of textual and institutional practices embodied in the notion of a British documentary movement can thus be reappropriated or recontextualised by considering them in relation to a series of ideological and economic/productive practices operating around certain notions of 'independence' at a specific moment. Although these practices may well be considered as in some senses interrelated, this is not to lose sight of their specificity. 'Independence' had a variety of inflections according to the economic, ideological and political functions of given practices. Therefore, the location of the documentary movement within a context of 'independence', rather than producing a new homogeneity, is the precondition for any examination of the precise conditions of its existence as a set of 'independent' film practices operating within a particular form of state sponsorship, the film unit system. On the ideological level, the positions discussed above were played out within a set of general and specific conjunctural relations whose aim was to make the notion of state propaganda less problematic or to mask it under the guise of 'art'. Politically, these conditions are perhaps to be understood in terms of the populist character of some left and radical politics in the 1930s in Britain. For instance, at that time fascism embraced a variety of left and social democratic positions in a relatively homogeneous way: the anti-fascist films made in the middle and late 1930s, especially those produced by the Progressive Film Institute in support of the campaign for arms and medical help for the Spanish Republic,[12] would certainly suggest this. In such a situation, in spite of political and aesthetic differences, independent film could sustain a degree of pluralism, and any relationship with the British state could be viewed as relatively unproblematic in political terms, particularly given the conditions in which state sponsorship operated for the film units.

Fundamental to the thrust of independent film practice was a preoccupation with education. This was evident, as for example in *Cinema Quarterly*, in the need felt to offer readings of the films and to encourage various forms of independent film-making; and less explicitly, in putting forward a notion of film production, distribution and exhibition as a unitary intervention. In this situation, state sponsorship *per se* and its institutional character concretised in the film unit structure (rather than through, say, the sponsorship or patronage of individuals or one-off projects) operated in a set of conditions *within which the state as such was not seen as the site of struggle*. State sponsorship was indeed seen as the vehicle of a practice, but having no central significance in itself. Such a position could be maintained for a decade or so alongside continuing state finance of independent film production only because the government-sponsored film units managed to negotiate and operate within a contradictory set of determinations.

CONDITIONS OF SPONSORSHIP

It is perhaps appropriate to recapitulate briefly the nature of these conditions.[13] During the period when the British documentary movement emerged, state sponsorship of 'independent' film-making took the exclusive form of funding production units attached to government departments. The Empire Marketing Board Film Unit (1928-1933) and the Post Office Film Unit (1933-1941) were the concrete examples of this. The activities of both units, since they operated as part of a government public relations programme, were ultimately delimited by the requirements of state propaganda. This must be seen in the context of the consensus view of the state as the benevolent mediator of mass democracy embodied in the notion of propaganda, a position publicly adopted as the rationale for the film units' existence. In Grierson's view, propaganda was 'elucidation' and 'understanding', aimed at 'civic understanding and civic co-operation . . . education in a world where the state is the instrument of the public's enterprise.'[14] This meant that any 'social' concern could not readily inform a politically oppositional film practice. However, this is not to argue that the state as sponsor occupied a monolithic or unitary position vis-à-vis the units, but merely to point to the character of the determination in the 'last instance' in this particular example. On the contrary, it is evident that the institutional repository of sponsorship was at various moments either indefinite or heterogeneous.

Moreover, and this is particularly important, the film unit system had built into its structure a certain distance from the sponsor. The principal means of maintaining this distance was the system whereby the bulk of production work was contracted out to a commercial firm. For instance, in 1935 the GPO Unit's contract for the provision of 'operational services' went to Associated Talking Pictures (to which Ealing Studio was associated), which was directly responsible for the employment of most of the production staff. Post Office funds for film-makers' wages were paid periodically to the contractor as part of a lump sum covering all services. This meant that the Treasury, which was ultimately responsible for monitoring the financing of the unit, had no day-to-day control over its expenditure. Until he resigned in 1937, Grierson, as Film Officer, controlled all decisions involving both production and administration. Therefore, so long as the total expenditure remained within the Treasury vote for the film unit, little direct control over production decisions could be exercised. However, built into the unit's structure after 1935 there was a check which could be brought into operation if it was seen to exceed the limits of film production for Post Office public relations.[15] In fact, no serious attempt was made to use this device.

An examination of the history of the working of these state-sponsored film units indicates that they operated within a set of determinations which provided recurrent moments of risk and recuperation. This particular form of organisation also meant that certain contradictions—which might seem to be inherent in that situation from the point of view of independent film practice today—either remained unexpressed or gained expression in a displaced form. The adoption, for example, of a craft/collaborative model for the organisation of the film production labour process obviously relates to the fact that people were prepared to work in the film units for relatively low pay or for no pay at all. The implications of the characteristically 'pre-capitalist' relations of production which appear to have prevailed stand in evident contradiction with the overt political radicalism of many of the units' personnel. That no attempt appears to have been made to unionise the GPO Unit, for example, is particularly significant in the light of the fact that some of its members were nonetheless active during the 1930s in the formation of the ACT and the organisation of the industry. As far as can be gathered, conflict around the labour process did not arise as such within the GPO Film Unit: on the contrary, as has already been suggested, the collaborative character of production relations was seen as a positive achievement in line with the particular position on independence embodied in the practice of the documentary movement—the rejection of alienating capitalist relations of production.

Also relevant to the question of internal conflict is the fact that the film unit system was an institutional expression of corporate sponsorship: the state as sponsor acted as producer rather than as patron. In this situation, those who worked in the units were employees, either of the government department concerned or of the contractor, and not clients: that is to say, they were not responsible as film-makers for negotiating the conditions of sale, distribution or exhibition of the products of their labour, since all rights rested in the producer. The question of conflict over rights, therefore, simply did not arise. This may be seen on the one hand in relation to the specific character of production relations in the units, and on the other to the fact that, given their contractual position, rights would have no financial implications for the film-makers themselves. Against this, however, the repeated recourse to notions of artistic freedom and individual creativity in defence of the unit would seem to indicate a potential, but as such largely unexpressed, concern over authorial rights. This concern expressed itself in displaced form, for conflicts in the area of authorship have tended to be depoliticised and rendered as interpersonal disagreements over, for example, screen credits.

The question of control on the part of the sponsor over the management of the film units and, relatedly, the nature of the films produced in them, is therefore not a simple one. There must undoubtedly have been limits in both cases, the transgression of which would have invited the closure of the units, but those limits were rarely put to the test: the public controversy over *Song of Ceylon* and *BBC—The Voice of Britain* which arose with the transfer of the EMB Film Unit to the GPO[16] probably constitutes the only major exception here. It seems clear that a good deal of autonomy in production decisions was possible, certainly until Grierson left the GPO, at which time administrative and production responsibilities formerly taken by the Film Officer were divided between two separate posts. It seems clear also that, given this autonomy and the precise character of the limits laid down for the unit's film production practice, a certain amount of space existed for 'experimental' work on documentary and other forms of representation. The fact that the unit constituted itself as a training ground, and that it was not required to recoup its operating costs through film production, would also indicate as much. And related to this is the tendency within the 'craft' model of production relations to foreground the notion of talent, genius or individual creativity, fostered in the hothouse atmosphere of the studio (in the Renaissance sense) or the workshop: in this view, collaborative work is seen to bring out rather than to suppress the talents of individuals. The recourse to conceptualisations of creativity and artistic freedom in defence of the—according to Civil Service standards—apparent inefficiency of the working of the units in this sense is not in contradiction with the ideal of collaborative production. On the contrary, it is this, together with the fact that the source of the units' sponsorship, the state, was not seen as the site of struggle, which largely explains how the notion of propaganda becomes deproblematised and can be claimed for 'art' in the work of the film units.

REALISM?—DOCUMENTARY AND EXPERIMENT
The mobilisation in turn of the 'film-as-art' model, combined with the rejection of cinematic fiction in favour of 'reality', accounts for the power of Grierson's dictum about documentary film as 'the creative interpretation of actuality'. In this view, it is the work of the film-maker to create art out of everyday life. However, to proceed from this to an unquestioning acceptance of the Griersonian position on realism as a means of approaching and understanding either the films in whose production he was involved, or of documentary film in general, is to invite either confusion or a premature and untheorised apprehension of those films as embodying a form or forms of realism. Besides the confusion which continues to attend the notion of realism whenever it is employed as a general category not related to specific textual practices or instances, such an approach tends to entail, on one level, a view of the output of the film units as a more or less undifferentiated sameness; and on another, a readiness to define the British documentary movement exclusively in terms of a limited number of film texts which come closest to contemporary definitions of 'realist documentary'. Films which do not fit easily into this category can then only be marginalised as 'idiosyncratic experiments'[17]—the fate of, for instance, all of Len Lye's work at the GPO, of much of Cavalcanti's, and also, though in a different way—by his elevation to the position of the GPO and Crown Film Unit's *auteur par excellence*—of the work of Humphrey Jennings.

To rescue such work from its marginal place and to site it within the *oeuvre* of the British documentary movement would require a long-overdue reexamination of the assumptions which lie behind taken-for-granted notions of realism as currently *applied* to a limited body of texts—largely those known as 'poetic documentaries', as indicated at the beginning of this paper. In other words, it would necessitate new approaches to the reading of the films themselves and a more theoretically elaborated use of the critical concepts at hand.

Any adequate examination of the relationship between the work of the state-sponsored film units and 'documentary realism', and of the relationship between both of these firstly with the work associated with other independent film practices in the 1930s and today, and secondly with the various forms of realism in the products of the British film industry and in certain television forms, must have as its precondition an awareness that the body of textual and institutional practices which constitutes the 'British documentary movement' is itself by no means homogeneous.

Any attempt to rewrite the history of the documentary movement must therefore constitute a demand for a reorientation of the issue. It calls in the first place for a questioning of the very notion of an autonomous British documentary movement and for the resiting of that movement in terms of 'independence' in film practice. In this way, the conditions of existence of this specific form of 'independent' practice, the limits to its 'independence', and the contradictions at work in its institutional operation become crucial topics of investigation. And secondly, because such a recontextualisation would necessitate a questioning of what constitute the textual practices which make up such a set of institutional operations, it would demand a reconsideration of the critical categories, notably 'realism', which have hitherto informed the understanding of some of the films concerned and have relegated others to the marginal and dehistoricised status of 'experiments'.

NOTES

1. Elizabeth Sussex, *The Rise and Fall of British Documentary*, University of California Press, Berkeley, 1975, p. 172.
2. See, for example, Sussex, ibid.; E. Orbanz, *Journey to a Legend and Back: the British Realistic Film*, Volker Spiess, Berlin, 1977; P. Rotha, *Documentary Diary*, Secker and Warburg, London, 1973.
3. A. Kuhn, '"Independent" Film Making and the State in the 1930s', in *Edinburgh '77 Magazine*.
4. See the articles by Claire Johnston, Trevor Ryan and Paul Marris in this book.
5. A. Lovell and J. Hillier, *Studies in Documentary*, Secker and Warburg, London, 1972, p. 25.
6. *Cinema Quarterly*, vol. 1, no. 1, 1932, p. 3.
7. Cited in Lovell and Hillier, op. cit., p. 15.
8. Cinemathèque Française, *Hommage au GPO Film Unit*, Paris, 1966.
9. Kuhn, op. cit., p. 46 and footnote 1, p. 54.
10. Six Empire Marketing Board Films bought by Gaumont-British for distribution and exhibition in normal commercial cinema programmes. All were originally silent films, with sound added by the distributor.
11. *Cinema Quarterly*, vol. 2, no. 1, 1933, p. 3.
12. *Defence of Madrid* (1936), *Refugees from Catalonia* (1936), *International Brigade* (1937), *Behind the Spanish Lines* (1938).
13. A full account is given in Kuhn, op. cit.
14. F. Hardy, *Grierson on Documentary*, Faber, London, 1946, p. 285.
15. Kuhn, op. cit., p. 53.
16. Ibid., footnote 4, p. 55.
17. Lovell and Hillier, op. cit., p. 30.

The Avant-Garde Attitude in the Thirties

Deke Dusinberre

In the autumn of 1966, in the midst of that period of prolific art activity in London, a telegram was composed for (though never despatched to) Jonas Mekas in New York, advising him of the imminent arrival of the London Film-Makers' Co-operative. And in the short lifetime of the London Co-op, this telegram has achieved almost mythic status: it finds its way into every history of the English avant-garde scene, and a reproduction of the telegram still graces—despite several changes of location and personnel—the office of the Co-op. Part of the charm of the telegram resides in its formulation: LONDON FILM-MAKERS COOP ABOUT TO BE LEGALLY ESTABLISHED STOP PURPOSE TO SHOOT SHOOT SHOOT SHOOT SHOOT STOP NEVER STOP NO BREAD NO PLACE TO LAY OUR HEADS NO MATTER JUST MIND IF YOU WANT TO MAKE MONEY STOP IF YOU LIKE BRYAN FORBES STOP IF YOU READ SIGHT AND SOUND STOP IF YOU WANT TO MAKE FILMS I MEAN FILMS COME ALL YOU NEED IS EYES IN THE BEGINNING STOP GEN FROM 94 CHARING CROSS ROAD W.C.2 PARTURITION FINISHED SCREAMS BEGIN STOP

It is generally considered to be—as the text itself implies— the birth certificate of the Film-Makers' Co-op and the avant-garde film movement it spawned, and therefore the telegram retains an insistent fascination for those who draw their identity from it. Like personal birth certificates, like very first photographs, there it *is*, irrefutable proof of one's existence, of one's formal entrance into history.

The validity of this document has never been challenged; that is to say, Britain claimed no avant-garde cinema prior to 1966. Hence it is with an eerie sensation—almost a shudder on recognition of an earlier incarnation— that one begins to unearth unmistakable traces of a coherent and productive avant-garde film practice in London in the Thirties. Of course, the work of Len Lye has long been acknowledged, as has the magazine *Close Up*; but these two incidents were never recognised as corresponding to a 'movement' or an identifiable corpus of work—they remained peripheral to the over-determining influence of the documentary movement fostered by John Grierson.

The term 'avant-garde' is intended toward those films (and that film criticism) which seek an alliance with modernism in the other arts, which demand a consistent interrogation of the medium; they challenge the industry

34

not only on the levels of content and of production/distribution/exhibition, but also on the level of the aesthetic/representational postulates on which the industry's commerce is based. In the Thirties, the characteristic ambiguity of the term was amplified, since 'the avant-garde' was manifest only through an institution of criticism (not, as in the Sixties, through an institution of production/distribution/exhibition). The avant-garde was thus really an attitude formulated by a series of film periodicals, an attitude which comprehended a disparate body of film-making practice. This in turn devolved on an intricate relationship between the avant-garde attitude and films produced by the documentary movement, the political newsreel movement, and even certain commercial (advertising) films. The common relationship existed on the level of a shared progressive aspiration, an aspiration which varied in degree and goal (from reformist to revolutionary) as well as in strategy but which nevertheless lent, at times, a spirit of unity among those who anticipated a progressive intervention from the cinema.

Indeed, the entire history of film could be written in the light of the progressive aspiration and its frustration. Annette Michelson has observed that ' . . . a certain euphoria enveloped the early film-making and theory. For there was, ultimately, a real sense in which the revolutionary aspirations of the modernist movement in literature and the arts, on the one hand, and of a Marxist or Utopian tradition, on the other, could converge in the hopes and promises, as yet undefined, of the new medium.'[1] When those hopes were squashed by the pressures of capitalist society, those who retained revolutionary fervour had to adopt a position of opposition rather than one of enthusiastic participation. The first reaction came with the first real consolidation of the industry: the avant-garde of the Twenties, capped by the combined aesthetic and political goals of the surrealist movement. And, until the production and financial changes wrought by the introduction of sound technology eventually polarised the situation, the emerging counter-cinema was able to contain contradictory versions of the progressive vision within a pluralist perspective. It is this pluralist perspective which yielded an avant-garde movement best characterised as an 'attitude'—as distinct from a specific aesthetic style or a specific production situation—which in turn leads to a certain ambiguity as to which films adhere to that avant-garde attitude.*

The initial focal point for avant-garde film activity in Britain was the film review *Close Up*, which commenced publication in July 1927 under the editorship of Kenneth Macpherson and Bryher. Edited from London and from Switzerland, *Close Up* immediately acquired an international reputation and, in conjunction with the exhibition work of the Film Society, established London as the site of an intellectual approach to film form. Writing of the intellectual film enthusiasts at the close of the silent film era, Richard Griffith says: 'Their leadership came mainly from Britain, which, though it had produced few films and no good ones, seems to have been a

---

*Further ambiguity is engendered by the incompleteness of the research for this article. At the time of writing too few of the films have been unearthed and too little of the documentation examined; my observations and apparent conclusions thus remain intellectually obstetric. [D.D.]

fertile field for the ideal of cinema perfectionism.'[2] If its opposition to the dominant industry could be construed as 'perfectionism', *Close Up's* eclectic endorsement of alternatives to that industry embodied an ambivalent attitude which remained characteristic into the first half of the subsequent decade. This ambivalence is expressed in Macpherson's introductory editorial where he asserted that 'really good art IS commercial' and expressed the wish that the film industry would awaken to the possibilities of the medium; but he felt it was more important to consider 'the film for the film's sake', conceding that 'the hope of the cinema lies with the amateur.'[3] *Close Up's* cultural sympathies with the avant-garde are suggested by its publication of contributions from people such as the imagist poet H.D. (who often wrote reviews and criticism and occasional poems), Gertrude Stein (who contributed a short story, *Mrs. Emerson*) and Man Ray (who published some photographs and a short piece on his film work). H.D.'s poem for the first issue, titled *Projector*, evokes the utopian expectations of the silent cinema which anticipate similar aspirations on the part of the 1960s' 'underground'. Hailing the power of the projector, she describes how it arrives:

'in a new blaze of spendour
calls the host to reassemble
and to readjust
all severings
and differings of thought,
all strife and strident bickering
and rest . . .'[4]

Close Up concentrated its film criticism on assaults on Hollywood 'mediocrity' and support for UFA and Soviet 'art' films, occasionally covering what it described as 'cine-poems' as well as documenting the work of the well-known French surrealists and the less-organised activities of independents such as the Belgian Charles Dekeukeleire and major individual figures such as Eggeling, Richter, Ruttmann and Lye. It also noted the formation of avant-garde production groups like Neofilms in Paris (under Cavalcanti) and Excentric Films in America (Herman Weinberg and Robert van Rosen).

The magazine similarly encouraged the production of cine-poems and other independent films in Britain. Pool Films sponsored H.D.'s attempt to make the 'first free verse film poem', *Wing Beat*, in 1927 (Pool Publishers produced *Close Up*). After two initial announcements of the work as 'in progress', *Close Up* was silent on the project; the lack of any trace of the film today or of any mention or review of it at the time have led me to assume that it was never completed. However, Oswell Blakeston—a film-maker and critic associated with *Close Up*—recollected in a recent interview[5] that the film was in fact finished and that *Close Up's* silence was due to an obscure embarrassment, either between H.D. and Macpherson or over the film itself. At any rate, no other record of the film's completion or screening has yet come to light. Blakeston himself made *I Do Like to be Beside the Seaside* (1927?), acted by H.D. and others, as something of a spoof on the pretentiousness of 'intellectual' film criticism. Described by a contemporary reviewer as '. . . a brilliant and amusing commentary on the technical devices of many well-known producers of films' (Dulac, Man Ray, Leni, Dreyer and Eisenstein are subsequently cited), it was contrived around 'an airy thread of story' involving a typist.[6] Blakeston advises that the only print of the film was destroyed by fire during the Second World War. Blakeston, who was to become one of the main apologists for an avant-garde attitude in the Thirties, also worked closely with the photographer Francis Bruguière. The two made *Light Rhythms*, an abstract film, in 1930. 'Pure' in conception, the 5-minute film represents a radical statement in film aesthetics, '. . . in which the material consisted of static designs in cut paper over which various intensities of light were moved. The appeal of the film lay in the changing light values, which were revealed by the cut paper patterns.'[7] A look at the graphic 'score' detailing the light movements reveals five sections or 'movements', each with six sequences. The symmetry and dynamism evoke the patterned structures of Eggeling or perhaps Richter, while stills suggest a more complex surface of light and shadow than is offered in either *Diagonal Symphony* or the *Rhythmus* series.[8] In addition, the musical score, by Jack Ellit, who was later to work with Len Lye (on *Tusalava* and at the GPO), was composed to enhance the sensation of progression and permutation.

If, in 1930, *Light Rhythms* and *Tusalava* [9] represented one pole of independent activity—that most comfortable with the epithet 'avant-garde'—that pole was nevertheless linked to other poles representing the progressive aspiration for the cinema. Two important developments—the political crisis in exhibition forced by film censorship and the aesthetic crisis in production following the advent of sound—cut across the independent sector and illustrate aspects of unity and difference.

The alignment of forces over the censorship issue suggests that association with specific film groups is not a sufficient guide to political position. Huntly Carter, in *New Spirit in the Cinema*, surveyed the positions as they were drawn in 1929-30, mobilised by the London County Council's recalcitrance in granting private exhibition permits for Soviet 'propaganda' films (*Potemkin, End of St. Petersburg, Storm over Asia*) to those groups formed expressly to circumvent the public censor. Carter writes: 'The combination of forces thus brought about for the purpose of making war on censorship, and obtaining a free hand in the importation and exhibition of "artistic" and social pictures and the reduction or abolition of Custom duties, is a very unusual one. It is a strangely variegated legion . . . broadly speaking it falls into three divisions answering to those of the three present political ones: Right, Centre, and Left.'[10] Carter lists the Film Society as 'Right', the Masses Stage and Film Guild as 'Centre', and the Federation of Workers' Film Societies as 'Left'. The Masses S.F. Guild is appropriately labelled 'Centre' due to its support by many members of government and the established theatrical profession, with Fenner Brockway as the President and six other MPs on its 25-member Advisory Council. The Film Society is labelled 'Right' apparently because of its aim (according to Carter) 'to act as a body supplementary and useful to the commercial film world in introducing to its study the work of talented newcomers and experimenters who might later contribute to its progress', and because its Council is comprised of 'The Honourable Ivor Montagu' (much is made of his parentage) as well as Iris Barry, Sidney L. Bernstein, Frank Dobson, Edmund Dulac, E. A. McKnight-Kauffer and W. C. Mycroft, and because of its association with *Close Up*, whose objects are 'in some respects similar to that of the Film Society'. (Macpherson is singled out as the editor and Blakeston as a principal contributor.[11]) Carter's 'Left'—the FOWFS—paradoxically has a Provisional Council which includes Montagu, Macpherson and Blakeston along with Harry Pollitt, W. Gallacher, Monica Ewer, Henry Dobb and G. P. Wells. Carter adds that although he is not sure that the Masses S.F. Guild is represented formally on the Council of the FOWFS, 'I think I am right in saying that it is affiliated with the FOWFS'. Carter then attempts to dismiss the paradox that is raised by his schematic divisions by subdividing the Federation into a 'Right', 'Right Centre', 'Centre', and 'Left'. Thus Carter misses the significance of the obvious conclusion that, on issues such as the political censorship of films, political distinctions were blurred, *even on an institutional level*. Macpherson and Blakeston had dubious credentials as political activists, but their commitment to a progressive role for the cinema merited their inclusion on the Council of the FOWFS.

Carter does point to an important difference between the groups, exemplified by the fact that the Film Society had an easy time with the censor by minimising the political aspect of the films in question. He cites a grievance raised by the *Daily Worker* of 9 January 1930: 'The Censors have allowed the film *New Babylon* to be shown to The Film Society, but the Workers' Film Society is refused permission to screen it . . . Why is The Film Society permitted to exhibit these films at one of the largest West End cinemas, and workers' societies are not? It is not hard to say why. The Film Society and *Close Up* clique have always done their best to convey the impression that they are obsessed far more with technique than with social content.'[12] This useful observation leads Carter to make an obtuse conclusion that, 'Indeed it is doubtful whether the leaders and members of these two groups have any knowledge of sociology and the transformation which present-day society is undergoing. The game is quite plainly to promote the idea that the moving picture must be detached from actuality and infuse it with a new aesthetic having nothing whatever to do with actual fact or a life-centred society.'[13] Thus Carter dismisses the likes of Blakeston, Macpherson and the Honourable Ivor Montagu.

The complex interdependence of progressive attitudes informed the production situation as well as the exhibition situation, and the production situation was of course further complicated at this point by the introduction of sound technology. At this juncture, Macpherson mounted an ambitious feature-length production titled *Borderline*. Incorporating a socially progressive theme into a 'psychoanalytic drama' (Bryher and H.D. collaborated on the film and both later were to be analysed by Freud), the film explored the social and sexual tension generated by the shifting passions of an interracial

38

foursome (black Americans Paul Robeson and Eslanda Goode Robeson played starring roles) which found itself in a small European town. The film was silent and, as is obvious from an illustrated review in *The Architectural Review*,[14] camera angle and mobility were exploited in the best silent technique for expressive purposes. A relatively disinterested description of the film was written some time later by Peter Noble from the perspective of *The Negro in Films*. His slightly condescending tone is balanced by his admiration for the thematic ambitions of the film and for Macpherson's 'delicate' handling of those themes.[15] The film was apparently not well received by the press, as Macpherson was compelled to defend it in the pages of *Close Up* after the film had its run, and it vanished from sight. Whatever the reasons for its disappearance,* an irresistible conjecture is that part of its problem lay in its non-specificity: not radical enough in form to adopt a marginal avant-garde status; not, as a silent film released in the summer of 1930, accessible enough to reach the mainstream. I would guess that it looked rather stylised and perhaps sadly 'rear-guard', certainly not qualities sought by those who consider themselves avant-garde.

It is now a cliché to attribute the 'decline' of the international avant-garde during the Thirties to the crippling effect of the added production costs of sound technology. Like most clichés, it offers a crude truth which masks a more subtle understanding of the issue. Silence itself was not considered a virtue (as would become the case in many avant-garde films of the Sixties and Seventies), as even the 'silent' avant-garde productions of the Twenties were invariably presented with musical accompaniment, but the 'talking picture' did frustrate one of the original aspirations of the silent cinema to formulate an 'international language'. Avant-garde critics welcomed sound, albeit warily, as yet another tool for creative production. From the modernist perspective it offered another level of control over the signifying relationship between image and sound and, as a progressive intervention, suggested new modes of formulating the internationalism promised by silent movies. Thus they railed against simple talkies as reactionary theatre, and lauded 'true sound pictures' which treated sound-image in a problematic vein. Blakeston, writing in 1931, cites as examples of 'the most intelligent contemporary use of sound' Fischinger's 'sound abstracts' (images derived from sound), Buñuel's *L'Age d'Or* (visual-aural counterpoint), and the *Secrets of Nature* science series (image motivated by word/text).[16] A few years later, in an article titled *Enslaved by Sound*, avant-garde film-maker Andrew Buchanan continued to complain of the turgidity of 'dialogue films' and admired documentaries for remaining 'sound films' in which '. . . dialogue is practically ignored, and the sound track is kept at bay . . . It is this freedom from microphones which enables documentary producers to create the maximum of movement, nothing hampering the picture, either during shooting or in the cutting room.'[17] Hence the advent of sound initially reinforced the pluralist attitude toward progressive counter-cinema in so far as it endorsed all practices aligned

*A print of the film is still in existence and may be acquired for preservation by the National Film Archive. [Ed.]

against the commercial talkie. The crisis it fomented within the avant-garde (which subsequently had a polarising effect throughout independent cinema) resulted not simply from the threat to the existence of avant-garde production through oligopolistic control of sound technology, but from a concomitant threat to the role and *identity* assumed by avant-garde film-making: silent avant-garde films were suddenly rear-guard, the cutting edge of their vanguard formal practice blunted and the films rendered effete. Silent films no longer represented the wave of the future, and that constituted a serious challenge to the avant-garde attitude. As private production became less feasible, many film-makers looked toward marginal industrial or advertising film-making or to state-sponsored production units, all of which, from the pluralist perspective of the time, retained at least the possibility of working within the avant-garde ambience, if in somewhat compromised circumstances.

Whatever the ultimate reasons for *Borderline's* lack of success, Pool Films made no more ventures into film production.[18] *Close Up's* spirit seems to have followed the stream of European directors who were drawn to Hollywood's studio attractions in the early Thirties. The magazine retained a Hollywood correspondent and became more sympathetic to the industry, finally folding towards the end of 1933.

Its role as 'voice of the avant-garde' had already been usurped earlier in that year when, in the spring of 1933, B. Vivian Braun published *Film*. With the next issue, the quarterly became *Film Art* and continued publication, somewhat irregularly, until 1937. While under Braun's direction, *Film Art's* masthead proclaimed itself as the 'international review of advance-guard cinema'. The magazine's tenure is perhaps most notable for its efforts to co-ordinate production and exhibition with the criticism it offered. Braun, like Macpherson, understood that critical intervention was only part of his role in the avant-garde and he completed several films, one of which, *Beyond This Open Road*, was screened by the Film Society in November 1934. Made with Irene Nicholson, then an assistant editor of *Film Art*, it was 'symphonic treatment of the open air'. The programme notes to the Film Society performance offer a laconic description of the production: 'This silent film was made in thirteen days and shot with a hand camera. The director was given waste material amounting in all to 1,500 feet, out of which in the final cutting emerged 1,000 feet of completed picture.'[19] The production is credited to the 'Film Art Group' which announced itself at that point as the 'First Cinema Unit for the production of Specialist Films' and eighteen months later listed five films for distribution, of which three were credited to Braun, including *Beyond This Open Road* distributed in a sound version. Additional films were made under the magazine's aegis, such as Nicholson's *Ephemeral*, a seven-minute 'film poem of light and passing time', and a mathematically abstract film by Robert Fairthorne and Brian Salt designed to demonstrate visually the equation of its title, $X + X = 0$ (distributed in 9.5, 16 and 35mm versions), and so on. Most impressive, perhaps, is the fact that *Film Art* almost immediately launched a 'Cinema Art Course' offering practical and correspondence courses in film-making, devising parallel courses for those with and those without access to 16mm equipment. It apparently became quite popular: the notice which re-advertised the course claimed that the first session 'met with enormous success—many persons having to be refused admission'; and maintained correspondents in America, Germany, Ireland and England.[20] The need for systematic film-making courses grounded in aesthetic theory was perhaps partially inspired to combat the 'amateurishness' of the 'cine clubs'. Writing in the first issue of *Film*, Judith Todd refers to the function of 'Exhibiting Film Societies' as distinct from the film-making 'Cine Clubs': 'They should realise that they [Exhibiting Film Societies] are at present fulfilling two functions: that of shewing [sic] films and that of understanding cinema. The latter, to which far too little attention has been given, is the active side and implies far more than shewing films; it must, of course, include making them, which is at present largely left to the cine clubs.' Whom she proceeds to dismiss: 'From examples of their work one would say that they exist, and will exist, chiefly as a means of using up film. Hence their name, as they start from the apparatus end, and are good customers of the makers of and dealers in cinematograph apparatus. The 16mm camera in the right hands is no toy. The pity is that the Film Societies, in concentrating on the exhibiting side, have not made more use of it for inexpensive experimental work.'[21]

Film Art was not to ignore the importance of exhibition, however. In 1923, Robert Herring complained in *Close Up* that 'London has no *salle d'avant-garde*. There is no place in London where good pictures can be regularly seen . . . It is absurd and maddening to go on cooing over the cinema when, in England, one is ignorant of Dulac, Dreyer, Epstein, Gance even . . .'[22] The same year did see the Avenue Pavilion Theatre in Shaftesbury Avenue dedicate itself to showing 'art' and 'absolute' (i.e. abstract) film. Although still very much a commercial venture, it did offer opportunities for public exhibition of non-commercial work. Blakeston recalls that the Avenue Pavilion, enthusiastically supported by *Close Up* and for a time the venue for Film Society screenings, was supportive of his work (*Light Rhythms* ran there) and was consistently willing to programme his and others' short films. The Avenue Pavilion sustained its policy for only a few years, but in the pilot issue of his periodical Braun could allude to two London cinemas [The Academy and The Everyman?] which were at least sympathetic to non-commercial films. In the same editorial he declared that '*Film* is not going to devote a certain amount of incidental space to good cinema, but is going to be entirely devoted to the film as an art. We shall seek a film-form, and attempt to solve the problems which prevent a realisation of that film-form.'[23] Good to his word, issue two of *Film Art* proudly announced the opening of the Forum Cinema in Villiers Street as 'London's Advance-Guard Cinema'. The Forum's organisers were M. Hatzfeld, B. Vivian Braun and Irene Nicholson. A year later Braun could list 'London's four worthwhile cinemas: the Forum, Villiers Street, the Curzon, Mayfair, the Academy, Oxford Street, and the Everyman, Hampstead.'[24] Despite its supportive image, the screening record of the Film Society was not particularly good. From 1925-1939 the only *British* avant-

41

garde films it programmed were *Light Rhythms* (1930), *Beyond This Open Road* (1934), $X+X=0$ (1936), and four films by Lye: *Tusalava* (1929), *Kaleidoscope* (1935), *Birth of a Robot* (1936) and *N. or N.W.* (1937). In fact, the Film Society's selection of British films was habitually confined to scientific films, sporting films, or documentaries.[25] Exhibition opportunities for London's avant-garde film-makers seem to have been at least as good through commercial cinemas as through the various film societies.

The concerted efforts of those involved in *Film Art* to produce, distribute, exhibit and criticise avant-garde film were impressive, but their impact was almost certainly weakened as a result of internal dissensions. Following a nine-month hiatus after issue five of *Film Art*, number six appeared with Nicholson and John C. Moore as editors and Braun presumably banished. The masthead dispensed with references to 'advance-guard cinema' and described itself as 'An Independent Quarterly devoted to The Serious Film'. The magazine did not change drastically in either style or content (articles on abstract film, on photography by Blakeston, etc, continued to appear), but it took a swipe at the 'advance-guard' six months later on the appearance of the rival *New Cinema*: 'The *avant-garde* film movement died in France many years ago, and *New Cinema* has only just realised it.'[26] *New Cinema* was edited by . . . B. Vivian Braun. It incorporated the familiar slogan of 'An International Review of Advance-Guard Cinema' and added, for those with any remaining doubt, that *New Cinema* was the 'Only Cinema Review in the World *Solely* Devoted to Art in Cinema'. *Film Art's* snide forecast of a single-issue publication for *New Cinema* turned out to be accurate, despite *New Cinema's* promising beginning with articles by Blakeston and Herman Weinberg and Robert Fairthorne (regular contributors to *Film Art*) and a particularly good one by Moholy-Nagy, all of which were quite theoretical in tone. Confusingly, however, the British films that were covered in the review section are uncompromisingly commercial: Paramount's *The Scoundrel* and *The Crusaders** and Hitchcock's *Thirty-Nine Steps* for Gaumont-British, etc.

Film Art carried on for another year, during which Nicholson and Brian Montagu left for Trinidad to make a film for the *Trinidad Guardian* about 'the varied life of Trinidad, its industries . . . and its cosmopolitan population', production stills from which graced the final issues. It is unclear whether the film was ever completed.

Film Art and *New Cinema* had sustained the avant-garde attitude (during a decade of limited avant-garde production) within the progressive aspiration as inaugurated by *Close Up* and the activities of the late Twenties. This attitude constituted itself as a vaguely progressive political line and a specific formal radicalism as the best strategy to combat the hegemony of the film industry. A manifesto published in the third issue of *Film Art* distills many of the ideas which informed that attitude. The language and visual style of the manifesto (reprinted here in Part IV, page 175) invoke those of Dziga Vertov, and in tone it attains the stridency of a political manifesto; yet

---

**The Scoundrel*, by Hecht and MacArthur; *The Crusaders* by DeMille. [Ed.]

its priorities remain clearly aesthetic: 'To analyse the potentialities and solve the aesthetic problems of cinema art' is listed first and 'to encourage the use of the cinema as social reformer . . .' is listed last.[27] Those, uncynically, were its priorities. The manifesto even asserts that *Film Art* would remain 'as non-political as possible', for example, but also that articles would be printed as received, 'except when space demanded cutting'. That is to say, while *Film Art* (Vivian Braun) could be identified with left wing politics, it affirmed the liberal pluralist tendency of the avant-garde to avoid an explicit political line, defining its role as one of open access to those with political ideas related to the cinema; hence it published articles on political film, by Herbert Marshall, then in the Soviet Union, and an anti-fascist article by John Sydney titled *Films and Internationalism*, etc. Braun himself would write that: 'The newsreel's (one might say the cinema's) two greatest tasks are: (1) the prevention of international war via the promotion of international understanding . . . and (2) the putting before the public facts concerning the conditions under which those persons some call 'workers' (others, more aptly, 'slaves of capitalism') live.'[28] Typically, Braun subsequently feels obligated to qualify that position: 'Our [i.e., *Film Art's*] interest in films is judging them first and foremost as art . . .'[29]

The attitude of openness, encouraging contact and co-operation ('Always in contact with our readers. CONTACT. And co-operation. Two essentials.'[30]) extended to an eclecticism regarding the production situation and stylistic tendencies of all non-industrial cinema. Thus the avant-garde attitude treated sympathetically the early GPO Film Unit and advertising films. For instance, Irene Nicholson reviewed Basil Wright's *Liner Cruising South* in 1933: 'If a little of it is ordinary it is the fault of the super producers . . . But the photography has a fine feeling for surface textures and the opening and closing sequences are pure poetry.'[31] Braun meanwhile described Wright's *Cargo from Jamaica* as an 'exquisitely photographed, beautifully mounted essay', noting Wright's 'eye for sculptural beauty'.[32] In addition to the vocabulary used (poetic, painterly, sculptural) these comments are characteristic in that they are highly selective, stressing certain qualities or points in the film and understating less attractive aspects of such commercial/institutional commissions. Hence a relatively brief sequence in Arthur Elton's *Aero-Engine* could be hailed as follows: 'For pure visual thrill, and impressionistic beauty, and cinematic value, the sequence of the aeroplane's first flight is unsurpassed. This sequence is a film in itself, and at that one of the finest that has ever come from England.'[33] This selective encouragement of certain sequences paralleled the celebration of individual film-makers as the bastion against industrial production-line anonymity. The avant-garde ambience thus sought to include not only those who financed and executed their work entirely alone, but also those who had chosen a slightly different production route. Nicholson would laud Paul Rotha's documentary *Contact* because it was 'a film directed, mounted and photographed by one man, an artist . . .'[34] Similarly, Wright is described as exemplary 'because he is, with Arthur Elton, and one or two others, one of the few men in England making real films which he writes, directs, AND EDITS.'[35] Since the best strategy for the formal radicalisation sought by the avant-garde seemed to lie in selective encouragement of those production aspects which permitted formal experimentation, it developed the 'selective pluralism' in which certain advertising films and documentaries were recruited as part of the avant-garde project (particularly those which experimented with sound/image signification). As early as 1931 Bruguière and Blakeston made a short advertising film, an entirely abstract film again involving the movement of light and shapes which eventually delivered a lettered message: 'Empire Buyers are Empire Builders.'[36] Blakeston defended the advertising efficacy of such an approach with the comment that through such abstraction 'the screen [was] used as the ultimate nerve end'. He also optimistically assessed the creative and economic potential for film-makers: '. . . an experimental approach can only be found in the new possibility of the advertising film. Indeed, the advertising film provides an economic basis for all pioneer work at the moment.'[37]

The search for an economic base for their work actually led pioneers, who had previously relied on private patronage, in three directions: the fringe of the industry, the advertising film, and state funding. Apparently several of the avant-garde film-makers tried stints at the studios (Blakeston among them) but only Andrew Buchanan appears to have had some success. Buchanan produced a fortnightly 'cinemagazine' (first known as *Ideal Cinemagazine,* then as *The Gaumont-British Magazine*) which ran as a support to commercial features. The flexible format of the magazine permitted some degree of experimentation and Buchanan directed sequences which explored dance and movement through experimental montage, which he theoretically justified in the pages of periodicals like *Film Art* and *Cinema Quarterly*.[38] Similarly, despite Blakeston's claims for advertising work, only a few European animators managed to support themselves in this manner, George Pal being the only one to work in England for any period. However, the term 'advertising work' included the commercially sponsored films like Lye's *Birth of a Robot* and Wright's *Liner Cruising South*, which were designed not so much to sell a specific product as to sell a corporate image (arts patronage eventually becoming part of that image). Though this type of work provided only occasional support for avant-garde film-makers in the Thirties, it did lead in the direction of the more substantial state patronage, for selling the corporate image was often coincident with selling the state image. And, indisputably, the most significant new economic base for pioneer film work was the one provided by state patronage in the form of the Empire Marketing Board and GPO Film Units headed by John Grierson.

The history of the Film Unit is sufficiently well documented to obviate the need for further discussion here, except in so far as the Film Unit influenced the notion of an avant-garde practice. As mentioned above, the avant-garde apologists perceived state patronage as a potential ally. By stressing the 'poetic moment' in otherwise unadmirable (to the avant-garde) films and by emphasising individual control over specific projects (even where control may have been ambiguous[39]), the avant-garde critics intervened in a clearly contradictory production situation in hopes of tipping the balance their way. This means that in the mid-Thirties the productions of the Film Unit were often perceived as within the avant-garde ambience. This suggests that documentary and promotional films should be re-analysed for evidence of their contribution to a modernist interrogation of the medium and, more importantly, that to the financial security and progressive connotations of working within the Film Unit should be added the attraction of enhanced *artistic* possibilities.* Thus Len Lye and Norman McLaren no longer pose a serious contradiction within the history of the Film Unit, and the attraction of the Unit for young artists such as the painters Coldstream and Jennings, the composers Ellit and Britten, and the poet Auden, becomes not only understandable but, given the progressive aspirations still associated with the medium, almost inevitable.

But the demands of state sponsorship (as well as commercial sponsorship, of course) inflected the films away from those values of incisive formal experiment and complete individual control. Although freed from the requirement to yield profit, Grierson considered mass exhibition and mass comprehension a palpable goal. Wright gently formulates the contradiction: 'The price to be paid for the privilege of aesthetic experiment was therefore the discipline of public service.' But Grierson was known to expect firm discipline. He is reputed to have introduced the young McLaren to the Film Unit with the following admonition: 'What you will learn here is discipline. You have enough imagination, you need not worry about that. But you are going to get disciplined.'[40] In addition, Grierson's conception of the propaganda role for the Film Unit[41] militated against the ambiguous or problematic formulation of ideas accruing to aesthetic innovation, and the documentary movement increasingly adopted a 'realist' aesthetic. Finally, state control could impose more direct forms of censorship as well: one of McLaren's finest GPO films, *Love on the Wing*, an animated fantasy about a new airmail service, was suppressed by the minister responsible for the GPO, who found its linear transmogrifications 'too erotic and too Freudian'.[42] These factors frustrated the avant-garde spirit, and after the demise of *Film Art* in 1937 there was no voice to assert the avant-garde attitude within the contradictions of state patronage.

State sponsorship also inflects history. The state tends to preserve (when it does so at all) its own films, not other films by those working occasionally for the state, much less those by Bruguière, Blakeston, Fairthorne, Salt, Buchanan, Macpherson, Braun, Nicholson, etc, who worked completely outside of the state apparatus. If those films were (or prove to be) extant, no doubt a different history, one with a space for a distinct avant-garde ambience, would emerge. Yet there are other factors which suggest themselves as contributory reasons for the absence of any 'history' of the avant-garde in the Thirties. It is striking that none of the relatively established visual artists in Britain

---

*See e.g. the arguments for the masking function 'art' fulfilled in relation to propaganda by and for the imperialist state in A. Kuhn's essay and C. Johnston's analysis of the interrelation of discourses, both in this book [Ed.].

had any regard for the cinema, and none explored its visual possibilities. In Paris, artists such as Leger, Duchamp, Man Ray (not to mention the surrealist celebration of cinema) elevated its status and imbued those avant-garde productions with an immediate historical value, a value which increases not just through film history, but also through the increasing art historical value of these artists' other work. It is impossible to assert that Robert Fairthorne and Brian Salt's abstract film $X+X=0$ is any less interesting or successful than, say, Man Ray's *Emak Bakia*; but it is obvious that Fairthorne and Salt's anonymity works against the film ever being found and, if rediscovered, equitably evaluated. It is equally difficult to ascertain why London-raised artists ignored the progressive aspiration of the cinema. One can only allude to the presence of a general anti-modernist trend within the milieu that professed modernism in terms of a hesitation, a reluctance to assume the logical extensions of that position or to relate it to film; so that a group of important young artists who named themselves 'Unit One'—Barbara Hepworth, Ben Nicholson, Henry Moore, Edward Wadsworth, Paul Nash, Frances Hodgkins and Edward Burra—restricted their call for modernism to the most traditional of arts. Nash asserted that 'Unit One may be said to stand for the expression of a truly contemporary spirit, for that which is recognised as peculiarly *of today* in painting, sculpture, and architecture'.[43] In relation to 'modern' art, cinema was doomed not even to a marginal role, but to a non-existent one. (Consequently, attempts to integrate cinema as a modern art were not notably successful.) *The Architectural Review* did cover avant-garde film for a period, but ceased to do so in 1935. *Cinema Quarterly*, founded in 1933, initially drew on an eclectic list of contributors which included the art historian Herbert Read (ironically, the author of the article on Unit One), the poet Hugh MacDiarmid and the designer McKnight Kauffer (who did the cover) as well as Blakeston, Braun, Buchanan and Fairthorne. But *Cinema Quarterly* shifted its commitment to realist documentary in a trajectory which describes the rise of the Film Unit and the decline of the avant-garde. It is paradoxical that consistent support for the cinema as a radical visual art came from literary directions. Macpherson, Bryher, Herring, Nicholson all had literary connections and careers, and it is their efforts to promote the avant-garde through literary periodicals which dictate this sketchy history.

And yet there is a further reason for the sketchiness of this history: the very a-historicism of the avant-garde attitude. That attitude stressed the newness, the nowness, of the work being done (cf. the crisis provoked by technological supersession of sound). It stressed *action*. This is evident not only in *Film Art's* manifesto but also in Blakeston's recollection of the period; it was not the films but their immediate impact which was crucial. Blakeston resists the idea of restoring and institutionalising the films made during that period but adds: 'If you could capture the *impact* of those films and put it in a museum, that would be ok . . .' He claims that he simply wanted 'to do something quick and magic'. Such an attitude was reinscribed in the mid-Sixties in London when the founders of the Film-Makers' Co-operative drafted their telegram affirming that ALL YOU NEED IS EYES IN THE BEGINNING. Not to be confused with an *aloofness* from history, this almost infantile fascination is necessary to sustain that level of commitment to a marginalised and as yet powerless mode of representation and expression. And such an a-historical fascination condemns one to (rewards one with) eternal rebirth.

NOTES

1 Michelson, *New Forms In Film* (Exhibition catalogue), Montreux, 1974, p. 10.
2 Griffith (with Paul Rotha), *The Film Till Now*, London, 1967, p. 416.
3 Macpherson, *Close Up*, no. 1, July 1926, p. 46.
4 H.D., 'Projector' in *Close Up*, no. 1, p. 46.
5 Subsequent unattributed quotations are from an interview between Blakeston and this author in December 1977.
6 Mercurius, 'The Pipes of Pan' in *The Architectural Review*, vol. 67, p. 341. Mercurius was James Burford, a friend of Blakeston's who, with his brother Robert Burford, was also associated with *Close Up*. Blakeston later assumed J. Burford's role as regular film critic for *The Architectural Review*.
7 Rotha, *The Film Till Now*, p. 342n. Rotha admired the film.
8 Mercurius, 'Light and Movement' in *The Architectural Review*, vol. 67, pp. 154–155.
9 For a description of the films of Lye see, for example, David Curtis, *Experimental Film*, London, 1971.
10 Huntly Carter, *New Spirit in the Cinema*, London, 1930, p. 285.
11 *Ibid*, p. 286.
12 *Ibid*, p. 290.
13 *Ibid*, p. 290.
14 Mercurius, 'Art, Fact and Abstraction' in *The Architectural Review*, vol. 68, p. 258.
15 Noble, *The Negro in Films*, New York, 1970, p. 144.
16 Blakeston, 'Film Enquiry—3' in *The Architectural Review*, vol. 70, p. 47.
17 Andrew Buchanan, 'Enslaved by Sound' in *Film Art*, no. 2, p. 54.
18 Apart from H.D.'s *Wing Beat*, Pool also sponsored Macpherson's first film, *Monkey's Moon*. I surmise, although I have no evidence, that much of the money behind Pool Films and Pool Publishers came from Bryher, whose given name was Annie Winifred Ellerman, of the Ellerman shipping firm.
19 Programme note, The Film Society, 25 November 1934.
20 *Film Art*, no. 4, pp. 4 and 86.
21 *Film*, no. 1, pp. 12–13. The relationship of the avant-garde to the burgeoning amateur film movement of the Thirties remains ambiguous. Although encouraging amateur production, avant-garde apologists were dismissive of the amateurs' attempts to ape the industry. Some of this was perhaps due to an élitist attitude, some of it perhaps to a reasonable defence of different criteria. See, for example, Ralph Bond, 'The Amateur Convention' in *Close Up*, vol. 5, no. 6, pp. 479–483.
22 Herring, *Close Up*, May 1928, p. 56.
23 *Film*, no. 1, p. 3.
24 *Film Art*, no. 5, p. 31.
25 Film Society programme notes. In fact, through its eclectic programming the Film Society reinforced the pluralist aspect of independent cinema during this period.
26 *Film Art*, no. 8, p. 39.
27 *Film Art*, no. 3, p. 9
28 *Film Art*, no. 4, p. 55.
29 *Ibid*, p. 55.
30 *Film Art*, no. 3, p. 4.
31 *Film Art*, no. 2, p. 53.

32 *Ibid*, p. 53.
33 *Ibid*, p. 53.
34 *Ibid*, p. 52.
35 *Ibid*, p. 50.
36 *Commercial Art*, no. 10, p. 65 (illus, p. 68).
37 *The Architectural Review*, vol. 69, p. 137.
38 See, for example, *Film Art*, no. 2, p. 63, and *Cinema Quarterly*, vol. 1, p. 165.
39 See Annette Kuhn's essay in this book, p. 24.
40 *Norman McLaren*, catalogue by Scottish Arts Council, Edinburgh, 1977, p. 11.
41 See Annette Kuhn's essay in this book.
42 *McLaren*, p. 13.
43 Herbert Read, 'Unit One' in *The Architectural Review*, vol. 74, p. 126.

APPENDIX: Provisional List of English Avant-Garde Film-makers

Below is a list of the names of those principally identified with the avant-garde in London in the 1930s, followed by titles and, where films are obscure (or not extant), a reference to a description or mention of the film. Although the argument of this article is that the avant-garde attitude during this period was a pluralist one (selectively encompassing, for example, the work of the film units or certain aspects of commercial productions), this list is limited to those film-makers who worked exclusively within the avant-garde ambience and therefore have been completely overlooked by conventional film history (Lye and McLaren excepted, of course). Any additional information on film-makers (their whereabouts) or prints (ditto) would be greatly appreciated.

Oswell Blakeston: *I Do Like to be Beside the Seaside* (1927)—*The Architectural Review*, vol. 67, p. 341.
Light Rhythms (with Bruguière, 1930)—*The Architectural Review*, vol. 67, p. 154.
Empire Buyers are Empire Builders (with Bruguière, 1931)—*Commercial Art*, vol. 10, p. 65 and *The Architectural Review*, vol. 69, p. 137.

Guy Branch: *Punch and Judy* (1936?)—*New Cinema*, no. 1, p. 31.

B. Vivian Braun: *Exhilaration* (1933?)—*Film Art*, no. 1, p. 18.
Beyond the Open Road (with Irene Nicholson, 1934), also known as *Beyond This Open Road*—*Film Art*, no. 5, p. 33.
Terrific Adventure (1936?)—*New Cinema*, no. 1, p. 31.
Rustic London (1936?)—*New Cinema*, no. 1, p. 31.

Francis Bruguière: *Light Rhythms* (with Blakeston, 1930); *Empire Buyers are Empire Builders* (with Blakeston, 1931); *The Way* (?) —*Film Art,* no. 10, p. 24.

Andrew Buchanan: Produced fortnightly (sometimes weekly) 'cinemagazines', including the following sequences—
Machine (1933?)—*Film Art,* no. 2, p. 63.
Time (1933?)—*Film Art,* no. 2, p. 63.
Chess-Bored—*Film Art,* no. 5, p. 38.
Dance Flaws—*Cinema Quarterly,* vol. 1, p. 165.

Robert Fairthorne: $X+X=O$ (with Salt, 1936)—*Film Art,* no. 9, p. 18.

H.D.: *Wing Beat* (completed? 1927).

Brian Desmond Hurst: *The Tell Tale Heart* (1933?)—*Film Art,* no. 1, p. 28.

Len Lye: *Tusalava* (1928); *A Colour Box* (1935); *Kaleidoscope* (1935); *The Birth of A Robot* (1936); *Rainbow Dance* (1936); *Trade Tattoo* (1937); *N or NW* (1937); *Colour Flight* (1938); *Lambeth Walk* (1939); *When the Pie was Open* (1939–40).

Norman McLaren: Untitled (1933); *Seven till Five* (1933); *Camera Makes Whoopee* (1935); *Colour Cocktail* (1935); Five Untitled Shorts (1935); *Hell Unltd.* (with Helen Biggar, 1936); *Book Bargain* (1937); *News For the Navy* (1937); *Many A Pickle* (1937-38); *Love on the Wing* (1938); *The Obedient Flame* (1939).

Kenneth Macpherson: *Monkey's Moon* (1928?); *Borderline* (1930)—*The Architectural Review,* vol. 68, p. 258.

Brian Montagu: Trinidad film (with Nicholson, completed?)—*Film Art,* no. 7, p. 8; no. 9, p. 23; no. 10, p. 9.

Irene Nicholson: *Ephemeral* (1934)—*Film Art,* no. 5, p. 42; Trinidad film (with Montagu, see above).

Brian Salt: $X+X=O$ (with Fairthorne, 1936).

Postscript

This article, completed some time ago, is ageing rapidly. Some of the films I described as lost have already come to light. A print of *Borderline* is in the collection at Eastman House in Rochester, New York, and fragments of *Wing Beat* have recently been deposited in the Museum of Modern Art, New York. The latter surfaced through the timely efforts of Mrs. Perdita Schaffner (H. D.'s daughter) and Anne Friedberg (in connection with her research on her doctoral thesis for the Cinema Studies Department of New York

University). I have not yet had the opportunity to see the films, and thus have decided to let this article stand unaltered.

However, I would like to make one correction. In a brief illuminating discussion with Friedberg, she asserted that *Wing Beat* was primarily Macpherson's film, despite my inclination to credit it to H. D. and in spite of the discovery of the fragments within H. D.'s estate (the film is described in *Close Up* simply as 'a Pool film'; H. D. is identified as the star). After a quick review of the meagre documentation currently available to me, I am inclined to agree with Friedberg that although the film relied on the contributions from H. D. and Bryher, it was probably the inspiration of Macpherson, and should be credited either to him or to the Pool group as a whole.

Deke Dusinberre
July 1979

Film and Political Organisations in Britain 1929–39

Trevor Ryan

The present interest in the relationship between film and the workers' movement in the two decades before the Second World War stems in part from a complex rethinking of relationships between political and cultural struggle over the last ten years. Two areas can be mentioned as having contributed to the re-examination of the way in which, if any, film has been considered as a weapon in the class struggle. Firstly, recent theoretical and political developments within Marxist currents have placed a crucial importance on notions of class struggle, both in opposition to tendencies of economism within the workers' movement, and in recognition of the significance of ideological factors in mediating social and political forms. Secondly, since the mid-1960s, the work of several independent film groups in Britain, Europe and the USA has been directly related to various struggles and campaigns fought by different sections of the working class.[1] This type of agitational work, in the context of a broader development of 'independent' cinema, has posed two related questions on the use of film as a political tool: firstly, in terms of the film's aesthetic construction and presentation of political ideas; and, secondly, in terms of the institutional relationships regarding funding, distribution and exhibition of the films, between official institutions (political parties, trade unions, etc.), campaign organisations, the politically conscious independent film-makers and distributors, and the audience (potential and actual) whom the films address and/or reach.

Any enquiry into 'independent cinema' or 'film and the workers' movement' in the 1930s, based within a 'left' framework, has to beware of simplifying or mythologising those activities so as merely to produce a teleological correspondence to the current situation, as if to provide a legitimating ancestry for contemporary practices. Accounts written by participants about their experiences, at the time or after many years, have too often provided the precedents for these present-day reconstructions.[2] A problem with this kind of history has been its inability to take an analytical–critical position on the subject it reconstructs (a previously unrecorded history, in opposition to dominant bourgeois reconstructions). The work of Bert Hogenkamp on film and the workers' movement has tended to continue within this methodological tradition.[3] It is beyond the scope of this article to engage in a general theoretical critique of Hogenkamp's published work, and there is no wish to minimise its importance in opening up the subject and providing a firm basis for future research. However,

Hogenkamp's reconstructions present as resolved—or fail to formulate adequately—a number of questions which are central to any discussion of 'independent cinema' or 'film and the workers' movement'. Any such discussion needs to be situated within the contradictions inherent in the labour movement generally; and the specific relations between film groups and the various political and campaign organisations need to be traced as the requirements and strategies of these latter bodies evolved, contingent upon a series of conjunctural factors which need to be analysed. These film groups responded to changing political situations in different ways, reflecting differing political perspectives, and resulting in differing filmic and political practices. The debates which took place within and between these groups vis-à-vis film and the class struggle need to be traced and contextualised. There was, for example, no linear development of the Film and Photo League in Britain: there was considerable tensions between political activists wishing to make films as an attempt to combine cultural practice with the overall political struggle, and the film enthusiasts with liberal and left-wing sympathies who came to dominate the League.

As a working paper this article aims to provide a clarification of the institutional relationships between these film groups and political and campaign organisations. Necessarily this involves a discussion of the formation of these groups and the political-ideological contexts in which they operated. Because so much basic research needs to be done, and because of the limitations of space, this treatment unavoidably simplifies an intriguingly complex conjuncture. No adequate analysis, for example, exists of the labour movement in this period. Of more immediate relevance, the relations between Kino, the Film and Photo League (FPL) and the Progressive Film Institute (PFI), for example, were never static, but were determined by fluctuating memberships and changing political perspectives; their development cannot be seen entirely in terms of separate organisations, as many of the more active participants were members of both Kino and the FPL.

The development of the use of film by fractions of labour has its origins partly in the work of Workers' International Relief (WIR) and the cultural export strategies of the Soviet Union, and partly in the theoretical response of the left in Britain to the emergence of film and radio into political and cultural prominence. The WIR had been set up by Willi Muenzenberg in 1921 for the organisation of relief to the millions in Soviet Russia starving as a result of the civil war; one of its main activities had been the production and exhibition throughout Europe of films depicting this starvation to raise funds and support. Conscious of the need to 'present a little of the truth about Soviet Russia' to the rest of the world, the WIR established a film production company, Mezhrabpom Russ, in 1924.[4] Thereafter Muenzenberg 'went into the film business in a big way . . . His was the direct influence behind Meschrabpom Filmgesellschaft, which employed four hundred people in its main studios in Moscow, and sponsored such classics as *The End of St. Petersburg, Mother, The Road to Life* and *Storm over Asia*. For such films, the

Prometheus-Filmgesellschaft acted as sole distributing agent in Germany: director, Willie Muenzenberg.'[5]

By 1929, WIR national sections were operating in most countries of the world, and film departments had been set up within the majority of western sections.[6] These activities coincided with a major cultural operation in the West, organised in Moscow: 'Soviet culture had been creating an increasingly favourable impression in the West . . . In the field of culture, the Russians conducted a vigorous export trade, despatching to the West distinguished actors, directors, dancers, musicians and writers'.[7] This in turn coincided with the initiation of the 'third period' by the Executive Committee of the Communist International (CI), and the policy of 'class against class'. This policy was based on the assumption that capitalism was soon to be confronted with a severe world economic crisis, in which internal and international antagonisms would sharpen dramatically, creating a potentially revolutionary situation. War against the Soviet Union being an inevitable outcome of this crisis, the tasks of the communist parties, according to the CI, were to place themselves in the forefront of these rising struggles, and organise 'class mass action' against war and in defence of the Soviet Union.[8] A major Comintern organisation, the Red International of Labour Unions (RILU), laid down at its 4th Congress in 1928 that these tasks required the integration of industrial and educational-cultural work, and established an agit-prop department accordingly.[9] Educational-cultural work was to be based on the tasks immediately facing workers in struggle at the point of production, but geared also to educating workers about the Soviet Union, and co-ordinating the various cultural leagues for the mobilisation of large numbers of workers in revolutionary organisations. In Germany this policy was successful, the basis for the building of mass revolutionary culture which already existed politically and organisationally. For example, in Berlin, in 1929, a Workers' Cultural League was formed consisting of the WIR, the Federation of Proletarian Writers, the Association of Revolutionary Writers in Fine Arts, the Workers' Radio Federation, the Workers' Sports and Culture Amalgamation and the International Federation of Victims of War and Toil.[10]

In Britain, however, the situation was entirely different. The 1924–39 period was one of class defeat for labour, which can briefly be indicated by, among other factors: the alignment of the TUC with the state (formally acknowledged by Bevin only as late as 1937 at the TUC Annual Conference); the dominance of social democratic principles and practices within the labour movement (such as economism), and the concomitant ascendancy of the Labour Party as *the* political organisation of labour; the political dominance of the National Government, the maintenance of striking class inequalities, and the perpetration of wide-ranging repressive measures to sustain them; the dramatic vacillations and extreme rightward shift of the Communist Party (CPGB) after the triumph of Stalinism in the 1927–29 period; the outbreak of European war in 1939; and lastly, the pervasive ideological and political fragmentation of labour, which both underpinned and was sustained by these other developments.

In such circumstances there were no mass revolutionary organisations which could maintain a network of people in struggle and give sustenance to those struggles. Even the Communist-inspired Minority Movement failed to achieve widespread support in the early 1930s.[11] In the absence of mass revolutionary organisations, no mass revolutionary culture could emerge. It is in this very specific situation that the London Workers Film Society was launched in November 1929. The Society, and Atlas Films, the distributor formed to supply the Federation of Workers Film Societies (FOWFS), have their origins in the work of the RILU agit-prop department and the WIR. Both were set up to show and make available 'Russian and other working-class films', 'to aid and encourage the workers in their fights against capitalism'.[12] Atlas acquired virtually all its material through Prometheus Films and Weltfilm in Berlin; and, just as the American section of the Friends of the Soviet Union (the WIR organisation in the USA) established a film production unit from a workers' photo league, merging this with its own film distribution department,[13] so the British Friends of the Soviet Union (FSU) played some part in launching the London Workers Film Society, Atlas Films and the FOWFS. Of those involved in the formation of the LWFS, Ralph Bond, Ivor Montagu, Emile Burns and Eva Reckitt were all members of the FSU. Bond was also the official copyright holder for all Soviet photographs in Britain,[14] and the FSU, with its own 'workers' photo section', regularly offered large collections of photographs for meetings and exhibitions throughout the country. Furthermore, Ivor Montagu was the treasurer of the FSU, and continued to be so until at least the end of 1936.

The importance of the FSU both as an organisation informally connected with the Comintern and in the development of independent film groups in Britain is more apparent in the period after the demise of the FOWFS, first when no independent film organisation was operating in the 1932–33 period, and secondly during the transitional period of Comintern strategy (1934–36). In the former, the FSU arranged film shows, screening such films as *Soviet Russia Past and Present*, and probably acted as the repository for Atlas Films' production after the company had folded. In the latter, it responded to the Comintern's call for measures to strengthen the international defence of the Soviet Union, by building up its own collection of films, mainly visual records of trips to the Soviet Union which it had organised and whose production it had sponsored, but also Soviet shorts: 'The National Committee has decided to break down all barriers to the truth about the Soviet Union . . . A big campaign by meetings, lectures, conferences, films and the issue of printed and illustrated materials is being worked out to reach hundreds of thousands'.[15] The FSU expanded this work as Kino and the Progressive Film Institute extended their film collections, buying copies of a number of their Soviet films and arranging frequent and widespread screenings as an integral part of political and cultural meetings.

With the accession to legal authority of the NSDAP and its rapid establishment of control over German labour, Stalin's foreign policy took a major turn towards alignment with France and friendship with Britain. This required the dismantling of the RILU in 1933, the termination of the 'class against class' policy, and the abandonment of a number of front organisations in an attempt to create a more favourable atmosphere in these two countries towards the Soviet Union. In this context, cultural propaganda to generate broad-based support for the USSR assumed increasing importance, rendering obsolete the cultural-educational work geared to promoting the growth of a revolutionary opposition.

The destruction of the German Communist Party (KPD) had been accompanied by the dissolution of the Berlin-based WIR, and the severe disruption of Comintern propaganda work generally. There were, however, two organisations based in Moscow which had already been established to mobilise intellectual support for the Soviet Union and, through such personalities, to disseminate pro-Soviet views, dovetailing with the work of the RILU's agit-prop department in relation to factory workers: the International Union of Revolutionary Writers (IURW) and the International Union of Revolutionary Theatre (IURT). These two bodies were now to be used by the Comintern as central channels for the organisation of 'broad support for the USSR, and, as the popular front strategy took shape in 1934–5, for the organisation of anti-fascist fronts, in defence of the Soviet Union and against war.[16]

The first fruits of the joint work of the IURT and the IURW were the Association des Ecrivains et Artistes Révolutionnaires, founded in March 1932, and the International Music Bureau, founded in December 1932. By the time of the International Workers Theatre Olympiad in Moscow, in May 1933, an International Cinema Bureau had been formed as part of the IURT, and at a conference convened by the Bureau at the Olympiad it resolved to build up an international workers' film movement, using the existing Workers Theatre Movement (WTM) organisations. Emphasis was placed on building organisational support for a workers' film movement within existing revolutionary groups and sympathetic cultural bodies, popularising revolutionary films, and bringing the attention of workers to the class basis of bourgeois films through discussions, articles in journals and demonstrations outside cinemas.[17] The showing and discussion of films at political and cultural meetings was seen as providing further opportunities for 'consciousness raising' and the building of revolutionary fractions within labour organisations and educational-cultural circles.

The British section of the WTM had sent representatives to the May Olympiad, and on its return a film group consisting of three people was formed to arrange shows of Soviet films. The group gave its first shows in July 1933, had formed itself into 'Kino' by December, and by May 1934 had been established as the sole distributor of 16mm Soviet films in Britain, with over sixty subscribing members.[18] By this time, however, Comintern strategy was changing, and the focus of cultural work, now channelled largely through the IURW and the IURT, changed with it. The formation of the Workers' Film and Photo League can be located in this shifting emphasis. Formed in

November 1934 from Kino's London Production Group and members of the Workers' Camera Club, to continue with film production while Kino devoted its resources to the distribution and exhibition of Soviet and other workers' films, the League immediately reasserted its adherence to the Programme of Cinema Bureau of the IURT in its Manifesto, published shortly afterwards:

> Workers' Film and Photo League thinks the time has come for workers to produce films and photos of their own. Films and photos showing their own lives, their own problems, their own organised efforts to solve these problems.

> For this purpose there must be joint co-ordinated activity by all working-class film and camera-club organisations, all individual workers, students, artists, writers and technicians interested in films and photography.

> Workers' Film and Photo League exists to provide this co-ordination.

> The League will produce its own films giving a true picture of life today, recording the industrial and living conditions of the British workers and the struggle of the employed and unemployed to improve these conditions.

> It will produce newsreel magazines of current events of working-class interest.

> It will popularise the great Russian films and endeavour to exhibit them to the widest possible audiences.

> It will carry on criticism of current commercial films in the Press and in its own literature, and expose films of a militarist, fascist, or anti-working-class nature.[19]

The Progressive Film Institute had similar political-ideological and cultural origins to those of Kino and WFPL, although, unlike Kino, there were no concrete links with Comintern organisations. The immediate occasion of its formation in mid-1935 was the need for a distributor to import and register the 35mm film *Free Thaelmann*, which had been produced in the USA by Kino's counterpart, as part of the campaign of the Relief Committee for the Victims of German Fascism (RCVGF) for the release of the KPD leader.[20] A more long-term source was the experience of Ivor Montagu in dealing on behalf of the Film Society with the Soviet Trade Delegation for the procurement of Soviet films for the Society's private showings. The PFI was the first British distributor to negotiate an agreement with the Soviet agency whereby the latter would supply films regularly, free of charge.[21] Bela Balazs of the Executive Committee of the IURT considered that the work of the Film Society had facilitated the insertion of Soviet culture into British intellectual circles and therefore represented 'fertile soil for our propaganda', and that the work of Montagu needed to be encouraged.[22]

More fundamentally, the PFI was formed during the transitional period in Comintern cultural work, in which the emphasis was increasingly on building broad fronts of workers and intellectuals in opposition to fascism, and in defence of the Soviet Union. The PFI was formed to distribute standard films which could not otherwise get a distributor in Britain. In practice, this meant predominantly Soviet productions. As the PFI's founder, and apart from his senior position in the CPGB and the FSU, Montagu already had connections with commercial cinema in Britain and was therefore well placed to extend the struggle to the 35mm circuits. The added attraction of the PFI's work was that the 35mm films imported could be reissued by Kino on 16mm stock, and they appear to have worked in close co-operation with Kino on this basis up to the outbreak of the European war.[23]

The work of these film groups has its origins also, and no less fundamentally, in the prevailing view within 'left' circles of the Hollywood system, and, concomitantly, in the unspoken assumptions with which they addressed the question of a 'workers' cinema'. Little theoretical work had been done after Lenin which had reached Marxist circles in Britain, or which had survived the Stalinisation of the CPGB. A crudely formulated and incomplete theory of ideology and the nature of the class struggle prevailed within Marxist currents, one of the central elements in which was a notion that 'truth' was independent of ideology, and accessible if only the veil of ideology could be penetrated. The intuitive response to the growth of the 'Hollywood dream factory' was therefore a theory of manipulation, in which the media were posited as comprising a concrete entity consciously performing a repressive function by transmitting a monolithic ideology to the masses. The corollary of this was an assumption that ideology could be penetrated by gaining control over the means of production of the media, and that the basis for a revolutionary or 'true' content resided in such control. The central importance of film was assumed to be, implicitly, that it offered this possibility of capturing the 'truth' because of its transparency: the filmic image was deemed capable of being exempt from connotation, recording the world 'as it is'. Moreover, it would appear that the notion of the 'audience' was also based on these assumptions. The presentation of the 'real' on film was thought self-evident and supposedly unproblematic to the audience: it was assumed that the audience was also a unity, possessing a unified political consciousness, at one with the subject on the screen. The implications of these assumptions for 'independent' film practices were considerable: control over production, distribution and exhibition as pre-conditions for any workers' cinema; virtually exclusive reliance on 'realist' techniques of cinematography; concentration on representing 'workers in struggle'—presupposing that the significance of this experience was readily apparent to workers in other spheres, thus overlooking the ideological and political fragmentations which characterised that audience. Such views were largely unarticulated, and, to some degree, merged with other currents which coincided with them in their effect. For example, the emphasis on visual accessibility had its source both in the reliance on 'realist' film techniques, and in the acknowledgment of the low visual literacy of the potential audience. Nevertheless, they were important pre-dispositions mediating the demands for a 'workers' cinema' from the political-ideological and cultural currents which operated within the orbit of the CPGB.

These specific inputs (the film work of the WIR, the Soviet cultural export strategy, the work of the RILU agit-prop department and the IURT, and the theoretical response to the dominant form of cinema) had profound and lasting consequences for the development of 'independent' cinema in the 1930s. There was, above all, a priority given to screening Soviet films, both as a cultural necessity and political strategy, and as a requisite of a cinema which consciously posed itself in opposition to the bourgeois media, destroying the veil of manipulated truth which they had constructed. The FOWFS disintegrated because there were insufficient new Soviet sound films available in 1932 to meet the demand: there were only two made available that year in Britain—Nikolai Ekk's *The Road to Life* and Trauberg and Kozintsev's *Alone*. Kino split with its production group to devote all its resources to the task of obtaining and distributing Soviet films, while the PFI was formed to distribute foreign films, a large number of which were from the Soviet Union. Only the Film and Photo League did not follow this pattern; yet this was due largely to the influx of new members in 1935, which transformed its political orientation and diverted the general thrust of its work away from its declared intention to 'popularise the great Russian films and endeavour to exhibit them to the widest possible audience'.

Where groups did engage in production, emphasis was placed on a realist reportage of events of importance to the working class, employing the newsreel form as the most appropriate (and the most practical) for its non-exclusive appeal. To some degree, film production can be said to have conformed with the strategies of the CPGB. During the period of the 'class against class' policy, attempts were made to produce films on workers' struggles as part of specific campaigns organised by the CPGB or its associated organisations, such as *1931* and the various Hunger March films. With the gradual transition to a popular front policy the emphasis changed to the Spanish struggle and the films depicting the unity of labour in opposition to fascism and war: for example, the numerous May Day films.[24] Such changes can also be seen in a wider context. They were in phase with the mood and atmosphere prevailing within substantial sections of labour which remained outside the sphere of influence of the CPGB. Nevertheless, although the 1937–39 period was one of massively increased industrial militancy, only one film was made in Britain depicting workers engaged in struggle against employers or the state, and this, *Busmen's Holiday*, a short item intended for a newsreel, was mostly devoted to the striking workers' day out on the coast.[25] The very specific origins of these film groups, and the political commitment of their leading members to the CPGB, ensured that their operations resided firmly within the political-ideological context of that Party. The FPL partly drifted away from this context in 1936–38, and, in response, some of its more politically motivated members left the League and formed a joint production group with Kino called the British Film Unit, to make a film on the Stepney rent strike covering the CPGB's campaign there.

Reference has been made to these film groups as being 'independent'. Before any discussion can take place of the relationships these groups evolved with political organisations it is necessary to explain briefly in what this 'independence' consisted. As already suggested, this 'independence' resided in developing alternative means of production, distribution and exhibition under the groups' own control, or that of similar oppositional groups. As argued in Claire Johnston's essay in this book, there was no substantive development in new forms of cinematic expression, based on an articulated theory of ideology. Consequently, relying on 'realist' techniques, recording the 'real' on film, enabled the 'real' to speak for itself: the voice of the film was the voice of the workers filmed. Presupposing the general empathy of audiences for the reality depicted, film was conceptualised (without necessarily being articulated or consciously posed) as a commodity, containing a view to be accepted or 'consumed'. The way in which the political positions of the film-makers were inscribed within the film was not at issue; nor, indeed, were the scenes depicted in any particular film. Film was seen largely in terms of providing visual confirmation of views already generally held by the audience, and in so doing, 'raising' political consciousness. The emphasis was placed on showing films as a means of attracting people to political meetings, since film shows were considered a tremendous opportunity for recruiting new members to whichever organisations had arranged the meetings.[26]

This maintenance of the dominant relations of consumption was underpinned by a strong tendency to objectify film-making as a task separate from political struggle: Montagu and Bond did not see themselves as political film-makers engaged in a struggle in ideology. The notion of film-making as a political practice in itself had not been developed. This was in large part due to the severe limitations on resources, with a consequent small turnover and minimal profit margins, and the relatively low level of cultural struggle in Britain. Where money and time were available for film production, the eternal question seemed to be 'how best to make our contribution with the means available'. Moreover, there was no theoretical precedent for such a notion residing in the work of Soviet film-makers, the most influential source for 'independent' film work in Britain.[27] However, as Brecht observed, 'The practical methods of the revolution are not revolutionary, they are dictated by the class struggle.'[28] One of the most significant aspects of the history of these film groups is that they materialised within a rarefied theoretical and cultural atmosphere and survived. In the absence of mass revolutionary organisations and a widespread oppositional culture, these film groups had to develop strategies enabling them to build bases of support which would be adequate for survival in a field of work which was objectively expensive. In relation to the resources available to them, the cost was considered prohibitive and therefore of very low priority for direct funding by any British labour organisation. The opportunities for establishing deep roots within the 'advance' sections of labour were severely limited. One indication of this is the lack of success of both Kino and FPL in promoting local production units throughout the country. The League did succeed in 1938, after four years of work, and in a different political situation—but only through its cultural alignment with the Left Book Club as a distribution and exhibition network. Paradoxically, by this time the League's internal organisation was disintegrating. The point clearly underlines that the relations between film groups and political organisations are highly significant and must enter into any account of the formation, development and function of 'independent' cinema in any given socio-political process.

Although the political-ideological origins of the independent film groups had a considerable effect upon their development, the formal connections between them and the CPGB or with Moscow were non-existent; there is no proof of manipulation or 'wire pulling' via the CPGB by the RILU or IURT agencies. These operated to provide guidelines and directives to national sections commensurate with overall Comintern strategy, and, where possible, to help co-ordinate work between national sections. Necessarily, this work was decentralised after a certain point, relying on local initiative and the abilities of section agents. The work of IURT sections coincided with IURT directives in so far as these directives coincided with the work of the communist parties and in so far as it was related to CP activities, but always on the basis of local initiative. In short, there was little IURT involvement and it would appear that by 1935 the IURT network had collapsed. As a former member of the American Film and Photo League observed, 'It wasn't necessary for anyone on the outside to press buttons to tell us our task was to cover the breadlines, flophouses, picketlines, hunger marches, etc.'.[29] The prominence of CPGB members in executive positions within the LWFS, Kino, FPL and PFI and as fractions among their memberships was sufficient to guide the work of these groups within the orbit of the CPGB and its associated organisations. Only the Film and Photo League moved away to some degree from the Party (symbolised perhaps by the transfer of the League's account from the Moscow Narodny Bank to a CWS bank in June 1936), and by 1937–38 its active members were predominantly film enthusiasts with left-wing sympathies, who had little or no experience of political work.[30]

As far as can be determined there were no funds provided for the FOWFS, Kino, FPI or PFI by political organisations (as distinct from campaign groups). The LWFS was launched with money loaned by Eva Reckitt, and the Federation derived its funds from membership.[31] Kino was launched with several personal loans from the first wave of members, and secured funds for putting Soviet films on to 16mm stock by arranging premieres and pre-release shows of its films in London and provincial centres, and securing a number of guaranteed advance bookings for particular films. From 1935 Kino's films were in such demand that it was able to maintain a financially stable position, dependent only on the profits it made from its films.[32] This appears to have been sustained until late 1939. The Film and Photo League derived its funds from members, often requiring personal loans to enable film productions to continue. As the League often had only one copy of many of its films, by 1938, despite the demand for films, FPL's distribution system became so overstretched and disorganised that only the personal sacrifices of its secretary, Hugh Cuthbertson, kept the League going. The financial basis of the PFI was provided by the relatively substantial income Ivor Montagu derived from his work in the commercial film industry. The Institute's distribution work, however, was never very successful and little income derived from this, although occasional runs at the Academy and Forum cinemas provided some money.[33]

The links between the FOWFS and the CPGB were through the communist fraction which originally set it up: Bond, Montagu, Reckitt and Henry Dobb, among others. The FSU was run mainly by prominent CPGB activists: E. H. Brown, Albert Inkpin, Isabel Brown and Ivor Montagu. Many of Kino's functionaries were CPGB members: Charles Mann, Ivan Seruya, Basil Burton, Frank Jackson, Bill Megarry; but its General Council also included many liberal personalities and cultural figures, such as H. G. Wells, Alberto Cavalcanti, J. D. Bernal, Julian Huxley, Lancelot Hogben, Victor Gollancz, Viscount Hastings, D. N. Pritt, Lord Strabolgi, Bertrand Russell, Aneurin Bevan, Joseph Reeves and the Bishop of Birmingham. Although the FPL did not secure such illustrious patronage, many of its leading activists were members of the CPGB: Jean Ross, Albert Pizer, S. Freedman, Sime Seruya; with several others apparently sympathetic to the Party, such as Charles Gralnick, Sam Serter and J. Harris. Moreover, these fractions within Kino and the FPL were interlocking, as many were on the executive committees of both groups. The PFI occasionally employed others, on specific film projects, such as Herbert Marshall, Sidney Cole, Alan Lawson and other Party members in the Association of Cinematograph Technicians, some of whom could not otherwise find employment. The Institute was informally, but effectively, a Party organ, yet it attracted to its directorial board Alan Bush, Dudley Collard, the Earl of Listowel, D. N Pritt, Wilfred Roberts, Dorothy Woodman, Louise Morgan, Geoffrey Vevers and Joseph Reeves.[34]

Lastly, little is known of Unity Films and International Sound Films. The former had been set up by Elsie Cohen of the Academy Cinema in 1937 as a distribution company for non-commercial films, and planned to go into production in 1939. The Academy and the Forum, both in London, were perhaps the foremost theatres in Britain for 'serious' cinema. For example, *Bed and Sofa*, a highly controversial Soviet film directed by Abram Room, was put on at the Forum for a run of six months. Both cinemas occasionally ran PFI films. International Sound Films (ISF) grew out of International Films, which was formed at the end of 1934 by Ivan and Sime Seruya. It shared the same address as Kino and the WFPL until 1936, moving with the League that year, becoming ISF and, eventually, on the basis of a financial loan from the League, setting up separate offices in January 1937. It folded in early 1939. Throughout, it was concerned with the distribution of 16mm and 35mm 'working-class and progressive films', acquiring the distribution rights of several such films in advance of Kino—notably the Irish film *The Dawn*. Members of its Advisory Committee included Aneurin Bevan, Ellen Wilkinson, Maurice Dobb and Stuart Legg.

Despite the overwhelming influence of communist fractions within these 'independent' film groups, the Communist Party had an ambivalent attitude towards the use of film for political-cultural purposes. There was a general awareness that film shows at political meetings related to the Spanish struggle or the 'popular front' were very useful and an effective means of raising money for these campaigns. In this respect, party branches were usually enthusiastic. Nevertheless, none of the senior members of the Party displayed any interest in film work, dismissing whatever importance it may have had for them, because they considered the resources required for such work to be disproportionately large in view of the meagre resources at the Party's disposal, and because they were uncertain about the value of 'film propaganda'. Ivor Montagu recalls that the initiative for *Peace and Plenty* and the 1938 Congress film came from him. Had he not provided the £900 necessary to produce the former, it would not have been made.[35] The idea of producing 'quality' films for profit does not appear to have been considered a possibility.

No organised policy was arranged for film production or exhibition, either through the CPGB leadership or the party's area committees. Consequently, though the Central Committee claimed in its report to the 14th Party Congress: 'We have made some progress in developing other forms of propaganda, including films . . .', in the same month Ivan Seruya wrote to the 'Party Organiser' claiming: 'The propaganda activities of the Party have in the last year or so become much more attractive and less stereotyped than ever before. It is true to say, however, that in general branches have been very slow to take up the showing of working-class and progressive films in the districts . . . It has apparently been thought that the showing of films was a subject to be left to FSU's and other non-party bodies, as it was not of sufficient political importance. Recently, this attitude has, in part, been dispelled through the amazing results achieved by the showing of the film *Defence of Madrid* . . .'[36]

The CPGB left film work almost entirely to the independent film groups, and to the initiative of local branches or individual members. The main organisations which used the libraries of these film groups in any systematic way were campaign groups, and it was within such bodies that Kino and the PFI established their bases of support. Kino, the WFPL and the PFI materialised within a network of cultural and campaign organisations which proliferated in the aftermath of the Nazi takeover of power in 1933. Willi Muenzenberg had already established a remarkable series of organisations to promote the Soviet Union and the work of the Communist International. These ranged from daily papers to banks, publishers and other commercial institutions. On installing himself in Paris in mid-1933, together with Otto Katz, as a member of the International Relations Section, 'the heart of the Comintern', he embarked on the task of making the popular front idea 'internationally popular among the intellectuals'.[37] Two of the most important organisations which he set up for this purpose were the World Committee Against War and Fascism, and the Relief Committee for the

Victims of German Fascism, both in mid-1933. Anti-war councils and relief committees were subsequently set up throughout Europe and the USA, which brought together more widely based peace and anti-fascist currents, with intellectuals and prominent personalities. This in turn led to the formation of such influential bodies as the League of American Writers (in 1935) and provided channels for influence within such movements as the International Peace Campaign and the League of Nations Union. These organisations apart, a series of cultural alignments formed in Britain with similar origins: Left Theatre, under the inspiration of Andre van Gyseghem and Herbert Marshall; the Artists International Association, with James Boswell, James Fitton and Elizabeth Rea; and Writers International, British section of the IURW, whose journal, *Left Review*, was edited by Montagu Slater, Tom Wintringham and Randall Swingler.[38]

It should be emphasised that the 'independent' film groups therefore formed part of this larger cultural movement under the auspices of the popular front, and their function was attractive to both oppositional and liberal campaigns. The political alliance of communist and some social-democratic forces was reflected in the new-found expression of 'cultural harmony' of such organisations as the Left Book Club. In this context, the political function of the films changed from agitation and recruitment for communist campaigns, to fund-raising for non-communist groups and gathering expressions of ideological support for more broadly based liberal campaigns. Of these liberal campaign organisations, the National Joint Committee for Spanish Relief (NJCSR) was one of the more widely supported, with over 150 relief groups in Britain involved in raising funds for Republican Spain under its auspices. The NJCSR used several films, notably *Modern Orphans of the Storm* and *Defence of Madrid*, as a major element in this campaign, and later sponsored the production of *Help Spain*, encouraging local relief committees to use this film by offering it free of charge.[39] One of the leading members was the Earl of Listowel; he was also a member of the FSU, the Relief Committee for the Victims of German Fascism, and on the PFI Board of Directors. Isabel Brown, a prominent CPGB organiser, was the Committee's Secretary for part of its existence. Ivor Montagu recalls that he acted as 'film consultant' to the Committee.[40]

One of the more prominent oppositional campaign organisations was the Relief Committee for the Victims of German Fascism (RCVGF). Although little information on it is available, a reading of left papers and journals of the period reveals that its activities were quite extensive. The Committee internationally sponsored the production of *Free Thaelmann* and organised its showing widely in Europe and the USA. In Britain it enlisted the support of a large number of liberal personalities and co-ordinated its work with that of other bodies such as the National Council for Civil Liberties and the NJCSR in a general campaign against fascism and encroachments on civil liberties. Of its more prominent members, D. N. Pritt was also associated with the FSU, Kino and the PFI; Lord Marley with the FSU; and Dorothy Woodman with the PFI.

Appropriately, the campaign organisation which appears to have been the most important in relation to the showing of Kino, FPL and PFI films was the Friends of the Soviet Union. Its key members were all leading activists in the CPGB; but it enlisted broad support for its own work, including that of Robert Boothby, Sir Robert Hadfield and even Harold Macmillan, and became involved in the work of groups such as the International Peace Campaign. By the end of 1936 it had sponsored the production of several films about the USSR, and arranged regular film shows as an integral part of its work, both nationally and locally. The audience figures for Kino shows for 1935–36 suggest that the FSU was the main 'customer' for Kino. Of the approximately 1,000 shows of Kino films in that year, half were arranged by Kino; and of the remainder 30% were given by FSU branches, 12% by film societies, 10% by united film bodies, 10% by CPGB and Young Communist League branches, and 6% by trade union branches, the rest being given by peace organisations, the National Unemployed Workers Movement and private hirers.[41]

The bulk of politically based 'independent' film work was therefore undertaken in connection with the activities of CPGB branches and campaign organisations. There were few instances of official social democratic institutions arranging regular shows of Kino, FPL or PFI films, or sponsoring film production by them. There were one or two instances of local trade union branches supporting the FPL to produce films on their particular situation: *Construction* and, possibly, *Revolt of the Fishermen*. However, the National Union of Seamen was the only trade union executive to sponsor film production. On their behalf, the PFI made *Britain Expects*, a film about the bombing of British shipping by German and Italian forces off the Spanish coast and Chamberlain's policy of non-intervention. The National Association of Co-operative Education Committees' Film Department hired four of Kino's films in 1937–8, having assumed responsibility for the film work of the Co-operative movement's 'Milk for Spain' campaign; and the Workers' Film Association, formed in November 1938, and sponsored by the Labour Party and the TUC after much campaigning by Paul Rotha and Joseph Reeves, acted as agents for Kino and PFI, offering 14 Kino films in its programmes and hiring Kino films on approximately 40–60 occasions in the ten months between its inception and the outbreak of European war, for between 20–40 shows out of a total of 90–100 film programmes hired from the Association.[42] However, neither the Labour Party National Executive Committee nor the TUC General Council displayed any interest in or were associated with the work of Kino or that of the PFI.

Finally, some indication of the extent of these film groups' work. The filmography in this book reveals many films produced or made available from abroad. There are, unfortunately, no figures available for the FOWFS and PFI's number of shows or total audiences. Although there is little direct evidence for the FPL, there is sufficient to give some indication of the level at which the League was operating. Between 1936 and the end of 1938 the League's subscription-paying membership varied between 60 and 100, and by

1938 it had 30 groups affiliated. However, even when the League was expanding through its alignment with the Left Book Club, its distribution network, and therefore its capacity for showing its films, was never extensive. In February 1938, in reply to an enquiry from an LBC group, the Secretary admitted: 'We had, I think, better refer you to Messrs. Kino Ltd of 84 Gray's Inn Road, as we are a production society, and not organised or equipped for projection outside London except where we have members in the locality, or others willing to lend their projectors . . .'[43] Seven FPL films produced in the 1935–6 year were shown a total of 162 times in that year, collecting approximately £29 in charges.[44] By 1937, the League was offering 30 films, but was severely handicapped by possessing only one copy of many of these.

With the largest network of agents and contacts as well as the largest film library, Kino's distribution work was probably the most wide-ranging and extensive of all these film groups. Audiences of up to 1,000 for Kino shows were not uncommon: West Lewisham Labour Party showed *Spanish Earth* to 1,100 people. The same film was shown by London Region Spanish Youth Foodship Committee to 1,000, and *Defence of Madrid* was shown in Manchester to 1,000.[45] Kino's audiences ranged from 250,000 in 1935–6 to 330,000 in 1938, with the number of shows increasing from 764 in 1936 to 1,372 in 1938.[46] The most widely shown films were probably *Defence of Madrid* and *Spanish Earth*: 20 copies of the former were distributed in England and 'since the spring two shows a night have been continuously given'; other reports reveal that it had been shown in over 400 centres in only five months.[47] More typical are figures for *Storm over Asia* (120 shows) and *Mother* (75) in Kino's first year as a non-profit-making company.[48]

The use of such empirical information needs to be qualified: it only gives an *indication* of the extent of these activities. Firstly, it would be misleading to correlate the numerical size of Kino's audience with admission figures for the commercial cinema: this would confuse two very different practices—the one building small politically conscious audiences to engage in political activity, the other necessarily trying to achieve the widest possible market for the realisation of profits. Secondly, the reliability of the figures quoted is uncertain and the full records of these groups have not been located. Nor do they take into account the activities of autonomous local groups. Glasgow Kino was perhaps the most important. In February 1937 it was reported to be often showing films five times a week to audiences of between 300 and 1,300, and between January and March 1938 it arranged a total of forty shows. Such activity produced impressive financial results: while a regular show could take £10–£15, a prestige screening could take £30, and weekly takings often reached £100.[49] The point to be emphasised is therefore not so much the reliability of the figures, or their comparison with audiences for commercial screenings, but their testament to a considerable organisational presence, and the existence of a sizeable and regular audience.

A number of tentative conclusions can be made. The extent to which the relationship which developed between various film groups and political organisations of the left was partially tied to the particular political and organisational line of the Comintern, at least until 1935, is of considerable importance. Both the film organisations themselves, and their subsequent relationships with left-groupings, were forged out of political needs and perspectives, no matter how attenuated by British circumstances; they had their origins largely in Comintern requirements, which focused ultimately on the defence of the Soviet Union. Wider sources and considerations obviously guided the political trajectories which these film groups followed, and specifically British conditions, both political and ideological, were of paramount importance in providing the terrain and setting the limiting boundaries of these activities. The influence of notions of film art, documentary and dominant codes of representation in commercial film, are considered elsewhere in this volume.

It is doubtful whether a revival of similar notions of ideological struggle could be expected to do anything more than repeat the political errors perpetrated during that period. Although the principal film groups were not isolated from the main elements of cinematic apparatus, there being many points of contact, notions of a socialist film practice were effectively contained within a political-ideological sphere, by no means hermetically sealed, but partially determined by the Communist Party. That this framework corresponded to some degree with wider currents of thought and practice within the labour movement, particularly after 1936, is less a tribute to the Party's political acumen, and more a guide to a remarkable series of adjustments within the larger movement to the dangers of fascism; yet it is precisely in the cultural and more broadly based campaign work of the Communist Party, rather than in 'party political activity', that the most important contribution to 'socialist' politics can be located. It is in this respect that the film work of groups such as Kino assumes a greater significance than would be apparent by extrapolation on the basis of more conventional reconstructions of Party history. A major consequence of this containment, it would seem, was that popular frontist notions of cultural harmony could be accepted without contradictions. The legacy of this strategy has seen the continued domination of so-called socialist film practices by pragmatism and utilitarianism based upon an outmoded theory of politics. If there are any connections to be made between the film work of the Thirties and of the present, a recognition of the link between the lack of an adequate theory of ideology and the crisis in a theory of politics during the Thirties could serve as a starting point for further elaboration of the issues at stake.

¹ For clarification of the theoretical issues involved in identifying the 'working class' at economic, political and ideological levels, see A. Hunt (ed.), *Class and Class Structure*, London 1977.

² For example: W. Hannington, *Unemployed Struggles 1919–36*, Wakefield, 1973; A. Hutt, *British Trade Unionism*, London 1975; W. Gallacher, *Last Memoirs*, London 1966. (One attempt to provide a legitimating ancestry for contemporary practices is Eva Orbanz's *Journey to a Legend and Back: The British Realistic Film*, Berlin 1977. Ed.)

³ B. Hogenkamp, 'Het Gebruik van Film door de Britse Arbeidersbeweging 1929–39' in *Skrien* 51, July/August 1975. Most of this essay is easily available in translation as 'Film and the Workers' Movement in Great Britain 1929–39', in *Sight and Sound*, Spring 1976; 'Workers' Newsreels in the 1920's and 1930's', in *Our History* no. 68, 1977.

⁴ Report of the English and French delegations of the WIR on 'Productive Enterprises in the USSR' in the *Workers' Red Cross: The Work of the Workers' International Relief in the Union of Soviet Socialist Republics*, London 1925, pp. 10–11.

⁵ D. Caute, *The Fellow Travellers*, London 1977, p. 57. Prometheus-Film was formed in 1925 and continued to distribute WIR films until it was compelled to close in January 1932 as a result of the bank crash of July 1931. (It should be noted, however, that Caute's implication that Prometheus was somehow merely a 'front' organisation for Comintern activity conceals a more interesting situation. Prometheus was in fact run extremely commercially, making profits from its distribution network, and was by no means solely involved in producing 'communist propaganda'. It distributed 'quality' films and did not officially have control over rights for Soviet films. Muenzenberg also made a point of employing people who were considered politically suspect by the German Communist Party. Emil Unfried, for example, was taken on as a film producer and distributor by Muenzenberg after being expelled from the Party in 1924 as a 'rightist'. What is of interest, therefore, is rather the range of the company's legal, financial and organisational autonomy from the German Communist Party or the WIR.) (Editorial note).

⁶ Quoted in translation from a Soviet report of 1929 by W. S. Sworakowski in *The Communist International and its Front Organisations*, Stanford 1965, p. 456.

⁷ D. Caute, op. cit., p. 53.

⁸ See H. Dewar, *Communist Politics in Britain*, London 1976, pp. 88–102; M. Woodhouse, B. Pearce, *Essays on the History of Communism in Britain*, London 1975. Discussing the results of the Sixth World Congress of the Communist International, J. T. Murphy asserted that 'the outstanding conclusion . . . [is that] the fight against the oncoming imperialist war [. . .] is the dominating issue of every day.' *The Communist Review*, Vol. 1, no. 8, August 1929, p. 433. The *Review* was the theoretical and discussion journal of the CPGB.

⁹ See 'Regulations for Bureaus for the Directing of Educational Work, Initiated by the Trades Councils of Revolutionary Trade Union Organisations' in *Trade Union Propaganda and Cultural Work*, no. 1, October 1928, pp. 2–3. This journal was the bulletin of the Agit-prop Department of the RILU. The RILU was founded in 1920 in Moscow, to build independent revolutionary trade unions and split off revolutionary elements from the social democratic International Federation of Trade Unions. In Britain this policy was modified to one of building revolutionary minorities within existing unions, which quickly developed into the 'National Minority Movement'.

¹⁰ *Trade Union Propaganda and Cultural Work*, no. 12, September 1929, pp. 23–4.

¹¹ On the position of the 'minority movement', see for example, *RILU Magazine*, no. 11, July 1931.

¹² R. Bond, 'Labour and the Cinema' in *The Plebs* (reprinted in this collection) August 1931; *Close Up*, November 1929, p. 438.

¹³ See 'Pioneers: An interview with Tom Brandon' in *Film Quarterly*, Fall 1973; Russell Campbell, 'Film and Photo League: Radical Cinema in the 30's' in *Jump Cut*, no. 14.

¹⁴ *Russia Today*, no. 26, March 1932, p. 8.

¹⁵ Ibid, no. 66, July 1935, p. 15. See also no. 59, December 1934, p. 15. The aims of the FSU, formed in 1927, were: 'to spread the truth about the Soviet Union; to counter anti-Soviet propaganda; to build fraternal solidarity between Russian and British workers; and to

mobilise British workers against the attempts by capitalism to destroy the Soviet Union'. Ibid, no. 35, December 1932, p. 14.

16 See, for example, S. Ludkiewicz, 'The Anti-Fascist Cultural Front' in *International Theatre*, no. 4, October 1933, pp. 92–99. The IURW was formed in Moscow in November (?) 1930. The IURT was established by the Agit-prop Department of the RILU as the International Dramatic Workers Union in 1929; it became the IURT in November 1932 under Heinrich Diament, former head of that Department.

17 B. Nichols, 'The American Photo League' in *Screen*, vol. 13, no 4, Winter 1972/3, p. 108; cf. B. Hogenkamp (1977), p. 18.

18 *Daily Worker*, 3 August 1933; *Cinema Quarterly*, vol. 2, no. 4, Summer 1934, p. 262. See also Tom Thomas, 'A Propertyless Theatre for the Propertyless Class' in *History Workshop Journal* no. 4, 1977.

19 'Manifesto of the Workers' Film and Photo League' (1934) in the *Film and Photo League Collection*, file (2), (hereafter *FPL* (x)). The collection has not been catalogued; file numbers refer to the provisional sorting made by Victoria Wegg-Prosser. For a brief but valuable introduction to the League and its films see Ms. Wegg-Prosser's article 'The Archive of the Film and Photo League' in *Sight and Sound*, Autumn 1977. For an account of the formation of the WFPL, see *FPL*, (2), item: no name, no date; handwritten notes opposing A. Pizer's resolution at the 1936 AGM that the League should dissolve and join Kino.

20 Ivor Montagu, in an interview with the author, 14 April 1978.

21 Ivor Montagu, interview with author. See also I. Montagu, 'Old Man's Mumble' in *Sight and Sound*, Autumn 1975.

22 B. Balazs, 'Let Us Create an International Union of Revolutionary Cinema' in *International Theatre*, no. 4, February 1933.

23 Ivor Montagu, interview with author.

24 Some indication of the importance of the Spanish struggle for the Comintern, and therefore the CPGB, is given by Felix Morror, a leading member of POUM, a Spanish communist current which rejected Stalinism: 'Internationally, the prestige of the Comintern and the USSR would have collapsed with the fall of Madrid . . . Madrid absolutely had to be held.' F. Morrow, *Revolution and Counter-Revolution in Spain*, New York, 1974, p. 222.

25 For information on stoppages, see *British Labour Statistics: Historical Abstract 1886–1968*, London 1971, Table 197.

26 See, for example, *Russia Today*, no. 15 (new series), March 1937, p. 15.

27 Ivor Montagu, interview in *Screen*, vol. 13, no. 3, Winter 1972. The quotation was from 'Pioneers: an Interview with Tom Brandon', op. cit., p. 16.

28 Quoted in C. MacCabe, 'Realism and the Cinema', in *Screen*, vol. 15, no. 2, Summer 1974, p. 17.

29 David Platt, letter in *Jump Cut*, no. 16.

30 In conversation with David Brotmacher, former treasurer of the FPL, November 1977.

31 Ralph Bond, in an interview with the author, 2 June 1977.

32 *Kino Annual Report* (1936).

33 Ivor Montagu, interview with author. The PFI consisted of Bill Megarry and Eileen Hellstern: one in charge of the films (titling, repair work, etc.), the other dealing with orders and general administration. Ivor Montagu acted as 'consultant'.

34 Ivor Montagu recalls that none of these became involved in the PFI's day-to-day work.

35 Ivor Montagu, interview with author.

36 *Report of the 14th Congress of the CPGB* (1937), p. 251: *Party Organiser*, May 1937, p. 32. For comparison with the French 'workers' film movement', consult, besides B. Hogenkamp (1977), E. G. Strebel, 'French Social Cinema and the Popular Front' in *Journal of Contemporary History*, no. 12, 1977, pp. 499–517; G. Fofi, 'The Cinema of the Popular Front in France' in *Screen*, vol. 13, no. 4, Winter 1972/3.

37 G. Nollau, *International Communism and World Revolution*, London 1961, p. 119; W. G. Krivitsky, *In Stalin's Secret Service*, New York 1939, p. 79; see also, R. N. Carew Hunt, 'Willi Muenzenberg', in D. J. Footman (ed.), *International Communism*, London 1960.

38 For information on these bodies, consult *International Theatre* and *International Literature*. See also J. Symons, *The Thirties: A Dream Revolved*, London, rev. ed. 1975. In 1936 two small

publishing firms amalgamated to form Lawrence and Wishart, placing itself at the disposal of the CPGB.

39 *Spanish Relief*, no. 13, June 1938, p. 3; no. 16, October 1938, p. 2. This was the monthly bulletin of the NJCSR.
40 Ivor Montagu, interview with author.
41 *Kino Annual Report* (1936). Unfortunately there are no figures available for later years. The pages of *Russia Today* regularly reveal details on FSU film shows.
42 There are no readily available figures. Those given have been calculated from the information available in the WFA's *Annual Report* 1939 and its Cashbook and Ledger.
43 *FPL*, (6). Hugh Cuthbertson to Shildon LBC, 17 February 1938.
44 *FPL*, (8). 'Production During 1935–6'.
45 *Left News*, November 1938, p. 1053.
46 *Kino Annual Report* (1936), PRO HO 45 21109, 'Memorandum of Evidence Submitted to the Cinematograph Advisory Committee to the Home Office on Sub Standard Films', by Kino and PFI.
47 *Daily Worker*, 9 June 1937; *Report of the 14th Congress of the CPGB*, 1937, p. 251.
48 *Kino Annual Report* (1936).
49 I am grateful for this information to Doug Allen, who is at present completing a PhD thesis at Glasgow University, Drama Dept., on 'Political Film and Theatre in Scotland in the 1930's'.

Politics and 'Independent' Film in the Decade of Defeat

Paul Marris

> To *understand* the history of the working-class press in Russia, one must
> know, not only and not so much the names of the various organs of the
> press as the *content,* nature and ideological line of the different sections of
> Social Democracy.
>
> V. I. Lenin, *The History of the Workers' Press in Russia,* April 1914.

The films to be examined in this essay are the products of groups more or less
closely tied to political parties, the parties of the British labour movement. It
might immediately be asked, can they then be said to be 'independent'?

On one of the few occasions on which he wrote on cultural questions, Lenin
reiterated a fundamental point which today threatens to become an overlooked commonplace:

> We must say to you bourgeois individualists that your talk about absolute
> freedom is sheer hypocrisy. There can be no real and effective 'freedom' in a
> society based on the power of money . . . This absolute freedom is a
> bourgeois or an anarchist phrase (since, as a world outlook, anarchism is
> bourgeois philosophy turned inside out). *One cannot live in society and be
> free from society.* The freedom of the bourgeois writer, artist or actress is
> simply masked (or hypocritically masked) dependence on the money bag,
> on corruption, on prostitution. (my italics)[1]

Claims for any sector of cultural production that it is somehow 'independent'
of class forces and their expression through institutions and apparatuses are
hollow. No work in this sense can be 'independent'. Lenin continued:

> And we socialists expose this hypocrisy and rip off the false labels, not in
> order to arrive at a non-class literature and art (that will be possible only in a
> socialist extra-class society), but in contrast to this hypocritically free
> literature which is in reality linked to the bourgeoisie, with a really free one
> that will be openly linked to the proletariat . . . Today literature . . . must
> become party literature.[2]

For Lenin, the struggle for an 'independent' culture—one in opposition to
the dominant institutions of the pre-socialist state—was integrally bound up
with the struggle for an *independent* working-class politics, whose central
thrust is towards the overthrow of the state and the building of socialism. The
directing and crystallising agency in this process is the Social Democratic
(later Communist) Party. Lenin's views on the question of 'independence' thus
lead directly to the production of works that are politically and materially

dependent on an apparatus. From a Leninist standpoint, it is not only admissible but essential to incorporate films produced by the socialist parties into any discussion of 'independent' cinema. But the status of the characterisation 'independent' is thus shifted: it is not a question of whether the work is institutionally dependent or not, but whether the particular institution—the party—can be said to be *politically* independent of imperialist politics.

It should be noted that a study of Lenin's text leaves little doubt that he was writing from the standpoint of a party apparatus on the field of literary and artistic production *as a whole*. In 1967, the Italian Marxist intellectual Fortini broached similar questions in the light of further decades of experience for the workers' movement and from the standpoint of another term in the relationship, that of writers and artists. He commented that in the Twenties 'writers and artists demanded of the political organism, not just a mediation with an audience, but an institutional "social mandate", a situation, a status'. He concluded that the development of such a mandate was—and implicitly is—impossible: 'What was demanded, indeed, was not so much a function of propaganda as one of revelation and discovery. But the formal character of artistic and literary expression is such as to render all contents ambiguous . . . Hence a conflict which is permanent and, to the extent to which its real terms remain mystified, useless.'[3]

The issues that Fortini raised are of the highest importance for those engaged in resolving the relationship between artistic practice, politics and the institutions of the workers' movement. But in this context, Fortini's words will serve primarily only to orient a discussion of the British labour movement films of the Thirties. For practically all these films do have, to quote Fortini, a function of propaganda. It is worth making this distinction. These films do not inhabit the realm of 'art'. Lenin's text confounds expectation by speaking of the literary field as one—a field where it has formerly been traditional to speak of distinct kinds, of the scriptural or the epic, the leaflet or the poem. But for cinema no such distinctions have been widely elaborated or accepted. It is necessary to insist on the differentiation between sectors of production, of their terms and functions, as preparatory groundwork in developing more sharply the critical practices of cinema. So it is not unimportant here to designate a sector of production and its function, propaganda. While socialist cultural workers may find it to be true of *all* representation that, in Fortini's words, 'the formal character of artistic and literary expression is such as to render all contents ambiguous', propaganda is one sphere where the relationship party–party line–expressive artefact is less problematic than others. The British labour movement films of the Thirties thus belong to that domain for whose producers the 'mandate' is plainest: 'One made a particular picture for the Party because the Party asked for one for a particular campaign, that was all. The Party man who was running the Party's campaign against Chamberlain wanted *Peace and Plenty*'.[4] The Party here is of course the Communist Party. The Communist Party of Great Britain (CPGB) was at that time the British section of the world Communist Party, the Third International or Comintern. Party influence was strong among those who pioneered the use of film within the British labour movement, ten years before the production of *Peace and Plenty*, and the initiative can be traced back, not formally but indirectly, to the Comintern, as Trevor Ryan and Claire Johnston point out in their essays in this book.

Wherever film came to be used in the labour movement, members of the national Communist Party were at the forefront. Within the various national developments, the distribution and exhibition of features and documentaries from the Soviet Union invariably came first, both chronologically and in financial importance. Production, when it emerged, followed upon these activities. In the United States, for example, the WIR section was distributing Soviet films throughout the Twenties. In 1930 some of its members began filming local protest demonstrations, and from that a production group, the Workers' Film and Photo League, was born. In the Netherlands the WIR exhibited Soviet films in the Twenties, and in 1928 the Vereeniging voor Volks Cultuur (Association for Popular Culture) was founded by the Communist Party to help ward off censorship of these screenings. Two years later the VVC began production. When production began in Britain, it too followed on from distribution and exhibition. The Federation of Workers' Film Societies was started in London in late 1929 and developed a network of local exhibiting groups. Atlas Films was the company set up to distribute Soviet and German films to the societies. At its 9 March 1930 screening of *Turksib*, the London Workers' Film Society gave the premiere of the first indigenous production, *Workers' Topical News No. 1*, for which Atlas Films was the production company. This short film depicts the rally at Tower Hill and the march to Mansion House against unemployment which took place in London on 6 March 1930, organised by the National Unemployed Workers' Movement. The Communist Party provided the leadership of the NUWM throughout this period, and the campaign was consequently opposed by the labour bureaucracy.[5]

The short time—three days—between the event depicted in the film and its first showing indicates how technically unambitious the film is in its construction. Made on 35mm, it is silent, consisting of documentary-style long shots with some closer shots edited together by Ralph Bond. These are probably shown in much the same order in which they were shot: short series of two or three shots, introduced by title cards that briskly name the items depicted. This topical newsreel set the basic pattern for many of the films produced within the labour movement throughout the decade: films that simply sought to record labour movement events, usually those in which the Communist Party had a leading organisational and political role. This kind of work straddles the crucial reorientation of Communist Party politics in the middle of the decade following the Comintern's change of line in 1935.

In the earlier part of the decade there had been attempts to found a national *series* of newsreels, or rather counter-newsreels, whose central function would be the dissemination of a visual record of events and activities ignored by the bourgeois newsreel companies. *Workers' Topical News* achieved probably four editions in all, of which the third (1931) is no longer extant, and the fourth is presumed to be a surviving film of the 1932 May Day demonstration found in the Film and Photo League archive. The *Workers' Newsreel* series also made four short films, produced first by Kino and then by the Workers' Film and Photo League between 1934 and 1935. A 1933 attempt by the Labour Party-connected Socialist Film Council to 'show the true picture of the world today' through a series entitled *What the Newsreel does not Show* never got beyond its first edition on the Soviet Union.

In the second half of the decade, except for two editions of the *People's Newsreels* produced by the Sussex District of the Communist Party as a record of its regional activities of 1938 and 1939, there were no further attempts at making such series. But surviving films of the *National Hunger March* of 1934, the *March against Starvation* in 1936, the *Empress Hall Rally* for the return of the British members of the International Brigade in 1939, and of the *Youth Peace Pilgrimage* in 1939, along with many others, reveal that this rudimentary newsreel-style production continued to form a staple diet throughout the decade. One of the most attractive of these films is the charming *Busmen's Holiday* on the London busmen's strike which took place during the Coronation 'celebrations' in May 1937. A London busmen's Rank and File Movement had arisen in August 1932, initially out of dissatisfaction with the trade union officials' attitude in negotiations, and in November it began to issue a newspaper called the *Busman's Punch*. The movement, led by Communist Party members, had developed into an impressive example of an organised left wing at the base of a trade union—in this case, Ernest Bevin's Transport and General Workers' Union, which by 1937 was the largest trade union in the world. Busmen's Rank and File members won a majority on the Central Bus Committee, and in the spring of 1937 they called a strike to force a reduction in working hours. The first part of the film, which is partly shot in colour, records the busmen's demonstration in London on May Day morning. Then the contingents climb into their buses and drive to Brighton, where they have a slap-up meal in a hotel, hear Tony Mann deliver a speech, and then go down to the beach for tea and a sing-song. This delightful film is shot and assembled in 'amateur' naive style, like the 'mass' holiday-movie that it is. Noteworthy are the different lights—the early morning light on Waterloo Bridge, the mid-morning sun flashing on the buses as they set off, the smoke-filled interior light in Brighton's Regent Hotel, etc. The events portrayed convey the spontaneous assertion of a potential life-enhancing use value to the machines that the busmen must drive daily. The cheerful tone, however, contrasts harshly with what was to prove the strike's outcome. After Bevin had manoeuvred so as to isolate the London busmen from other London Transport workers and from provincial busmen, the strike was defeated. Bevin then expelled the rank and file leaders from the union, which ensured the disappearance of the *Busman's Punch* by Christmas 1937. The film exhibits at its best the kind of grass-roots 'democratisation' of film-making that the Film and Photo League regarded as the central contribution necessary to a socialist development of the medium, and which they sought to bring about.

Workers' Newsreel No. 1, made in 1934, is a little different from the other newsreels and takes one step beyond the mere 'transparent record' format of the newsreel-style films. It is an assembly of five news items: a *Daily Worker* sporting gala, the opening of a new Co-op store, a protest picket against the Hendon air pageant, a youth anti-war congress, and an anti-war demonstration in Hyde Park. Titles state that 'The workers create/whilst capitalism destroys./Workers make planes/to destroy workers./But the masses are organising.' This newsreel organises its various items around a political axis which ties together the different current activities that it records, and brings to the viewer's attention their political coherence.

Several other films are also organised around this basic opposition, capitalist class/working class. *Jubilee* sets film of the 1935 royal jubilee 'celebrations' against shots of East End housing conditions, queues outside the labour exchange and war veterans on crutches. A 1936 FPL short, *Winter,* on which Ralph Bond collaborated, contrasts rich Piccadilly shoppers with their poorer counterparts in Leather Lane Market; slum dwellers shovel snow from the streets while the wealthy leave Victoria Station for their winter sports holiday, and so on. *The Merry Month of May*, like *Jubilee*, sets royalist celebrations (in this case, the Coronation in 1937) against opposing events such as the republican struggle in Spain (drawing on footage from *Defence of Madrid*). *Communist Party Home Policy*, a silent film for most of its length, intercuts shots of the living conditions of the rich with those of the poor—in housing, shopping facilities, health care, and even military service. The last quarter of the film introduces a sound-track, an address to camera by a Communist Party member, who urges that the way to begin resolving these problems is to cast a vote for the Party. These other films take a single step beyond primary unordered recording, to articulate the fundamental class contrast, though only as it is available to the camera at the level of appearances, in combination with a simple dualistic notion of montage. *Communist Party Home Policy* takes a step further, and urges a preliminary resolution through a vote for the Communists: it is noteworthy that it introduces sound to do this.

All the films mentioned so far carry for us now an undoubted archival fascination, satisfying a simple antiquarian appetite for the appearance of the past. This role as document, as 'witness' to the various depicted events, was also the major function they fulfilled at the time. For example, in 1930, Ralph Bond edited ('constructed' as the credits say) for Atlas Films 'from material available in this country' a film about the Soviet Union; it was aptly entitled *Glimpses of Modern Russia*. The only issue in the intended series *What the Newsreel does not Show* was also about the Soviet Union: 'Our first journey will be to Russia/to show you the completion of the First Five Year Plan'. These opening titles are intercut with shots of the film crew boarding ship; again we have the theme of bearing witness, of seeing is believing. In the case of the footage and sound brought back by Ivor Montagu from Spain in 1938, this function constituted a particularly direct political intervention. The material was assembled into *Prisoners Prove Intervention in Spain* and

74

Testimony of Non-intervention, which specifically aimed—as their titles suggest—to testify, to prove, that the Italian and German fascist governments were violating the five-power agreement not to give material aid to either side in the Spanish Civil War.

Undoubtedly, the primary reason that so many of the films were restricted to an elementary recording of events deliberately neglected by mainstream newsreel production was the financial limitation. Shortage of money and time, and consequently of the opportunity to accumulate much beyond a scattered and sporadic experience of intervention through film, largely dictated the rudimentary quality of the output. Steve Neale, with co-author Mark Nash, has succinctly described the aesthetic of these films as 'no coherent point of view, no coherent strategy of address in the sequencing of images'.[6] They appropriately label this an 'amateur' aesthetic. The BBC-TV programme *Caught in Time* has recently shown examples of the home movie-making of the Thirties. The edition of 19 March 1978, for example, broadcast a film of the 'Walking Day' in Warrington. The stylistic resemblance between this amateur film of 1934 on a local annual procession and the contemporary films of labour movement demonstrations is striking. But this very resemblance points up a difference of another kind. Neale himself has written on this: 'What has been considered here is propaganda solely as a system of textual address . . . However, this is to isolate the . . . films from the apparatuses of their production, distribution and consumption, and both text and apparatus from the conjuncture, thus to restrict the concept of address solely to an abstract text-subject relationship. I would want to argue in fact that "address" is not simply synonymous with textual address; that although the latter can be analysed and has an effectivity, particular positions and modalities of position are a product of textual address in conjunction with the immediate discourses that necessarily surround it within the apparatuses that support it . . .'[7] As the passage indicates, to give a full account of the films' intervention it is necessary to recall the institutional apparatuses by which they were produced and disseminated.

All the films were exhibited non-commercially. When *Kino News* promoted Kino's library of films, it told its readers to 'bring your own organisation into this work. Your club, your film society, your school, your trade union branch, your co-operative guild, your local Labour party'.[8] Although it is difficult to reconstruct with any precision the exhibition life of these films, they were shown predominantly by political bodies within the labour movement, such as Co-op, Labour Party, Communist Party and ILP branches, and by local committees of international solidarity campaigns. Early in the decade the Workers' Film Societies showed such films, and later Left Book Club branches played a part in exhibiting them. The choice of these venues and the use of the 16mm gauge after 1932 was partly a ploy to avoid the censorship regulations. When asked much later where his *Defence of Madrid* (1937) was shown, Ivor Montagu replied: 'Oh, halls, Co-op halls and things like that, because they're outside the censorship, you see.' But the reason was more than that alone, as Montagu recognises in the same interview: '[With *Defence of*

Madrid] we collected money for the Medical Aid—people will pour the money out for a film then because it's a thing that touches their hearts. But you can't do that commercially. But I expect the same people would have resented it if they'd gone to the cinema expecting to be entertained and had seen *Defence of Madrid*.'[9] With this last point, Montagu indicates the importance of the basis on which audiences are convened in governing the reading of a film and hence its effectivity.

Steve Neale has also pointed out that: 'Generally speaking, propaganda is produced as an intervention from a particular apparatus (a political party, the State, the Church and so on) . . . One of the frequent traits of propaganda is that the apparatus concerned will be given discursive representation within the text.'[10] This comment is extremely pertinent to the British labour movement films of the Thirties. A high proportion depict nothing other than the activities of the unofficial movement of which they are a part—hunger marches, rallies, demonstrations, and so on. For instance, as we have seen, *Workers' Topical News No. 1* had depicted the NUWM rally and march in London on 6 March 1930. It also included shots of a *Daily Worker* seller, and of a WIR relief kitchen. The shorts on British activities acted as a political bridge between the society that the audience inhabited and the socialist society of which the Soviet films were an expression, which is what the political movement whose activities the shorts depicted ostensibly sought to do within the wider social process. Overall, the showings of these films participated in the reciprocal process of the building of a political movement: they helped constitute this movement, and in turn their role was constituted by that task.

The active convening of the political meeting as the site of exhibition, however, was not arrived at without debate. Dissension regarding the appropriate kind of institution for socialists to exhibit films—and, therefore, reciprocally, what kind of films to produce, and how—occurred in the Thirties, and we can get a feel of the terms of this debate from its imprint in two publications. First, early in the decade, the activities of the Federation of Workers' Film Societies brought forth an attack in the pages of *The Plebs* from Huntly Carter.[11] In the November 1930 issue, Carter seemed to urge some kind of wholesale labour takeover of the cinematic institution, and complained that 'there has not been any concerted action by Labour Parliamentary representatives, big Labour Unions, Co-operative bodies, and others to establish a Labour Cinema on true Labour principles.' But it is not wholly clear from this article what a true Labour cinema meant for him, although his concluding sentence in his next *Plebs* contribution on the topic, in June 1931—'what this country needs is the planning and centralisation of the Labour cinema world, and a British Labour Five Years' cinema plan'— suggests that he was groping towards some concept of nationalisation of the industry, presumably by the serving Labour government. What Carter was certain of, however, was that the FOWFS constituted an obstacle; furthermore, in line with the worst traditions of the British labour movement, he claimed that this was because the Federation's initiators were implicated in a politically and morally corrupt conspiracy, intent on 'the subordination of revolutionary and social content to the technique of aesthetic'. Carter's political impulse towards a much fuller labour movement transformation of the cinematic institution was a healthy one. But if he had been serious about this, he might have sought to develop a movement for a socialist cinema policy to be urged upon the Labour government by its supporters, as part of the overall struggle for socialism. Any such movement would obviously have begun by building its base of support among the membership of the FOWFS, giving priority to accelerating the resolution of unionisation problems within the industry's workforce.[12] For the central political forces for any socialist transformation of the cinema come from the joint struggle of that public dissatisfied with the product of the bourgeois cinema, and the workers in the industry dissatisfied with the conditions of production, their role in it, and the nature of the product. Instead, however, Carter had launched into a gratuitous and sectarian attack on the FOWFS organisers.

The April 1931 issue of *The Plebs* saw a reply from 'Benn', film critic of the Independent Labour Party weekly, *New Leader*. Against Carter's moralism, he set forth an overall account of the main factors governing the social role of cinema, concluding that 'working-class cinema, like capitalist class cinema, must arise from and be an expression of working-class political rule.'[13] Taken baldly, Benn's position as expressed in this article is more like an ultimatum, potentially disregarding any steps taken along the road on the grounds that the end of the road has not yet been reached. The article does not point to any activities which might constitute the passage from here (capitalist-class cinema) to there (working-class cinema). Benn himself, however, in a series of three articles in his *New Leader* column in 1929, had been a pioneer of the scheme for a Workers' Film Society that would both exhibit and produce films, especially 'socialist newsreels'. In *The Plebs* polemic, his bald account was complemented by a contribution in the August 1931 issue from Ralph Bond, who, through his involvement with the FOWFS and Atlas Films, was at the very centre of such production, distribution and exhibition activities as then existed in the labour movement. Bond recognised that short of a situation of dual power, the project of developing a working-class cinema can only remain an embryonic, parallel activity, inevitably subordinate to the capitalist cinema. He proposed two activities for socialists: 'Exhibiting the films of the only country where the workers are the ruling class', and 'Making their own films . . . to aid and encourage the workers in their fights against capitalism'.[14] These were to be the active steps in the sphere of cinema for the passage from capitalist-class rule to working-class rule. And, one may perhaps add, steps in developing film-making personnel and class-conscious film-goers as the agents for carrying through that transformation of the cinematic institution as a whole in the context of socialist revolution.

According to the report in their second news sheet, Kino's first annual general meeting in April 1936 grappled with similar problems regarding the relationship between exhibition sites and the films exhibited there: 'Mr. George Elvin said that the official Labour Party attitude to films was that they should produce films which were films first and propaganda second.

77

Distribution of films through the medium of the Labour Hall, Trades Hall, Co-op Hall does not get to the film going public and is mainly preaching to the converted. Film propaganda must be done through the medium of the commercial cinema. Mr. Elvin pointed out that a film made for the commercial cinema would have to be first class technically.'[15]

The 'official Labour Party attitude' to which Elvin referred was then contained in the circular *Labour Cinema Propaganda* signed by the general secretaries of both the TUC and the Labour Party and issued in the same month as the Kino AGM. 'It is most desirable that we should not preach to the converted,' it stated, a sentiment echoed by Elvin. But the circular had in fact continued: 'It is suggested that the best method [for] Labour [to] organise its own Film Propaganda without delay, will be for Local Parties to take the initiative in the formation of Film Societies.'[16] It is reported that at the AGM Ivor Montagu disagreed with Elvin, pointing out that 'to make "good" films in the commercial sense would be almost impossible without an immense expenditure.'[17] Montagu stressed the financial limitations within which he and other labour movement film makers were working.

In 1929, in a pamphlet entitled *The Political Censorship of Films*, Montagu had drawn attention to further limitations imposed by the censorship regulations. He had personally acquired concrete experience of these limitations when he tried to get the Progressive Film Institute's version of *Free Thaelmann* passed by the censor so that it could be shown in licensed cinemas. The film was a call to campaign on behalf of the German Communist Party leader jailed by Hitler in 1933, and contained various smuggled documentary materials (film and still photographs) on the situation inside Germany, which had first been assembled into a film by the New York Film and Photo League. The British censor refused the film a certificate on the grounds that it supported a criminal, despite the fact that Thaelmann, as the film brought out, had not been tried by any court.[18] Like most of the films distributed by the Progressive Film Institute, *Free Thaelmann* was on 35mm (with a 16mm version handled by Kino), so there was no technical impediment to it being shown in cinemas. At the Kino AGM, Montagu alluded to this additional obstacle, over and above the strictly financial ones, to exhibition in the cinema—namely, the political opposition of the controlling interests in the industry. George Elvin was actively stressing the use of the commercial cinema and professional production, for political reasons also: first, because a growing semi-amateur production sector with a local non-professional exhibition network would have seemed to him to pose a contradiction between his concerns as a trade unionist[19] and his concerns as a socialist; and secondly, because his socialism was to the right of Montagu's, he envisaged a less radical political position for these future films than Montagu did, and anyway attributed less importance to the activity of labour movement organs at the base in the overall progress to socialism. The position that Kino adopted on these issues was Montagu's, as can be seen from their news sheet's editorial comments on the TUC–Labour Party circular (reprinted in this book pp. 150–152).

Although the debates of both 1930–31 and 1936 address similar questions (where to locate socialist film work) and come up with formally similar answers (within the institutions of the labour movement), the difference in the terms of the debate are also striking. In 1931 the protagonists were trying to think through their activity in the light of the overall class struggle, and particularly in the battle to change the class control of state power. Five years later, the aim had become the use of film 'for Peace and cultural progress', terms drained of all class content.

At the AGM, Montagu had suggested that Kino concentrate on documentary production, and although the group distributed several Soviet features, it had made no attempt at the production of fiction. Nevertheless, there were one or two attempts at fiction films by other groups within the Thirties labour movement in Britain. The first of these was *The Road to Hell*, made in 1933 by the shortlived Socialist Film Council. This was a social democratic organisation, and the credits for *The Road to Hell* include Labour Party chief George Lansbury's daughter Daisy, and her husband, labour historian Raymond Postgate, plus Naomi Mitchison, and as the film's director, Rudolph Messel.[20] The film tells of the effects of unemployment on the Smith family. It is constructed with some care and skill: not only does it contain rather self-conscious shots—such as those through a line of railings, or from a low angle at the riverside—there are also examples of sophisticated space construction, as when the younger son crosses the bedroom and his movement is conveyed by a swift insert of a daytime shadow on the wall. But the political import of the film is so wretched that it caused even John Grierson to criticise it in his *New Clarion* review.

In true social democratic fashion, the film alleges that it is not the economic system of capitalism that causes unemployment, but the careless evil of the capitalists: in this case, Mr. Smith becomes unemployed when he is knocked over and injured by a fast car driven by a rich youth. And what is it that is wrong about unemployment? It leads people to contravene Methodist morality! In this case, the elder son Fred, short of money because he is on the dole, takes part in robbing a jewellery shop: it is not the practical unwisdom of this activity that is highlighted, but its character as a 'moral horror'. This Methodist tone also suffuses the film's attitude to sexuality. In the opening scene, Mrs. Smith—who 'had a house you could be proud of', as a title announces—is at home with her younger son Arthur, who has an art scholarship from the local council. She snatches from his hand a postcard of a Greek statue, because the figure is nude. This brittle gag sets the tone for the censorious yet sexually fascinated morality that informs the rest of the film. When Fred and his girlfriend Gladys kiss, the film cuts away to a zoo sign that reads 'Warning: these monkeys are dangerous'. The irresponsibility of the rich young man who knocks over Mr. Smith is established through his gesture of cuddling his girlfriend as he races along in the car. A montage signifying Fred's anticipation of the benefits from a share in the loot if he participates in the jewel robbery associates him with this driver, by including a shot from his point of view as he too races along in a fast car in this imaginary future. The montage also incorporates images of him in the company of a good-time girl to amplify the lurid picture of his coming moral fall.

This overall Labourist thrust is illuminated by an episode in the film that can be compared to one in Brecht–Dudow's *Kuhle Wampe* (1931). The younger son, unable to find work, puts aside a small personal luxury (in *Kuhle Wampe* this is a wristwatch, in *The Road to Hell* a fountain pen) and commits suicide by leaping from an upper-floor window—metonymically indicated in both films by a hand gripping the window jamb and then releasing it. Whereas in *Kuhle Wampe* the incident has a strong representative (class) resonance, in *The Road to Hell* it does not transcend individual tragedy. The end of the film consists of an empty gesture towards the notion that unemployment is a social phenomenon to be fought collectively, when, quite unexpectedly, the final image proves to be a fluttering red flag with the words 'Workers of the world unite' superimposed on it. This image bears no relation whatever to the preceding drama, merely serving as a cover for the Labour Party's failure to back the NUWM.

In sharp contrast to this moralistic posturing stands *Bread*, a fiction film made the following year, again about unemployment leading to crime. *Bread* tells of an unemployed worker denied relief by the Charity Commissioners (because his wife has a small income from cleaning). To feed his hungry family he steals a loaf from a baker's shop, but gets caught and sentenced to jail. The film concludes with shots of NUWM contingents on the 1934 Hunger March, cited as the non-fictional 'real' agency for the resolution of the kind of problem presented in the fiction. This call to collective action flows from the film's presentation of its protagonist's predicament. The scene in which he faces the board for relief assessment can be compared with a similar scene in *The Road to Hell* in which Mrs. Smith is the supplicant. In the latter, the board members are smug and inattentive; their 'fault' is a lack of compassion. In *Bread*, the commissioners are shown and reshown in a quickening montage of low angle close-ups, whose lighting renders the faces ugly and sinister; these men are not 'morally flawed', they are the personification of the (class) enemy. When the protagonist comes up before the magistrates for stealing the bread, his case is preceded by the trial of several upper-class undergraduates who have overturned a tradesman's cart for a lark. The undergraduates are let off with a caution. In *The Road to Hell* the crime reveals (to whom?) the 'moral wrongs' that unemployment gives rise to; in *Bread*, what is wrong with crime is its ineffectiveness as a method of fighting back against the conditions of unemployment, compared to the collective activity of the NUWM. These two fiction films, although about similar topics, speak very different politics. *Bread*, made by Communist Party member Sam Serter, is the most exciting and imaginative film in the surviving collection of the Film and Photo League. Various details, such as the montage of commissioners' faces noted above, or the close-up of the protagonist's clenched fist beside the kitchen table when he has to face his family without food for them, are reminiscent of the Soviet cinema. Indeed, Serter reports that he was inspired to make the film after attending a lecture in London by Eisenstein.[21]

80

In a seminar held in London to mark the changes in French left-wing film culture since the events of May and June 1968,[22] Serge Daney of *Cahiers du Cinéma* observed that in the immediately succeeding years there was an upsurge in the production of two kinds of work: *cinéma militant* (that is, 'cinéma direct' and agitprop documentaries) and *films tableaux noirs* (loosely, didactic works of theory and political argumentation). He pointed out that it was not until 1972–3 that the impact of the events could be seen in fiction film production, and suggested that this was because the ideological effects of fiction are less immediately foreseeable than those of other kinds of work by socialist film makers, a view echoing that of Fortini in the essay mentioned earlier. In the film work within the British labour movement of the Thirties, fiction also came a little later than documentary production. And it was even more scattered and infrequent than the tiny documentary output.[23] By and large, fiction work at a particular level requires more time and resources than documentary work at a comparable level. It was for such reasons that Montagu made his call at the Kino AGM for a concentration on documentary.

Shortage of resources is a persistent problem for radical propaganda currents in the cinema. Periodically, capitalism enters a slump; it destroys accumulated capital values and drives down the living standards of the masses, for these are the only measures for the resolution of the crisis within its framework. If the greatest opportunities for developing the subjective will to end the reign of capital can be said to occur at this time, then the urgency of the need for propaganda intensifies during the very period that the available financial resources within the working class, and therefore its political institutions, are likely to be at their lowest. A comparatively expensive medium such as film is rendered less accessible to the working-class movement as a propaganda instrument at the moment it is most required.

Just as, in order to understand the documentaries produced within the British labour movement, it is necessary to have a knowledge of the politics of the contending parties within that movement, so in order to grasp these politics, an overall understanding of the central features of the class struggle worldwide is required. Since this obviously cannot be attempted here, a brief sketch will have to serve.

The Thirties was a period of profound defeat for the working-class movement. The world economic crisis which opened the decade was so far from being resolved in the interests of the working class that the imperialist powers were able to launch a new war at its close. The single largest defeat—the victory of fascism in Germany in 1933, and the consequent destruction of the workers' organisations in that country—prompted a change in Comintern's world strategy in the middle of the decade. But this new strategy was to prove as incapable of defending working-class interests as the previous 'third period' line had been. The Comintern was concerned to defend the Soviet Union from imperialist aggression, a necessary component of any socialist policy. But the Soviet Union had come to be dominated by a bureaucratic caste, with interests distinct from that of the working class, and it was the political vehicle of that caste—the Communist Party of the Soviet Union—which was hegemonic within the Comintern. At its crucial Seventh Congress, held in July–August 1935, the Comintern resolved to adopt a new, rightist policy. The central strategic intention was to find a stable alliance for the Soviet Union with one or other of the imperialist powers in the hope of ensuring military aid in the event of invasion. In its first phase, this took the form at the international level of seeking military pacts with the so-called 'democratic' powers, especially France, in an 'anti-fascist' alliance against Germany, and at the national level of seeking electoral pacts for the Communist Party with 'anti-fascist' bourgeois parties that would be prepared, if in government, to come to some accommodation with the Soviet Union through the League of Nations (which the Soviet Union had joined in 1934). These electoral pacts were called 'People's Fronts' or 'Popular Fronts'. They were to be built round the slogans of 'peace', 'social justice', 'anti-fascism' and 'national independence'. As these slogans were empty of all class content, they chiefly served to hold back the development of an independent working-class programme and leadership within the labour movement, to subordinate the proletariat to bourgeois politics, and to demobilise the struggle for socialism. Essentially, the CPSU was seeking to trade, in exchange for military and diplomatic pacts with various powers, the Communist Parties' influence within the local labour movements, to help hold back the working class from any profound challenge to bourgeois legitimacy. Thereby the defence of the Soviet Union was weakened, and imperialism, along with its internal contradictions which drove inexorably toward war, was strengthened. In its second phase, the policy was to take the form of a military pact between the Soviet Union and Hitler's Germany.

The adoption by the Comintern in 1935 of the first phase of this policy, the Popular Front phase, is the major watershed in the history of the European labour movements of the Thirties. No phenomenon in the socialist movement of that period is comprehensible without a grasp of the nature of the Popular Front. It was a thoroughly counter-revolutionary strategy, whose implementation threw away the pre-revolutionary situation in France and sabotaged the Spanish revolution, thus almost opening the way to the loss of what it sought minimally to defend, the basis of the existence of the bureaucratic caste—social ownership of the means of production in the Soviet Union.

Unlike several of its European counterparts, the Communist Party in Britain, since its founding in 1921, never had sufficient weight in the labour movement seriously to rival social democracy for the overall leadership of the working class, although it had had the leadership of many important particular struggles and campaigns during its history. The reason for its weakness, in contrast to other European Communist parties, probably lies in the fact that it had to struggle to build itself in a country with a long-established labour aristocracy grown fat on the surplus extracted from the masses in the 'colonies'. Through making real concessions to its domestic

82

labour movement in the period before the 1914–18 war, British imperialism had successfully established a thoroughgoing class accord with the Labour bureaucracy which saw it safely through the General Strike and the slump period. In the late Thirties, the British Communist Party could not be said to have determined the outcome of the class struggle in Britain. But it was the national section of an international party whose policy did determine the fulfilment or otherwise of an essential political precondition for the socialist revolution in Britain at that time. That precondition was a successful revolution in Europe, with the immense political impact on British workers which would have ensued. But the implementation of the Comintern's Popular Front policy in continental Europe was to furnish the exact opposite: the checking of the rising tide of class struggle in France, and the aborting of the Spanish revolution.

In Britain, the Communist Party set about trying to implement its version of popular frontism. In building support for this, it looked to different social layers than before. In the early Thirties, the memory of the forceful industrial agitation by the Party-initiated National Minority Movement, plus its continued championing of the struggle of the unemployed through the NUWM, had ensured a small continuing base of working-class support for the Party, although the composition of this base had tended to shift away from advanced industrial militants towards the unemployed. In the latter half of the decade, the Party's appeal came to be much more slanted towards the middle class and intellectuals, and with comparative success. In magazines such as *Left Review* and *New Writing*, in cultural organisations such as the Left Book Club and the Unity Theatre, many of the activists were likely to be—and did in fact prove to be—drawn from the middle class, and Communist Party influence here grew strong. Perry Anderson pointed out that 'A spontaneous radicalisation of the traditionally dormant English intelligentsia occurred, spurred by the political gravity of the time'.[24] But it has to be recognised that this was only a 'radicalisation'. The Communist Party, armed with the Popular Front policy, moved closer to the milieu of radical liberalism, with its fascination with Stalin's Russia, its preparedness to defend bourgeois democracy in Spain, and its utopian hopes in the capacity of the League of Nations to prevent war. The cosy smugness of this sub-Bloomsbury milieu can be glimpsed in the film, *Red, Right and Bloo*, which spins a mildly misogynous tale from footage taken at the Left Book Club summer school at Digswell Park in 1937.

The change in the character of the left in the British labour movement following the 1935 change in the Comintern line is evident from a comparison between the May Day demonstrations of 1933 and 1937 as portrayed in two extant films. The 1933 film is the earliest surviving labour movement material apart from the *Workers' Topical News* series. The demonstration was the first following a United Front agreement between the Communist Party and the ILP, and the first title reads: 'The Workers' United Front in Action. All out against fascism. Despite the orders of the leaders, the workers are determined that all workers shall be allowed to march to Hyde Park thus showing a REAL

United Front against the National Government and the Capitalists.' The 1937 demonstration has a far less militant, more 'cultural' character. Floats are used, people dress in costume—some as Left Book Club books, others as the Spirit of May Day—there are contingents from sporting clubs, the Unity Theatre, scientists (whose banner reads: 'Science makes socialism imperative. The alternative is barbarism'), and from the Film and Photo League itself (banner: 'Show Workers' Films'). The film also records the preparations for the demonstration, showing the Basque refugees making their huge floats and the cut-outs being made up for the Left Book Club members who were to personify various titles. This changed style of the May Day demonstrations in the later Thirties is evidenced too by *Challenge to Fascism*, which depicts the May Day demonstrations in Glasgow in 1938. This demonstration also incorporated several floats—for instance, an anti-Nazi one organised by a Socialist Sunday School, and Kino's own, which called for 'Arms for Spain'. The inclusion of details of the preparations for the procession, such as women sewing banners, men constructing and painting the floats, horses and carts being decked out, might be thought to reveal a particular interest on the part of the film's credited director—art school-trained Glasgow Kino member Helen Biggar—in a kind of popular cultural activity (Biggar was later to design sets for feature films). However, the inclusion of similar details in the previous year's London May Day film would suggest that such an interest was more generally shared. In the January 1937 edition of *Left News*, Victor Gollancz, founder of the Left Book Club, wrote: 'The Popular Front is not the policy of the Left Book Club, but the very existence of the Left Book Club tends towards a Popular Front.'[25]

When the 'People's Front' campaign proper was launched in 1938, the milieu for such a campaign was already well developed and the Communist Party well placed within it. The campaign's aim was to throw Chamberlain's National Government out of office, and replace it with another all-party government that would implement a policy aimed at curtailing Hitler's external activities through a joint show of collective military force by Britain, France, the United States and the Soviet Union. Strenuous efforts were made by the Popular Front campaigners to draw in Liberal MPs such as Richard Acland and Tory critics of Chamberlain. The Labour Party national executive was thus able to take a position to the left of the Communist Party, and pose as the defenders of the working-class movement's independence, threatening to expel constituency parties that supported the campaign.

Most of the labour movement film activity in Britain in the Thirties took place in the second half of the decade within this post-popular frontist milieu. Just as it was influential in the Unity Theatre groups and the Left Book Club, the Communist Party was also the predominant influence in the sphere of left wing film. This had of course been true even before the popular frontist period. As Trevor Ryan points out in his article in this book, party members had made a major contribution in the first stirrings of film activity at the beginning of the decade through their part in Atlas Films and FOWFS. Again, party members played the leading role in the founding in December 1933 of

84

the distribution and production group Kino, which was set up to implement decisions taken at an international cultural workers' conference held in Moscow a few months earlier. In 1934, the production wing became part of a distinct new organisation, the Workers' Film and Photo League (later, simply the Film and Photo League). Kino continued to grow as a distributor, and re-formed a production group of its own in late 1935, no longer automatically accepting FPL productions for its distribution library. Kino co-distributed several films with another Communist Party-dominated organisation, the Progressive Film Institute, founded by Ivor Montagu. The PFI handled the 35mm versions and Kino the 16mm ones. The FPL put its stress on grassroots film making, and its leadership grew away somewhat from the Communist Party, although this had little effect in local areas. Kino had more of a cadre conception of film activity, showing more technically and politically elaborate films to larger audiences, and raising sums of money on a bigger scale, either to enable their importation of Soviet films, or as donations to political campaigns. In the summer of 1937, John Lewis, organiser of the Left Book Club local groups, urged his members to work with the FPL, explaining: 'The Film and Photo League does not aim so much at big public performances which cost a lot of money, but rather at the projection of quite short films, which are very easily obtained, as a frequent feature of ordinary Group meetings. They therefore work very largely with 9mm [sic] films . . . They do not infringe upon the excellent work which is being done by sub-standard distributors for the larger shows with gate money. They have come to a mutual understanding with Kino and they will chiefly be catering for shows in rooms and small halls, and encouraging production of films by amateurs.'[26]

Many of these 'larger shows with gate money' were screenings of documentaries on the Spanish Civil War, aimed at building support for the Republicans and raising money for medical supplies. The first of these was *Defence of Madrid*, documenting the results of Franco's bombing raids on the city in 1936 and released at the beginning of 1937. Soon after came *Crime against Madrid, News from Spain*, and a version of *Refugees in Catalonia*. In the face of the neglect by the bourgeois media in reporting Francoist atrocities and the Axis powers' involvement in them, these films performed an essential political function. Despite the expense, and at times the physical danger involved in securing footage, the British film makers managed to produce many films on Spain. On occasion they had to re-use shots and sequences from their own earlier films, and borrow sequences from Soviet documentaries in Spain. In 1937, however, in Spain itself, the counter-revolutionary results of the Comintern's insistence on keeping the Republican supporters confined within the 'bourgeois democratic stage' were increasingly apparent. In May, in Barcelona, there was an armed clash between government forces—mainly represented by forces of the Spanish Communist Party—and the POUM, backed by the Anarcho-Syndicalists. This was a striking expression of the general conflict during these months as the socialist thrust of the worker and peasant masses continually came up against the pro-bourgeois policies of the Spanish Communist Party as directed by the Comintern. It would obviously be inappropriate to give a full history of the Spanish experience here, but readers are referred particularly to the account by Fernando Claudin, who participated in the events as a member of the Spanish Communist Party and later served on the party's central committee.[27] For our purposes, it is important to observe that the continuing stream of films on Spain released by Kino and the PFI—including *Spanish ABC* (1938, produced by Ivor Montagu, directed by Thorold Dickinson and Sidney Cole) and *Behind the Spanish Lines* (1938, directed by Sidney Cole)—remained silent on the political situation behind the lines, and continued to disseminate, implicitly and uncritically, a version of the struggle that accorded with the Comintern's.

In September 1938, the British Communist Party held its fifteenth congress, at which party secretary Harry Pollitt made the keynote speech entitled 'Peace and Plenty'. He put forward the leadership's perspective on the coming period: 'As the whole situation develops, as dissatisfaction with the Chamberlain policy grows, if the labour movement is united and actively fighting Chamberlain, then the differentiation amongst millions of people not organised in any political party, as well as in the Liberal and Tory parties, will increase and take a more crystallised form that will place the organisation of the people's front as a practical and immediate proposal.' *Peace and Plenty* became the title of the twenty-five minute sound film made by party member Ivor Montagu on behalf of the party for the anticipated 1939 General Election that was never held because of the outbreak of war.

In France, where a Popular Front government had come to power in 1936 based on an electoral alliance between the social democratic party (the SFIO), the French section of the Comintern and the bourgeois Radical Party, the Communist Party had also produced an election film. Entitled *La Vie est à Nous*, the film was directed by Jean Renoir, and was also based on the speech made by the general secretary at the preceding party congress. The London Film Society, of which Montagu had been a founder member, had shown *La Vie est à Nous* in 1937, and the opening of *Peace and Plenty* owes much to the opening of Renoir's film. Both begin with mock versions of conventional, lyrical documentaries extolling the national heritage, which are then sharply disrupted. In *La Vie est à Nous* the source of the 'commentary' over the images of the 'riches of France' turns out to be that of a teacher whose pupils go on to ask themselves why, given France's wealth, their fathers are out of work. *Peace and Plenty* opens with the strains of classical music over images of the Union Jack and the white cliffs of Dover, followed by shots of the countryside in bloom and factories at work. A voice intones: 'Our country . . . with its wealth . . . its industry . . . its traditions . . .'; abruptly, the music ceases, and the voice harshly observes: '. . . all this is ruled by Mr. Chamberlain and the members of his National Cabinet'.

This sharp introduction sets the biting polemical tone for the entire film. Whereas *La Vie est à Nous* went on to mix documentary with fictional episodes, the basic device of *Peace and Plenty* is the visual elaboration on the image track of a critical monologue on the sound track, a monologue that sets out the state of Britain under the Chamberlain government and attacks

86

Chamberlain and the members of his Cabinet on their Tory political records. The empirical detailing of the bad housing, educational and welfare conditions of the masses is extremely vivid. For example: 'For this child of an unemployed family, for food, clothes, everything, is allowed three shillings. The minimum of food per week reckoned as necessary by the British Medical Association costs today five shillings and three pence. To keep this young chimpanzee in good health, the necessary food alone costs the zoo authorities one pound and ten pence per week. Three bob for a child: one pound and ten pence for a chimpanzee.' This declaration, for which Montagu, as a professional zoologist, was well placed to gather the facts, is accompanied on the image track by shots of the child, a chimpanzee, and two different piles of coins on a table. In its realisation the entire statement is simple, arresting and powerful. The listing of the family and business connections of several leading Cabinet ministers is punctuated by a single derisive percussion beat on the cut to a still of each in turn. 'Truly, it is a government for the best people by the best people. They own the banks, they own the press, they own industry through holding combines, they staff the civil service, they form the general staff and staff college, to say nothing of the police college. And Chamberlain has ever been their faithful puppet.' At this point a little mannequin of Chamberlain with rolled umbrella and top hat clambers up from the floor, jerked by marionette strings. The film then proceeds to detail some of Chamberlain's hated Tory policies enacted during his past career: the 1926 reduction of relief scales, the 1929 rates reduction for big industry, the unpopular tea tax of 1932. Over photographs of Chamberlain with Mussolini in Rome, and with Hitler in Berchtesgaden, the commentary accuses: 'Friends with Hitler, friends with Mussolini.' There follows a sketch of the foreign affairs situation, and the civil defence measures then being prepared by the National Government are criticised as either meagre (air raid shelter provision) or tyrannical (the 'National Service' White Paper which threatened industrial conscription). The last section of *La Vie est à Nous* had included snatches of speeches by French Communist Party leaders, and similarly the final sequence of *Peace and Plenty* consists of a speech delivered to camera by Harry Pollitt.

Peace and Plenty is a propaganda film with an attacking edge and vigour unrivalled in the British cinema. The opportunity to use sound gave a major advantage over most of the previous unofficial labour movement films, and is put to full advantage. The soundtrack functions throughout as the dominant axis of the film, and this results in a structure of *argument* unattained in the earlier work of the decade (excepting the silent *Hell Unltd.*). Montagu commented: 'I did it in the style of how I'd write an article, a literary article, and then translated it into visual terms. The logic of it would be the logic if I'd sat down to write a pamphlet or a leading article.'[28] Faced with the task of illustrating, symbolising and explaining the soundtrack, the image track displays a wealth of imaginative invention, despite the poverty of available financial resources. Maps, graphs, optical effects, titles, stock-shots, stills[29] and the notorious Chamberlain mannequin are all employed in the exposition, setting fragments of 'reality' (film) against the less concrete, more conceptual representations. At one point, even the arch-agent of the didactic method—blackboard and chalk—is used.

An impressive work, but to what end? The film largely confines itself to criticisms of the National Government's policies. The Communist Party constituted the left face of the would-be Popular Front, and its criticisms are undoubtedly from the left. The film's domestic politics are the same as those of the British Labour Left's traditional policies of militant reformism. But the conceptual links between the National Government and the bourgeois class, the crisis of its mode of production, and thus the underlying causes of the approaching war, are not attempted: the overall *context* of the election, and the terms of the resolution of the problems of poverty and war, are taken as given: capitalism; parliamentary democracy; the diplomacy and repressive apparatuses of imperialism. Symptomatic of this is the claim that Chamberlain was 'friends with Hitler, friends with Mussolini'. This masks the salient point that the very *antagonism* between a declining British national capital and a reinvigorated German capitalism was a major factor propelling the world towards a new war.

When the film needs to go beyond criticism of the National Government's policies, and make explicit its own platform—the place from which it speaks—then its political shortcomings are most sharply revealed. Pollitt, who sets forth this platform, puts the Popular Front position within the labour movement, as he had done in his 'Peace and Plenty' congress speech. 'The defeat of the Chamberlain Government,' states Pollitt in the film, 'is the supreme task of the labour and democratic people in Britain . . . the time has come . . . for *all opponents* of the Chamberlain Government to get together and elect a government which . . . will defend the British people from Fascist aggression, by joining hands with the people of France, the Soviet Union, and the United States . . . Make *common cause* against Chamberlain, the enemy of the British people. This is the way forward.' (My emphases.) (Any doubts as to which class the euphemism 'the people of the United States' might refer to is dispelled by the accompanying image, which is a still of Roosevelt.) Pollitt's capitulation before imperialism is confirmed when he neglects the elementary duty of all communists, so often urged by Lenin—the absolute refusal to cede any legitimacy to an imperialist power in its rule over 'its' colonies—and instead grasps utopianly for a 'democratic' imperialism: 'Defend British liberties and *extend them to the countries of the Empire*', he cries. (My emphases.) The strengths of *Peace and Plenty* are the strengths of its realisation, the marriage of labour movement militancy with a bold didacticism derived not from the Soviet documentary but from the British documentary stripped of its 'poetic' aspirations. The film's weaknesses are political: its popular frontist politics.

However, popular frontism and its international policy had by no means been the only political response in the British labour movement of the late Thirties to the growing threat of war. There was a range of responses to the National Government's programme for rearmament which had begun in

1936.[30] The Labour Party right wing unequivocally supported the rearming of British imperialism. Another current of Labour opinion took a rather contradictory position, favouring disarmament by international agreement while supporting British participation in implementing any collective action called for by the League of Nations. There was also still a strong strain of moral pacifism in the Labour Party, though this had been weakened by the resignation of party leader George Lansbury over that very issue, precipitated by the 1935 party conference majority's final repudiation of a pacifist policy. The Labour left was opposed to rearmament by the National Government, and favoured the rearming of a 'socialist Britain'. The meaning of the latter term shifted ambiguously between a Britain with the dictatorship of the proletariat, and a capitalist Britain with a Labour government, though it mostly meant the latter.

1936 saw a three-minute film, *The Peace Film*, made by Paul Rotha and others, which pitted itself against rearmament from a pacifist position. The films *The People who Count* and *Peace Parade*, made in 1937 for the London Co-operative Society, record pacifist demonstrations. More importantly, the same year produced *Hell Unltd.*[31] This was a collaborative work by two students at the Glasgow School of Art: Helen Biggar of Glasgow Kino, who made *Challenge to Fascism* the following year; and Norman McLaren, who a few months later worked as a cameraman in Spain on Ivor Montagu's *Defence of Madrid*, and went on to become internationally known through his work for the GPO Film Unit and the National Film Board of Canada. The anti-war politics of this film are extremely interesting. Asked in a recent interview whether the film was shot to order, McLaren commented:

> Oh no! This film was my idea because I was then politically very committed. At the time I was a member of the Scottish Communist Party. We had seen Hitler growing in power for four years. It was terrifying. I wanted to do my best. I know that a film cannot stop war, but I wanted to make my contribution.
>
> Q: You have said that you were a communist at that time. Does the film to some extent put forward the view of the party on war?
> No.[32]

The change in the Comintern line during the preceding year indicated emphatically that the film did *not* represent the party view. But the nature of its account of contemporary war brought it far closer to constituting an authentic communist agitational instrument than all the *Imprecor* bulletins.

Hell Unltd. is a fifteen-minute silent film that uses stills, stock-shots, graphics, fast montage sequences, and extensive animation and pixillation in a barrage of images and ideas. Early titles announce, 'This film is addressed to all who are made to pay each day for their own and other people's destruction, to all who are taxed just now to pay for the future murder of millions of men, women and children, and especially to those who sit back and say "we can do nothing about it".' Animated graphs reveal the growing proportion of the

British budget spent on armaments. The massive death and destruction during the first imperialist war is recapitulated, and a title asks '1914–18. For what?' The failure of the 1927–28 Disarmament Conference is ridiculed, and the interests of munitions manufacturers in the continuing threat of war and therefore in sales of arms is shown up. The film is not afraid to name names, and denounces Krupp, Vickers, Mitsui, Dupont, ICI, Schneider–Creusot and the Bethlehem Steel Company. The increased taxation necessitated by rearmament, and the way this money finds its way into the pockets of the arms manufacturers, is attacked. In what is perhaps the least successfully realised sequence of the film, there is an attempt at indicating the horrific effects of a future war, with its death, disease and human misery.

The final section encourages the fight back. 'No war can be waged without the masses,' declares a title, 'Act now.' Film of a mass rally follows the title 'Demonstrate'. 'If that fails, then mass resistance is better than mass murder. /Strike/Act now.' A hand shuts off a machine, and there are shots of a city not at work—the idle locomotive, a pit-wheel at a standstill, a factory chimney without smoke. 'No government can contemplate war with things at a standstill.' In the form of pixillated models, the citizens join together to push armaments off the world-chessboard. The three-dimensional graph of arms expenditure falls over, the arms capitalist drops dead, people cheer, and the models link arms and dance round in a circle. The film is caught uneasily between a naive humanistic anti-war sentiment and the full bolshevik revolutionary defeatist position. In 1936 the two-year-old Peace Pledge Union, which was a Christian-led movement to 'renounce' war, already had 10,000 members, an index of the extensive support for moral pacifism at the time. It was this political tendency that was to come to full flower in some of McLaren's later solo animation and pixillation work. But in *Hell Unltd.*, it lies in curious coexistence with a more militant working-class anti-war thrust. The film approaches the politics summed up by German bolshevik leader Rosa Luxemburg: 'Either the class struggle is the imperative law of proletarian existence also during war . . . or the class struggle is a crime against national interest and the safety of the fatherland also in time of peace.'

In August 1936, Helen Biggar travelled from Glasgow to London to persuade Kino to distribute the film. It was accepted, as McLaren later mentioned ('What I can say is that many copies were made and that we received very small royalties from them.')[33]. But the acceptance of the film for distribution by the Communist Party-initiated Kino was not entirely smooth, and it seems to have been the section on the fight against war that caused the problem. McLaren had to defend the film's advocacy of industrial action against imperialist war, arguing: 'Other means have been failing for years. We mean one day strikes to protest against the present policy of governments and to show what resistance will have to be met with, in the case of outbreak of war'.[34] It is not surprising that there was some political doubt about the film. When war did come, the Communist Party—at least from 1941, with the ending of the Hitler–Stalin Pact—opposed all strikes, supported conscription and backed Churchill wholeheartedly. That in 1936 this film could be made by

90

young Communist Party members was probably in part because the Comintern line, and the changed view of inter-imperialist war that it implied, had not fully seeped through. But the production context is also important. The intersection of two apparatuses (film makers with Communist Party connections in an art school context) produced a film that was distinct in form from any other political work of the period (whether 'documentary' or 'fiction'), and politically distinct from the line of the Communist Party.

Overall, the achievements in labour movement film work in Britain in the Thirties were small. This is not surprising, given the political weakness of the labour movement in general despite its continuing organisational strength. Resources were pitifully lacking, and a logical solution might have been to tap the financial resources of the official movement. But this would have tied socialist film makers to the policies of a labour bureaucracy which was busy witch-hunting communists with its 'black circulars' of 1935, and signing joint planning agreements with management. Only at the very end of the decade, when the politics of the Communist Party had converged with those of sections of social democracy, and could be seen to offer little threat to the labour bureaucracy as a whole, did the official movement begin to take a serious interest in the use of film. The Co-operative movement, through its Co-operative Film Committee, produced one or two films in 1938–9, of which the most interesting is Ralph Bond's *Advance Democracy*. The eventual outcome of the deliberations of the Joint Film Committee of the Labour Party and the TUC was the emergence of the Workers' Film Association late in 1938, in which the Co-operative Film Committee participated. The WFA produced no films of its own, other than *The Builders*; and for its screenings it drew on Kino's library of films.

CONCLUSION

It is the contention of this essay that it is possible in the sphere of propaganda films to 'read off' the politics of a film more straightforwardly and unproblematically than with films from other spheres of production; to read off the politics partly from the political apparatus that produced the film and from which it takes its function. Indeed, in the case of the simpler documentary records, it could be argued that the films are incomprehensible outside of that apparatus. Practically all the films which articulate any more complex political meanings are caught up in a political stance that did not fight for an independent working-class position in the face of the impending war. This is true not only of films from the organisations of the official movement, but also of those from the unofficial movement. They are therefore *not* 'independent' films in a strict Leninist sense of the term. For popular frontism saturated cultural work on the left in Britain in the latter half of the Thirties. This can be seen even in the tiniest detail. For example, the series begun in 1934 by Kino was called *Workers' Newsreels*; when members of the Sussex district of the Communist Party began to make their newsreels, they chose to call themselves *People's Newsreels*. Shifts in terminology of this kind are not arbitrary: they

91

indicate profound changes in political direction. It is important to stress this general political ambience of the left in the late Thirties. For today, socialist cultural workers, seeking to link their potential contribution to the contemporary working-class's struggle for socialism, are returning to an examination of the activities of the Left Book Club, the Unity Theatre groups, the workers' film movement, and so on. Especially because, taken on their own terms, some of these activities 'flourished', it is necessary to remember that their overall setting was a decade of defeat for the working class. It is essential that any re-examination of the cultural work in Britain in the Thirties does not take place outside of a full understanding of the strategic questions of the time for the socialist movement or a knowledge of the answer that was provided.

Over the last decade, in Europe and elsewhere, a rebirth of agit-prop film making has taken place. In Britain, unlike in the Thirties, this has not occurred in relation to a particular party, a single political apparatus. This state of affairs seems likely to continue into the immediate future. However, agit-prop film work will necessarily, if sometimes unwittingly, be a participant in the struggle for the development of the kind of revolutionary socialist current in the labour movement that can, among other things, authoritatively furnish a mandate to socialist film makers. Many of the films produced and/or distributed in the socialist movement in Britain during the Seventies were dominated by the legacy of a particular aesthetic, a more sophisticated descendant of the simple visual recordings that comprised the majority of the Thirties labour movement films. However, this *militant vérité* aesthetic intrinsically tends simply to reflect the political level of the particular struggle it represents, and to reproduce this for its audience. Thus, it can only one-sidedly fulfil the tasks of socialist propaganda work. For in order to explain or argue politically within a given context of struggle, it is necessary to uncover the ideological and political forces that *produce* appearances, and re-present them. So it is important to find ways of constructing representations that cut against the commonsense versions of the world as it is/as it is represented.

The technological properties of cinematography enable the reproduction of the appearances of the moving world, and for the ideology that surrounded the birth of this technology and much of its early use this was one-sidedly regarded as its function. Even now, the capturing or recreating of the image (and the sound) of the specific in its apparent 'unity' is still the overriding aspiration of a great deal of documentary and dramatic film and television. But if socialist agitation is to work in a constant dialectic between the specific and the general struggle, then methods of argumentation, of dialectically transcending representations of the existing world, need to be developed. It is to this dialectic that agit-prop film makers must attend; and they are partially blocked from doing so because of the dominance of work in cinema as a whole that actively seeks to stay prisoner to the specific. Colin McArthur has drawn attention to the prevailing view of the capacities of the audiovisual, citing a piece written about television: 'The medium . . . does not lend itself to the detailed analysis of complex events; it is difficult to use it to relate coherently complicated narrative histories, and it is quite hopeless at portraying abstract ideas'.[35] In this claim about what the medium cannot do is delineated well the very tasks which contemporary agit-prop film makers increasingly find posed for them: 'We had a lot of things to say that did not lend themselves to being said in the *vérité* style that those of us who were most skilled as film makers knew. We were trying to find a way—a stylistic way—to say some of those things . . . We said "Okay, these problems are inherent in this film. Let's not ignore them. Let's work with narration, work with problems of abstract ideas, work with the problem of bringing in a whole historical analysis" . . . From the beginning we try to put [the concrete struggle] in a larger context. But it's hard. The forms don't exist to do that kind of thing dramatically and effectively.'[36]

It is from this perspective that the importance of *Peace and Plenty* and *Hell Unltd.*, can be seen. In Britain, the pressing problems of the period wrenched into existence two bold, vivid and pioneering films which strove to interact politically and ideologically with socialist argument. At the same time they intervened implicitly against the predominant ideology of filmic representation already echoed in the labour movement, an intervention which made that argument possible. Both films point the way for a militant cinema that is needed again, a non-fiction cinema that goes beyond the ideology of *vérité* documentary. We can learn from them and their achievement about the direction and development needed for a new cinema of intervention, one that can play a genuine part in the continuing struggle for socialism. But today, no less than in the Thirties, this struggle must include the fight against the politics of the labour aristocracy, i.e. that layer in the labour movement that acts on behalf of and is dependent upon imperialism. It is only in this context that the term 'independence' has meaning.

NOTES

Any study of this topic is indebted to the scholarship of Bert Hogenkamp. This piece owes much to 'Film and the Workers' Movement 1929–1939', an abridged translation of an article in the Dutch periodical *Skrien*, July–August 1975, published in *Sight and Sound*, Spring 1976; and to Hogenkamp's 'Workers' Newsreels in the 1920's and 1930's', *Our History* pamphlet no. 68, 1977. Thanks also to ETV Films Ltd., Metropolis Pictures Ltd., and the National Film Archive, for the opportunity to view films in their collections.

[1] V. I. Lenin, 'Party Organisation and Party Literature', November 1905, *Collected Works*, Vol. 10.
[2] Ibid.
   In view of a persisting tendency to read Stalinism back into the history of the Bolsheviks, it is worth noting that Lenin was making a political call, not laying down a coercive precept for a future socialist regime. He went on to say: ' "What!" some intellectual, an ardent champion of liberty, may shout. "What, you want to impose collective control on such a delicate, individual matter as literary work! . . ." Calm yourselves, gentlemen! First of all, we are discussing party literature and its subordination to party control. Everyone is free to write and say whatever he likes, without any restrictions. But every voluntary association (including the party) is also free to expel members who use the name of the party to advocate anti-party views. Freedom of speech and the press must be complete. But then freedom of association must be complete too.'

3   Franco Fortini, 'The Writer's Mandate and the End of Anti-Fascism' in *Screen*, Vol. 10, no. 1, Spring 1974.

4   Interview with Ivor Montagu, conducted by Peter Wollen, Alan Lovell and Sam Rohdie, *Screen*, Vol. 13, no. 3, Autumn 1972.

5   In 1932 the TUC General Council even urged local trades councils to establish rival Unemployed Associations, which could only serve to dampen down the fight back by the unemployed: 'They were certainly not intended as instruments of unemployed agitation' (Ralph Miliband, *Parliamentary Socialism*, London, 1961).

6   Steve Neal and Mark Nash, 'Film: History/Production/Memory' in *Screen*, Vol. 18, no. 4, Winter 1977-8.

7   Steve Neal, 'Propaganda' in *Screen*, Vol. 18, no. 3, Autumn 1977.

8   *Kino News*, no. 1, 1935, reprinted in this book p. 147.

9   Interview with Ivor Montagu, op. cit.

10 Steve Neale, op. cit.

11 Huntly Carter, 'Labour and the Cinema' in *The Plebs*, November 1930, and 'Where are the British Labour Films?' in *The Plebs*, June 1931, Reprinted here p. 139.

12 At this time, projectionists were organised either into a special section of NATE (the National Association of Theatrical Employees), which had a right-wing collaborationist leadership, or into the ETU (Electrical Trades Union). Poaching disputes between NATE and the ETU were not finally resolved until 1947. Camera operators and laboratory technicians were not even organised at all (the ACT was formed in 1933), although studio craftsmen were generally members of the union for their particular crafts. For an excellent survey of trade unionism in the British film industry in the years before 1940, see Michael Chanan, *Labour Power in the British Film Industry*, BFI, London, 1976.

13 Benn, 'The Cinema. An Instrument of Class Rule' in *The Plebs*, April 1931. Reprinted here p. 138.

14 Ralph Bond, 'Labour and the Cinema. A reply to Huntly Carter' in *The Plebs*, August 1931. Reprinted here p. 140.

15 *Kino News*, no. 2, 1936. Reprinted here p. 150.

16 TUC-Labour Party circular 101, 'Labour Cinema Propaganda', 1936. Reprinted here p. 153.

17 *Kino News*, no. 2, 1936. Reprinted here p. 150.

18 Ivor Montagu relates this incident in the documentary film *Before Hindsight*, a 1977 production of the British Film Institute, directed by Jonathan Lewis and Elizabeth Taylor-Mead.

19 Elvin took over as Secretary of the ACT in 1935, and contributed immensely to 'putting the Association back on its feet.' (Chanan, op. cit).

20 Rudolph Messel was a film correspondent for *New Clarion*. After *The Road to Hell*, Messel made *Blow Bugles Blow*, also for the Socialist Film Council. This anti-war film, which I have not seen, presumably expressed a Lansbury-style moral pacifism. The SFC never released the film: Lansbury's view was rejected at the 1935 Party Conference. Messel later helped on *March against Starvation* (1936). In some unpublished notes, Victoria Wegg-Prosser has speculated that he may have been responsible too for the fiction film *Strife* (1935; see note 23). In 1938, Messel left the Labour Party and joined the Independent Labour Party, which had an anti-war policy. *Blow Bugles Blow* was then released through the ILP.

21 Sam Serter in an interview with Terry Dennett, 1977.

22 National Film Theatre, London, 12 July 1978.

23 Besides those mentioned in the text, there survives another fiction film. Entitled *Strife*, it was made in 1935. Bob, a young worker, shares his father's anti-red prejudices, but is nevertheless sacked along with some active trade unionists, following a factory meeting in work time held in response to a 10% wage cut. Bob is eventually reinstated, because—magically, off screen—the active trade unionists have won union recognition and a reinstatement agreement from the management. Bob is found sleeping rough in Whitehall by his colleagues and informed of this new agreement, whereupon he consents to join the union, starts work again, and is reunited with his father. The construction of the film thus turns away from presenting the collective action that forms the lynchpin of the narrative, and focuses instead on an individual Prodigal Son parable. Somehow the film contrives to be simultaneously perfunctory and rambling, but

employs the occasional appealing device, such as the mood montage in which Bob is shown in a variety of postures taken from different camera angles and framings as he decides against committing suicide by jumping off Tower Bridge. *Advance Democracy*, made in 1938 for the Co-operative Film Committee by Ralph Bond, is also a fiction film. For a brief account, see Bert Hogenkamp, 'Film and the Workers' Movement 1929–1939' in *Sight and Sound*, Spring 1976.

24 Perry Anderson, 'Components of the National Culture' in *Student Power*, ed. Cockburn and Blackburn, Penguin, 1969.

25 Victor Gollancz, *Left News*, January 1937.

26 An amalgamation of quotes from two articles by John Lewis, in *Left News*, no. 14, June 1937, and no. 16, August 1937.

27 Fernando Claudin, *The Communist Movement: From Comintern to Cominform*, Peregrine, 1975. See also Leon Trotsky, *The Spanish Revolution (1931–1939)*, Pathfinder, 1973.

28 Ivor Montagu, interview, op. cit.

29 'I used an enormous number of stills. We found stills with each of the politicians in some utterly ludicrous position. For example, Chamberlain in a top hat, in a conservatory, in this attitude (Montagu mimed it) looking at a bunch of grapes.' Montagu, ibid.

30 The information in this paragraph is derived from Miliband, op. cit.

31 The title is often written *Hell Unlimited*. But it appears on the credits to the film as *Hell Unltd.*, and since this is intended to mimic the style of writing company names as well as referring to the infinitude of the hell of war, I use the version on the credits.

32 Norman McLaren, interview in *Sequences*, October 1975; English translation in *Norman McLaren*, Scottish Arts Council, 1977.

33 Ibid.

34 Quoted by Anna Shepherd, 'Helen Biggar and Norman McLaren' in *New Edinburgh Review*, no. 40, February 1978.

35 Jerry Kuehl, in *The Historian and Film*, ed. Paul Smith, Cambridge, 1976, quoted in Colin McArthur, *Television and History*, BFI, London, 1978.

36 Gordon Quinn, speaking of *The Chicago Maternity Center Story* in 'Film for the People', interview with the Kartemquin collective in *Jump Cut*, no. 17, April 1978.

PART II

Censorship and the Law

Introduction

The texts in this section outline different aspects of the struggle against censorship and other laws. They cover such topics as the founding of the London Film Society and the growth of the film society movement, the licensing and safety procedures for running film shows; examples of harassment by both local councils and police; the illegal filming of a demonstration; and some of the activities of the British Board of Film Censors (BBFC) in the period.

The introductory notes and anthologised material are designed to serve two purposes: firstly, to map out the principal institutional, legal and political discourses involved, and secondly, to provide a guide to some key figures and events informing the dynamic of these discourses as far as the censorship debate is concerned. The aim is to suggest that the pattern of censorship and the issues involved constituted an ever changing process, a constantly shifting set of relations between institutions and the discourses impinging on them. However, the attention to empirical detail inevitable in the presentation of this type of material is bound to reproduce to some extent the ideology of the legal apparatus prevailing at the time, stressing classic empiricist notions such as 'legal precedent'. But hopefully, in spite of this drawback, the main point still comes across: the lack of a theory of the way that legal institutions and the discourses they organise are articulated to and within the social formation cannot but make that apparatus appear as a labyrinthine system impregnable to rational political analysis. The production of this appearance invites attempts to reduce the complexity of the issues involved and the analyses required, to replace the complex systems of articulations with notions of direct linear causality and manipulation attributable to a class conceived as a monolith: 'Law is the expression of the rule of the capitalist class'.

The issue of censorship did in fact become a major unifying factor of 'independent' film practices in the Thirties. What all their disparate activities had in common was that they constituted an actual or potential challenge to legality. However, the notion of 'legality' involved was a complicated one. Indeed, it would be misleading to ascribe a fictitious unity to the fundamentally different types and levels of 'censorship' during the period by lumping them together under the generalised heading 'the censor' or 'censorship measures'. 'Censorship' was not, and never has been, the activity of one centralised institution, but a network of interrelated and contradictory institutions. Because of this, the struggles against censorship, which at least

96

implicitly regarded it as precisely such a unified institution, the monolithic intervention of a monolithically conceived class, became a severe strategic problem for the movement against censorship.

On the one hand, the identification of a single issue around which to rally support from sectors of the working class and among the radicalised or democratic factions of the British petty-bourgeoisie did help to provide some coherence and unity to a number of struggles. But simultaneously, the theoretical and political identification of the censorship issue as a single monolithic target (a failure to understand the potentially contradictory relationship between censorship as, firstly, a set of institutional and discursive practices and, secondly, as political practices) produced a tendency for 'anti-censorship' struggles to fragment. This threw up and accentuated contradictions within the movement which could not be coped with or properly understood without questioning the very basis of these struggles themselves. The side-stepping of this contradiction in favour of the maintenance of a vague and intuitive notion of a united front against 'censorship', conceived along traditional lines as 'anything impeding untramelled freedom of expression', guaranteed the ultimate fragmentation of the forces temporarily (and illusorily?) unified under one rather patched together banner.

FILM CENSORSHIP IN THE THIRTIES

As Ivor Montagu explains in his article (see below) and in his earlier pamphlet *The Political Censorship of Films* (1929), the ambiguity over what exactly constitutes 'censorship' of film in Britain arises in part from the interpretation of the 1909 Cinematograph Act. This act had originally empowered local authorities to safeguard halls from the acute fire risks involved in projecting 35mm nitrate films. In 1923, with the introduction of new smaller gauges of film (the so-called 'sub-standard' gauges of 16 and 9.5mm) for non-commercial exhibition, a problem arose because the film stock for these gauges was a safety stock, i.e. slow burning (technically 'non-inflammable'), and it was therefore not subject to the provisions of the 1909 Act. In the Thirties the efforts of the trade and local authorities were directed towards getting the exhibition of films on safety stock under licensing control. This meant that if the BBFC gave a certificate to a film, a local authority could still ban it. As a corollary, if the BBFC were to ban a film, it could still be shown legally either on safety stock if there was a sympathetic local council, or to the membership of a private club. The BBFC itself, however, never had statutory powers. Set up by the industry in 1912 as a self-protective body, it was appointed by the Kinematograph Renters' Society (KRS) and the Kinematograph Manufacturers' Association (KMA). Despite the fact that its President had to be approved by the Home Office, it did not possess the official standing held by the Lord Chamberlain, for example, under whose censorship theatres and music halls operated in London. Although the Board had no higher authority to back it, this did not prevent it from having a clause in the contract which anyone who submitted a film had to sign, forbidding the person to seek redress elsewhere should the Board reject the film. A critical report by the

Film Council, an investigative team sponsored by Grierson's *World Film News*, summed up the situation: 'Its limits are set by its own discretion. Yet its constitution involves no loyalty except to the bodies who elect and pay its members. It is responsible neither to the government nor to the public'. (*World Film News*, August 1936)

The BBFC itself served a function similar in some respects to the Hays Office in America. While the exploitation of 'sex and violence' in films had made good economic sense for the American studios in the British as well as in the American market, it increasingly contradicted their ideological representation as respectful of 'moral standards'. Censorship had to be self-imposed by the trade so as to secure the maximum market and avoid legal intervention from local authorities, external pressure groups, decency leagues and so on. Eventually a political intervention by the Hays Office was necessary to stabilise this contradiction between economic and ideological interests.

In 1931 the BBFC was faced with the influx of gangster pictures that accompanied the introduction of sound and rejected more films than in any previous year on grounds of 'collusive divorce', 'offensive political propaganda', 'prolonged and gross brutality and bloodshed', and 'suggestive themes acted throughout by children'. In January 1931 the President of the Board, the Rt. Hon. Edward Short, complained of 'films . . . in which the development of the theme necessitates a continuous succession of grossly brutal and sordid scenes, accompanied in the case of auditory films with sounds that accentuate the situation and nauseate the listener.' Protests were voiced against the destruction of 'King's English' by American accents, and there was an outcry against American films, emanating from established officialdom, religious groups and the letter columns of *The Times*, as well as demands for a parliamentary inquiry into the matter.

It is important, therefore, to distinguish between:

(i)   the national, non-statutory award or refusal of certificates by the BBFC, and

(ii) the local, statutory powers of local authorities and their related agencies such as regional police forces, civil servants and so forth.

The county councils received additional administrative powers in the local government reforms introduced by Chamberlain's Local Government Act of 1929, and the prerogatives afforded them by the ambiguities of the 1909 Cinematograph Act were zealously guarded as additional powers. The county councils themselves followed no single line, varying widely in their application of 'national' censorship regulations at a local level. Birmingham, for example, complained of the BBFC's leniency in giving films an 'A' certificate (banning all children under 16 years unless accompanied by a *bona fide* adult guardian); Manchester accused the Board of being too strict. In Liverpool and many other cities, children were excluded from all 'A' films. The Bishop of Croydon organised a local committee to select 'Sunday films', for which even 'U' films (for universal exhibition) were not always thought suitable. This erratic application of regulations worried cinema exhibitors. From their point of view, and especially at the time of a depression, anything that stopped the constant flow of people into the cinemas (around twenty million admissions per week) was to be avoided. However, after about 1935, with the mandatory application of the Hays Code in America, there was much less call for censorship of American films. Studios staked commercial success on uncontentious, 'wholesome' stories, musicals and comedies to avoid censorship difficulties and irregularities, and thereby ensured the achievement of the widest international market for their product. By 1936, in Britain, the Public Morality Council registered its appreciation of the increase in 'wholesome stories'. The children's market was expanded with children's cinema clubs, while Shirley Temple became the number one box-office star. The idea of the film societies' unlicensed halls competing with regular cinemas was also not welcomed by the trade, but it was soon realised that any straight competition could be rendered minimal by the application of the same *legal* means that had initially caused trouble for the trade (as instanced by the banning of *Scarface* by Birmingham City Council in 1931).

If the BBFC and the local councils covered the preliminary stages of preventing the exhibition of both 'commercial' and 'independent' films, other levels of harassment were also used. There are instances of police raids before or even during film shows, allegedly to check fire and membership regulations which were rigidly enforced anyway. In Glasgow, for example, guests were allowed in (maximum one hundred per night) on a ticket which had to be bought two days in advance, from a named agent's shop, by a fully paid-up member, who could not introduce more than two guests per performance. In January 1933 the film shows of the Scottish USSR Society (Glasgow branch) were closed down by the authorities for an alleged infringement of their rigorous set of rules*. There are cases of 'organised letter-writing' to cinema managers, recounted by Ivor Montagu, complaining of left wing political propaganda on the screen, thus enabling the managers, with due demonstrations of regret, to bow to the 'wishes of the customers and public opinion'. Organised disruptions of screenings were also frequent occurrences (cf. *Daily Worker*, Jan. 9, 1934). Moreover, groups of film-makers were physically assaulted by police when filming demonstrations, and laboratories were put under pressure to withhold prints or to 'accidentally' spoil negatives.

In the periphery of this area an immediate point of attack for left groups and liberal opinion alike in the mid to late Thirties was the 'political bias' of the newsreels which were shown as cheap support programmes in commercial cinemas. The avoidance or the trivialisation of controversial issues by the newsreel companies had made it unnecessary for the government to have recourse to forms of legal pressure, and there were only very few instances of such direct intervention. However, in October 1934 the Home Office issued a circular which offered the licensing authorities the possibility of prohibiting 'films likely to be offensive to public feelings', a regulation which had previously only applied to feature/fiction films, as newsreels were not officially subject to BBFC review. In this context of the direct relation between the state

---

*I am indebted to Doug Allen for this information

and the media, the importance of the radio had been realised in 1926 at the time of the General Strike when it became virtually the only means of national communication. Until 1928 the government had used its power to forbid any 'controversial' material on radio, but in the 1930s self-censorship prevailed with a ban on 'editorialising', reaffirmed by the Ullswater Committee on Broadcasting in 1936.

It is important, however, to discern the different shifts in attitude to the problem of censorship in radio in the Thirties. For example, in 1931, between the time of the formation of the National Coalition Government and the opening of the election campaign in October, no Labour speaker was allowed to broadcast. Following this, Attlee demanded 'equal time' in broadcasting for the three major political parties. But it was not until 1933 that Parliament established the principle of broadcasting being shared between the 'major political parties' instead of being wholly at the disposal of the government of the day. It is important to stress that this acceptance of the principle of 'access' as a *political* aim ignored any question of a fundamental restructuring of broadcasting in Britain. It forced debates on broadcasting and the media to remain on the level of a gradual extension of 'freedom of expression', thus promoting the impression that legal, technological and organisational aspects (indeed the very concept of broadcasting) existed by default in a politically neutral area. This acceptance of 'access' occurred in conjunction with a re-organisation of the internal structure of the BBC in 1933. Administrative and managerial power was effectively divided up, creating for example the post of an 'output controller' who became responsible directly to the director-general, and a heavily bureaucratic structure was installed throughout the departments of the BBC, necessitating an increasing number of staff: the number of employees doubled between 1931 and 1933 and was to double again between 1935 and 1939. Therefore, while the Labour Party was to be guaranteed equal access to airtime and thus to become 'representable to the nation' as a party fit to govern, decisions on overall BBC policy and on specific incidents tended to become 'departmental affairs' internal to the BBC. Such incidents included, for example, the 'error of judgment' in allowing hunger-marchers to express their opinions in broadcast interviews, and the resignation of two directors of the 'General Talks' programmes after accusations of 'left wing bias'. What could be seen as a kind of progress in respect to censorship is therefore significantly modified by the compensating factors of managerial reorganisation. In effect it demonstrates the limitations of a struggle based on the notion of 'censorship' as an essential given, a single empirically definable and unchanging thing considered to be separate from and outside of the dynamic of concrete social formations.

The film societies movement, which had initially served as a focus for a progressive front against the existing censorship laws, can best be seen as providing a kind of 'pioneer spirit'. They enabled films to be shown outside the cinema theatres, accompanied by meetings and lectures intended to contribute to discussion. However, despite their numerical growth, after the early Thirties they increasingly became mere providers of an 'alternative' service—a venue for 'unusual' films. Without a sustained input of 'uncensored' new films they became dependent on a staple diet of subsidised certificated documentaries and 'art' films of the kind promoted by the magazine *Cinema Quarterly*. The anti-censorship issue was soon isolated from any explicitly political questions and the film societies gradually began to form a kind of art-cinema circuit.

The issue of censorship can thus be seen in relation to four main groups: (i) central government; (ii) local authorities; (iii) the film industry; (iv) private organisations/pressure groups. The relation between government, the BBFC and local authorities made official state censorship unnecessary, despite a statement by the Prime Minister in 1935 that the government was ready to consider any practical steps to create one. This situation in Britain was in contrast to examples of a much more centralised administrative control, such as in France. There, although formal decisions were taken by a communal authority, such as the mayor, this process was monitored and supervised by the 'prefect', who was an organ of central government. To define censorship as intervention by the state is therefore misleading. The BBFC acted precisely as a protection of the industry from official censorship, for primarily economic reasons. The role of the BBFC was 'legitimated' (a different status from 'legalised') both by a long series of circulars from the Home Office advising local authorities to accept the Board's decisions, and by the practice of appointing a President of the Board who was 'acceptable' to the Home Office. Of the two Presidents during the 1930s, the Rt. Hon. Edward Short (President 1929–35) had been Chief Secretary for Ireland from 1918–19 and Home Secretary from 1919–22; while the Rt. Hon. Sir William George Tyrell (President 1935–47) had been Under-Secretary of State for Foreign Affairs (1925–29) and British Ambassador to Paris (1929–34) before assuming the Presidency at the age of 69. Only during the war was there a direct institutionalised chain of command from the government's War Office or Ministry of Information to the BBFC. The conflict between local and national governments was compounded when faced with the national and international bodies of the film trade which were radical opponents of local or national censorship on purely economic grounds, but were forced to modify their strategies in the light of opposition. In another context, any simple identification of the BBC with the 'voice of the state' during the period would similarly have to take account of both the administrative changes mentioned earlier and the development of the ideology of the 'soulful corporation', creating its own methods of defusing conflict under a paternalistic authority figure (Reith) and antagonistic to state intervention.

It is important to see how such a situation threw the left 'anti-censorship' forces out of gear. The immense regional variation in local applications of censorship/safety/membership regulations meant that local authorities were more politically effective at a local level than the BBFC. This situation, largely dependent on the ideology that 'freedom or denial of expression' was primarily the responsibility of functionaries within a social-democratic electoral system, was therefore supported by left groups because of the relative autonomy of individual local authorities, which in turn enabled Labour-controlled authorities to allow more 'freedom of expression' than others. However, this support for the system approved by the government distracted attention from the BBFC's role in refusing certificates on political grounds. Part of the weakness of 'oppositional' film practices was to represent themselves in terms of a negative definition (e.g. anti-censorship, anti-Hollywood) which would only preserve its identity, and political force, so long as the chosen objects ('censorship'/'Hollywood') retained their coherence. The conditions of existence for film censorship in the 1930s, however, straddled contradictory legal, economic and ideological grounds which completely escaped the analyses offered at the time.

A fundamental contradiction draws on the ambiguity of film's status as an object commodity and as a (potential) series of representations/ideas. In a society which accepts the principle of 'freedom of speech', there has nevertheless always been a problem as to what extent this applies to film. This problem was tackled differently in terms of the relations between national and/or state institutions, their legal apparatuses and the trade interests. In the USA, where 'ideas' are protected by the Constitution, for a long time cinema was not considered serious enough to have a major ideological/political impact. In contrast, Soviet Russia immediately recognised films as an ideological weapon of great importance to the class struggle, with censorship imposed by the state as a deliberate act of policy. The American situation was based on a 1915 court decision that cinema was 'business', analogous to the selling of food or motor cars, and thus did not constitute a form of expression which could be constitutionally protected. Neville Hunnings (1967) summarises the situation: 'It is only when the expression *reaches the realm of ideas* (and, apparently, *when it is uttered in a form recognised as a medium for ideas*, e.g. print, speech, dramatic performances, and now film) *that it is cognisable.*' (my italics—Ed.)

The importance of this distinction is that it marks a shift in the ideological (socially cognisable) status of 'film' between the end of the First World War and the Thirties, from being defined exclusively as a commodity to the status of being also a form of expression. This can in turn be related to the production of the ideology of film as an 'art' with the concomitant notion of an 'author' who owns and can express such ideas. In Britain, before the First World War, films were also subject to law in a manner similar to other commodities: the 1909 Cinematograph Act regarded film as a commodity which is potentially unsafe, like a car with a faulty engine or contaminated food. Film on nitrate stock was considered a risk to life and limb, and therefore to the public, those who worked with it and who sold it, and all of them had a legal right to be protected from the risks, which might result in physical injury and in claims for financial compensation to insurance companies or to 'responsible authorities'. Films were not considered as conveying complex ideas, but as merely working as slogans, pointing to simple moral lessons, against drunkenness, infidelity, etc. Consequently, by the Thirties films were in effect 'legally' censored only as commodities. The political controversy arose as this particular legal fiction became increasingly impossible to maintain. Thus the situation in the Thirties was one in which the combination of political and ideological pressures exposed the legal fictions and anomalies raised by the 'censorship' issue, but also one in which the contradictory implications of that exposure could not be surmounted. The dominant left-wing notion that the law expressed the interests of the capitalist class could not adequately comprehend the situation beyond its immediate social effects (banning of Soviet films, police raids on workers' film societies, etc.). The anomalies in the legal situation showed that no single group had responsibility for 'censorship', and that it was precisely this institutional separation which was an important factor in the complex transformations of the British state in that period.

THE FILM SOCIETY

Editorial note: *The foundation of the London Film Society (usually known as 'The Film Society') in 1925 was an important event for the social context of cinema in Britain and its relation to censorship. The following article, written in 1932 by Ivor Montagu, one of the Society's founders and its leading spokesman, is important for two reasons: firstly, as a retrospective account of the founding of the Society, and secondly because of its emphasis on the changing role of the Film Society from a* salle d'avant-garde *in the late 1920s to being a 'grandmotherly' institution in the early 1930s.*

The LFS was founded by Montagu and others just after leaving Cambridge, where in the immediate post-war period several of the European art films had been smuggled in and screened privately, producing a very small group of people interested in the 'art of the film'. Montagu mentions having seen The Cabinet of Dr. Caligari *there, while Basil Wright recalls Bertrand Russell arranging a secret projection of Pudovkin's* Mother. *The institutional inspiration for the LFS came from two directions: firstly, there was the film-maker and critic Louis Delluc's idea of a cine-club network in France in the*

early 1920s which produced both a proliferation of clubs throughout large towns in France, as well as a number of specialist cinemas in Paris which screened avant-garde films not generally distributed; secondly, the idea for a LFS was derived from the Stage Society of London, founded in 1889, which had been set up to produce plays which either for reasons of censorship or of commerce stood little chance of being performed in a West End theatre. Similar in many ways to the work of the Film Society, the Stage Society introduced the work of Ibsen, Strindberg, Gorky, Wedekind, Pirandello, Cocteau and many other new foreign dramatists to London audiences. It established both the precedent of Sunday performances (still illegal under the Sunday Entertainments Act), and the precedent of police raids (the first performance of Shaw's play You Never Can Tell *was raided by police for infringing the Act). The Society's main achievement was the introduction of naturalist theatre and, later, the presentation of avant-garde styles to the London intelligentsia. But although still in existence in the 1930s its role had gradually been assumed by commercial theatre, and the Society closed down at the outbreak of World War II.*

The Film Society's 'golden age' came in the

103

period 1925-29 with the growth of a 'serious public' for the flowering of the silent film, and in particular the new so-called art film. During this period the cinema gained a new intellectual and social respectability in Britain, both in terms of patronage by the progressive intelligentsia, and in the development of an interest in film criticism as opposed to exclusively publicity-oriented reviewing practices. George V and Queen Mary were occasional visitors to the cinema, and it was rumoured that nineteen members of the royal family ventured out to see Ben Hur in London in 1926. And although there had always been a trade press and fan-magazines, a number of the 'serious' daily papers began to publish film criticism from the mid-20s on, sometimes as an addition to drama reviews. Books focusing on the artistic nature of film began to be published in London, with such titles as The Art of the Moving Picture and The Mind and the Film. Eric Elliott's Anatomy of Moving Picture Art was published by Pool, whose owners, Kenneth Macpherson and Bryher, also edited and published the critical magazine Close Up from 1927 to 1933.

The Film Society catered for this growing interest in the 'art of the film' with its showing of imported, subtitled prints of films from France, Germany and Soviet Russia to a select audience composed largely of intellectuals willing and able to pay the annual subscription fee of 25 shillings. Some idea of the Society's backing from the English liberal intelligentsia can be gleaned from the list of founder members, which included Lord Ashfield, Anthony Asquith, Anthony Butts, Lord David Cecil, Roger Fry, J. B. S. Haldane, Julian Huxley, Augustus John, E. McKnight Kauffer, J. Maynard Keynes, George Bernard Shaw, John Strachey, Dame Ellen Terry and H. G. Wells. The original council of directors for the non-profit making limited company included Iris Barry (film critic), Sidney Bernstein (cinema exhibitor and owner of the Granada chain of theatres), Frank Dobson (sculptor), Hugh Miller (actor), Ivor Montagu, Walter Mycroft (film critic), and Adrian Brunel (film director). Later, Sidney Cole, Thorold Dickinson, Robert Herring (critic and author), Basil Wright, Ellen Wilkinson (later Labour MP for Jarrow) and John Grierson also joined the Council.

Potential opposition to the Society came from two main sources—the cinema trade,

and the London County Council. The trade, anxious at any sign of competition from whatever source, soon became reconciled to the idea of having an artistic fringe, and once it became clear that no economic harm was likely to result, the Society was at least tolerated. Eventually certain films shown at the Society, such as Ruttmann's Berlin, Leni's Waxworks and Reiniger's Cinderella, also received showings at other cinemas in London such as The Academy in Oxford Street which opened a season of silent Soviet films in September 1931. The Film Society was required to ask permission for its Sunday shows at the New Gallery (a commercial cinema, 35mm, with an orchestra) from the London County Council, as the films had not received a BBFC certificate. But this permission was granted, and continued on the grounds that the shows remained private and to a restricted audience only. However, a third kind of opposition came from critics such as Huntly Carter, writing in The Plebs, who criticised the Film Society for being élitist, and consisting of formalist intellectual aesthetes who were far happier concentrating on the aesthetics of Soviet Russia's films than showing films by British workers. Despite the occasionally vitriolic and self-contradictory nature of Carter's argument, the criticisms are important for what they reveal about the Film Society's own contradictory character within the British context. It is immediately noticeable that, at the time, the London Film Society's outlook had more in common with Paris or Berlin than, say, Manchester or Glasgow. Its period of growth from 1925-29 was nevertheless a period of transition away from the purely cosmopolitan Twenties culture from which it derived much of its ideological perspective. From the early years of the century, London had become the point of concentration of English national culture, pre-empting the role of large provincial cities. It was the capital of an Empire, the centre for world trade, finance and shipping, and until immediately after World War I it shared the role of European centre of modernist culture with Paris. But by 1930 London had lost this status, while Paris continued to function for another decade. However, in between these dates, the Film Society seems to have continued and transformed, albeit in a muted form, some elements of that pre- and post-First World War international avant-gardism as it appeared in the British context: the aristocratic traits of dandyism and extra-vagance; the purely urban, metropolitan or cosmopolitan emphasis; the aestheticism and formalism of a select and prestigious coterie possessing enormous influence—the presence of all these elements mark the LFS as part of the end of a declining era.

The programme of 10 November 1929 can serve as a convenient historical point of transition for the Film Society. Two months earlier Montagu had been in Switzerland for the ill-fated International Congress of Independent Cinema where international experimental film-makers had gathered to make future plans for international co-operation and expansion, a programme rendered impossible by the political and economic crises of the next few months and years. The special 10 November programme consisted of Jean Epstein's The Fall of the House of Usher, Walt Disney's The Barn Dance, John Grierson's Drifters and Eisenstein's Battleship Potemkin. The audience included both Eisenstein and Grierson, Aldous Huxley and also several members of the future so-called documentary movement—Basil Wright, Arthur Elton, Stuart Legg (all fresh out of Cambridge) and Paul Rotha. While the next decade was to be dominated by the films made by Grierson's group, a success made possible by the approval given to Drifters at this premiere showing, the context and aims of Grierson's movement were to prove a radical development from the Film Society's milieu. The lead given by the Society's select, upper-class metropolitanism was taken over by completely different values: as opposed to a privately financed club for a select audi-ence, Grierson sought state finance to reach a mass audience of middle-class (but repres-ented as classless) 'citizens' whose interests were firstly regional rather than metropolitan and international. Contrary to the formal aestheticism and the less virulent anti-intellectualism of the Film Society, Grierson saw artistic practices as possessing a pre-dominantly social function, as a pragmatic tool for 'mass education' in the new demo-cracy.

By 1932, when Montagu wrote the follow-ing article in the first issue of Cinema Quarterly, his point of view was already one of retrospection, his style superseded by its context. The Film Society was able to con-tinue until 1939, but by then it had been an anachronism ('grandmotherly' in Montagu's

words) for almost a decade. At its last performance, the 108th, at the New Gallery, Regent Street on 23 April 1939, it showed a silhouette film by Lotte Reiniger in Dufay-color (HPO), a film by Sidney Cole and Paul Rotha (Roads Across Britain), and Eisen-stein's Alexander Nevsky.

The Film Society, London

The Film Society of London is not quite the oldest body interesting itself in the ambig-uously named 'unusual'* film—that distinc-tion belongs to the Vieux Colombier in Paris, where Tedesco, a Rumanian, started a cinema on repertory lines in winter 1924—but it is the second oldest, and the doyen of all that have attempted to act along non-commercial lines. It came about in the following way. Soon after Warning Shadows was shown in London, Ivor Montagu was in Berlin (autumn 1924) doing a special cor-respondent tour of the German studios for The Times, an assignment which, in the end, he never wrote up. Angus MacPhail (now Gainsborough scenario editor) was with him, and together they saw Nju[1] (Jan-nings, Veidt, Bergner) and other stuff they knew their friends at Cambridge would give their eyes to see, and ran into Hugh Miller, an English actor now in America. On the train back Miller and Montagu got together. 'Why shouldn't there be a Film Society for films no one in England would ever see otherwise, just as there's a Stage Society?' In London Miller knew and added Brunel (at the premiere of Lubitsch's Forbidden Paradise), and Iris Barry, not yet of the Mail. Montagu, meeting McKnight Kauffer over a book advertisement, pressed him into service to design the Society's monogram, a much-admired, bold F.S. with a tiny attenu-ated figure attached, deciphered variously as a Cupid and as a Red Indian. Iris Barry brought in Sidney Bernstein, who brought in Dobson. Reading through the papers and

---

*A good epithet for our quarry is hard to seek. 'Artistic' is pretentious, 'cultural' bunkum; Captain 'Jock' Orton, on a hunting expedition with us in Paris once, announced to a L'Herbier cocktail party that we had come over 'pour chercher les films curieux,' with what instan-taneous success may be imagined.—I.M.

liking their criticisms of *Warning Shadows,* the conspirators enlisted also Mycroft of the *Standard* and Atkinson of the *Express.* That, substantially, was the group that got down to it. Brunel dropped early off the Council, though he still helped with the editing; Atkinson—for reasons no one else has ever known and which he has possibly by now forgotten himself—thought it wiser suddenly to attack the Society for trying to get Russian films he himself had recommended to it; Miller went presently across the seas to star for Gloria Swanson; Iris Barry has now followed him. But the rest of the veterans are still on duty with the new blood.

The procedure adopted after a number of cabalistic confabulations between the above was as follows. First, a list of possible programme material was assembled based on (a) Montagu and Miller's Berlin report; (b) world-wide gossip in Mycroft's and Atkinson's possession; (c) answers of the Russian film people to a questionnaire drawn up by Montagu and Atkinson and put by the former on a visit made to Moscow for the British Museum; (d) some of the shorts in Tedesco's programmes. Next, guarantees of support were canvassed (very successfully) from eminent unimpeachables like Lord Ashfield and the late Dame Ellen Terry (G.B.S. and H.G.[2] are the most notable survivors) to lend an air of respectability to the whole scheme. Third, detailed plans were got out for a system of shows (at the New Gallery, free, thanks to Lord Ashfield's generosity) exactly on Stage Society lines. Finally, all was burst on to the press and trade at a banquet in the best tradition.

This was summer 1925. The reception was—from the press, cordial (except by Lejeune,[3] who called us bloated plutocrats, and said that no scheme that couldn't include annual subscriptions at tuppence was worth tuppence to the cinema's great heart)—from the trade, cautious. The trade was right to be on its guard. Its view, most clearly expressed by Fredman[4] (now running the *Referee*), was that the Society might be used by the ill-informed as a stick to beat the trade. Success of a film at an F.S. show, he pointed out, would be followed by abuse of the trade for not having shown it to the general public, a totally different type of audience. For the Society it was replied that the difference of the publics was clearly recognised; the error would never be made

by us. Meanwhile all we wanted was toleration of our public, a chance to study stuff that his didn't demand, no cash but help wherever it didn't cost anything. On these lines we should do no harm, might bring new publicity and interest new people. And these have been our relations ever since. The trade has never grudged its help, and I think it recognises we've not been hurtful.

I shall never forget that first show.[5] From the moment the curtains drew apart punctually (in itself a triumph), and in silence (in itself an experiment), to disclose Ruttmann's absolute *Opera 2, 3, and 4,* the Society was made. The main film was *Waxworks,* poor Dr. Leni's best (it has never since been shown properly in England; for some unearthly reason the eventual distributor changed the ends round back to front and the B.B. of F.C.[6] insisted on Jack the Ripper being called Spring-Heeled Jack), and we finished with *Champion Charlie.*

But this first show nearly didn't take place at all. Just like so many of our juniors after us, we had casually assumed that what is allowed to plays must surely, in equity, be allowed to films, forgetting that English law broadens down from accident to precedent, and nothing is ever as anybody would expect. It turned out—what nearly everyone knows now—that though this boastedly democratic country has never passed a Bill on the matter, and never even discussed it in Parliament, the clumsy wording of an incompetent lawyer has not only established a film censorship, but given it powers over private shows as strict as over public. In short, we needed L.C.C.[7] sanction. This, of course, we found out about two days before our show. The L.C.C. Theatres Committee very generously let us have it for the emergency, 'without prejudice,' deciding to discuss our death or continued life afterwards. And, afterwards, the discussion, at the full L.C.C., voted 'life' by 69 to 66! Not so bad, when you think what the movement now has grown to—the younger societies all over the country, and, seven years later, the Home Office throwing bouquets about our work in the Commons and specifically amending the Sunday Observance Act so as to enable it to go on.

Well, what have we done since then? Times have changed, and it is not easy to recapture some of the highspots of those early days. *Raskolnikov,* when we tried a two-hour show with no music but a battery of coughs; *The End of St. Petersburg*, when a naughty journalist, writing over three different names in about twenty different papers, tried to pretend there was a riot, and only the happy accident of the presence in our audience of a Conservative M.P. saved us from a knuckle-rapping in the Commons; Léger and Murphy's *Ballet Mécanique*,[8] when there really was a riot, but not about politics, and Clive Bell said 'Marvellous,' and Dobson, overhearing, confessed ruefully: 'Begins to make one wonder what they say about one's own work, doesn't it?' There were fights and quarrels a-plenty, and I do not think it is conceit to claim that, in the midst certainly of plenty of dull drivel, we did introduce to England new techniques, new workmen, and new films that have not always been infertile. But what now? To repeat, times have changed. Counting to the favour of our past all the parallel movements we have aided, in the provinces and in other countries, occasional bright innovations such as Eisenstein's lecture course and less bright, if braver ones, such as our ventures into production, measuring also the fruit of our spade-work by the success now apparently fixed (Hurray!) of the London repertories, well—aren't these very repertories, these very new societies, beginning to make our work super-erogatory? Aren't we growing grandmotherly? Why don't we shut up?

This is a question we often ask ourselves. (And this year will be the third in succession that the Council has split on whether or no it should recommend the A.G.M. to wind up.) Prosperity, yes. Members, plenty. But when you can see films like *Hauptmann von Koepenick*[9] in the West End, and like *M* and *Turksib* and *Le Million* all over the place, it really is worth asking ourselves whether we have any excuse for being. Our prime object is, as on the day of foundation, 'to make available for study films (whether entertaining or not, whether 100 per cent of them or only as little as 5 per cent is worth study), not available elsewhere.' Last year we had one score; *Maedchen* was our *Journey's End*.[10] But one swallow doesn't make a summer. This year, two months before the season opens, our prospective programme includes exactly 0 names. Why then do we carry on? Well, even in London we still have a task. We are needed as a protection to the student against censorships hiding anything worth while. Though films banned or un-

submitted have always formed less than one-seventh proportion of our programmes, it is still important for us to be on the spot for this function in case of need. But there is a wider task; our object must be interpreted in no narrow sense. Except for those censored, provincial society and London repertory can show our films, true. But both live as yet insecurely on the bank of a volcano. The whimsies and perversities of each local Licensing Council threaten the societies in every province. An inelasticity of the Quota Act has menaced the repertories since their inception. We fight for a Charter of Uniform Recommendations from the Home Office for the first, an Agreed Interpretation by the Board of Trade for the second. I cannot reveal here in its fullness the essential part we play in keeping both alive even now. Should we abandon the struggle, withdraw the aid of our experience and fade away just because our members can no longer endure the tripe that is all we can dish up for them nowadays after scouring the corners of the earth, second in the queue to the Oxford Street Academy?[11] Fie! They must grin and bear it a little longer. And then, perhaps, who knows, one day soon or late, we may hit on a new function, a new unusualness, and the old lady will lift up her skirts and once more go trotting gaily on.

IVOR MONTAGU
Cinema Quarterly
Vol. 1, no. 1, Winter 1932-33

Notes
1 *Nju*—dir. Paul Czinner, Germany 1924; eventually screened at the FS's 5th performance, Feb. 14, 1926.
2 George Bernard Shaw and H. G. Wells.
3 C. A. Lejeune, film critic for *The Observer*.
4 Ernest W. Fredman, founder and editor of the *Daily Film Renter*.
5 The first performance of the FS took place at 3.30 p.m. on Sunday, 25 October 1925 at the New Gallery Kinema, Regent Street. The programme was Walter Ruttmann's 'Absolute Films' *Opera 2, 3 and 4* (1923-5); *How Broncho Billy Left Bear County* (USA 1912), part of the LFS's 'Resurrection Series'; *Typical Budget*, an unreleased burlesque by Adrian Brunel (GB 1925); Paul Leni's

Waxworks (Germany 1924); and *Champion Charlie*, an early Charlie Chaplin produced by Essanay Films (USA 1916).

6 British Board of Film Censors.

7 London County Council.

8 Montagu is referring to these performances: *Raskolnikov* (dir. Robert Wiene, Germany 1923) at the 3rd performance, Dec. 20, 1925; Pudovkin's *End of St. Petersburg* at the 29th performance, Feb. 3, 1929; Léger's *Ballet Mécanique* (France 1924) at the 6th performance on March 14, 1926.

9 *Hauptmann von Koepenick* (dir. Richard Oswald, Germany 1931), a satire on militarism adapted by Carl Zuckmayer from his play.

10 *Mädchen in Uniform* (dir. Leontine Sagan, Germany 1931), shown at the 53rd performance, Feb. 28, 1932; *Journey's End*, a successful stage play by R. C. Sherriff.

11 The Academy Cinema, opened in 1931 playing Soviet, German and other continental art films.

WORKERS' FILM SOCIETIES

Editorial note: In the following article taken from the magazine Close Up, *Ralph Bond traced the resistance and antagonism to the foundation of workers' film societies back to the first attempts to organise them in 1929.*

The annual subscription of the Film Society (*founded in 1925*) had been fixed at 25 shillings. Although theoretically anyone could join, with the earnings of an average industrial worker of the period at about 49 shillings per week, in practice the fee excluded all but the well off. The London County Council argued that the London Workers' Film Society's reduction of membership fees to 1 shilling really did bring membership within reach of anyone, thus making its shows virtually 'public'—and thus, by definition, potentially abusing the privilege of showing uncensored films to a private and restricted ·audience (*reported in* Bioscope, *26 February 1930*).

The winter of 1929-30 passed with such skirmishes, but in April 1930 West Ham Council allowed a public screening of Pudovkin's Mother *in Canning Town, and*

in the same month the film was also shown privately at the Edinburgh Workers' Film Society. As a result of the agitation caused by these events, the LCC began to reconsider its attitude to film societies other than the London Film Society. The principle of allowing 'recognised' film societies to show films which had not been submitted to the BBFC was approved in May 1930 by the Theatres and Music Halls Committee, and in October it produced a new set of rules to apply to film society shows which was approved by the full council in November.

The rules set the minimum annual subscription per person at not less than 10 shillings, with additional powers for the council to demand that all documents relating to members' subscriptions be available for inspection. Seven days notice was to be given if uncensored films were to be screened, and there were restrictions on guest tickets so that 'the total number of guest tickets issued in respect of an exhibition shall not exceed the total numbers of the society'. But the rules still did not allow films to be shown which had been submitted to and rejected by the BBFC. In such cases the LCC banned the films unless they were approved after a special viewing.

Following these guidelines from November 1930, film societies underwent a massive growth. Workers' Film Societies had grown up in major industrialised urban centres such as London, Glasgow, Bradford, Manchester and Salford. But also other film societies emerged in more middle-class areas, suburbs and small towns. They were the ones especially favoured by the British Film Institute, founded in 1933 to 'encourage the art of the film'. The official legal status of societies encouraged the formation of 'film-appreciation groups' under suitable 'educational' auspices. When societies wanted to show Soviet or British workers' films to working class audiences, however, police raids and harassment were still in order to check, as official justifications had it, that the intricate membership and safety regulations were being observed.

Acts under the Acts

Friends and foes who feared (or hoped, as the case may be) that after the rejection of

108

the *Close Up* petition nothing more would be heard for some time about the Film Censorship in Britain, will rejoice (or curse) in the knowledge that this question has suddenly become a storm centre of heated discussion and fierce controversy.

So numerous and involved have been the incidents of these last few weeks that it will do no harm to get some little order out of the chaos.

Act 1.

It is now well known that in November 1929 the London Workers' Film Society applied to the London County Council for a licence to exhibit privately uncensored films on Sunday afternoons. The application was summarily rejected without explanation or reason despite the fact that the Film Society had long enjoyed these same privileges. The Workers' Film Society said that the L.C.C. decision was actuated by class bias; that they were not far wrong will shortly be seen.

In January 1930 the Workers' Film Society again applied to the L.C.C., this time for a permit to show *Potemkin* on one specified occasion to its members. The L.C.C. replied saying that the Council had decided that under no circumstances could *Potemkin* be shown in any Cinema licensed by them under the 1909 Act. Back went a letter pointing out that *Potemkin* had been exhibited by the Film Society as recently as 10 November, 1929 in premises licensed by the L.C.C. under the 1909 Act. Would the L.C.C. please explain?

No explanation was forthcoming. Another letter was sent. This time the L.C.C. replied dealing with another matter altogether and strangely enough completely omitting any reference at all to *Potemkin*!

Act 2.

The Film Society announces that it will show *Storm Over Asia* at the Tivoli on 23 February. Great sensation. The Lord's Day Observance Council is very upset and calls on the L.C.C. to prohibit the exhibition. The audience at the Tivoli is assembled. A copy of a letter received by the Tivoli management from the L.C.C. is flashed on the screen. Fearing the worst, and straining our eyes we read:

'Clause 8 (a) of the Rules of Management, etc., etc.

'No cinematograph film shall be exhibited which is likely to be injurious to morality or to encourage or incite to crime, or to lead to disorder, or to be in any way offensive in the circumstances to public feeling or which contains any offensive representation of living persons.

'I am to add' (proceeds the letter) 'that should any disorder occur at the premises during the exhibition of *Storm Over Asia* the Council will hold the licensee of the premises responsible.

'I am Sir,

'Your obedient servant'.

The Film Society laughed. So would a cat. But can you beat it?

Act 3.

The I.L.P. Masses Stage and Film Guild announces that it will show *Mother* in a London cinema on 2 March. An application for the necessary permit is confidently sent to the L.C.C. A week or so before the date of the proposed exhibition the Council in full session assembled rejected the application.

The Masses Guild then says that it will show *Mother* in the Piccadilly Theatre, a theatre licensed by the Lord Chamberlain.

Theoretically, this was possible. The L.C.C. has no control over this theatre, and the Lord Chamberlain, it was assumed, had no authority to prevent any film being shown in one of his theatres on a day when his licence was not operative.

But prevent it he did. Nobody seems to know why, and it would appear that the Chamberlain himself is not very sure of his grounds for it is expected in some quarters that he will lift his ban. By the time this article appears he may have done so.

Act 4.

Meantime, Miss Rosamund Smith, Chairman of the Theatres and Music Halls Committee of the L.C.C., has been giving the low-down on the whys and wherefores of the decisions of that remarkable body. It all boils down to the fact that the minimum subscription to the Film Society is twenty-five shillings, whereas anyone can join the other Societies on payment of one shilling. Which means, according to Miss Smith, that *any* member of the general public can join these latter societies. You see, if you pay twenty-five shillings to the Film Society, you are not a member of the general public.

Class bias? Oh, no! Anyway, the combined entrance fee and subscription to the Workers' Film Society for a season of eight performances is 13s., which is just about half that of the Film Society, so when is a

109

member of the general public not a member of the general public? Answer—twelve bob! *Act 5.*

These extraordinary events, following so rapidly one upon the other, seem at last to have convinced various people that the British censorship and its attendant licensing regulations are the most reactionary in Europe. It takes a long time to get some people moving, but an All-Party Committee has been organised and has promised to raise the whole question of the censorship in the House of Commons and in the L.C.C.

The first step of this Committee of M.P.s was to arrange for a deputation to the L.C.C. to ask for a change in the regulations governing private societies.

For this meeting the Theatres and Music Halls Committee of the Council prepared a special report. From this it appears that they asked the Board of Censors whether in its opinion the films *Mother, Potemkin, Storm Over Asia* and *Modern Babylon* are provocative or likely to cause a breach of the peace if shown (a) publicly, or (b) privately. 'The Board's opinion is definitely in the affirmative', we are told.

Well we all know the Board of Censors. (The Company controlling *Modern Babylon* recently re-submitted it to the Censors who rejected it on account of its 'constant alternation of brutality and bloodshed, with scenes of licence in many cases', and 'indecency'.)

The Committee recommended to the full Council that no permission be given for the private exhibition of *Mother* and the report was couched in such terms as to suggest that the Film Society itself might have its privileges withdrawn.

The reference back of the Committee's report was defeated by 69 votes to 38!

So there you are. Comment seems quite superfluous; it is quite painful enough merely to record such events as these.

One other thing. A certain film critic on a London newspaper, who is famous for his admiration of Russian films and for his complimentary remarks concerning Russian film directors, professes to see the whole business as part of a 'well concocted scheme' to undermine the censorship. Almost a Bolshevik plot, in fact, with Ivor Montagu as the chief conspirator and villain of the piece!

This gentleman rushed in to assure the great British public that (1) the cinema industry is perfectly satisfied with the present system (which may or may not be true, but has nothing to do with the case), and (2) that if Moscow's propaganda films are rigorously excluded, their directors may eventually be persuaded to make films of a 'more commercial and entertaining character'.

Which, when you come to think of it, is a very significant remark. What a pity that our friend is going to be disappointed.

RALPH BOND
Close Up, April 1930

Dirty Work

So we are exposed. The sleuths of the Tory Central Office after months of snooping around, have blown the whole dirty conspiracy sky high. Their fearless bloodhounds, noses to the ground, have unearthed the dastardly plot to undermine the very foundations of civilisation. The universe totters. The millions gasp with wonder and lift their voices to High Heaven in thankful praise for their deliverance.

But let us get to our muttons. The sleuths have discovered that Russian films are being shown in England. And shown publicly, too. In fact, the REPORT containing the exposure emphasises by italics that one London cinema ran *The End of St. Petersburg five times daily*. Just think of it. By paying sixpence you could see 'St. Petersburg' continuously from 1 p.m. to 11 p.m. Horrible!

And just think of the inflammable propaganda of some of these Russian films. Among others mentioned in the REPORT as guaranteed to pollute the minds of the great British public are *The Postmaster, The Station Inspector, The Marriage of the Bear,* and *Polikushka.** Again we say, Horrible.

The real trouble seems to be the distressing habit of these Russians for making films that cause people to think. The REPORT quotes Eisenstein in *Close Up* ('a monthly film review') as saying that the Soviet films are 'a powerful weapon for the propaganda of ideas.' And, as we all know, the last thing a film should do is to make people think. All the most 'successful' box office films are those without any ideas at all, and it is only

110

right that the Russians should be told off for busting such time honoured and valuable traditions.

Of course, you could scarcely expect the sleuths to be over accurate. *Turksib* was apparently made by a man called Torin, of whom we have never heard. *C.B.D.* had 'panics and riots in every corner,' (this is too rich!). *Potemkin*, according to the REPORT, was shown by the Film Society at the New Gallery when as everybody knows it was the Tivoli. We learn that the Workers' Film Society exhibited *Men of the Woods* in May 1928, whereas this film did not arrive in London until months after.

I merely mention these little points in case the REPORT is given a second edition. Even our comic literature should be accurate.

Who is behind this plot? Who are the enemies within the gate? Well, according to the REPORT, the villains of the piece are:

The Film Society.
The London Workers' Film Society.
The Atlas Film Co.
Close Up ('A Film Magazine').
The Komintern.
A five-headed monster.

But the activities of the sleuths are not confined to ferreting out Russian films in England. Edgar Wallace must turn green with envy when he contemplates the international ramifications of the bloodhounds, for they have discovered that Ivor Montagu is in America, or about to go to America (they are not quite sure which).

A few weeks ago Wardour Street was agog with excitement. Rumours were thicker than cans of film. All work was suspended. First came the news that Ivor Montagu *had* been arrested in Hollywood. Then, Ivor Montagu *was* going to be arrested *when* he arrived in Hollywood. Then, Ivor Montagu *would* be arrested when he stepped off the boat at New York.

Wardour Street went back to work.

Meanwhile Russian films continue to be shown in British cinemas and audiences seem to like them.

RALPH BOND
Close Up, August 1930

Notes

* *The Postmaster* and *The Station Inspector* also known as *The Station Master*, are in fact

the same film, directed by Yuri Zhebiabuzhsky in 1925 in the context of a collective based in the Moscow Art Theatre troupe. This collective was set up in 1919 to film *Polikushka*, released in 1922, directed by Alexander Sanin. *The Marriage of the Bear*, also known as *The Bear's Wedding*, was directed by K. Eggert and V. Gardin from a script by A. Lunacharsky. *Men of the Woods* is probably a reference to the film by G. Stabovoi, *Man of the Woods*, released in the USSR in 1928. *C.B.D.* is a reference to Trauberg and Kozintsev's film *S.V.D.* (1927), also known as *The Club of the Big Deed.*

ACTION OVER POTEMKIN

Editorial note: *These extracts from the Daily Worker, since January 1930 the daily newspaper of the Communist Party of Great Britain, indicate the kind of official and unofficial harassment experienced by the organisers of screenings of Soviet films: checks on membership, threats of prosecution, government circulars to film laboratories were all used in attempts to prevent screenings. Eisenstein's* Battleship Potemkin *was the most infamous case during the decade, and as a result gained widespread notoriety, adding greatly to the film's subsequent popularity and helping it to become the classic film par excellence.*

The person identified as 'Seruya' in the advertisement was Ivan Seruya who, together with his mother, was a founder member of the Workers' Film and Photo League in November 1934, and, as a member of Kino, was prosecuted during the Jarrow Test Case in December 1934 (see Ivor Montagu's article on 'Film Censorship' below p. 113). He went on to become a founder in 1935 of International Films (later International Sound Films) which distributed foreign sound films on both 35 and 16 mm. Seruya was a member of the Film and Photo League's central committee until 1937; and International Sound Films had ceased to operate by March 1939.

L.C.C. again bans 'Potemkin'
Show stopped in East London.

For the second time within a few weeks the
L.C.C. has stopped the showing of the
famous Russian film 'Potemkin'.

The Jubilee Street (East London) cell
of the Communist Party arranged a
private show of the film in the King's Hall,
Commercial Road, for Friday evening last,
but a day before the show the proprietor
of the hall received a letter from the clerk
of the L.C.C., which declared:

'I am directed to point out that the
premises are not licensed by the Council
under the Cinematograph Act 1909, and
that the proposed exhibition must not,
therefore, be held.

'I am also to state for your information,
that the Council in May 1928, decided not
to consent to the exhibition in premises
licensed by it of the film referred to.'

A protest meeting against the banning of
the show was held on Friday night. The
organisers state that all those who bought
tickets for the film show, can have their
money refunded if they apply to those
from whom they purchased tickets.

In connection with the banning of
'Potemkin' reported above, KINO, the
film section of the Workers' Theatre
Movement, writes:

'The King's Hall is not licensed by the
L.C.C. and they have no legal jurisdiction
whatever concerning the exhibition of
16mm non-inflammable films in such a case.

'Nevertheless, quoting a 1909 Act,
which did not apply, the L.C.C. sent a letter
to the owner of the hall threatening proceedings if the film was shown.

'Similar methods were used by the L.C.C.

at a Hampstead show of the same film on
Thursday last, but alternative premises
were found, and the film shown four times
to crowded audiences successfully on
Sunday at another address.

'Local organisations should arrange an
exhibition at unlicensed premises. Full
details may be had from Kino, the Workers'
Film Organisation, at 33 Ormond Yard,
London WC1.'
Daily Worker, January 9, 1934.

Government act against 'Potemkin'
New Move Follows L.C.C. Ban Failure.

Kino, the workers' film organisation,
reports that so great has been the demand
for the film 'Potemkin' that further copies
were required to meet it. These were ordered
from the film-printers in the usual way.

Delivery not being made on the date
promised, inquiries to the printers produced
the reply that 'the matter is being held up
owing to a Government circular having
been received which cautions us against the
reproduction of Russian propaganda films.'

This direct interference by the Government reveals to what lengths they are
prepared to go to stop working-class
audiences from seeing these films although
no law exists to prohibit their exhibition.

Kino has succeeded in circulating
'Potemkin' extensively in the Greater
London area despite the L.C.C. ban, and
the fact that workers are actually seeing
the film has undoubtedly frightened the
government . . .
Daily Worker, February 19, 1934

IVOR MONTAGU ON
FILM CENSORSHIP

Editorial note: *This summary of the
censorship situation by Ivor Montagu
appeared in the first copy of* Kino News, *a
four-page bulletin issued by the Kino
organisation. Two issues of* Kino News
*exist (December 1935 and Spring 1936) and
further issues have not been traced. Montagu
had previously written a pamphlet on* The

Political Censorship of Films, *published by Victor Gollancz in 1929, but the present article was written much more within the institutional base provided by Kino, which was by this time distributing 16mm copies of Soviet and British films on the non-theatrical circuit throughout Britain.*

The most recent signs had been encouraging in the continuing battle against censorship and the Home Secretary, Sir John Gilmour. Gilmour, who had been promoted from Minister of Agriculture to Home Secretary in September 1932 in MacDonald's Second National Cabinet, had suffered a heavy defeat in the attempts to stop screenings of workers' films with the famous Jarrow Test Case of December 1934 in which Kino had been involved as the distributor, and Kino member Ivan Seruya had been one of the defendants.

Trevor Ryan writes that 'the Jarrow Test Case was the first instance of proceedings being taken by the police against the exhibitor and distributor of an uncensored non-standard film after they had refused to comply with police instructions to cancel the showing under powers conferred by the 1909 Cinematograph Act. The Home Office, in the process of considering a revision of the 1909 Act with a view to bringing the exhibition of 16mm films under control of licensing authorities by suggesting that all types of film are inflammable, saw this prosecution as a test case. The defendants were successful in maintaining the illegality of the police action, and the bill which was being drawn up by the Home Office was dropped on the basis of a judicial decision which restricted the operation of the 1909 Act to 35mm inflammable film stock.'

This victory in the courts did not, however, prevent further action being taken by the police or local authorities in similar cases, although it did remove even the pretext of any legality for such action. The fact that 16mm film stock was now considered legally as non-inflammable film should have taken it out of the jurisdiction of local authorities' censorship powers altogether. But the results of future actions confirmed the political basis for censorship in ever clearer terms. The National Council for Civil Liberties (the article's 'Council for Civic Liberties'), founded in 1934, had been involved in the Jarrow case and much of their work was devoted to opposing censorship, working closely with Kino up to the outbreak of World War II. *They produced a pamphlet on* Non-Flam Film *in 1934.*

Film Censorship

We live in a democratic country, so some people never tire of telling us.

The people makes its own laws.

But there is a film censorship established by law, and curiously enough, it was never discussed by the people, never voted or even discussed by Parliament. The people just woke up and found it there. How did this come about?

In 1909, some years after a terrible film fire at a charity fete in France, Parliament passed a law about inflammable films. The law was entitled: 'for the Protection of the Audience against Fire,' and it established that local governing bodies, the town and county councils, shall lay down conditions for film shows each in its own area.

But these councils did not confine themselves to regulations about fire protection in the conditions of the licences they granted —how many exits and no standing in the gangways and the like—they started to control a hundred and one other things, like *No Sunday performances, no German to be a cinema owner* (during the war) and *censorship.* So hungry was their appetite to control things they even made a condition *No non-inflammable films without our permission in a place we license for inflammable films.*

People went to law and complained:

After a lot of expensive litigation, the judges decided for 'law and order'. They said, 'It is true Parliament meant the law to be only for fire protection, but the law is not what Parliament meant, but what it said, and it said county councils can make conditions, so we must agree that they can make any conditions they like'.

Needless to say, one of the first conditions that the councils liked was censorship. (No council in the whole country *needs* to put on a film censorship if it doesn't want to, but not one of them has ever taken it off the licence conditions.) But censorship is hard work, at least it takes a lot of time, so most of the councils delegated their powers to sub-committees of magistrates and the like, and said to the trade: 'If you film business people will appoint and pay your own censor, we will accept his decisions.'

Democracy?
The film business people were, of course, delighted.

And everybody is happy.

The trade is happy because it has its own censorship.

The censors are happy because they are censoring.

The government is happy because it always gets its own way (it can and does whisper in the censor's ear: 'Be good or we'll bring in a new Bill for State Censorship and you'll be out of a job') without having to answer for it. ('The censorship of films is not a government institution,' see any Home Secretary's answer in the House of Commons any time.)

Not so very democratic? No, perhaps not, but, you see, everybody's happy.

Everybody?

Everybody except the working class.

One of the fires that the censors all agree on protecting the working class from, is revolutionary fire.

Standards of what is allowed or not allowed change and alter, save always in one respect. Anything that deals seriously with any real social problems has to be kept vigorously off the screen. And this applies not only to Soviet productions, or films submitted by working-class bodies, such as the 'documentary' showing news-shots of events in Germany and Thaelmann addressing meetings, but equally to such a film as *The Weavers*, a story of the struggle against unemployment by the nineteenth century 'machine wreckers', made in Germany and submitted some years back by an ordinary trade firm.

Loopholes
In English law, one of the penalties for our rulers getting their own way in this underhand sort of fashion is that the situation is so complex that loopholes are sometimes left. As a rule this is not a great inconvenience to them, for by power of money they can and do exploit these loopholes themselves in case of need.

But when the working-class movement tries, without money, but by its own energy and effort, to use these same loopholes, then every method is used to prevent it, even to illegal threats and intimidation by the Special Department of Scotland Yard.

And now these last loopholes are smashed by yet another treacherous Act passed ostensibly for another purpose—the Quota Act to help British Film Production. By a fortunate 'accident', this Act also happens to have been phrased in such a way that, as a side issue, it cuts out any possibility of a working-class body arranging the showing of films and restricts said privilege to big business men with plenty of capital.

Any possibility? No not *every* possibility. If we show on 16mm (small size) film instead of 35mm (full size) we are exempt from the Quota Act.

If you use small-size film you are exempt from the power of the Board of Trade.

If you use non-inflammable film you are exempt from the power of the police.

If you use an unlicensed hall (a private house or a hall without any sort of licence) you are exempt from the power of the magistrates and county councils.

And this is equally true, whether you show a censored or uncensored film, in public or to a private society, admission free or paid at the door.

Don't be intimidated
Kino's use of these opportunities has already led to weeping and wailing. First: the police and councils tried to ban the shows. They then looked up the laws and found they could not. One disappointment. Next: the police and councils began to send illegal and intimidating letters to the house or hall owners in whose places the shows were proposed, threatening that if there were any breach of the law (knowing all the time perfectly well that there was none) these houses or hall owners would be held responsible. Visits to the house and hall owners and even to the film-printers took place by the C.I.D. Some of these owners—with guts—carried on. No prosecutions followed, simply because there was no reason for prosecution. The bluff was blown up. A second disappointment. (Note: In one or two places where the bluff has not yet been thoroughly exposed, improper threats of this kind are still sometimes used. Where they are used in writing, send them in to Kino, for they are an actionable and illegal interference with trade.)

The Chief Constable of Cardiff then hit on a new one, since imitated by other Chief

Constables. He announced that all film shows, allegedly inflammable or allegedly non-inflammable, required his sanction. Why? Because, *in his opinion,* there was no such thing as non-inflammable film.

Take notice friends—if you have a call from your local police and they ask to be given and test and burn a piece of your film, refuse to allow it. If they bluster, laugh and order them away. Your film is, of course, non-inflammable within the meaning of the law, but suppose it wasn't. No policeman has any right to oblige an accused person to provide evidence against himself. And even more, the piece of film he wants to burn isn't your property to let him burn it, even if you wanted to. It belongs to Kino. You've only hired it. If you let him burn it, or if he burned it in spite of your refusal, Kino could get damages from you or from him. Tell him to write to Kino for permission if he wants to make a test. Tell him to prosecute or get a warrant if he thinks a breach of the law is being committed. He won't. He'll bluff.

The Jarrow Test Case

Not so long ago, the then Home Secretary Sir John Gilmore [*sic*], declared that all films were inflammable and consequently, that all films were subject to fire-protection laws. He proposed not to make stricter laws for non-inflammable film (nothing so undemocratic), but to relax the rules for 'slow-burning' films. *Relax* rules that had never been applied. Very kind of him. But not even Home Secretaries can make the law without going through the Parliamentary forms. The Council for Civic Liberties [*sic*] did valiant work challenging him, and in the end he was forced to bring a case.

At a police-court prosecution at Jarrow, of Kino and a miners' lodge which gave a show of *Potemkin*, the authorities were forced to give battle. A battle which ended in defeat all down the line.

The law has not defined 'inflammability'. So called non-inflammable film does, when heated and if the heat be great enough, undergo a chemical change. In so doing, the part heated shrivels away for an instant before the change ceases. If conditions be hot enough and dry enough, even a sort of momentary and disappearing flame accompanies the shrivelling. But precisely the same is true of anything that will combine at all with oxygen. *Precisely the same is*

true of steel. But nobody in their right sense would call steel or other metals 'inflammable'. Kino's defending lawyer had no difficulty in showing that, by the definition claimed by the Home Office 'expert', all sorts of material like toughened woods would be inflammable, *although their use is insisted on in various Home Office regulations against fire for the very reason that they won't burn.*

After Jarrow, Gilmour talked of an appeal. It petered out. There was nothing to appeal about. For even if he could overcome commonsense, and induce the courts to accept his contentions about the nature of fire-raising, he dare not. More than law and order is involved in this case. If the law courts did decide that no film is non-inflammable, the cat would certainly be among the pigeons with a vengeance. All the schools, all the public houses and hotels, all the advertising agencies, all the film societies, would need licences. And have to rebuild their premises to get them, or give up using film. And all the shekels invested in non-flam apparatus, non-flam stock, non-flam distribution would disappear into next-to-nothing. And could that be? No, my friends, it could not.

So carry on with your shows. At present there is nothing to fear. Later, new legislation may be introduced to bring non-flam films under some form of censorship. But this will be fought and, we trust, defeated!

IVOR MONTAGU
Kino News, Winter 1935

FORMATION OF FILM SOCIETIES

Editorial note: *This advice from Ralph Bond on how to start a film society formed part of a series of articles devoted to giving groups and individuals in the regions the elementary knowledge necessary to run a film society legally, safely, and at a profit—hopefully. It was important for Kino to build up regular groups if it was to survive financially. Given the small membership and the rigorous Comintern line during that period (1929-34) of the Communist Party of Great Britain, denouncing all social-democrats (the Labour Party and the Independent Labour Party) as 'social-fascists', expansion of audiences was unlikely. Expansion was, however, desirable both for the sake of securing a return on the limited capital investment in new prints, and for the new tasks of running a production group. However, such expansion could not be guaranteed other than by securing new audiences or by increasing the costs to existing audiences, either by raising prices or by more frequent attendance—with the concomitant necessity for an increased number of new films for that market. Specification and financial exploitation of this market was, however, directly linked to the identification of new political allies. While the Communist Party's strength lay in its mobilisation of unemployed workers, a broad audience giving financial security was out of the question. It was therefore only with the Comintern's belated call in the summer of 1935 for a policy of anti-fascist unity with social-democratic forces in a 'People's Front' in context of the Spanish Civil War that a larger audience became politically and commercially possible. This was also evident in different political and commercial contexts in Britain where, for the first time, progressive and left-wing ideas found an eager consumers' market, based on the 'need to know' the facts about the world situation.*

In 1935 Penguin launched their 6d. paperback series which by 1938 had reached previously unheard of initial print runs of 50,000 copies, and in 1937 they launched their Pelican series with books by left-Labour figures such as Laski and G.D.H. Cole plus Tawney, Shaw and Wells. Collet's Bookshop had been formed in 1934 and Lawrence and Wishart merged in 1936 to give a large number of groups involved in selling explicitly 'progressive' literature. Victor Gollancz's Left Book Club (founded in May 1936, and whose selection committee included both Laski and John Strachey) achieved a similar success with 57,000 members and 1,500 'Left Discussion Groups' by 1939, reaching a nationwide audience which had previously not come into contact with radical literature. Although Kino was a small cadre organisation with limited resources, by the winter of 1935 it was possible to start expanding the range of its activities and widen the basis of its support. In 1935 Kino provided films for about 1,000 shows to an estimated audience of 250,000 people.

Why Not Form a Film Society in Your Own Town?

The enthusiasm that has everywhere greeted the showing of the great Russian and other films which are obtainable from KINO—has stimulated a desire in many districts such as Sheffield, Doncaster, Birmingham, Manchester, Warrington, Glasgow, Gateshead, Tonyrefail and many others to show and produce films of real cultural and social value.

The task is not really so formidable as it sounds. First of all get a meeting of all the people who might possibly help. Invite representatives of all the workers' political organisations, trade unions, co-ops, and working-men's clubs. If there is a local amateur film society, rope them in too, their technical experience will be useful. Get a note about the proposal in the local papers and invite anyone who is interested to get in touch with you. Discuss the idea in broad outline, and then appoint a small committee as widely representative as possible, but at the same time active, to work out the plans in detail, and draw up the programme of shows and activities.

The First Show

Book a suitable hall for your first show, and do not be afraid to take a reasonably large one. As Kino films, and films from other libraries (16mm) are all on non-inflammable stock, the usual fire, safety, and censorship regulations will not apply.

Now, as to projectors—these can be hired from Kino but, particularly if you are in the provinces, it is a great advantage to have your own, which can then be used by other groups in and around your area for a small charge. To start with, however, you should be able to hire one—two would be preferable to avoid the intervals between each part of the film—from your local photographic dealer. If an amateur film society exists, you should be able to arrange with them to borrow theirs, and they will probably be able to supply an operator and a screen as well.

Advertise your first performance well. Send notices to all the working-class organisations, as well as to any cultural bodies, such as photographic, literary, debating, dramatic and similar societies. If you can, distribute handbills outside your local factories, etc., and do not forget to send a free pass to the local press—they will appreciate it and may give you a good write-up that will be valuable publicity.

Getting Members
See that the show is stewarded properly, and have someone to make a short announcement in the interval explaining the purpose of the society, and appealing for members. Membership forms should be handed out at the same time. The subscription can be anything from 3d. to 1/- a month (if you are giving monthly shows), the exact amount depending largely on local conditions, such as the cost of the hall, possible attendance, and degree of prosperity in the district. The one thing that is essential is to cover your expenses, so that losses are not accumulated.

Your group should affiliate to the Film and Photo League, whose headquarters are at 84 Grays Inn Road, London, WC1, and which exists for the purpose of co-ordinating the work of similar groups throughout the country. It can supply valuable advice, organisational material, exhibitions, lecturers, and help you in the purchase of any apparatus you may require.

Once you are well established, you should raise money with which to get your own equipment. A good projector suitable for a large hall can be secured for quite a reasonable figure, and on easy payments if necessary. A second-hand model can probably be obtained, and will save a good deal of money, but be sure and get expert advice before buying it, as a bad machine can (and will) give a lot of trouble. If you are in difficulties Kino or the League will be able to help you.

Making your own Films
After a time you won't be satisfied with showing other people's films only, but will want to make your own. Those of your members who are interested in this side of the work should levy themselves a bit extra to cover the cost—or you could run special functions, perhaps, to raise the necessary money. Movie cameras can be had at prices ranging from £5 to £150, according to what you have to spend, the age of the camera, its quality, or its number of special refinements. Here again the League could assist you—by advising on the model for your needs, and if necessary, looking out a good second-hand model for you; they can also obtain a discount off the cost of film-stock if you are affiliated.

Once you have mastered camera technique you should be able to make some quite interesting short films. For instance, a local news-reel from the workers' standpoint would attract a lot of interest, or you could make a picture of housing conditions, or some other problem in your town. You will want good weather before you can 'shoot' outdoors, and here you will find a couple of reflectors invaluable. These can be knocked up at practically no expense. A cutting-bench for editing could be fixed up in someone's room quite simply.

If your films are reasonably good, and of interest outside your own district, as they easily can be, there is a good chance of their being distributed by the Film and Photo League, in which case you would probably get back the money spent on them, and this would enable you to go on making others.

Start Now!
So why not go ahead? There are great possibilities, and enthusiasm will overcome any number of difficulties. The headquarters of Kino and the League will do all they can to assist you. It's up to you to make a start.

RALPH BOND
Kino News, Winter 1935

POLITICS ON THE SCREEN

Editorial note: By the summer of 1936, the increasing frequency of political censorship of mainstream, liberal or pacifist inspired films further exacerbated the crisis of the ideological/epistemological status of film in relation to the institutions of censorship, and the ideology of 'freedom of expression'.

With the outbreak of the Spanish Civil War, growing fascist aggression throughout Europe, and calls for an anti-fascist People's Front in Britain, the non-interventionist line of the British National Government was extremely sensitive to criticism and the possibilities of a radicalisation of 'public opinion'. However, while films produced about Spain by Montagu and others via the Progressive Film Institute were banned from theatres in Britain, the ideology of the commercial newsreel came under scrutiny from a number of liberal/commercial perspectives.

The March of Time *series was a monthly newsreel started in 1935 by Richard de Rochemont as the 'third great publication' from the giant American firm Time-Life Inc. In contrast to the 'light entertainment' offered by other newsreels, they worked upon the populist ideology of 'hard-hitting journalism' for citizens with 'a right to know'. Linked by a narrating 'voice of God' derived from the* March of Time *radio series in the USA, the films combined conventional newsreel footage with the re-enactment of current events which had not been 'recorded' by the camera, which also increased its 'dramatic effect'. The series was innovatory both in its fast editing style and in its dramatisation of current events, which became its selling point. It is essential to note that it was the product of a 'news' company and that it was widely advertised in the hope of attracting potential customers. It was selling* news *as a product, and initially it was reviewed in the 'news' rather than 'cinema' columns. It was therefore markedly different, in certain respects at least, from the movie companies' newsreels which were produced to provide cheap and entertaining programme fillers for cinemas.*

The notion of 'film as witness' recording an unmediated view of reality thus came under pressure, politically, ideologically and commercially, from the changes noted in the texts which follow: the 'disappearance of the old impartial presentation of news' (World Film News) *with the addition of the 'partisanship' of an enunciating voice; the new sense of 'news' as 'melodrama', and as an increasingly viable commercial product (see e.g. Dangerfield's 'selling history at a profit'); the construction of 'news' according to notions of 'screen value' (Grierson) and the consequent differentiation of roles between visual and written information. For the* World Film News *correspondent, this crisis is to be remedied by an appeal to the public's supposed hatred of 'bias': 'Whether this bias is to right or left, it is any case to be regarded as dangerous. The public must be warned'. 'The public' is taken as a neutral entity of undoubted integrity, innocence and fair-mindedness which should not have 'violent political lobbying on [its] screens'. Moreover, a link is made between the true interests of 'the public' and the 'indisputable authority' of* The Times, *which has been disturbed by unscrupulous/commercial/politically motivated interests. For the historian George Dangerfield, the newsreel has to 'photograph roots rather than branches' to regain its truthfulness and honesty, an unexplained remedy which is left wide open to Grierson's apologies for 'screen values' and 'dramatic focus'. Grierson locates the chance of this dream coming true in those institutions which would be representative of the 'thinking public' (film societies, adult education, literary societies, church groups, and, in the future, television) rather than the mass idiom of the entertainment cinema: 'Every progressive who has a sense of direct action comes to realise this distinction and organises the non-theatrical field for the great public service it can perform'.*

The ideological/epistemological assumption of 'film as witness', however, found difficulty in accounting for the 'manipulative function' of 'biased' commentary, since this went against dominant notions of a non-discursive ordering of images, i.e., images which 'unfold the real' rather than constructing a discursive reality from an enunciating position. Although at the time newsreels were supposedly guaranteed as ideologically neutral by their status as 'records of current events', the foregrounding of a structure of address ('propaganda') caused problems for the 'fiction/news' distinction based on the real/fantasy status of the image.

Politics on the Screen

Lord Tyrrell, who was appointed President of the British Board of Film Censors in November, 1935, in his paper delivered at the annual conference of the Cinematograph Exhibitors' Association of June 17th, drew attention to 'the creeping of politics into films'. 'From my past experience I consider this dangerous,' he stated.

'Nothing would be more calculated to arouse the passions of the British public than the introduction, on the screen, of subjects dealing either with religious or political controversy. I believe you are all alive to this danger. You cannot lose sight of one of the first regulations in your licences, which states that no film must be exhibited which is likely to lead to disorder.

'So far, we have had no film dealing with current burning political questions, but the thin end of the wedge is being inserted, and it is difficult to foresee to what lengths it may go, or where it may ultimately lead, unless some check is kept on these early developments.

'The Board has been attacked for having passed certain innocuous dramatic films, which irrational partisans have looked upon as containing insidious propaganda against the State. This is an attitude of mind with which we can neither agree nor sympathise. Indeed, Mickey Mouse has been so assailed on more than one occasion . . . Consequently, I think it would be well, in this early stage, to have some definite pronouncements from your organisation as to what will be your attitude towards these films, if, and when, they make their appearance.'

Referring to *People of Britain*, Lord Tyrrell stated that there was no question of the Board's banning it and that 'as a matter of fact, the certificate was issued for the film the day before the attacks were made in the Press'. Explaining the cuts recently made in the *March of Time*, Lord Tyrrell stated that *The Times* had said that the amendments suggested by the Board had improved the film and that the distributors had asserted that they did not in any way militate against its interest. Referring to the attacks on the Board in the Press in regard to these films he stated that as they were quite unfounded 'we did not think it necessary to give any public explanation.' Lord Tyrrell made no reference to the alleged political propaganda in news reels. News reels are exempt from censorship as being records of current events.

Sight and Sound, Summer 1936 (extract)

Newsreels Show Political Bias
Editing of Spanish War Scenes
discloses partisan views

The newsreel cameraman is the new war correspondent. He represents all the bravery of the great journalists of fifty years ago, who sketched—for they had no cameras—scenes of fighting on the battlefield itself. He brings to life, more vividly than any words, the plight of common people whose daily life has been suddenly spoilt by the drama of war.

But what happens when the material he has shot gets to the editorial cutting-bench? A check on recent newsreel tendencies shows that the old impartial presentation of news is disappearing. A partisan spirit has arisen. There is a strong measure of political bias. And it is time to face up to the implications behind this vital change of style.

The brilliant work by the newsreel companies on the Abyssinian invasion and now on the Spanish civil war was at first sufficiently sensational in its presentation of the violence and grimness of the modern battlefield to be simply the highspot of every issue. But as time goes on, it is a little depressing to find such material pushed down to the lower level of baby-shows and beauty parades. On such vital situations this banal and negligent treatment should be avoided at all costs.

But the question of partisanship raises a much more serious problem.

Up till quite recently the newsreels presumably regarded themselves mainly as entertainment and information caterers (chiefly entertainment). Their aim was to serve up a popular hors d'oeuvre of the week's sport and any other items of snob-value, thrill-value, or amusement-value. They would indignantly have repudiated accusations of propaganda or the deliberate plugging of controversial issues in a one-sided manner.

But almost imperceptibly the new racket has started. In recent newsreel issues about Spain the pro-rebel bias has been too obvious to escape notice, as witness a note on this page and also the fact that the Rothermore-controlled British Movie-tonews blatantly uses the terms 'Red' and 'Anti-Red'.

This propagandist element in the newsreels is bound to have a telling effect on the average audience. Shots of unkempt militiamen contrasted with Mola's[1] smart regulars, backed by a carefully worded and tendentious commentary, impel the innocent middle-classes to side with the better-dressed. And when the film uses its subtle technique of assertion by implication, the cumulative effect of atrocities and desecrations (nearly always by Government forces), becomes terrific. Many people have noticed the fact that newsreels which in previous issues had been well sprinkled with 'Red' atrocity stories presented the fall of Badajoz without reference to the mass executions of prisoners which took place there.

With typical guilt-complexes several newsreels have been careful to proclaim their impartiality. Items complimentary to the Government forces are indeed not unknown. But this does not alter the fact that no intelligent person can fail to notice the bias and political partisanship which is so rapidly establishing itself on the newsreel screens.

Whether this bias is to Right or Left, it is in any case something to be regarded as dangerous. The public must be warned. And, what is more, impartiality must be regained. If the newsreels themselves are unwilling or unable to re-attain it, there will very soon—if there is not already—be a crying need for a truly-balanced newsreel, which will give both sides of the picture with equal fairness, avoid violent political lobbying on public screens, and in general keep a check on the more unscrupulous of its contemporaries.

If cinema is to have its Yellow Press, it must also have its 'Times' and its 'Manchester Guardian.'

The whole problem is recommended to the newly formed Film Council[2] for its early attention.

World Film News, October 1936

Notes
1 General Mola—extreme right Falangist leader of Franco's army in Northern Spain, died in an aeroplane accident in June 1937.
2 Film Council—investigative body established by *World Film News* to examine aspects of the film industry.

March of Time under the Scalpel

Is it Fascist?

(With acknowledgments to the *New Republic*) Recent issues of *The March of Time* (screen version) have created a good deal of excitement in my local theatre. The demonstrations started last spring with the episode dramatising the dilemma of the League of Nations. This episode seemed to revel in the contemplation of might and disaster: it invited us to join in the spree—to hurry to and fro like Eden, shriek like Hitler, wear Mussolini's helmet, weep with Cecil of Chelwood. And we did; very surprisingly, for my local theatre is normally a drowsy place. We were emotional, we hissed and cheered. And all the time the narrator's voice rose serenely above our distressing clamour, talking behind the screen like a Greek actor behind his mask. Just such a voice, I feel sure, would have been hired to speak the lines of one of Euripides' suave male gods—those gods who appeared so opportunely at the end of a tragedy, when everything was going up in flames and agnosticism, and explained matters away. Nobody has ever been quite sure what those gods believed in or whether they even believed in themselves; and this gives them a real affinity with the voice that does the talking for *The March of Time.*

The March of Time has come in for a good deal of criticism at one time and another. It has been criticised for being (a) clever (b) melodramatic (c) fascist. The accusation of cleverness could hardly have worried it, cleverness being quite the thing these days, witness the circulation of *Time* magazine. And it is only the very, very sensitive who complain of melodrama. They don't like the assumption that time does not pass but marches; and they say that when the immediate past is resurrected, tied up, recreated in pictures, it is very trying to be informed, by implication, that none of these things could have taken place if time had not been something like a military band and history something like a circus. This has reason in it, but one has to realise that *The March of Time* is selling history at a profit, and this can't be done without a trick or two. Besides, there *is* a tendency towards melodrama in human affairs, and this tendency produces its heroes and its villains, and just occasionally one of them bobs up in national affairs. I like *The March of Time's* melodrama. Its heroes are all that heroes should be; they are energetic, human, fallible...

It is only when *The March of Time* gets off to highly controversial subjects that its melodrama disappears and something careless and complacent takes its place. If only it had absolutely refused to go any further than Devil's Island and dope rings and automobile disasters, which are human and important! But it wants to go further. It wants to thrill us with the collapse of a civilisation; and last year it was confronted with the most serious accusation of all. People of all shades of opinion swore it was going fascist. In one episode it appeared to suggest, with approval, that the C.C.C. boys were about to creep up on democracy, like Birnam Wood upon Dunsinane, behind the disguise of a reforestation scheme. Another episode showed the U.S. Army manœuvres. A third, and this was the worst, was very kind to the Croix de Feu.

A formidable thunder rolled, from right to left, from *The Herald Tribune* to *The New Masses*; and *The March of Time*, alarmed at this unanimous attack, hastily scrambled back to safer ground. To have sent such an episode into so many theatres was an infuriating gesture, even if an unintentional one; and the evidence against its being unintentional was overwhelming. If the Croix de Feu was news—this being *The March of Time's* excuse—wasn't the People's Front news too? No answer ...

Like the Deity, it (*The March of Time*) observes without prejudice, or pretends to. It claims to present both sides of every question, and that is an admirable claim: except that there is generally a third side to every question, and frequently a fourth and fifth. In its last year's episode, dealing with Bergoff's strike-breakers, it first of all allowed Mr. Bergoff to have his say, who protested that he stood for law and order. Then it showed how Mr. Bergoff's thugs were driven out of Georgia at the request of Governor Talmadge, who had been persuaded—with not too much difficulty, I should imagine—to re-enact his part in this fight for justice. At the end of it all, the Euripidean voice announced that the social conscience of America had taken a considerable step forward. But there was a third side to this question which *The March of Time* had neglected, and which the partial observer might think the most important side of all. It had neglected to inquire whether the textile strikers of Georgia would be much worse off when subjected to Mr. Bergoff's social conscience than when at the mercy of the Governor's. It had not pointed out that, while Mr. Talmadge sent Mr. Bergoff's employees away with one hand, with the other he continued to break strikes. That bit about social conscience

was the weak spot. If it had called this episode 'Bergoff muscles in on Governor's territory', it would have told a truth. As it was, it told a lie. Such are the effects of taking no sides ...

In one issue it managed to throw the same fog over the ministerial murders in Tokyo. It wanted to be fair both to the murderers and the corpses ... The episode had apparently taken no sides; it had praised the butchers and the butchered. But what did it really mean? ... You had paid your money, and you could take your choice.

That is the trouble: you have paid your money. There is a lot of money involved in *The March of Time*, and how can it afford to risk offending anyone by telling a deliberate truth? Against an argument like this, I realise that all I have been saying is not criticism but a wish, I suppose. I wish they would say—outright, beyond question— that somebody was right or wrong: even if that somebody was the Morgans, or Mussolini, or the masses. Then we could attack them or defend them, and they would be exciting their audiences honestly. But that is only a wish. Unless there really are liberal minds somewhere in *The March of Time* who would be glad to take a chance on photographing the roots instead of the branches. What an opportunity they have, if they could take it and would!

GEORGE DANGERFIELD
World Film News, October 1936

And a reply—Pity the Journalist

I agree with Dangerfield's analysis—and it is a brilliant analysis—but I wish I could agree with his conclusions.

In the first place, pay no attention to the charge that Richard de Rochemont is a fascist. I give you my word he is not. He is a deeper and more difficult problem. He is a journalist, and a film journalist at that. The real heart of Dangerfield's attack lies in his passage about punch. '*March of Time* picks out those bits of contemporary history which seem to pack the most punch'. The Croix de Feu was a story with punch and de Rochemont told it as a good journalist would.

But here is the sad part of the record, as I can testify in fact. De Rochemont wanted to balance his Croix de Feu with a slab of the Front Populaire and shot for it. But this, remember, was in the days before the Front Populaire was making the organised show it is today. It lacked screen value and the balancing factor (judicial, political, New Republic, Dangerfield or what you will) did not make the screen.

Blame de Rochemont perhaps. He ought, you may say, to have built the discussive huddles of the Front Populaire into something of screen value. The plain fact is that riding to the tempo of *March of Time* production and *March of Time* editing, the Front Populaire stuff was dull and it was out. De Rochemont, journalist, said, 'Hell, maybe we can get an angle on the Front Populaire sometime'. In his story of French peasants, he subsequently did. The discarded material appeared this time, and in dramatic focus.

There, I believe, is the real issue. *March of Time* is not fascist, complacent, irresponsible or any of the villainies charged. It picks the bits of contemporary history that pack the punch, as a screen journal must. Eight thousand theatres of circulation need tempo in the story telling, sensation, novelty, clash, suspense, in fact all those things which entertainment on a mass scale imposes on a film producer. But if, on the other hand, you were to show *March of Time* that the British Museum had the requisite elements of tempo, etc, etc, *March of Time*, I have no doubt, would do it.

One thing certainly that will not work is to *wish* that *March of Time* would do this, that or the other thing. Not in the theatres. As Dangerfield himself says, it is 'selling history at a profit and this can't be done without a trick or two'. 'Time ... something like a military band, history ... something like a circus': these are the conditions of showmanship. All we can ask is that the deeper aspects of time and history be turned into the idiom of military band and circus. Given a mass appeal the idiom of the cinema theatre rules. The theme, on the other hand, may be as deep as the producer knows how to translate into the idiom, and *Pasteur* is an example.

Taking sides doesn't solve the matter. The angle (hell, etc.) must be there—a dramatic angle or nothing. And a desire to show the entire four or five sides does not solve the matter, either. In the atmosphere

of the cinema, where political discussion is only a curtain-raiser to Garbo, complication is the devil. The danger is that we would have no *March of Time* at all. We might soon be back in the blithering grip of the newsreels.

There is, in fact, naiveté in Dangerfield's wish. If we are to show the 'roots instead of the branches', why the theatres at all? The real place for these deeper discussions and these more sober judgments is surely in the non-theatrical field, and in the prospect of television. That is where people —the same people—will sit down to think about things and discuss them. In the film societies and the adult education groups and the literary societies and the church groups (a hundred thousand of them) is where Dangerfield's dream has a chance of coming true.

I will lay a bet that in a couple of years *March of Time* will have realised the fact. In that case we shall have two versions of *March of Time* stories: the hotcha version for the theatres, because that is the way and mood of the theatres, and a more discussive version for television and the halls, because that is the way and mood of the halls. Every progressive who has a sense of direct action comes to realise this distinction and organises the non-theatrical field for the great public service it can perform.

But, my great respect to George Dangerfield, and I like the reference to Euripides. I have often wondered where I had heard the *March of Time* commentator before. I only pray he will not read the story and get himself a larger size in buskins. They are long enough—and so are his speeches.

JOHN GRIERSON
World Film News, October 1936

SURREY COUNTY COUNCIL/ N.C.C.L.

Editorial note: *This letter from the clerk of the Surrey County Council to a representative of the National Council for Civil Liberties in 1938 illustrates the continuing resistance of local authorities to the screening of Soviet films outside narrowly defined legal boundaries. Surrey County Council had long been* in the forefront of attempts to bring the showing of non-standard film under the control of licensing authorities. In June 1934 it had urged the Home Office to take steps to obtain control of non-inflammable film shows, but in the light of the Jarrow Test Case had achieved little success, despite its influence on the drafting of a comprehensive report on the cinema by the County Councils' Association in August 1935, asking the Home Office to be alert to the dangers of uncensored films being used for subversive purposes (quoted by Neville Hunnings, 1967). In November of that same year (1935) it had taken the unprecedented step of adopting a series of special rules which would bring control of non-inflammable film shows into its jurisdiction, enabling it to grant special licenses for such exhibitions. Despite the fact that this action had no legal justification, no objections had any effect on their bluff, and the Council were left to abolish their system themselves

after the start of the war. It is worth stressing that although their primary objective was to prevent the showing of left-wing films, their action also affected the trade, who were using 16mm in increasing quantities. Gaumont-British, for example, were issuing 100 films a week on 16mm by mid-1938. The letter makes it clear, however, that the question of the film's non-inflammable status 'does not arise'. The decision regarding screening was totally at the discretion of the Council although it would almost certainly have been held ultra vires (beyond their authority) if if had been challenged in court.

The investigation by the National Council for Civil Liberties formed part of its broader activities against censorship. Formed in 1934 to promote the rights of the individual and to oppose all forms of discrimination and abuse of power, it was a non-party organisation which secured the sponsorship of several intellectuals and personalities.

SURREY COUNTY COUNCIL
County Hall,
KINGSTON-UPON-THAMES.
7th December, 1938.

Dear Madam,

'Potemkin'

In reply to your letter of the 6th instant, the British Board of Film Censors declined to issue a certificate in respect of the film entitled 'Potemkin' on the ground that it was unsuitable for public exhibition. The representatives of the Public Control Committee of the County Council saw this film and decided to refuse permission for its exhibition in the Administrative County of Surrey.

The County Council's Regulation 23 (j) reads as follows:— 'No film, which has not been passed for "Universal Exhibition" or "public exhibition to adult audiences" by the British Board of Film Censors, shall be exhibited without the express consent of the Council.

Provided that such consent shall not be necessary in respect of any exhibition of films (known in the trade as "Topicals" or "Locals") of actual events recorded in the Press at or about the time of the exhibition, whether exhibited with or without sound effects or commentary.'

The question as to whether the film was a so-called 'non-flam' film does not arise.

Yours faithfully,
(Signed) DUDLEY AUKLAND,
Clerk of the Council.

To: Miss Sylvia Crowther-Smith,
The National Council for Civil Liberties,
Morley House,
320, Regent Street,
LONDON, W.1.

NCCL Files, Brynmor Jones Library, University of Hull

CARDIFF POLICE AND THE PEACE PLEDGE UNION

Editorial note: *This memo to the NCCL Central Committee illustrates an effective but illegal method of harassment by the police and fire authorities common throughout the period.*

The Peace Pledge Union (PPU) was founded in 1934 by Dick Sheppard as a non-party pacifist organisation which worked to promote pacifism by encouraging individual rejection of war, and it eventually became the British section of War Resisters International. George Lansbury, a Labour MP from 1922-40 and leader of the party from 1931-35, was a devout pacifist and a member of the PPU.

FOR G.P.S.C. 3.1.39.
Cardiff police and P.P.U. film show

P.P.U. local organisation in Cardiff wished to hold a film show on Dec 16th. Owners of the hall in which it was proposed to hold it told them that they thought it was necessary to get the permission of the police. Local P.P.U secretary wrote to the Chief Constable for permission.

Chief Constable wrote back asking them to submit synopses of the films to be shown and particulars of the certificates issued by the B.B.F.C. in respect of the films.

The films in question were 'Kameradschaft' [by G. W. Pabst] and three P.P.U. shorts of appeals by Dick Sheppard, Lansbury and Stuart Morris. All on 16mm non-flam stock.

Having received the letter from the Chief Constable asking for synopses etc, the Cardiff P.P.U. wrote to P.P.U. head office in London about the matter. P.P.U. head office asked our advice. I advised them to tell the Chief Constable that the films were non-flam and therefore he had no jurisdiction to lay down conditions relating to the *content* of the films. P.P.U. head office had considerable amount of argumentative correspondence with the Chief, who gradually reduced his demands in the course of the argument. P.P.U. carried on with the film show and held it and there has been no further trouble about it.

However, at the film show, two cops and one fireman were present. The fireman insisted that the operator make a roped-off enclosure round the projector, and that he should have a sand bucket and a fire extinguisher somewhere handy. The operator complied with these requirements to save a row and the risk of having the show stopped. The fireman also asked a lot of questions about fuses, double pole switches etc in the projector circuit. The operator was able to make sufficiently satisfactory answers to these questions.

The point is that this visit by the police and the fireman is *ultra vires*. The police appear to have been acting under Part 2 of the Cinematograph Regulations 1923, which relate to the use of portable projectors 'where the enclosure is not permanent' i.e. where there is no separate operating box and the projector is actually in the auditorium. But the point is that these regulations are made by the Secretary of State in pursuance of the Act of 1909. The Act of 1909 relates solely to *inflammable films*, and the regulations made pursuant to it can therefore relate only to such films. The action of the police and fire authorities in attempting to enforce flam. film regulations at a non-flam show, is therefore *ultra vires* and illegal.

What about protest to the Chief Constable and letters to the Cardiff papers?

NCCL Files,
Brynmor Jones Library,
University of Hull

FILM AS EVIDENCE

Editorial note: *This snippet of news highlights a use of film which was not developed until new technology was available after the war. Although the defects of the use of film in connection with speeding offences are fairly obvious for the reasons mentioned below, the use of film as an 'action replay' device in the courts brings the legal status of film during the period again into question. It is not known whether police were already recording demonstrations for identification purposes, but at a demonstration in South Wales where a 'workers' newsreel' recorded*

124

police brutality the film record was refused as evidence in the courts—one case where the ideology of 'film as evidence' proved to be officially denied.

Police use Cine-camera to Convict Speedsters

The Chesterfield police are trying to obtain evidence against dangerous drivers by securing records on moving film.

They have mounted a 16-mm camera in the front seat of one of their mobile cars. It is operated by a man sitting beside the driver, who shoots through the wind-screen of the car. When the hood of the car is up the camera is almost invisible.

The experiment was started in July last year, when films were used to convict street bookmakers. The pictures, screened in court, showed bets actually being received by the bookies.

Scotland Yard, when asked if they were doing anything along similar lines, said they had considered the idea but discarded it as impractical.

There certainly would appear to be many technical snags. If the police-car is travelling at high speed, the vibration would almost certainly reduce the picture to a blur. And who will check the camera speed? The most innocuous driving looks dangerous when the camera is turning slow!

World Film News, May 1936

125

PART III

The Labour Movement and Oppositional Cinema

Introduction

This section contains texts which deal with a variety of film practices and institutions relating to socialist politics during the period. It covers the period chronologically and includes the following topics: the early proposals around 1929 for a workers' film society and a socialist newsreel; the debate over the 'correct strategy' for a socialist film practice in Britain; the role of the Film Society 'intellectuals' in the movement and attacks on their 'aestheticism' and 'formalism'; the early agit-prop film units and their relations to the Workers' Theatre Movement; the expansion of National Government film propaganda during the period; the contrast between conceptions of Hollywood and the film industry and the social function of the film maker as both political agitator and artist; the construction of a socialist distribution and exhibition network; the response of the Labour Party and the TUC to the question of film propaganda; and the expansion and interlinking of film activities with the Left Book Club during the period of the Spanish Civil War and the movement for a Popular Front in Britain.

In providing a thumbnail sketch of the context for these practices, the complex relation between the cinemas of Hollywood, Soviet Russia and Britain in the 1930s needs to be taken into account. 'Hollywood' was received in a hostile manner by socialist organisations as a symbol of the economic and ideological phenomenon of 'Americanism'—the impact of America and American industrial methods on Europe after the First World War—which the British left conservatively and monolithically identified with the vices of capitalism. This contrasted with the meaning of 'Americanism' in the Soviet Union immediately after the revolution, where it functioned as a model both for socialist industrialisation and for, in Mayakovsky's words, 'sweeping away the dead culture of Europe'. In a socialist context in Britain, however, Hollywood was represented only as a dream machine, and the socialist movement generally allied itself with reactionary forces such as decency leagues and churches to portray American films as brimming over with psychopathological and irrational forces unleashed and exploited by capitalism, capable of providing only illusory pleasures as 'dope for the workers'.

In contrast, Soviet cinema was read as an exemplary model for 'artists' putting their artistic energies in the service of the working class. But because of the romantic individualism that still dominated discourses about art, artistic practice was conceptualised as the expression of someone's point of view.

Soviet film makers, living in what was assumed to be a workers' state, were then supposed to be giving expression to the point of view of the working class (for the shift from 'individual artist' to 'working class' as expressive subject, see Claire Johnston's essay in this book). Therefore, as the question in Britain was precisely, according to the same romantic ideology, to present the working class's point of view, the Soviet cinema came to be the exemplary cinema. This, of course, was in the face of the contemporary champions of 'art cinema', who, applying the traditional literary and theatrical canons of 'excellence' to the new medium, were equally enthusiastic about the work of Eisenstein, Pudovkin and Dovzhenko, to name but a few. There were, of course, more pragmatic reasons for promoting Soviet cinema. As the political practice of the Soviet Union came to be increasingly problematic and was accompanied by virulent attacks on theoretical work and intellectuals in general, aesthetic practices such as cinema provided the terrain where compromises could be reached. The Soviet Union derived prestige and admiration from its cultural exports, while intellectuals could sidestep the more risky and intractable problems posed by the Comintern's politics. Moreover, the contemporary ideologies of 'art' allowed the CP intellectuals to articulate their cultural-political practice with ideologies dominating the radicalised intellectuals of the British petty-bourgeoisie.

The British cinema during the decade saw an increase in the representation of the working class on the screen, both in the low-life musicals, in the comedies of George Formby, Jessie Matthews and Gracie Fields, and in the 'serious' documentaries associated with the name of Grierson. The reasons for this are multiple and complex. Of course, the need to cope in one way or another with the increased militancy of workers and of the unemployed, together with the need to sell a programme for the capitalist reorganisation of the industrialised countries under the hegemony of the USA, were two factors which contributed to the increased visibility of the world of work in the cinema. However, the actual forms this increased visibility assumed in British films can only be understood if examined in the context of the discursive forms and institutions regulating British films as a specific regime of representation. This is a subject that still needs to be studied.

Audiences stayed away from British films in droves, associated as they were with middle-class theatrical antics and southern accents which northern audiences found it easy to resist. Similarly, the Formby films, for example, did not play in London's West End. Not only did the majority of British cinemagoers have more opportunity to see American films because of the American film industry's economic and political muscle, British audiences also felt more at home with Hollywood films. Hollywood's products were not just well made and massively advertised; they also allowed the British audiences to 'overlook' the class problems which indigenous films could only emphasise even as they tried to ignore them. This in turn—or simultaneously—cleared the way for and increased the effectiveness of the various pleasure-producing and identification mechanisms inherent in mainstream narrative cinema, codified into genre categories and mobilising

127

apparently 'a-political', 'innocent' emotions. In other words, Hollywood films appeared to be more 'entertaining'. These introductory notes are not, however, the appropriate place to elaborate on these 'pleasure-producing and identification mechanisms' in mainstream cinema: for a detailed account of these aspects, see Stephen Heath's 'Narrative Space' in *Screen*, vol. 17, no. 4; Laura Mulvey's 'Visual Pleasure and Narrative Cinema' in *Screen*, vol. 16, no. 3; and Paul Willemen's 'Voyeurism, The Look and Dwoskin' in *Afterimage* no. 6.

In contrast to the entertainment industry, the GPO film makers were at times represented as anti-capitalists because of their 'serious' approach to the working class and because of their role as 'artists' fighting against the individualism and the profit motive by which, in their judgment, Hollywood was ruled. The space for a self-styled socialist or oppositional film practice in Britain developed its characteristics within these limits. While Grierson's films had largely recovered the significance of the Soviet films and alone possessed the funding suitable for professional productions likely to be accepted by the monopolies for theatrical release, the independent workers' film groups concentrated on non-theatrical screenings at political meetings. The stress on the social use of film against so-called 'aesthetic fetishism' by cinema revolutionaries had its counterpart in debates on Soviet cinema in the late 1920s. This view had emphasised that 'the social and class distinctions which characterise an art product are not to be sought intrinsically within the art product itself—[but] are extrinsic to it and located in the methods of production and consumption'. It also, and somewhat rashly, located 'the essence of bourgeois cinema in the existence of the network of film theatres which gather together film audiences' (Arvatov, 1928). The tendency in Britain towards the socialisation of the aesthetic function helped subordinate any theorisation of the relation between politics and aesthetics to a subsidiary role, and reduced the interaction between politics and film making to the immediately observable aspects of the political context.

Throughout the pre-war decade, however, the attention of the workers' film movement was focused on the production of documentary newsreels of contemporary events 'from the working-class point of view'. These were specifically designed to counter the cinema newsreel, which concentrated on the monarchy, military affairs and sport, and played to mass audiences each week. Most workers' newsreels were shot silent, on 16mm, with a hand-held camera. This was necessary, first, because of limited financial resources; and secondly, because of police harassment of those filming demonstrations unofficially (i.e., not on behalf of one of the major newsreel companies). The film makers had therefore to be extremely mobile, using the lightest possible equipment and occasionally using a van so that they could masquerade as an official newsreel group.

Although these newsreels were to some extent informed by an ideology of 'news' similar to that of the press and the commercial newsreels, their conditions of production and their functional aspect in recording an event for a politically conscious audience gave rise to a number of differences. These can be summarised as follows:

1. Problems arising from the need to order the silent images.

Editing facilities were extremely limited, and the use of sound was prohibitively expensive, making a commentary or a music track economically unviable. Apart from occasions when the newsreels were shown to audiences who were directly involved (as in the case of the *Sussex Communist Party's People's Scrapbooks*, 1938–39), there was still a need to 'explain' the visual images, to link them to the intended reading. Using too many titles tended to fragment the continuity of the films, as in *Hyde Park Demonstrations, May 1933* and *Revolt of the Fishermen* (1935) by the Film and Photo League. So more usual devices were: (a) the inclusion of information in the pro-filmic event, for example contemporary newspaper headlines, banners and placards, so as to convey the maximum dramatic information and explanation without breaking up the fictional world; and (b) a structuring of the pro-filmic event so as to produce reading via framing, such as the image of a man framed against a huge poster of Lenin in *Against Imperialist War—May Day 1932*. In this context it should be stressed that the consistent use of images of people making speeches at demonstrations or meetings without either sound or titles implies that the film is addressing an audience which already knows what is being said from non-film sources, such as party or union meetings, the left press, etc.

2. Problems arising from identification of temporal or spatial co-ordinates, placing films within history.

The debate in Soviet Russia over the merits of 'acted' and 'unacted' films had ranged over the historical documentaries of Shub, Vertov's editing of *Kino-Pravda*, and the fictional portrayal of historical characters and events in Eisenstein's *October* and *Battleship Potemkin*. Although these debates were not explicitly articulated in the British context, a variety of practices illustrate the divergences around such notions as 'reality' being observed or constructed:

(a) *The use of stock shots*: film material was used and re-used as needed, not being tied to a 'real' location, but in order to construct other 'newsreels'. This is conceivably a case of economic constraint enforcing a contradiction which went unacknowledged. There was in any case no monolithic 'belief' in film capturing a pure reality or as simply and only being a witness to an event. Instead, film was used as an interchangeable representation of struggle, a 'class weapon' in agitation. For instance, *Against Fascism* (1934) contains material from *Workers' Newsreels* 1 and 2 and from *National Hunger March* (1934), in addition to new footage.

(b) *News*: the ideology of 'news' made problems of narrative and fiction of subsidiary interest. A title from *Workers' Newsreel* 1 (Kino 1934) proclaims: 'This is an attempt to present News from the working class point of view. It covers events up to August 1934.' Such films were seen more as intervention in newsreel coverage than in 'the cinema' *per se*—the polarity of 'news' and 'fiction' was accepted.

(c) *Identification of time*: specific historical moments were identified by posters, newspapers or titles within the image. Usually the items retain a unity of time and action, as in the coverage of a march or demonstration on a specific day (*Hyde Park Demonstrations—May 1933*; *We are the English*, 1936) or over a number of days (e.g., *National Hunger March 1934*); or the films are split into integral periods of time as in orthodox newsreel coverage. Occasionally, within the newsreel format, items are juxtaposed to illustrate a 'timeless' maxim: e.g., *Workers' Newsreel* 1 (1934), in which shots of a new co-operative store are intercut with shots of a plane crash at an air pageant, with the titles 'The Workers create/whilst . . . Capitalism destroys'. The thematic use of seasons in *Winter* tries to politicise the traditional moralism (the 'hardship of the poor') by intercutting shots of political meetings with seasonal shots.

How Labour Can Use the Films

This is not so much a note on amateur film societies, and a plea for the extension of the idea to the socialist movement, as a demand that the labour, co-operative, and socialist movement sit up and consider the effects that films have on the lives and on the outlook of the workers in general.

There are two sides to films—production and projection; the moulding of ideas and the determining of artistic standards (euphemistically called catering for public opinion) can be exercised at both points. The film producing companies make what they consider the public should want; the film distributing companies choose what they consider the public really desire, and, between the two, the filmgoer is tossed about like a shuttlecock and, finally, exercises his power of choosing what is forcibly fed to him. Generally he has no definite artistic standards and is quite content to accept, and to take kindly to, the dope; but, even if he has any fairly strong and independent views about films, he finds it almost impossible to get, at all regularly, films of a standard that may not be an insult to his intelligence.

The Monopoly Complete
The process of control is then carried a step

further. Control, when exercised at two points, generally leads to conflict, and, as in all capitalist industry, when there is a clash of interests the problem is generally solved by an amalgamation, merging or simply buying-out. This is what happened in the film industry and today most of the big American producing companies (Famous Players Lasky, Fox, Metro-Goldwyn, Mayer, etc.) each own some hundreds of picture theatres, and are thus provided with a ready-made market in which to dump their products.

Can this monopoly, so strong and so complete, be broken? And, if so, how is it to be done? As well ask whether the Press monopoly can be broken, for the answer, necessarily a trite one, is that neither the power of the Press Lords nor the power of the film magnates can be broken while industry and Government remain under capitalist control. And yet something, small as it may seem in the beginning, can be done; a breach in the wall of control can be made by forceful and co-ordinated effort. For even under individualist monopolistic ownership of the Press there has been a strong Labour and Socialist press, not strong financially and not powerful by reason of tremendous insurance impelled circulations, but exercising, nevertheless, an influence out of all proportion either to its puny financial resources or to its relatively meagre circulation.

130

Socialist Film Society

If then, by dint of determined effort, a Socialist Press has been built up, there seems very little reason why the Movement should not found its own Film Society with the object of producing and projecting its own films. A start has already been made—in Germany the Social Democratic Party has produced a film (Erno Metzner's *Freie Farht**) that is said to be a remarkably fine piece of work, while in Belgium the Labour Party has decided to establish a cinema in Brussels.

In Britain it seems as if we do not realise that there is any need for putting the workers' point of view in the Cinema; we realise the necessity of a Trade Union Movement, a Co-operative Movement, a Socialist Press, Workers' Dramatic Groups, etc., if working-class needs are to be met, and yet in the Cinema we are content enough to accept what our masters are kind enough to give us. So far, the only breakaway from the commercial cinema has come from small amateur film-producing groups, and their work, interesting though it may be, has had no definite Socialist tendencies. It is time that we decided quite definitely that in the cinema there is a workers' point of view to be put and that the only way in which it can be expressed is by the Labour, Socialist, and Co-operative Movement realising that the workers themselves are the only people who are ever likely to make films or show films that are likely to put a working class point of view. Now is the time to get a move on.

BENN**

The New Leader, 26 April 1929

Notes

* *Freie Fahrt* was a two-part propoganda film for the German Social Democratic Party. The first part consisted of a heroic, Soviet-style treatment of the German worker; the second part, according to Siegfried Kracauer, was a 'pictorial manifesto' devoted to SDP activities. The film was reviewed in *Close Up* (February 1929), to which Metzner occasionally contributed as a writer. Metzner was a well-known set designer who worked for Pabst on *Kameradschaft* and also directed experimental films such as *Überfall* (1929).

**The identity of 'Benn', who wrote frequently on film for *The New Leader*, is unknown. Fenner Brockway, editor of *The New Leader*, remembers him as being an intellectual of the Independent Labour Party. Later, however, he became a member of the Labour Party, and was reportedly found to have been leaking secrets, whereupon he emigrated to South Africa. *The New Leader* was the paper of the Independent Labour Party. The edition of 26 April was an 'Election Supplement: the MacDonald Special'. At the General Election on 30 May 1929, Labour became for the first time the largest party in the House of Commons and formed a government under MacDonald within which the ILP had some critical influence.

A Workers' Film Society

In last week's *New Leader* I said that the Labour, Socialist and Co-operative Movement would have to realise that the workers are the only people who are ever likely to make or show films that will put a definite working-class point of view in relation to life and the problems of life. This has been proved in the commercial cinema, where only the Russians, because the Government and the people and the artist are all consciously working for the building up of a Workers' State which involves the development of a purely working-class philosophy and art, have been able to make films that are full-bloodedly and positively working class in sympathy, execution and outlook. America with *The Crowd* and *Our Dancing Daughters*, England with *Underground* and Germany with *Metropolis** tried to look at the world through working-class eyes, but all failed miserably and hopelessly. Try as they may, their approach to films must remain different, and this difference in approach is reflected in general conceptions, in type of story chosen, in artistic development, and even in angles, lighting and make-up. There is very little hope indeed from the ordinary commercial production channels, for even *Jeanne Ney***, perhaps the most sympathetic film of all, flopped rather badly towards the end.

Amateur Films

There is more hope from the amateurs, for in their case the terms of the problem are rather different. They are freelance, they do not produce for the commercial market, they are

131

not bound by box-office considerations. All these statements have to be qualified, however, by the consideration that although they do not produce with an eye on the commercial market, they do produce, in general, with brains steeped in capitalist conceptions and traditions. So their work, although it has greater possibilities of freedom, is generally moulded on somewhat similar lines to commercial productions.

But, in spite of this, the Amateur Film Movement is deserving of the greatest praise and encouragement, for it does mark a movement aiming at self-expression instead of blind assimilation, and it may mark a movement of reaction against the all devouring power of the gigantic Film Trust. The history of the Amateur Film Movement makes amazing reading, for in the short space of seven years it has grown from one or two isolated groups into a powerful 'movement consisting of perhaps 50,000 camera friends.

Although these amateur film societies have done much good work in the way of experiment and in the way of self-development, it is doubtful whether they have produced anything that would be of any specific interest to the Labour Movement. At Oxford they have made a short anti-Fascist burlesque for which the AWC&S Film Society*** has been formed with the object of making propaganda films, but in general, it is probably true to say that the amateur movement has made no definite break with the traditions of commercialism. After all, even though there may be many Socialists inside the amateur film movement, the movement itself is certainly not Socialist, and this must be reflected in the films produced. If, therefore, we want the working-class point of view in films, we can only get it, apart from Russian films, in films that we would make ourselves. A Workers' Film Society for production purposes is necessary; we have the talent and we have the energy—all that is needed is determination and that first initial united push.

Problem of Projection
We next come up against the problem of projection. To show films you must have a hall in which to show them, and, if you want to show them to the widest possible audience, your cinema must be open at the same times as all other cinemas. Perhaps it would be impossible to have even one cinema of our own (picture theatres are very expensive), and so we are thrown back on two alternatives. Whether

to limit our audience by working in conjunction with some movement such as the Repertory Cinema movement, started a year ago by Leslie Ogilvie, of the Avenue Pavilion. This movement has now spread from London to Leeds, Liverpool, Glasgow, Edinburgh, Oxford, Cambridge and perhaps Manchester ('what England says today, Manchester says tomorrow').

The objection to the latter suggestion is that we should be tying our hands; the initiative might tend to be diverted, and we would have to accept the terms of this outside commercial organisation. The advantage, on the other hand, would be that our audience would be as wide as possible, working-class films and Russian films could be shown to pretty nearly the whole of the working-class population. As for the formation of a Workers' Film Society on the lines of the London Film Society, here you are narrowing down your audience to a handful of people, with the perhaps inevitable result that you tend to become 'arty' and 'precious'. There is the compensation that even a limited membership Film Society has agitational value, but I think we want rather more than just an agitation of a shallow stream. These difficulties and these alternatives, then, have all been weighed up, and after they have been thoroughly considered, a united policy should be worked out to overcome the difficulties and utilise the possibilities to the greatest advantage. And when we have done this, when perhaps we have found our Workers' Film Society for production and projection, we can be certain of a tremendous response from the workers themselves. When once they have seen working-class films they will never again be satisfied with the hollow mockeries of Elstree, of Hollywood and of Neubabelsberg.

BENN
The New Leader, 3 May 1925

Notes
*The Crowd, USA 1928, directed by King Vidor; *Our Dancing Daughters,* USA 1928, directed by Harry Beaumont; *Metropolis,* Germany 1927, directed by Fritz Lang; *Underground,* GB 1928, directed by Anthony Asquith.

**Die Liebe der Jeanne Ney, Germany 1927, directed by G. W. Pabst.

***A reference to the Association of Women Clerks and Secretaries Film Society—

probably the only trade union film society organised in this period, and even pre-dating the London Workers' Film Society.

Why not a Socialist Newsreel?

It is rather surprising that in film criticism practically no attention is paid to the newsreel. The Topical Budget, Pathé's Gazette, Fox News, Eve's Pictorial Review* and the rest are regular features of every movie programme, and by the mere fact of their regularity must play a large part in the forming of popular ideas and in the moulding of public opinion. If it is the little daily dose that does it, it is worthwhile examining the composition of the pictorial daily dose, so as to find out how it is made up and what are the effects at which it aims.

Lickspittles and Jingoes
Take as an example the newsreel I saw last week. It consisted of the following items: first, two schoolboy football teams playing for some trophy or other; second, Princess Mary opening a building; third, the erection of a stand on a racing track, and racing ponies engaged in trial runs on the track; fourth, the Prince of Wales opening the Newcastle Exhibition; fifth, Captain Campbell failing in his attempt to beat Major Segrave's motor-racing speed record; sixth, the King being removed from Bognor to Windsor on his recovery from illness. Six items—three devoted to sport, and three showing the movements of royalty. No mention of the General Election of May 30, 1929, (perhaps it is not considered an item of news value at such a time as this), no mention of the industrial troubles in Yorkshire and Lancashire, no hint that there is a mill strike in Bombay, or a strike in North Carolina, no pictures of the Russian trade deputation. Nothing about art or music or industrial development of slumdom or the breakdown of the efforts towards international agreement on disarmament.

Simply sport and royalty, royalty and sport. And this newsreel that I have selected is only exceptional by reason of the moderation of its choice of events. Usually, one has pictures of Mussolini reviewing the Italian troops, of tanks in action somewhere in England, of gas-mask parades, of aeroplanes practising bombing raids, of naval manoeuvres—

pictures of the whole paraphernalia of slaughter, but never a picture aiming at the development of the will to peace and at the inculcation of the spirit of internationalism. Always militarism, jingoism, sabre-rattling or sport—never internationalism, peace, scientific advance or any matters likely to raise the intellectual and moral standards of the people.

This, then, is the newsreel. Its object is not to present news, but to breed a race of society gossipers, sport-maniacs, lick-spittles and jingoes. There is room here for a Workers' Film Society to photograph events of interest to the workers. We could have a newsreel showing industrial and political demonstrations; the social causes leading up to strikes; co-operative activities; the effects of the miners' eight-hour day on the miners and their families; the contrast of nine-to-a-room in workers' homes with one-in-nine-rooms in the homes of the upper class, etc. It could be fairly easy to film such events, and, if done internationally, we could have a newsreel that would act as a real educational weapon on behalf of Socialism and world peace, and a defence against the dope with which the cinemas are now flooded.

BENN
The New Leader, 31 May 1929

Note
*The Topical Budget was an old-established newsreel that never made it into the sound era. However, the Topical Press Agency, through its Commercial and Educational Film Company, made a number of commercials masquerading as educational magazine items. Fox News is a reference to British Movietone News, a subsidiary of American Fox Film Corporation. According to Rachael Low, 'It is generally believed that the company had a close unofficial connection with the Conservative central office.' (R. Low, *The History of the British Film 1929–1939: Films of Comment and Persuasion of the 1930s,* London 1979.) *Pathé's Gazette,* also known as *Pathé's Animated Gazette,* had been introduced into Britain by the French parent company around 1910. In 1929, it also issued the *Pathé Sound Magazine,* soon to be followed by a sound version of its newsreel. In 1936, *Pathé Sound Magazine* became the *Pathé Pictorial. Eve's Pictorial Review* is probably a reference to the short-lived American 'independent' newsreel called *Eve's Film Pictorial.*

First Steps Towards a Workers' Film Movement

The organisation of a workers' film movement in Britain is an event of some importance; the fact that the movement is meeting with the most encouraging response, and achieving positive results, is of even greater importance.

In matters of this kind Britain—as in so many other things connected with the cinema—has been very backward. In Germany the proletarian movement is firmly established and has intimate contact with hundreds of trade unions and other mass working-class organisations. In France and Austria, in the Scandinavian countries, and in America, similar movements have been undertaken with varying degrees of success.

But in Britain, up to a month or two ago, nothing practical had been accomplished. In November of last year, however, a group of enthusiasts got together, and laid the foundations for an organisation which, within a very short space of time, got things done.

A Federation of Workers' Film Societies was launched, with the object of encouraging the formation of local Workers' Film Societies on a private membership basis, arranging to supply films and apparatus to the local societies, and encouraging the production in Britain of films of value to the working class.

The Federation is governed by a large and representative Council, with a working Executive which includes John Grierson, Henry Dobb, Oswell Blakeston, Ivor Montagu, Ben Davies and the present writer.

London, naturally, was the first centre upon which the Federation concentrated its activities, and a London Workers' Film Society was formed. This Society has for its object, the private exhibition of films of outstanding technical, artistic, educational and other merit which are not easily accessible to workers. The lowest practicable subscription was fixed (13/- per season), and in order that workers should not be debarred through economic reasons from joining, provision was made for the subscription to be paid in monthly instalments.

The response was magnificent. Several hundred members were secured in the first few weeks. The initial performance was arranged for a Sunday afternoon in November, but a week before the date arranged the London County Council stepped in and refused permission for the cinema to be opened on a Sunday afternoon! Hurried alternative arrangements had to be made and the performance was held in a Co-operative Hall on a week-night. Five hundred members and guests gave an enthusiastic reception to a programme which included Stabovoi's *Two Days,* Florey's *Skyscraper Symphony,* and *Garbage* (*La Zone*) by Lacombe.*

Both before and after London's first performance, the Federation had been receiving letters from enthusiasts in many provincial towns, and from workers in the mining areas of South Wales and other coalfield districts. The Federation is now busily engaged in assisting these workers to organise local societies on a similar basis to the London Society. Early results are anticipated from Belfast, Cardiff, Edinburgh and other centres.

One of the first problems that had to be tackled by the Federation was a supply of suitable films. Some of the Russian productions were available, but a wider range was desired. Negotiations with the German workers' film movement produced gratifying results, and the Federation has now at its disposal several films from this quarter, including *Shanghai Document, Shadows of the Machine,* and *Hunger in Waldenburg***. This latter film, re-edited, and re-named *The Shadow of the Mine,* was shown with great success at the second performance of the London Society.

But the greatest difficulty of all was the Censorship (O Blessed Word!) and the licensing conditions. It cannot too often be said that the regulations governing private film performances are ridiculous and barbaric. Nearly all the local licensing authorities stand by the decisions of the British Board of Film Censors, both for public and private performances. If a private Society in London wants to show an uncensored film to its own members in an ordinary licensed cinema or hall, it must obtain the sanction of the London County Council. If the film were to be exhibited without or against this sanction, the licence of the cinema would be endangered. If a private film society in London wants to show a programme of censored films in a cinema on a Sunday afternoon (which is invariably the only time available) it cannot do so without the sanction of the LCC!

The London Society duly made application to the LCC for the necessary permit, and was met with a refusal! No reasons were given. The existing Film Society has a permit to exhibit

134

uncensored films and to give Sunday afternoon performances, but apparently a workers' society must not have the same privileges.

The Federation urgently needs finance to develop its work. In the early stages some assistance must be given by the Federation to the local societies, particularly in many of the industrial areas where economic standards are low. The offices of the Federation at 5, Denmark Street, London, W.C.2. will gladly welcome donations from friends anxious to help in its work.

While, for the time being, the work of the Federation and its affiliated societies will be mainly in the field of exhibition, it is firmly intended to undertake the production of suitable films in Britain at a later stage. The possibilities, and the material, for production work by a workers' film movement are immense.

R. BOND

Close-Up, January 1930

Notes

*Two Days is *Dva Dnya,* directed by Georgy Stabovoi, USSR 1927 (also known as *Father and Son* and *Shadow of Another Time*); *Skyscraper Symphony,* an experimental film in the 'city symphony' genre by the French/American director Robert Florey, USA 1928; *Garbage (La Zone),* directed by Georges Lacombe, France 1925.

**Shanghai Document, directed by Yakov Blioch, USSR 1928; *The Shadow of the Mine/Hunger in Waldenburg* was an English-language version of Piel Jutzi's *Unser tägliches Brot,* Germany 1929; *Shadows of the Machine* is a Russian documentary, *Teni Maschin.*

THE PLEBS DEBATE

Editorial note: The Plebs *was a monthly journal first published by the Plebs League for the Central Labour College. The Plebs League was a syndicalist and Marxist breakaway group from Ruskin College which challenged the adult education of the Workers' Educational Association. It sought to provide the facilities for a process of self-education of the working class—an education wholly under its control in terms of organisation and content, thus providing a training within a political tendency. In 1921 the National Council for Labour Colleges was founded to organise such education*

throughout Britain. One of the major participants in the Plebs *debate was the populist mystic Huntly Carter, a film and theatre critic who wrote* The New Spirit in the Cinema *(1930)—see Deke Dusinberre's article in this book—compiled an account of avant-garde and agitational Soviet theatre practices, entitled* The New Theatre and Cinema of Soviet Russia *(1927), and was a frequent contributor to the socialist press of the period.*

The film company referred to, Atlas Films, was formed to distribute Soviet and German films and those produced by the Workers' Film Movement, a small group centred on the London Workers' Film Society, for the Federation of Workers' Film Societies (FOWFS). The WFM produced three newsreels, a 20-minute documentary and a compilation film on the Soviet Union. It folded in 1932. The 'Sunday communist sheet' contemptuously dismissed by Carter was The Sunday Worker.

Labour and the Cinema

Labour is expressionally insolvent. It has not enough cultural assets to meet its cultural liabilities. It has far more problems than it has means to solve them. In other words, not only its economic and social but its spiritual liabilities far exceed its assets. A class may have ten million pounds, but if it owes more than ten million pounds, it is insolvent. Labour has a vast fund of vital ideas, but it owes more ideas to its own class and to the community than it has means to communicate, and therefore, it is, in this respect, insolvent. A Labour Cinema is a Labour asset of immense value. It is an asset to meet cultural, social and other expressional and interpretational liabilities.

Such is the true situation as regards Labour and the Cinema. How has it arisen?

In the September number of *Plebs* I dealt with the situation as regards Labour and the Theatre, and I stated its causes. The causes of the Cinema situation are partly similar, partly different. A difference is seen in the fact that, whereas the English Theatre since Shakespeare's day has been organised as a middle-class, commercial and aesthetic affair to exclude the workers, the Cinema, of more recent origin, has been organised throughout by the Hollywood Colossus to cater for the Mass and to drain its pocket. Resemblances appear in the lack of recognition by Labour leaders of the importance of the Cinema to Labour interests, and the lack of loyalty to facts on the part of those engaged in promoting a Labour Cinema Movement. On the one hand, there has not been any concerted action by Labour Parliamentary representatives, big Labour Unions, Co-operative bodies, and others, to establish a Labour Cinema on true principles. On the other, there is a failure to change with facts. Time has changed the facts on which the small group of promoters of the Labour Cinema Movement originally based their action, but the promoters have gone on assuming that the facts were unchanged; that the mind of Labour today is where it was, say, five years ago.

To the fixed attitude must be added a very grave element of corruption which has touched the promoters of the Labour Cinema Movement who have, in consequence, come under the influence of a hierarchy of cinema intellectuals and aesthetes, and by this means, have been delivered, bound hand and foot, to the philistines.

It is owing to this fixed attitude, to corruption and compromise, that the incipient Labour Cinema Movement is suffering from stagnation. There are no insurrectionary groups within the movement to breed fresh ideas, no attempt to appeal to the workers through a true concept of the Cinema. The ideas of the aesthetes sworn to carry on the campaign of aestheticising the Cinema to the exclusion of all social and human interests, and the ideas of the Russian workers of ten years ago, still dominate and determine action in spite of the fact that the 'art of the cinema' like the 'art of the theatre' stunt is as dead and rotten as the dodo; that the revolutionary impulse has died down in this country, and Labour is seeking salvation not along a path of blood and gloom, but of economic reconstruction. Corruption is doing its deadly work through alliances which the Left Wing enthusiasts are forming with the Right Wing individualists and reactionary aesthetes who are in a conspiracy to capture the cinema for their own use with the aid of the Labour forces.

It is of importance to consider the cause and effect of the strange alliance between opposing Right and Left Wing forces, and a means whereby the fluid Mass, drawn into and distracted by, on the one hand, the capitalist cinema, and on the other, the discussion of abstract theory by its would-be deliverers, may be attracted and drawn into a Labour Cinema Movement not led by a hierarchy of Film Society and *Close Up* intellectuals.

This may be done by a brief reference to the history of the Labour or, as it is called, Workers' Cinema Movement—the Movement that grew out of, and has now replaced the dead Workers' Theatre Movement.

The Workers' Theatre Movement in this country was largely the outcome of the book on the Soviet Theatre and Cinema which I published in 1925, and which, like my other books, except one on the Russian Theatre published last year, is now out of print, and acquiring a rarity value. That book was the first of its kind to give a truthful and comprehensive account of the new social use to which the Russian theatre has been put since 1917, and the cinema since 1919. It revealed that these two institutions had been organised to form an organic part of the people. They were the new Labour assets to meet social, cultural and other liabilities. Their business was to assist first of all, in securing the safety of the New Republic, and thereafter the reconstruction of its economic side. Their function was, in fact, first fighting and then building, fighting military adventurers, bourgeoisie and reactionaries, and building a Socialist State. But the reflection of home policy was mainly their function, such policy being, of course, largely a reflex of Soviet internal conditions and principles. The Russian cinema was, in fact, organised to record the consequences of the rapidly changing events of the internal movement towards socialisation and to explain to the Mass the causes—political, economic, industrial and social—that moved the Government to act for the common good (as no doubt the Soviet Government would say).

The book served its pioneering purpose (which, by the way, was my only reward). It went all over the world and its seeds fell on good ground. It stimulated widespread interest in the Soviet Theatre and Cinema, with the result that ever since its publication there has been a steady pilgrimage of students to the theatrical Mecca, as the German journalist, Scheffer, once called Moscow, to see its wonders for themselves.

A Workers' Theatre Movement sprang up in this country. I need not refer again to its unhappy career and end. All I shall say is that its concept was misunderstood, its true aim misjudged, and its methods distorted by the very people who claimed to be its friend.

It was succeeded by a Workers' Cinema Movement, and for a time the columns of a Sunday communist sheet were occupied by a cinema critic who, writing under the pen name of Henry Dobb, sought to impart the views of and to explain the concept of the Right Wing aesthetes, who appeared to hold him spellbound. Instead of explaining the true concept of a Labour Cinema to the worker readers, instead of pointing out the meaning and significance of the social content of vital films, he offered a dreary analysis of aesthetic and abstract technique and material in the Right Wing approved political vein. It was clear that both he and the paper had been captured by a hierarchy of aesthetes for the purpose of exploiting their concept of a 'Pure Cinema', a concept calculated to dope the workers and to attract their attention from a form of cinema aiming to fulfil a social function for them.

The 'Pure Cinema' according to the aesthetic concept, is a separate, independent and highly specialised tool for the production of abstract and poetical commodities that cannot be produced by any other tool, say, the Theatre or commercial cinema. This tool is meant to produce things by itself, and to be cut off from the life-blood of the interaction of vital tools, social and other. The cardinal error of this concept is quite plain. That its use was solemnly recommended in the columns of a communist sheet must have staggered the more sober-minded to whom the cinema suggests a tool of expression at once more scientific, economic and humane.

The sequel is soon told. During the autumn of 1929 there came a tendency in this country towards the formation of groups for the purpose of stirring up active interest among workers, in particular industrial workers, in films having a working-class appeal. Whether the intention was revolutionary propaganda, or whether to encourage the workers to build their own cinema and to produce their own films, is not clear. What is clear is that it was decided that the film-hungry workers must be fed on unusual foreign goods, Russian and German for preference, as these contained elements agreeable to the two groups—the Federation of Workers' Film Societies, and the Film Society and its followers—that were exploiting them for their technical and poetical (!!) material.

The simplicity of this discovery led to complications and combination. Intellectuals, aesthetes and the representatives of the workers' revolutionary and cultural interests found themselves faced with a common difficulty. In seeking to promote the importation and consumption of foreign goods, they came into conflict with the Censor. And they banded together to destroy him. Thus a battle of free versus restricted imports swept over the country instead of a wave of home-creative activities.

Then a strange thing happened. The extreme Right intellectuals got on to the council of the FOWFS organisation, and at once took charge of operations, as the Film Society-like official statements and the highly intellectualised composition of rules of the FOWFS plainly prove.

Of course, the aim of the Right Wing folk was not alone to slaughter the censor, but to have a voice in the importation and selection of Soviet films for distribution in this country. Their obvious game was the subordination of revolutionary and social content to the technique of aesthetic, to fix the attention of the workers not on Eisenstein's or Pudovkin's Marxian message, but on their 'montage'.

The result has been to narrow down the scope of the Workers' Cinema Movement to vanishing point—to the exhibition of Soviet films, in fact. Here let me say that my remarks are not meant to be a criticism of Soviet films. I have as great an admiration as anyone for the best of them. The worst are rotten. But this apart, I should perhaps say, 'almost to the exhibition of Soviet films', because there has been a leaven of American and British ones, no doubt for box office purpose. For there is plenty of evidence that the Movement is at present on a strictly commercial basis. The Film Society has a current programme of Soviet films which it is careful to label 'non-political' and 'interesting experiments with topical and poetical material', no doubt to soothe the conscience of its highly respectable patrons who are expected to pay as much as three guineas for a helping of half-a-dozen or so of Moscow's best. The Atlas Renting concern is also busy offering Soviet attractions for sale. Its programme, duly noted by the capitalist Trade Press, if you please, contains an assortment of Soviet films to be shown at commercial cinemas in London and the provinces. The FOWFS and affiliated groups are girding up their loins, or slackening their belts, for a feast of Soviet goods. Likewise the Masses Stage and Film Guild is preparing to sell one or two Soviet films to its expectant subscribers.

There is no harm in this particular traffic. The harm arises from labelling the imported goods—'The sole delight. Choose Soviet chocolates with the taste that thrills'.

In all this activity there is no evidence of a search for a principle upon which to build the British Labour Cinema, and to organise the British Labour World to be screened. Foreign goods, very tasty some of them, are offered for consumption; but there is no home labour production. This disparity between consumption and production is appalling. We look in vain for the incentive to production. Workers are invited to watch the extraordinary changes which Russia has undergone, to study the doctrines of revolution embodied in historical and recapitulation films. They are asked to study the first storey of the new Soviet edifice. But Russia is already under the Five Years' Plan, building a new economic storey, better proportioned and more unified. They are not, however, asked to study that glimpse in Turksib*—a film with which by comparison Potemkin, The General Line, and Earth, are old-fashioned Americanised products.

Nothing is being done by responsible Cinema folk to remind our workers that they are in the presence of new forces in their own country that cry aloud to be screened. The present mighty struggle between the old classical economic doctrines and the new life-centred ones surely offers unequalled stage and screen material, which, if handled effectively, would do more than all else to awaken the Workers' Theatre and Cinema consciousness.

The Theatre must be linked with the Cinema in an appeal to the workers to build their own new civic centre, their House of Vision, or their Outlook Tower on the amazing panorama of current Life and Labour. The poisonous concept of a 'Pure Cinema' fit for aesthetic heroes only, must be destroyed. Given the true concept, the most comprehensive scheme, the fullest co-operation, the spirit of the age, and incorruptible instructors, and British Labour may be trusted fully to realise its invaluable expressional assets.

HUNTLY CARTER
The Plebs, November 1930

Note

**Turksib,* directed by Victor Turin, USSR 1929, was a 'documentary' film about the building of the Turkestan-Siberia railway which became a very popular success abroad, and was widely hailed throughout the early Thirties in Britain by many of the British 'documentarists' as an exemplary film. The film was shown at the London Workers' Film Society on 9 March 1930, in the presence of Turin. Viktor A. Turin (1855–1945) had emigrated to the USA in 1912, where he studied at the Massachusetts Institute of Technology. On his return to the USSR, he became a documentary film maker. His most significant films were made between 1926 and 1935. His international reputation rests entirely on *Turksib*.

The Cinema:
An Instrument of Class Rule

There is no such thing as non-political cinema. The cinema is a propagandist organ, a weapon of class war. Class war is expressed through politics and political supremacy is maintained through the cinema. That is why, in those countries where class alignments and antagonisms are most direct, the cinema is most obviously a battleground. In Germany, for example, *All Quite on the Western Front,* an American talking-film with a sentimental pacifist message, has been banned by the Censors as a result of demonstrations by the Fascists, ostensibly directed against its anti-German tendencies, but really because of its possible effect on recruiting and the war-mind.

This is not the first occasion on which Germany has been a film battleground. As Huntly Carter reminds us in his latest book, *The New Spirit in the Cinema* (Shaylor, 30/-), when *Potemkin, End of St. Petersburg* and other early Russian revolutionary films were being shown in Berlin, Hollywood replied by entering the lists with Emil Jannings in *The Last Command** and so the industrial and political fight surged into the cinema and found its pro- and anti-red expression there.

Only as an expression of class supremacy can the cinema throughout the capitalist world be adequately explained. In Russia, for example, the early efforts at film making were definitely imitative in form of Hollywood films, with the simple exception that the worker (not as class representative, but almost

138

purely as an individual) was always good and noble, while the grand-duke or the boss was always villainous and vile. Then the Russian cinema found its feet and began to make epics of class struggle, in which the worker-hero became the mouthpiece of the mass, expressing mass suffering and urge towards liberation, and the boss-villain the mouthpiece of individualism and repression. This was the period of *Mother, End of St Petersburg, Potemkin,* etc., a period when there was urgent need to inform the workers of the realities of class war and the vital necessity for stamping out any remnants of the old ruling class and of capitalist domination. Then the fight shifted to the countryside, and there came the time when collective as against individual farming had to be propagated. This was the period of *The General Line* and *Earth*.

So with each change in the problems of Soviet industry came a change in the subject matter and technique of Soviet films. All these films flowered in the soil of class rule and were expressions of class needs. The latest type of Russian film, *Turksib,* which is based on man's struggle with nature and sings of the triumph of collective man plus the machine (symbol of collective work and collective effort) over his last enemy, has only been made possible by the demands of, and apparent success of, the drive of the Five Year Plan.

Now, seeing this, Huntly Carter asks: Why cannot we have a cinema of this kind in England: why do we not make English *Turksibs,* not English replicas of *Turksib,* but English films that, like *Turksib,* shall be rich in 'subject-power' that shall put the 'soul' of the English nation on the screen? By asking this question, Mr Carter shows that he has missed the fundamental motives animating the policy of the cinemas in capitalist countries. These necessary motives are, firstly profit, and secondly (and even more important) the maintenance of the profit-making system as a whole. This understood, it becomes apparent that English or American or German cinemas simply cannot make *Turksibs* because the object of capitalist cinema (though accomplished in multifarious ways) is to divert working-class thought from the problems of life, and not to concentrate attention on, and provide opportunities for, studying and discussing them. Study means understanding, and understanding spells the end of capitalist class rule. Let them have sex, crime, anything but the realities of life. This is the primary and fundamental reason underlying capitalist

cinema, and it cannot be altered either by tinkering with problems of aesthetics, or with problems raised by the capitalist cinema itself, or by attempting to set up hole and corner production of our own, no matter how fine underlying motives may be. For working-class cinema, like capitalist class cinema, must arise from and be an expression of working-class political rule.

BENN
The Plebs, April 1931

Note
**The Last Command,* directed by Josef von Sternberg, USA 1928.

Where are the British Labour Films?

For every £1 the workers spend on books, they probably spend at least £1,000 on 'the pictures'. The films, in nearly all cases, reflect the ideas and social values of the governing class. In this article, Huntly Carter asks what the Labour Movement is doing about it. Unfortunately, Labour still likes to send out its thinking, just as the middle class sends out its washing. [*The Plebs'* editorial presentation— Ed.]

Let us look at some cinema figures. In 1930 six American Production Companies made an aggregate profit of £10,000,000. In 1931 Hollywood is sending out 400 pictures and hopes to make more than £10,000,000 profit. It is spending no less than £25,000,000 on production, which means that someone is expected to pay £25,000,000 plus 12 per cent profit for Hollywood goods.

In 1930 the British Production Companies spent approximately £1,200,000 on production. In 1931 they calculate to spend £2,000,000 with a corresponding increase in profit. A hint at the rate of profit may be gathered from the fact that in 1930 there was a £700,000 increase in entertainment tax, due to the talkie boom. Talkies are, in fact, calling the tune which must be paid for by the general public.

Again, there are 4,300 cinemas in this country. Of these 2,700 have been wired and in this way are practically controlled by American interests. There are about 1,600 small cinemas still on their own, but facing competition and collapse.

On the whole a mighty commercial organisation. Where are the workers' cinemas? Echo answers, where? Who will consume this £25,000,000 American and £2,000,000 British, plus 12 or more per cent profit, worth of pictures? Who will pay for the wholesale exploitation of personalities and stage plays? In the words of the exploiters, 'the masses', or, if you like, the working class. Let some more figures speak. In Britain there are 20,000,000 cinema goers. For the most part they are in big industrial cities and towns. Birmingham, like the rest of the big cities with dense working-class populations, is throwing up mammoth 3,000 and 4,000 seater cinemas. For whom? The workers? It has now 78 cinemas, seating 85,127 persons, or roughly 1,700,000 on the week's three shows a day basis. Who are the 1,700,000 who contribute to the upkeep of Hollywood and the £1,000 a week Baby Beauty Queens? Who else but the workers or the 'masses' as the Film Kings rightly term the vast audiences for whom they cater and for whom they are now providing 'penny-in-the-slot' talkies, so that not a penny shall escape from the workers' pockets to the workers' own cinema.

Against these staggering facts, what have the workers to show? The annual reviews of the high-brows, middle and muddle brows, low-brows, and no-brows-at-all-brows, all mixed in a sticky dodging-the-censor mess!

What have the workers had during 1930 from the commercial folk to satisfy their real cinema hunger? Much useful stuff poached from their own grounds. Commercial-made epics, embodying the national spirit, engineering achievements, great industrial enterprises, world-wide business transactions resting on the workers' backs, railroad, aerial, covered-wagon films showing that pioneering, conquest and construction are mainly the workers' jobs.

What have they got from the semi-commercial folk? On the one hand the Righteous in Pocket, the Pure in Cinema aesthetes busy talking through their Freudian 'Clothes Up' sheets about technique, 'montage' and the 'cinema mind' and obscuring the socialism in films and loudly despising all films that need no technical tricks to make their socialist message clear. And on the other, the communist intellectuals who are chiefly concerned with marketing foreign goods, and forming consumers' associations on a subscription basis, and who, together with the Film Society, form themselves into Watch Committees—over what? What have the workers had from these fundamentally opposed schools of cinema thought?

Russian, German, French fare, with a mixture of Hollywood fare that is slightly 'different', in pictures into which the commercial producer has introduced a touch of the 'unusual' in a moment of dementia, and thus queered their money value, but otherwise retaining all the marks of the Beast.

A glance at the review lists of the intellectuals reveals the old familiar gang, uppermost Pabst (the beloved of the Aubrey-Flanagan–Henry-Dobb type of mind*) and Pudovkin—all good men in their own countries and own ways, but what are they doing to help the British workers to screen Labour Britain? Practically nothing. For, while the workers can crowd 300 or so into little stuffy dens in Shettleston, Clayton-le-Moor, Salford, Garnant, Burslem, and elsewhere, and dine off *Mother, St. Petersburg,* and the rest of the stuff meant for a population in a shockingly backward state, they will do nothing. These are the pictures they cannot, or need not, copy, for our workers have no such backward state to express, and is it not an insult to their intelligence to suggest that they are in such a backward state as to need such pictures? This does not rule out Russian pictures entirely. Let Moscow send us the new stuff—the Five Years' plan stuff of the *Turkish Breed.* It may be trusted to stir the British workers into activity. What this country needs is the planning and centralisation of the labour cinema world, and a British Labour Five Years' Cinema Plan.

HUNTLY CARTER
The Plebs, June 1931

Note
*Aubrey Flanagan and Henry Dobb both wrote film criticism for the *Sunday Worker,* and were founder members of the FOWFS.

Labour and the Cinema: A reply to Huntly Carter

In the June issue of *The Plebs,* Huntly Carter describes the gigantic capitalist domination of the film industry, the millions that are invested and the millions taken out in profits, and then plaintively asks 'Where are the workers' cinemas?' According to him the workers have nothing to show but the 'annual reviews of the high-brows, middle-brows and no-brow-at-all-brows'. If this were true, the stage would certainly be set for deep gloom and mourning. Fortunately, it is not true, and Mr. Carter should know better than to ignore and dismiss with such contempt the efforts of those who are striving to challenge the octopus of finance capital in the Cinema.

There is a Workers' Film Movement in Britain. This movement has only been able to grow because it fulfils a need, because it provides the workers with a chance to see the type of film that is so rarely shown in the commercial cinemas, the film that reflects and expresses the fundamental problems in the workers' daily struggle against unemployment, slums, wage attacks and capitalist oppression in the factories and the homes.

But Mr. Carter condemns the workers' film societies in London, Glasgow, Edinburgh, Manchester, Newcastle, Sheffield and elsewhere, because their audiences 'dine off Soviet films such as *St. Petersburg* and *Mother*'. To show such films, says the emancipated Mr. Carter, is to insult the intelligence of 'our workers' who are not in such a 'backward state' to need such pictures.

Perhaps Mr. Carter has never mingled with a working-class audience during an exhibition of *St. Petersburg*; perhaps he has never heard their applause and seen with what passionate interest they follow the events leading to the Russian Revolution, how they see in the suffering and struggles of Russian peasants and the Russian workmen of this film the counterpart of their own sufferings and struggles. The appeal of *St. Petersburg,* and indeed of nearly all the Soviet films shown by the workers' societies, is international. It is around such films as these that the Workers' Film Movement has grown. It is Mr. Carter's misfortune if he cannot share the workers' appreciation and understanding of them.

Labour Newsreels

I agree, absolutely, that it is not sufficient to witness and applaud the films made in other countries, but while Mr. Carter has been immersing himself in the outpourings of the high-low-middle brows (and incidentally greatly exaggerating the part they play) others have been borrowing film cameras and have gone to the docks, the Labour Exchanges, the slums, and the streets and squares, photographing real life and constructing newsreels and short documentaries of the class struggle.

Puny efforts, perhaps, but apparently overlooked by the Huntly Carters.

It is significant that Mr. Carter offers no concrete suggestions as to the methods or the character of workers' film production in Britain. Perhaps after all this is not surprising. If he cannot understand the significance of the Soviet film, it is scarcely to be expected that he can approach the problem here in England.

In a letter written by Mr. Carter to *The Cinema* (19/11/30) he acknowledges that he is not a member of any working-class film organisation. Perhaps that explains why he is so much out of touch with what has been done, and is so incapable of grasping the actual requirements of the moment.

Why the Mysticism?

In his work *The New Spirit in the Cinema,* Mr. Carter concludes with the words, 'May not wisdom and the English people build a splendid Theatre-Cinema temple to initiate all into a new philosophy and a new religion?' Such mystic and spiritual phraseology is basically contradictory to a Marxist viewpoint. The Cinema today is a weapon of the class struggle. So far this weapon has been the exclusive property of the capitalists. We cannot hope to wrest it completely from their hands until relations in society have been changed, but we can and must fight capitalist influences in the Cinema by exposing, in a Marxist manner, how it is used as an ideological force to dope the workers. That can be done by exhibiting the films of the only country where the workers are the ruling class, and by making our own films, not to initiate 'new spirits' and 'new religions', but to aid and encourage the workers in their fight against capitalism.

I suggest that out of the small beginnings expressed in the workers' film societies, in the newsreels and documentaries that they have made, will arise gradually the foundations for the mass British proletarian cinema of the future.

RALPH BOND
The Plebs, August 1931

141

Labour and the Cinema (II)

I have been reading Mr.Ralph Bond's reply, in your August issue, to my article, *Where Are The Labour Films,* and I am wondering whether I am entitled to waste your space by taking notice of it. But it seems to me that if I let it pass unanswered, my silence may be taken for flight.

Actually it is not a reply. It does not refute my facts or figures. It contains nothing material. Throughout Mr. Bond accuses me of speculating, but he speculates fast enough when he comes to cross-examine me. In this and other respects he very ingeniously follows the capitalist Press method of disposing of an argument that it does not like.

First, let me state the material points of my article.

(1) The big capitalist production companies are making millions yearly in this country out of the cinema. (2) Much of this money is coming out of the pockets of British Labour. (Mr. Bond refers to (1) but omits (2).) (3) Labour is being ruled in cinema matters by apes of the capitalists who, to serve their own interests, are feeding it on old-fashioned foreign goods, or foreign goods made to suit the peculiar political, economic and social requirements of other countries, as in Soviet Russia where the pre-Five Year Plan pictures were made for the consumption of 100,000,000 people in a state of savage ignorance that made Lenin shudder. (4) That Labour is encouraged by these self-appointed organisers of the Workers' theatre and cinema movements to polish the seat of its pants in little hole and corner dens instead of bestirring itself in the matter of planning and realising its own cinema world wherein all who like could watch or co-operate with British Labour handling its own problems of Life and Labour, such as the new gigantic political and economic struggle upon which Labour has just entered.

Bare Assumption

Now let me give a brief and illuminating example of Mr. Bond's method of meeting these essential points. He is anxious to show that I have no reasonable familiarity with the work of the WTM and LWFS; that, for example, I have made no systematic study of the doings of, say, The Red Star Players, The Red Blouses, and other Red Groups; that I have taken no part in a technical conference held in the East End (of all places in Britain);

that I have not played the exciting game of running round to the nearest dark and dreary docks and making little amateur newsreels. All this puts me beyond the pale as a writer on the Labour Cinema. And I may say, it is all bare assumption.

Mr. Bond does not bother about definitions or distinctions. For instance, he uses a number of terms to denote a section of the community known as 'workers'. But nowhere does he say definitely what he means by 'workers'. Does he mean industrial workers; Labour or more precisely labourers, for Labour is an abstraction; or all who work? It is important to know, because in one paragraph, 4, he assumes a familiarity with the cultural work, 'the appreciation and understanding' of workers, and suggests that I have no such appreciation and understanding. In the aforesaid paragraph he *suggests* that I have 'never mingled with a working-class audience during an exhibition of *St. Petersburg'*. He *speculates* on what I should have seen if I had done so. And he *infers* that because I have not had this experience I 'cannot share the workers' appreciation and understanding of the Soviet films'. From this I gather that by 'workers' is meant folk who attend a performance of Soviet pictures by the London Workers' Film Society.

Where were the Workers?

The short answer to this is that I have seen several performances of *St. Petersburg,* in Moscow, Berlin and London. On the last occasion but one I mingled with the LWFS audience at a large theatre, and I took the trouble to note its composition. So far as I could judge it consisted of 50 per cent East End Jews, mostly Russian, and 50 per cent foreigners—'high-hats', reformist bourgeoisie, teachers, 'unusual picture' fans, and a thin sprinkling of genuine labour-class folk. I took particular note of the effect of Mr. Ralph Bond's Russian travelogue* (wrongly attributed to British Labour) on two labour men seated by my side. They sat unmoved. At its conclusion they went out for a drink. It was a long drink, so long in fact that I thought they were having a bath in beer.

For the rest, a passage is torn from the conclusion of my book to exhibit terms that are assumed to be anti-Marxian. But no definitions are offered to prove that I use them in an anti-Marxian sense. It is suggested that I am wrong in saying that some of the Soviet pictures are not suited to Labour's present-day

142

requirements. But no scientific analysis of the pictures is put forward to prove that I am wrong. Later, I should like to make such an analysis in *Plebs* if there is space, not only to prove that the old Soviet pictures now being shown in this country are old-fashioned and out of date, but to prove that in saying so, I am not trying to underrate their great value as pioneers of pictures intended to perform a high social purpose. I should take *The General Line* as unsuited for consumption by British Labour. It is inconceivably old-fashioned. It is a mess of primitive magic and ritual, of religion (in the sense of god-making), of superstition, of faith in and fear of tribal gods and faith in and fear of the new god of machinery. Take the ceremony of the marriage of the Bull, wherein the Bull is deified and worshipped as the God of fertility as in early Greek days. The cow to be fertilised is beribboned and garlanded like a virgin about to be given in marriage. The Bull is led forth swelling visibly till it seems ready to burst with carnal desire. The excited peasants are dolled up in their holiday best like a lot of harlots shrieking with delight at the sight of the marriage being consummated, as it is in the original Soviet film. Is British Labour so unintelligent that it requires this mixture of primitive ignorance and idolatry to stir it to economic action?

HUNTLY CARTER
The Plebs, October 1931

Note
*Probably a reference to *Glimpses of Modern Russia* (Ralph Bond for the Atlas Company, 1930), distributed to the Workers' Film Societies.

NATIONAL GOVERNMENT PROPAGANDA FILMS

Editorial note: *It should be stressed that the direct sponsorship of film was not confined to left political organisations. In 1939 Ralph D. Casey, an American writer on publicity and propaganda, could write in the* Public Opinion Quarterly *that 'No political party in the Western democracies utilises political propaganda motion pictures as extensively as does the Tory organisation in Great Britain'. Despite this observation, a constant feature of the Tory propaganda was the tight secrecy which developed around its organisation and funding so as to bypass the articles of incorporation of many British companies which forbade financial contributions to political parties as such. Casey could write of the Tory propaganda machine as 'one of the most important of all British political devices, yet one which is unknown to the general public, and to most scholars both here [USA] and abroad'.*

Films had been produced for the Conservative Party as early as 1927 when a national publicity campaign was launched using new media and employing ex-military staff with experience of propaganda in Britain during the First World War. Film vans toured with propaganda films from 1927 onwards, and the high level of finance from businessmen and companies was such that the Conservative Party was reportedly able to implement sound technology in motion pictures before it was available in the commercial theatres.

In the early Thirties, however, with the coming to power of the National Government, the Conservative Party and the ruling alliance's campaigns shifted from a divisive and overtly political focus to a unified one based on the supposedly a-political notion of the 'national interest'. In 1934 plans were made in secret to form the National Publicity Bureau (NPB) as an independent organisation designed to unify the propaganda of the three parties involved in the government, to raise money for campaigning purposes, and to act as an advisory authority in formulating the National Government's election policy for the 1935 election. The NPB was therefore set up as a 'non-political' organisation intended to bring national unity during the recovery period of British capitalism on a non-partisan basis.

It was the brainchild of an unholy alliance between Ramsay MacDonald, Neville Chamberlain and Sir Kingsley Wood. Wood was at this time Postmaster-General and had supervised the transfer of Grierson's Empire Marketing Board Film Unit to the GPO in 1933, stressing in his preface to the GPO Film Catalogue the 'communications value' of the GPO and EMB films. His sponsorship of the GPO unit was combined with more blatantly propagandist activities for the National Government: the London Morning Post *of 4 March 1935 reported that 'an official announcement will shortly be made of the appointment of Sir Kingsley Wood, Postmaster-*

General, to be Director of Publicity and Propaganda for the National Government'. Despite the fact that the appointment was never officially ratified, Wood's activities caused fears even among members of the Conservative party that he was using the NPB to build up a big political machine, intending to form a national party which would obliterate the power and identity of the three groups that formed the National Government coalition.

Although the NPB was said by Wood and others to be a 'purely temporary organisation' for the 1935 election, it was still operating and even expanding in 1939. In fact, the NPB's public relations firm had engaged its propaganda and publicity experts in a five-year contract from the start, indicating that it was seen by its organisers as a long-term operation. The NPB's slogans, emblazoned on huge posters throughout the country and in its millions of copies of broadsheets designed to look like ordinary tabloid popular newspapers, gave a feeling of its type of work: 'THE NATIONAL GOVERNMENT IS YOUR SAFEGUARD AGAINST FASCISM, COMMUNISM AND DICTATORSHIP', 'IT'S TEAM-WORK THAT COUNTS', 'SHOW THE WORLD THAT BRITAIN IS UNITED', 'BRITAIN STILL FORGING AHEAD', and so on. In depressed areas such as agricultural Scotland, however, where wages were still pitifully low and provided little to enthuse about, the optimistic slogans displayed on English billboards were replaced by the more cautious claim that the National Government had 'Saved Scottish Agriculture from Collapse'.

In the 1935 election campaign the NPB joined forces with the Conservative and Unionist Film Association to put on film shows in virtually every important constituency. Even in a non-election year, however, such as the 1936–7 'indoors' campaign, the NPB is estimated to have conducted 2,048 showings in 304 constituencies, with an audience of 370,515. The Conservative Party had retained control of its 'outdoor' film-vans, but in 1935 the NPB purchased seventeen vans and equipped them with portable 16 mm equipment, giving continuous showings from March that year throughout the country. Despite the favoured 'low-key' approach to propaganda from about 1933 onwards, activities gradually increased during the decade.

It is significant in a British context that while the films produced by left organisations are usually presented as 'propaganda' in the sense of 'biased', these National Government films could be presented as 'explanatory' or 'informational', as suggested by the title of the 'story film with a moral, Without Prejudice'.

This short note cautiously advertising films by the National Government appeared in Sight and Sound.

National Government Propaganda Films

A number of propaganda films made to illustrate the work and policy of the National Government were shown recently at a private viewing in London. It was explained in a foreword that the films were intended as a review of the past and present activities of the Government and they are to be exhibited throughout the country on a fleet of self-contained travelling cinema vans. A speaker travelling with the van answers questions after each performance and distributes leaflets.

There are eight films in all. Mr. Ramsay MacDonald, shown speaking in close-up, gives a general introduction; Mr. Neville Chamberlain talks on the Budget; Mr. Elliott speaks at the conclusion of a film on English agriculture; Sir John Simon is shown speaking on the Government's foreign policy; while Mr. Baldwin gives a general survey entitled Britain Under the National Government. In addition there is a film on Scottish industries and another on Scottish agriculture, intended for distribution in Scotland only, and a story film with a moral, Without Prejudice. The Scottish films have a Scottish commentator.

The conditions under which the films are to be shown required the adoption of a slow-moving and simplified technique, with few remarkable features. Only in Mr. Baldwin's film was there any attempt at interweaving the speech with relevant scenes. The story film was possibly the poorest of the series in that it was so simplified as to defeat its end with certain audiences: the character of the Socialist was so limp as both to rob the film of dramatic quality and to miss a valuable opportunity, which the other films could not give, of dealing with some possible opposition arguments. The films are available on both standard and 16 mm. copies, which can be supplied through the local political agent for display in cinemas or small halls.

E.H.L. [Ernest Lindgren]
Sight and Sound, Summer 1935

144

FILMING THE MAY DAY DEMONSTRATION

Editorial note: *The period 1931–32 was marked by intense communist agitation, particularly during and after the formation of the National Government under Ramsay MacDonald in August 1931. The annual Labour Day demonstrations on May 1 grew into massive events with thousands of workers, many of them unemployed, taking part. Various organisations contributed to the celebration of the national 'workers' day' with dramatic sketches, new songs, posters and banners to accompany the marches and festivities. Similarly, those interested in the use of film contributed by making film records of the events, and several of the earliest surviving workers' films are records of May Day marches. The following account of the 1932 May Day march appeared in* New Red Stage *(formerly* Red Stage*), the organ of the Workers' Theatre Movement. That same year, the Communist Party (GB)'s agitational and organisational work culminated in the National Hunger March, the largest mobilisation of the unemployed in inter-war Britain, although the size and force of the Hunger March should not be attributed to the CP's work alone. Many other left groups, including non-party ones as well as the socialist wings of bourgeois parties (such as the Labour Party) and the socialist fringe of the CP itself (shortly to be branded as 'Trotskyite' and expelled from the Stalin-dominated CP) contributed to the organisation of the march.*

The event referred to below involved a cameraman filming the 1932 May Day march (using 16 mm film) from the roof of a van as it passed through Stepney Green and Hackney.

...The police, who were with these marchers, apparently took us for press-men, but our driver was ready to step on the gas.

This time the cameraman shot from the inside of the van, so as not to attract attention, but nevertheless the huge crowd of onlookers, which had gathered on either side of the pavement to greet the marchers, were very curious at the black van (they probably took us for Workers' Movietone); but fortunately for us, some Press photographers came up and asked permission to use our van. This was just what we wanted for it served as a camouflage for our work, and it was then a simple matter to film the magnificent demonstration.

We moved on to the Embankment, parked the van in a back turning, and made our way to the demo that awaited the arrival of East London. Here we found to our dismay that filming of any description was barred. As we looked round at the crowds, banners, tableaux, carts and cars covered with slogans, our cameraman nearly wept and we had to forcibly restrain him from filming. We then had a short discussion, and came to the decision that it must be 'shot' and that order was carried out.

Just off the Embankment, the road through which the demo had to traverse on the way to the park, we spied a Movietone van, and certainly if they could film so could we...

New Red Stage, June–July 1932

FILMS IN THE STREETS

Editorial note: *Although there is as yet no detailed investigation of the relation between the Workers' Theatre Movement and film work in the late Twenties and early Thirties, it would appear that the WTM was a much more coherent cultural and political grouping, with its roots in the use of dramatic tableaux and other types of 'theatrical' performance that had been a feature of European socialism since the 1870s. Even Engels and Lasalle wrote plays to be performed by workers' groups. But after the First World War, theatre came to occupy a particularly prominent place within the workers' movement as a whole, with the Soviet and German agit-prop and Living Newspaper groups. It may be seen as significant that the tradition of Living Newspaper performances was to filter back into British cinema via a detour through the United States: the so-called 'documentary movement' came into contact with this theatrical tradition in the USA, and thus, in a somewhat roundabout way, discovered an important aspect of the cultural traditions of the European workers' movement.*

In Britain in the early Thirties there was a fertile crossover of certain members of the WTM into film groups. What had started as 'special' activities—that is, the hiring out of films and projection equipment by individuals in the WTM to those who wanted to screen Soviet and British workers' films—became the organisational beginnings of Kino as a distribution service. Kino emerged out of the film section which the WTM had formed in August 1933. The distribution and production organisation which grew out of this, Kino, was constituted in November 1933 and held its first meeting in London on 3 December of that year. When Kino split from its production group in November 1934 to concentrate on the distribution and exhibition of Soviet films, the Kino production group became the Workers' Film and Photo League, dropping the term 'Workers' from its title during the short-lived Popular Front campaigns from about 1935. In April 1936, Kino once more formed its own production group.

Despite the relatively unambitious beginnings of their film making activities, one of the most dramatically successful experiments in Kino's agitational work was the film Bread, made in May 1934 by a former member of the WTM, Sam Serter. It must be acknowledged that the WTM's concerns significantly facilitated and encouraged the drift towards film activities: the concern to take 'theatre' out of the theatres; the concentration on short sketches and satires rather than full-length plays; the concern with contemporary news items; the rejection of the 'theatre of illusion', of costumes and make-up, all this shows a preference for the 'unacted', agit-prop type of performance which dominated the output of the film groups. Moreover, the screening of a film was far more 'repeatable' than a theatrical performance and could thus be seen as a legitimate complement to and extension of the cultural and political work of the theatre groups.

The WTM's introduction of street theatre, fusing traditions of political work and the carnivalesque, led to experiments with cinema-in-the-streets in the early Thirties. Film vans would be positioned at street corners and market places to project films on a screen inside the van to shield it from the light, thus building up a crowd and then using the occasion for the presentation of speeches.

The new film section of the Workers' Theatre Movement, on Sunday evening in the East End of London, gave the first practical demonstration of the potentialities that lie in the use of small film as the medium through which it intends to develop interest in its work.

With the aid of a car loaned by a comrade a section of the film *Soviet Russia Past and Present* was actually exhibited to audiences outside their very homes in this densely populated area.

The apparatus used was a small projector of the box type containing its own screen, and power was obtained through a generator connected directly with the accumulator of the car.

The effect was quite presentable, but owing to slow running a large amount of flicker was noticeable. A stronger battery would easily obviate this, and as an experiment the young men who evolved and presented the 'show' are to be congratulated on pioneer work which will lead to big developments.

Here is a new medium which will add yet another weapon of intense cultural and propaganda value. Nothing of the sort within so reasonable a financial outlay has been possible before in the scope of the workers' movement, and realms of possibilities are opened up.

We understand that this is only one of the plans on which the recently formed film section of the WTM hope to organise interest in the film as an invaluable medium in the class struggle.

Daily Worker, 3 August 1933

Film Notes

by Peter Porcupine*

Famous Producer Exposes Financial Dictatorship

It is impossible for me to give you in this short space any conception of the completeness or brilliance of John Grierson's Marxist analysis of the film industry under capitalism in the lecture which he gave on Sunday night for the Left Theatre**.

As a director and producer of documentary films he is well known to all students of the cinema. He and his GPO Unit have done more to develop the medium of cinematography as an artistic means of expression, to exploit its possibilities to the full, than possibly any group outside the Soviet Union.

According to bourgeois standards, Grierson has no grounds for complaint. He is rich and he is famous. What more, ask the capitalists, can a man ask? What more indeed? Except that in this case the man happens to be—that much-abused word—an artist.

146

And the aim of an artist, whatever medium he may choose, is to portray life, human emotions, his own thoughts.

Owing, however, to the complete dictatorship of film financiers, an artist is only free to show just what the financier wants him to show.

The fact that anyone who wishes to produce, act in, write, shoot or direct a film is, owing to the great expense of the necessary material and apparatus, dependent on the financier not only to produce the film, but also on those financiers who control the distribution of films, imposes the most effective and complete limits on his choice and treatment of subject.

Where individual artists have tried to break away, have tried to show life as it really is, where they have shown social problems and the real solution, they have either been blacklisted, exiled from the film industry, or they have had to climb down and accept the conditions imposed on them by the financial dictators of the industry.

No-one who was present at Grierson's lecture can wonder at the prevalent discontent in the film studios today or at the fact that even the highest paid workers in film are beginning to realise that the only solution is the overthrow of the capitalist system.

The only organisation which can make films about reality and which is not dependent on the capitalist class for finance is the Workers' Film and Photo League, with their silent sub-standard films. On Saturday they are giving showings of four of their films, beginning with *Bread*, their first effort, and ending with *Transport*,*** the latest. Details of time and place will be advertised later in the week in this paper.

This week has nothing much to offer in the way of general releases. Film exhibitors estimate correctly that after the Jubilee celebrations **** nobody (except the Reds) are likely to have any money left for going to the pictures...

Daily Worker, 21 May 1935

Notes

*The identity of 'Peter Porcupine' is unknown. However, it is of some interest to note that the CP (GB)'s newspaper could describe Grierson as capable of providing a 'Marxist analysis'.

**The Left Theatre was formed in April 1934, and was part of the gradual process of

'professionalisation' of the Workers' Theatre Movement. It used exclusively professional actors and actresses, and put on Sunday performances at the Phoenix Theatre, taking its shows to Labour and Co-operative halls.

***Bread was made by Sam Serter and other members of the Workers' Theatre Movement; *Transport* was made by FPL members including Frank Jackson, a CP member who wrote for *Left Review*. In fact, Peter Porcupine was slightly misinformed about these groups and films: *Bread* was produced by Kino before it became the WFPL, while *Transport* was made after the WFPL had chopped the reference to workers from its title. Moreover, as documented in this book, the WFPL was by no means 'the only organisation' that was not dependent on the capitalist class for finance.

****George V's Silver Jubilee, held on 6 May 1935, received saturation media coverage in a concentrated effort to revive past glories of national and imperial unity in a time of crisis, and to echo the jubilees of Queen Victoria. Any analogy with the function of more recent Silver Jubilees may not be entirely coincidental.

THE NEW ROAD TO PROGRESS

Editorial note: Kino News was a four-page news and information bulletin published by Kino Films. Only issues 1 (December 1935) and 2 (?April–May 1936) are known to exist, and there is doubt as to whether any further issues were produced. The two issues, however, contain extremely valuable information and reports of Kino activities.

Kino had originally been formed in December 1933 as a section of the Workers' Theatre Movement to provide shows of 16 mm Soviet films. It was closely associated in its work with the Communist Party in terms of its outlets and its personnel. The following statements appeared a few months before Kino, then a distribution organisation leaving production to the Film and Photo League, was to restart its own production group in April 1936.

Those of us who stand for progress have no time to lose: to-day the road is steeper than before. This is an age of monopolies, of immense vested interests, of mass destruction of the fruits of human toil, of bitter economic

147

rivalry and the ever-increasing danger of a new world war. There are powerful forces working, not for progress but for reaction and decay.

The election is still fresh in our minds. We cannot blind ourselves to the fact that a Government which has shown itself to be opposed to the interests of the people is again returned to power with a large majority. We cannot doubt that if the electorate had been convinced that the National Government stands for reaction and against progress, this Government would have suffered an overwhelming defeat at the polls.

Therefore, our first task is—Enlightenment.

We have no illusions that this will be easy, but twentieth-century science has given us the most powerful instrument for our purpose which we have ever known—THE FILM.

The film has been intensively exploited by the entertainment monopolies for super profits. Now is the time to challenge the conception of the film which they have created. Now is the time for every individual and every group who realise the need for progress to use the film for its real purpose—for culture, for education and for enlightenment.

Bring your own organisation into this work. Your club, your film society, your school, your trade union branch, your co-operative guild, your local Labour Party.

Lead them on the new road to progress.

Kino News, Winter 1935

To Our Readers

Our proper medium is the screen and we feel that a few words of explanation are necessary in print.

Kino is not an ordinary business. We do not run for profit. We issue neither shares nor dividends, and our capital (what there is of it) is made up of the loans, donations and subscriptions of our supporters. Our real capital and our reason for existence are the demands, the appreciation and the enthusiasm of the masses. We started two years ago as a small group of enthusiasts who were keenly aware of the possibilities of films apart from their 'box-office' value. We sense the growing dissatisfaction of the twenty millions who see the so-called entertainment films in the commercial cinemas of Britain every week, and we set out to offer them an alternative: films which dealt seriously with their own lives and their own problems; films which would derive their theme and inspiration from the people; films which would constitute a real factor for enlightenment and a vital force for social progress.

How We Started

We started with no capital, no films and no apparatus. We had enthusiasm and determination. We had decided that the only way to achieve our aims was to work with the small size (16 mm.) films and apparatus. This not only cut down the expenses, as compared with the very costly full size films and apparatus, very considerably, but non-inflammable films could be used, and thus we were able to avoid the very stringent regulations applying to inflammable film, and show in ordinary halls and meeting rooms. Films of the sort we wanted were few and far between, but we managed to obtain a 16 mm. copy of Eisenstein's famous film *Battleship Potemkin.* As soon as we began to show this, we met with political censorship, commercial boycott, and official opposition, but the enthusiasm with which the film was received all over the country enabled us to put up a successful fight and to acquire further films and apparatus.

We had not over-estimated the demand, and at the beginning of 1935 it became evident that if we were to cope with the situation, we should have to organise on business lines. We decided to form a nonprofit-making company, and on 4th March, we became Kino Films (1935) Limited. But although we run as a business and hope to make the films pay for themselves, we still depend largely on voluntary help, and we are still appealing for loans and subscriptions.

The Future

We have printed our first newspaper to widen our sphere of activities and to extend the distribution of our films. We have very ambitious plans for the next six months, and soon we hope to have sound films. We have gone only a little of the way towards the achievement of our aims, but we are on the right lines and we look to the future with confidence. Our success depends entirely on the support we receive from the organisations and individuals who show our films. Our slogan is : *The Film is the Art of the Masses.*

Kino News, Winter 1935

The Power of the Film

by a Member of the British Film Institute

The film has grown to its present position of importance as one of the foremost industries of the world through its development as an instrument of entertainment, of unprecedented magnitude. This does not constitute its only function, however, nor even its most important one, except in point of mere size. The film is also an instrument of scientific research. It can record and analyse movements too fast for the human eye to appreciate; it can as faithfully record and show in a few brief minutes the growth of a plant which may have taken weeks or months. It can record movements of microscopic size or, by diagrammatical or symbolic means, bring the movements of nations under the planets within the compass of a lecture room screen.

Character of the Audience

It is an instrument too, of historical record, perpetuating what has before remained quite beyond the historian's grasp, the actual movements of men and women, or, indeed, of cancer cells or of earthquakes. It is an instrument of education from the narrowest to the broadest senses, as a teaching medium in the classroom, or as a force of propaganda to sway the hearts and minds of a whole people. Even the most innocuous entertainment film, planned for the diversion of an idle hour, wields an all too subtle influence for good or for ill. How can this instrument be turned to its most rich and fruitful use?

The power of the film springs from its almost infinite capacity to convey ideas and feelings of all kinds. Ideas originate in the minds of men, and how far they are effective depends on how far they spread in the mind of *man*: and that, in turn, depends on how far men, as individuals, are prepared to maintain and battle for their ideals in face of *man's* conservative hostility. It is just here that the film, unless we take care, is most likely to break down. It has grown and draws its financial strength from the fact that it is, for purely technical reasons, an art of the people. It is a mass art, in which the individual is scarcely likely to find a foothold unless he is of a mind with the masses. Its very power, in short, may well prove its very weakness.

The solution lies in encouraging the individual element, in encouraging the growth of the specialist audience. Specialist audiences are of many kinds. They may be scientific societies, or schools, or film societies, or church clubs, or technical study groups. Whatever their character they all have one great value; they enable specialised films to be produced and compared. The very life blood of democracy is the tolerance which permits individual conceptions and points of view to exist and meet in conflict and stand comparison with each other. And what is here the life blood of democracy is the life blood of art in general and of film art in particular.

Yet the obstacles in the way of a growth of specialist audiences are well-nigh overwhelming. Censorship is not the least of them. It maintains the mass character of the film; for its certificates are awarded, not to exclude those films which would be unfit for anybody, but to pass those which are considered fit for everybody. Many films, as a result, which would be eminently suitable for audiences of a certain kind, fail to pass the Censor at all. This usually means, in effect, that they cannot be shown at all; for whereas banned plays may be shown by private societies, the restrictions of censorship are so effectively strengthened by the Quota Act as to exclude any such showing of films.

A Warning

Far from a relaxation of the restrictions there is every evidence of a desire to strengthen them. Attempts have recently been made to bring non-flammable films, at present one of the possible loopholes, under the same restrictions as flammable films. More recently it has been suggested by the County Councils Association that sub-standard films should be subject to censorship. It is important that those concerned in developing the full capacities of the film should be aware of such moves and, if need be, oppose them.

Ultimately, television may have a larger say in the matter than many now realise. A man will not stir outside his home to see a film unless it gives him something more than he can see on his television set. Cinemas, in short, will be emptied of the mentally lazy and compelled to cater for audiences that are selective and critical. The next few years will be of interest to watch from many points of view.

Kino News, Winter 1935

Making Films With a Purpose

Ralph Bond

If you were to ask Sam Goldwyn or Carl Laemmle or Alexander Korda why they made films they would probably answer quite frankly—'For the purpose of making money'. If you asked the Conservative Party why they produced films they would say—'For the purpose of getting votes for Tory candidates'. And if you put the same question to Shell or the Gas Light & Coke Company or Cadbury's they would answer—'For the purpose of selling more petrol', or gas or chocolate as the case may be.

So as everybody who makes films has a purpose in doing so, we had better ask ourselves the reason and purpose for Kino making films.

Selling Working-Class Ideas

Obviously it isn't primarily to make money, although our films should be good enough to get back their production costs. Have we something to sell? Yes, we are trying to sell working-class ideas and working-class politics through a medium that is popular in every town and village.

The cinema is probably the most powerful form of propaganda yet devised by modern civilisation. But like everything else, it is under the control of vested interests who use it not only to make profits but to put across propaganda for their own class interests. The same, of course, is true of other arts—literature, the theatre, and so on, but whereas in these it is possible for independent artists and groups to break through the stranglehold, the cinema is a far more difficult proposition because of its dependence on costly technical equipment.

Nevertheless, Kino has succeeded to a certain extent in breaking the monopoly, and has commenced production on sixteen-millimetre films. And just because of the expense involved in any sort of film production it is important that our directors should learn to get to the heart of their subjects in the most forceful and compelling images.

Our purpose in making films must be to dramatise the lives and struggles of the workers. The subjects available are inexhaustable—Unemployment, Victimisation, Housing, Children, Strikes, Hunger Marches, War. Our propaganda must not be forced or artificial: we don't want melodrama or false heroics and the message or lead must grow naturally out of the material. Our films must be positive in the sense that they must indicate the subjective factor of revolt and struggle against existing conditions, and it will be the task of those who make our films to learn how this can be most effectively achieved.

Our Films must be Real

For instance merely to tag a few slogans on the end of our films is not sufficient. It would be unnatural, dramatically and artistically weak. A film must have unity and lead up to its motivating point in such a way that the audience will be carried with it naturally and logically.

The documentary type of films is, I think, the one most suited to our aims. We can take our cameras out into the streets, and at the expense of little more than film, patience and an infinite capacity for taking trouble, photograph our material as it actually exists. To build sets is expensive and often unsatisfactory in the final result. We should aim at achieving naturalism and avoiding obscurity. Through the camera we can speak to the workers in terms they can understand and appreciate. And if we do this we are at the same time exposing the stupidity and false values of the commercial film.

We organise and we attack. That is our purpose.

Kino News, Winter 1935

Making Film History

The move towards unity on the part of working-class organisations has led to an increasing realisation that the film is a most powerful weapon of propaganda, and with this realisation has come an increasing use of films.

This was clearly brought out at the first Annual General Meeting of Kino which took place at the Conway Hall, London, on 26th April. The meeting was an unqualified success, there being over eighty delegates present from Trades Councils and T.U. Branches, Labour Parties, Leagues of Youth, Co-operative Societies and Guilds, Friends of the Soviet Union. Alderman Joseph Reeves was in the chair. Speakers included Ivor Montagu,

William Hunter and George Elvin.* Outstanding points in the Secretary's report were that during the year Kino had trebled its turnover; that shows had been given during the year to over a quarter of a million people. Provincial groups had been formed in Doncaster, Glasgow, Manchester and Birmingham. Shows had been given to all types of organisation; to Branches of the Friends of the Soviet Union, to Film Societies, to Trade Union Branches and Trade Councils, to Co-operative Societies and Guilds, to Labour Parties, Schools, L.N.U.** and Peace organisations

Kino has realised that potential audiences for progressive films have increased immensely and has made concrete plans to go into sound, and it was officially announced that a sound projector and one sound-film would be available this autumn.

There was a growing demand for films dealing with home problems and the newly set up Kino Production Committee was preparing to supply this demand.

Alderman Reeves, in his opening speech as chairman, considered that the increased interest and activity taken in the showing of films for the workers had justified the institution of the Company. In the midst of a great deal of trouble and anxiety Kino had been able to distribute and to show worthwhile films all over the country. 'There is no doubt' stated Alderman Reeves, 'that we have seriously to consider going over to sound, and that is going to mean a very great expense, but if we have the support of the working-class bodies, then it ought to make the problem of going over to sound an easy one.'

The Secretary of Kino pointed out that in spite of transport difficulties and the fact that in most cases it was not possible to purchase more than a single copy of each film, efficiency in exhibition had increased 100 per cent. during the year. He saw no reason why distribution organisation should not improve still further this year. In the last few months, progress in the provinces had been rapid, and the number of groups was increasing. In a critical situation like the present, it was essential to get on the Kino Council very much wider representation from the Labour Movement.

Mr. Hunter, speaking on *THE FILM AND EDUCATION*, said that there was not to date any real technique evolved for the classroom film. So-called educational films at the moment could be divided into two main kinds: advertising and propaganda films such as those made by Cadbury's or the E.M.B.; and films made to sell projectors.

Mr. Elvin said that the official Labour Party attitude to films was that they should produce films which were films first and propaganda second. Distribution of films through the medium of the Labour Hall, Trades Hall, Co-op. Hall, does not get to the film-going public and is mainly preaching to the converted. Film propaganda must be done through the medium of the commercial cinema. Mr. Elvin pointed out that a film made for the commercial cinema would have to be first class technically. 'The film' Mr. Elvin concluded, 'can be the most powerful weapon for Peace against War and Fascism'.

Mr. Montagu said he wished to take issue with Mr. Elvin. To make 'good' films in the commercial sense would be almost impossible without an immense expenditure. The one film which had been made for the Labour Movement had cost in the neighbourhood of £3,000. But £10,000 was considered by the film trade to be the very minimum cost for a respectable production. The major companies spent something like £60,000 or £70,000, on an ordinary film.

It followed from this that Kino would have to work out its own technique of very cheap production.

'A great deal of the propaganda in the commercial cinema,' said Mr. Montagu, 'was not deliberate but because in production on such a financial scale, interests had to be safeguarded and vested interests would not be willing to risk a Censorship ban on their films. But the Censor is in a very anomalous position and nation wide protest against the films we don't like would have a real effect both on the censor and on the type of story chosen by the trade.'

It was Mr. Montagu's opinion that Kino should concentrate on documentary films. Kino was in a position to make true documentaries, whereas a good many so-called documentary films were forged documents. He mentioned one very famous documentary film which had received a gold medal from one fascist dictator*** and had been purchased for distribution by another— on condition that the names of all Jews connected with the production were withdrawn. Yet this film purported to present a true picture of the life of the people.

Lively discussion followed these speeches and the recent circular issued by the T.U.C. and Labour Party was welcomed by the Conference, although many of the delegates considered this circular to be long overdue. Conference then witnessed a show of representative films: *Limestone*, an educational film directed for the Dartington Hall School Film Unit by William Hunter, *Holiday from Unemployment*, one reel of Eisenstein's classic film *Ten Days That Shook the World, Jubilee*, a reel of the interest film *In the Land of the Soviets*, and a reel of *Free Thaelmann.***** This last was so well received that the Conference immediately decided to send a resolution, demanding Thaelmann's release, to the German Embassy. A striking proof of the value of shows of Kino films.

Kino are confident that after this Conference, the Labour Movement will take an increased interest in the most powerful weapon of propaganda, and will use the film for peace and cultural progress.

Kino News, Spring 1936

Notes

*Joseph Reeves, a leading member of the Royal Arsenal Co-operative Society, became a Labour MP after the war. The RACS was closely connected in its political work with the Labour Party, and Reeves was in the forefront of the Society's educational work, which extended throughout South London. Through Reeves' interest in the use of film, these two types of work merged, resulting in the Workers' Film Association which, under Reeves' management, operated from 1938 to 1947.

William Hunter was the chief organiser of the Dartington Film Unit, a professional but non-commercial outfit engaging in educational projects.

George Elvin was the first Secretary of the Association of Cinematograph Technicians (ACT).

**League of Nations Union.

***Flaherty's *Man of Aran* obtained Mussolini's Grand Prix at the Venice Festival in 1934. It also obtained a prize in Berlin, and Nazi Germany wanted to distribute the film.

*****Holiday from Unemployment* was made by members of the Film and Photo League,

Oxford Trades Council and the South Wales Miners' Federation, and distributed by Kino from about 1935. *Jubilee* was a film on the 1935 Jubilee by the Green brothers (see Paul Marris's article in this book). *In the Land of the Soviets* was made by the Friends of the Soviet Union (they arranged trips two or three times a year to the Soviet Union on which some FPL/Kino members went—footage shot on these trips was edited into Communist travelogues). *Free Thaelmann* was edited by Ivor Montagu for the Progressive Film Institute, and used internationally in the campaign for the release of the jailed German Communist Party leader.

LABOUR CINEMA PROPAGANDA

Editorial note: Walter Citrine, General Secretary of the TUC from 1926–46, and J. S. Middleton, Secretary of the Labour Party, jointly issued this circular from Transport House in April 1936. It was the first official acknowledgment of film's importance, and of the contribution it could make to depicting the institutions of the labour movement as 'functional' in society rather than 'destructive'. This circular preceded the Kino annual general meeting of April 26. The pointed omission of any reference to socialist film making traditions in Britain before 1936 may stand as a significant indication of the circular's political thrust. Kino's reply to the circular makes the point that they had already set up the groups the circular was trying to call into existence, while warning against competing with the commercial industry on its own terms and addressing the need for political education via the non-theatrical sphere.

It should also be emphasised that, by the time of the circular, the Conservative Party had been operating an active film propaganda section for nine years, and the National Government's little-known National Publicity Bureau, a supposedly 'independent' body, was at that moment building on the considerable success of its propaganda operation in the 1935 election. While the traditions of propaganda in British political life were being broken in different ways by both Conservative and Communist groups, this official inauguration of 'Labour Cinema Propaganda' might well seem, as Left Review commented, a 'welcome, though belated thesis'.

152

Labour Cinema Propaganda

'The eyes are more exact witnesses than the ears'—*Heraclitus.*

Dear Secretary,

During the War the Cinematograph became a powerful instrument of propaganda in the hands of the Government.

Since then, with the development of talking films and the immense improvement in cinema technique, film production has become nothing short of a fine art, the propaganda value of which has been multiplied a hundredfold.

Indeed, the film has now become a weapon that can affect the minds of the multitude in a given direction without the multitude being aware of what is happening. It can create bias against which neither reason nor rhetoric can prevail. It can persuade and be understood by the ignorant as well as by the educated, for it works through the combined media of sight and sound, appealing to those senses which are the common property of nearly everybody—men, women and children alike.

In the interests of the Labour Movement, and of the working class generally, it is imperative that Labour should organise its own Film Propaganda without delay.

A Committee composed of representatives of the Labour Party Executive, the General Council of the Trades Union Congress, and a number of friendly experts was set up last year to consider the problems involved in Film Propaganda.

As a result of many discussions, during which the subject has been exhaustively studied, the Committee has decided to form a Central Organisation for the supply of information, projectors and films to those localities where suitable machinery can be established.

It is suggested that the best method will be for Local Parties to take the initiative in the formation of Film Societies.

It is most desirable that we should not preach merely to the converted. It is therefore proposed that association with these Societies should be available to members of other non-Party organisations with interests of an educational and cultural character, as well as to individual members of the general public.

It is suggested that, at the outset, you and your colleagues should convene a Conference of all the bodies associated with the Labour and Co-operative Movements in your district likely to be interested, including, where such exist, the Trades Council, the Workers' Educational Association, the National Council of Labour Colleges, the various Co-operative organisations in the district, etc., with a view to discussing the establishment of a Film Society on the lines indicated.

This is Most Important

A model Constitution and Rules for Film Societies will be sent to those localities where it is decided they should be instituted, while a Library List of Films is also in preparation for their service.

We enclose a Questionnaire with a view to securing information as to local conditions. It would, perhaps, be advisable to return this after the proposed Conference has been held.

It is obvious that the success of the scheme will depend upon the amount of support it receives throughout the country. So far, it has met with unqualified approval by all to whom it has been submitted, the general opinion being that the Cinema is destined to play an increasing and ever dominating rôle in propaganda and cultural and educational work generally.

Trusting, therefore, that we shall be able to count upon the approval and co-operation of your Executive in this important matter.

We remain, yours sincerely,
Walter Citrine
J. S. Middleton   *April, 1936.*

Labour Opens Its Eyes

'The eyes are more exact witnesses than the ears'—*Heraclitus.*
From the circular issued by the T.U.C. and Labour Party.

We welcome, and we are sure that the whole of the Labour movement will welcome, the recent circular issued by the T.U.C. and the Labour Party entitled *Labour Cinema Propaganda.* This circular is undoubtedly the response of the growing demand of the rank and file of the labour movement for new forms of propaganda. We can cite many instances of

153

local Labour Parties and Trades Unions who were well ahead of Transport House and who have run shows in co-operation with us. We can safely claim that we have not been an unimportant factor in the production of the circular.

The circular states that 'in the interests of the Labour Movement, and of the working class generally, it is imperative that Labour should organise its own film propaganda without delay; and proposes that a Conference be convened in each district of all bodies associated with the Labour and Co-operative Movements with a view to establishing Film Societies.' We have already initiated such groups in a number of districts throughout the country and their experience would be useful at these conferences. The circular also states that a library list of films is being prepared and we have already offered Transport House our full co-operation in this and also in making our projector service available to all societies and groups.

We have one criticism of the circular. In view of the astronomical expense involved in the production of films for the ordinary cinema (see the reports of Ivor Montagu's speech on our front page*) and of the consequent difficulty of using such films for Labour propaganda, we feel that it should be clearly pointed out that the majority of the work will have to be done at the start on 16 mm. or other non-theatrical stock and apparatus, and that the Labour Movement will have to work out its own special production and showing technique. There is no reason why this should cut down the effectiveness of the propaganda or why large sections of the general public cannot be drawn in. We are stressing this point as we are anxious to ensure that the movement will not be throttled by the very system which gives rise to it.

Only when the public as a whole is much more critical towards commercial films and insists on films of a different kind from those which it now sees, will it be possible to use the commercial cinema to any extent. The work of the Labour Movement in the non-theatrical sphere can do much to bring about that state of affairs.

Kino News, Spring 1936

Note
*The article 'Making Film History' included in this collection.

FILMS FOR LABOUR

Editorial note: *Frank Jackson, the author of the following article, was a Communist Party member involved in the Film and Photo League's production of* Transport. *He later became a founding member of the British Film Unit, formed by ex-FPL and Kino members, who made* A.R.P. (1939) *and the (incomplete?) production of* Popular Front Film No. 3.

Left Review, *a cultural review dominated by Communist literary intellectuals, paid very little notice to film. Of note, however, is an article by Arthur Elton entitled 'Realist Films Today'* (Left Review, *June 1936), which outlines the development of the 'realist film' in the work of the GPO Unit with the coming of sound: 'In* [Housing Problems], *instead of directing the players to "act" a scene, they were asked to address the camera, and to tell in their own words, unguided and unrehearsed, what they felt their own problems of living in a slum to be... Here the audience was transported into the skin of the subject... The modern realist film has given up the loving caress of industrial process and statuesque treatment of workers, for a racy intimacy with men and women which we hope will blow away the romantic cobwebs of an earlier vision'. This concept of a 'new realism' fitted into the problematic of* Left Review *in which '... two main problems seem to emerge. The first is: Is the real revolutionary art of today to be realistic or non-realistic? The second is: if it is to be realistic, what will this new realism be like?'* (Anthony Blunt, 'The Realism Quarrel', Left Review, *March 1937). In keeping with a tradition of Marxist writing on culture, the popular propaganda and agitational work of the theatre, press and film movements did not qualify for the accolade of 'art', and were therefore seldom discussed.*

Films for Labour

'In the interests of the Labour Movement, and of the working class generally, it is imperative that Labour should organise its own Film Propaganda without delay'. This is the welcome, though belated, thesis of a circular issued by the T.U.C. and Labour Party to their branches.

For a very long time now, the more live sections of the Labour movement have felt the need for up-to-date methods of propaganda and education. They have realised that the cinema is one of the most potent of these methods. The cinema plays a very real part in the national life; about 18,000,000 people visit the cinema every week in the British Isles. Already, steps in the right direction have been taken by Kino; their experiences have shown that there is a widespread demand for using the film as propaganda and education.

The circular makes the practical suggestion that local conferences should be called to discuss the establishment of a local Film Society. This conference should have representation from 'all bodies associated with the Labour and Co-operative Movements in your district likely to be interested'. In many districts, such film society organisations already exist.

'It is most desirable,' says the circular, 'that we should not preach merely to the converted. It is therefore proposed that association with these (Film) Societies should be available to members of other non-Party organisations with interests of an educational and cultural character, as well as to individual members of the general public.' With the second part of this statement there is no quarrel, but the ambiguity of the first could be the cause of great difficulty.

The circular seems to have its eyes on the commercial cinema.

There are several difficulties in the way of using the commercial cinema for working class education and propaganda. Leaving the Censorship aside for the moment, there is the great obstacle of cost. In the film trade it is reckoned impossible to make a good (in the sense of technically good) story film at less than £10,000. This is the minimum figure. Most competent commercial productions cost in the region of £60,000.

With the best intentions in the world, as soon as financial interests are involved to this extent, no producers are going to be fools enough to make such films as stand even the least chance of being banned by the Censor. It would mean that their money would be lost. Making films on this scale would mean squashing out every trace of propaganda or education; it would mean that the films would defeat their own purpose.

Latest information has it that the type of films which will be produced for the commercial market will be one- or two-reelers dealing with such subjects as 'A Day in the Life of a Railway Worker.' Such films would stand a chance of being shown fairly extensively, on condition that there was no 'propaganda' in them. And if these films are going to be in the tradition of the 'English School' of documentary, they would be shown only in the specialist cinemas, and again would not reach that wider public at which the circular aims.

The alternative is to use the 16 mm. film. It should be borne in mind that 16 mm. talkies are now as sound a proposition as the 16 mm. silent films. Even at the present moment it would be quite possible for an excellent library list of 16 mm. films to be drawn up for the use of such Film Societies as are envisaged by the circular. Initial cost for apparatus, etc., should be easily covered by an efficient society.

The circular adopts an unnecessarily gloomy attitude with regard to this question of 'showing to the converted.' After all, a film show in a Labour or Co-operative Hall is bound, if well organised, to reach a very much wider circle than merely the membership of the organisation which arranges the show.

FRANK JACKSON
Left Review, June 1936

To Our Readers

A most remarkable move towards unity has been recently observed throughout the working-class political life of the entire country. In a situation fraught with immediate danger of war, the working class is gathering together its scattered forces. Not since 1926 has this country seen such a general political awakening, which is not affecting hundreds but tens of thousands, which is bringing into activity people who hitherto had thought themselves not concerned, which is the only check to the war mongers.

One of the ways that will be used to whip up a war spirit and make a recruiting drive is the cinema. We have already seen attempts at this in the Duff Cooper newsreel,* and in the film Gaumont-British are making for the Army Council.

One of the means that the working class can use for peace propaganda is also the cinema. Not perhaps, to any large extent the commercial cinema. But the working class should and will make full use of the sub-standard film, for peace.

The situation, then, is that just now film shows will reach a very much wider audience than ever before. This means that the films must have a very wide appeal. There must be a supply of films dealing with English conditions.

With this in view, Kino has set up its Production Committee to make and get made films about English problems.

Kino is purchasing a sound projector and will have at least one sound film available for showing this winter, in all probability *Men and Jobs* or *Road to Life*.** These films will attract audiences that would not, perhaps, be so interested in a show of the great silent films.

This means that 16 mm. sound films are definitely on the order of the day.

We feel sure that all those forces working for peace will take immediate advantage of this potent means of propaganda.

Kino News, Spring 1936

Note
*The Duff Cooper newsreel was a recruiting newsreel for the army and navy which was distributed in all cinemas. It showed Duff Cooper (the Foreign Office commissioned the film) addressing the audience.

The Gaumont-British film for the Army Council was *On His Majesty's Service,* a feature which crudely promoted military service. It was released in March 1937.

**Men and Jobs,* directed by Alexander Macheret, USSR 1932, an early Soviet sound film employing 'naturalistic' sound, released in Britain in 1935.

Road to Life (also known as *A Pass to Life*), directed by Nikolai Ekk, USSR 1931, sometimes regarded as the first Soviet film to be conceived and written as a sound film, about 'wild' children and their social taming.

Film Production

Kino's object is to use the film as a force for social, political and cultural progress. With this in mind it has obtained and shown very widely such films as *Potemkin, Storm Over Asia* and *New Babylon*—on sub-standard, because there are no restrictive regulations applying to the showing of 16 mm. non-inflammable films. Kino has taken the film into the Trade Union branch meeting, into the political meeting, and has given shows in rooms holding ten people and in halls holding a thousand.

In only one way has Kino not fulfilled its aim. Very little has so far been done in the way

of creative work. Kino has practically no films which deal with conditions in this country. Such films are an urgent need at the moment. We cannot hope for very much in this line from the film industry proper, although we do not in any way minimise the great work done by the G.P.O. and independent production units. Yet the demand is very much larger than the supply. And, at the same time, there are about 200 amateur film clubs in this country, mostly making poor imitations of Hollywood productions, for want of anything better to do.

With these facts in mind, Kino set up its Production Committee. The jobs of this Committee are as follows:

1. To discuss and determine themes and treatments for films of social significance.

2. To form units throughout the country for production of such films, on sub-standard stock, and to act as a co-ordinating body to all such units and give assistance in every way.

3. To offer existing units a source of distribution for suitable productions in the substandard market, to assist and advise them on scenarios.

4. To undertake production for any organisations who feel that a film illustrating their work from a particular angle will aid them in their own sphere of activity.

While we cannot at the moment offer rising Garbos a chance, we should be very glad to send details to anyone interested in any branch of the work outlined above.

At the moment of writing, production is in initial stages on a film for the Kensington Labour Party, dealing with infant mortality; and on a film on Housing and Slums in co-operation with builders' unions.*

The Scenario Committee is also going strong, and has already proved of value to several units throughout the country.

Besides these, the General Production Committee meets at less frequent intervals to discuss general policy and report back on all work done in other sections.

We should be glad to hear from anyone interested, and ask all organisations and individuals who believe in our aims to aid us in the formation of production units and in the showing of our films.

Kino Production Committee
Left Review, June 1936

Note
*These films became, respectively, *Nursery School,* and *Housing Progress,* made by Matthew Nathan for the Housing Centre.

WORKERS PRODUCE PROPAGANDA FILM

Editorial note: *A group of building workers initiated a particular form of dramatised documentary with a film entitled* Construction, *an FPL production which was shown to trade union branches during 1936–37. Its titles read 'Made by the Men on the Job', and it was financed and shot by the builders themselves. The film combines staged sequences with candid camera and* cinéma vérité *techniques, using a concealed camera to shoot on the building site itself. The finance was raised by raffling a pound note and through the sale of photographs, as well as through personal contributions. The overall cost was £8, roughly equivalent to four men's weekly wage packets: the film includes a building worker opening his pay packet, showing the total to be £2.12s.6d.*

Workers Produce Propaganda Film

A ten minute film made by a group of building workers on the job has been causing something of a sensation in Trade Union circles. This film, *Construction*, shows more than volumes of talk, how films can be used to put over Trade Union propaganda to the least 'class conscious' audiences.

The story is very simple. A staunch Trade Unionist is shown recruiting on the job. He is victimised. After consultation with the Federation Stewards, the men organise a lightning strike. The strikers win complete and speedy victory, and the Unionist is reinstated.

The photography is by one of the building workers, who learnt to use the camera in a few days. Some of the scenes were taken from under a sack! This will give some idea of the difficulties encountered at every turn in the making of the film.

The total cost of the film was under £8. It has been shown, through Kino, to over 20 branches of Builders' Unions, and has been enthusiastically received.

So clearly does the film demonstrate possibilities of work in this sphere, that Kino organised a meeting at which *Construction* was shown to discuss further work on these lines. The meeting was attended by delegates from Building and Transport Unions, and by noted professional technicians. The film *Construction* was endorsed by the meeting as being the type of propaganda needed by the Trade Union Movement. Lively criticism and discussion resulted in immediate suggestions for future films on these lines.

A Committee was elected from the Meeting to discuss in detail plans for immediate production, and work is going forward apace on a film of Housing and Slum Problems from the working-class point of view.

Kino News, Spring 1936

TUC CONGRESS 1937

Editorial note: *In contrast to the activities of the rank and file workers with the film* Construction, *the TUC chose the quality productions ('first-class "documentary" and propaganda pictures') of members of the GPO Film Unit as their exemplary films:* Industrial Britain, *directed by Flaherty for the Empire Marketing Board, 1931;* Shipyard, *directed by Paul Rotha for Gaumont-British Instructional, 1935;* Housing Problems (*here called* Housing), *directed by Arthur Elton and Edgar Anstey for the British Commercial Gas Association in 1935;* Face of Britain, *directed by Paul Rotha for G-B Instructional, 1935;* Coal Face, *directed by Cavalcanti for the GPO, 1935.*

Cinema Propaganda

A joint committee of the General Council's officers with the Labour Party has been considering the possibility of equipping the movement with machinery for propaganda by cinema films. Evidence has accumulated to show that great interest exists throughout the movement in film propaganda. Effective educational and film propaganda organisation has been established in the Co-operative Movement. Discussion with technical experts on the productive side has been carried on by the joint committee, and it is resolved that, next to the problem of providing adequate machinery for the exhibition of films, the production of first-class 'documentary' and propaganda pictures, similar to such 'documentary' productions as *Industrial Britain, Shipyard, Housing, Face of Britain,* and *Coal Face,* which show graphically how the wage-earners live and work, is a problem of first importance. The supply of such films is limited. They are, moreover, costly to produce.

The joint committee has, therefore, framed recommendations for the consideration of the General Council and the National Executive of the Labour Party to prevent overlapping and duplication of productive schemes, and to pool available resources, with a view to joint productions of film propaganda and education in conjunction with the Co-operative film organisation, the Workers' Travel Association, and the Workers' Educational Association, as well as trade unions interested in the application of film publicity to their own trades and industries.

Report to the General Council,
TUC Congress 1937

FILM AND PHOTO LEAGUE/ LEFT FILM FRONT

Editorial note: *The following call for support was made by the FPL in their bulletin* Left Film Front, *issued in July 1937. This bulletin replaced their previous one of January 1936, called* Camera Forward, *which included an article by Irene Nicholson, an editor of the avant-garde film magazine* Film Art. *The sloganised call for support presents a truly weird mixture of ideologies, from that of the New Social Order via pacifism and professionalism to the notion of 'ideological warfare' and cinema as a 'machine-gun', foreshadowing some of Godard's more polemical statements. This heterogeneity gives a clue to the problems involved in the very concept of a 'united popular front'.*

Left Film Front (1)

For the building of a new Social Order and the exposure of the present. The camera with a purpose.

Co-ordinating amateur workers in 9 and 16 mm movie and still photography under guidance of professionals.

Production and projection groups everywhere, linked up with vital directive centre.

Working in conjunction with Left books, plays, artists and all United and People's Front Organisations.

Cine is the machine-gun of ideological warfare. Use and make films and photos for Peace, Freedom and Democracy!

Support the FILM and PHOTO LEAGUE.
Left Film Front, July 1937

Left Film Front (2)

RETROSPECT: Among the many mushroom growths in the progressive film field, the FILM AND PHOTO LEAGUE stands a firm plant with its roots in the earliest days of workers' films. Originally the production unit of Kino, it became an independent organisation in 1934, film making and distribution then being separated. With very limited purses and little spare time the early members bravely faced with the difficulties of pioneer work, making its witness amid the lavish and pampered display of the capitalist cinema. Today we are on the eve of a fuller recognition of the screen and camera as a powerful propagandist weapon, and the league is keen and ready to take up the challenge.

WE are building up this year almost from rock bottom. There was a stock of rather antiquated films, which when re-edited will be of real historic interest in the movement: there was a certain amount of equipment loaned by enthusiastic members and a great deal of accumulated experience. A new committee, which means business, was appointed, and with a vision that appreciates the phenomenal development of left-wing activity, the scope of our ambitions was enlarged.

THE FUTURE: The social situation is critical. Not only Spain, but the whole world is on the front-line trench of the struggle. Everywhere people are turning to the Left for guidance and enlightenment. We must not fail them through lack of unity or neglect of any weapon of imaginative propaganda. The cinema strikes straight home to brain and feelings. It can bring the whole realm of facts within the small compass of a screen. Everywhere there are poignant scenes in the breakdown of capitalism and stirring aspects of the birth of a new order ready to win new comrades for the Cause.

Left Film Front, July 1937

Film and Photo League
Report of Left Book Club Conference

In London on June 7th an important preliminary conference was held to discuss the co-ordination of sub-standard film work for Left propaganda. Among those attending were

158

delegates from Left Book Club and other Groups.

In opening the Conference, Michael Burke outlined briefly the history and development of progressive film organisations, and called attention to the need for further effort in the production and distribution of films 'with a purpose'.

Dr. John Lewis* then gave a most stimulating talk on the value of the film in supplementing the printed word. Because of the easier assimilation of facts presented through the eye, social education by this means can, he said, prepare the way for the appeal of literature. He would like the League's film *March Against Starvation*** to be shown to every one of the six hundred L.B.C. branches throughout the country. The film medium can, then, go hand in hand with the printed word, possessing with other forms of art, the ability to bring its message to life. As an example Dr. Lewis stressed the vitality and interest of the film in the presentation of such materials as statistics.

In the documentary sphere, the land or factory worker, seeing things from his own angle, can contribute more for our purpose than the most expert professional artist approaching the same subject lyrically and from the outside. Such effort must be enthused, trained and assisted in a way that only such a society as the F.P.L. can do.

The League recognises this Conference as the first step towards the formation of film units within all the Left Book Club and other regional Groups that will concentrate on the showing and making of realist films, availing themselves of expert guidance and training under the aegis of a vital central organisation. It hopes that other organisations will follow the lead that the Book Club has given.

The Conference ended with the showing of two productions of the League, one of them dealing with the public events of May, 1937, employing a new technique in the use of colour.***

THE FOLLOWING SCHEME was adopted as a basis for the working of such units as these which may be organised in connection with the Left Book Club:—

A. Formation of amateur units co-lateral with political and cultural groups.

(*a*) Showing and making films illustrative of the Left movement.

(*b*) Short films (10–15 mins.) to be a frequent feature of ordinary Group meetings.

B. Units to be co-ordinated with the League, as central body.

(*a*) Liaison with Central Committee.

(*b*) Lectures and practical instruction in use of camera, projector and technique. Advice in subjects and treatment.

(*c*) Pooling facilities in use and economic purchase of equipment and film-stock.

(*d*) A centre for editing and studio work in London for mutual use of various units and common meeting place.

(*e*) League as distribution centre for substandard films suitable for small audiences, to be rented at the most economic rates possible.

(*f*) All units to co-operate on subjects of national scope (as for example, the 1937 Hunger March).

(*g*) A monthly Bulletin to be issued dealing with film Group activities, problems involved, films available, etc.

C. Membership of units to involve membership of the League and receipt of all central publications.

D. Type of films to be made—local conditions, working class life, cultural problems. Story and documentary films, also subjects suitable for children. Exchange of films for material from foreign countries. Acquisition of useful film material from other societies and amateur workers.

The Secretary writes:—Following notices in the film and Left press, I have received a large number of enquiries. By far the most numerous have been for films to show. Shorts are wanted, and cheaply, for small shows. Many requests are for 9 mm., and in this connection may we say that a mistaken impression was given in a previous number of the *Left News*. Although the Film and Photo League encourages work with 9 mm., up to the present it has worked almost entirely with 16 mm. So that we have mostly 16 mm. material in stock at present. So great is the demand for films that we urge all Left Book Club Groups to co-operate in the production of new films in 16 mm. and where this is impossible in 9 mm.

The Film and Photo League are investigating the possibilities of music and commentary accompaniment to be played on ordinary gramophones, and hope to have special discs prepared in the autumn for the more important films listed below. In conclusion let it be said that excellent results can be obtained, and easily, with a simple paper or white rubber screen and a small 16 mm. projector in an ordinary room, all fixed up in a jiffy.

The second type of enquiry is for particulars of the League and for general information on the whole problem of cine work. This latter is more than can be answered in a letter or a bulletin! There is a real demand for an information bureau for beginners. The next issue of the Bulletin, as also our group at the L.B.C. Summer School, will seriously attempt to cope with this healthy desire for knowledge. In the meantime may I suggest that the columns of *Home Movies* and *Amateur Cine World* (6d. monthly) and various simple books for amateurs, as also a visit to your local cine-photo store will help you find your way about.

The most valuable thing you can do, if your Group is within the London area, is to ask one of our speakers to come to your ordinary meeting for a talk and discussion. A film will be included at low hire rates, plus 1s. a reel for projection.

FILMS FOR AUTUMN BOOKINGS

Nos. 1–10 available now. Nos. 11–14 release in mid-July. Nos. 15–25 release Aug.–Sept. Rates below per day (6d. a day extra) postage extra. Colour films on League's projectors only. One reel lasts 10–15 minutes.

16mm FILMS

1. CONSTRUCTION (1r).—By a builder on the job.   ..   ..   .. 2s.
2. WINTER (1r).—Cold weather for poor people   ..   ..   .. 2s.
3. BREAD (1r).—A study in the struggle against poverty.   .. 2s.
4. U.A.B. (1r).—Demonstration against this imposition .   .. 2s.
5. REVOLT OF FISHERMEN (1r).—The fishing strike   ..   ..   .. 2s.
6. HUNGER MARCH, 1934 (1r).— Documentary ..   ..   .. 2s.
7. JUBILEE (1r).—Questions '25 years of Peace and Progress' .   .. 2s.
8, 9. INTERNATIONAL NEWS REELS each   ..   .. 2s.
10. MARCH AGAINST STARVATION, 1936 (2r).—Why and how they marched ..   .. 6s.
11. One-reel version of the above   .. 4s.
12. DOCK WORKERS (1r).— Documentary of the London Docks   ..   .. 4s.

13. SPIRIT OF MAY DAY (1r).—May Day as part of historic process 1s.6d.
14. CORONATION MAY-DAY (2r with colour).—A satire and document .   ..   . 10s.
15. STRIFE (2r).—An argument for T.U. support   ..   ..   .. 4s.
16 to 22. BUILDING THE PEOPLE'S FRONT IN ENGLAND.—Seven separate films intended to run progressively in the style of 'The March of Time', including much historic material and aspects of political and ideological struggle from month to month each   ..   .. 3s.
23. A PENNY TO SPEND (1r).—How a penny can be wisely (and unwisely) spent ..   ..   .. 2s.
24. SPAIN, 1936–1937 (2r with colour) 10s.
25. GENEROUS SOIL (1r).— Documentary of work on the land   ..   ..   ..

Left News, August 1937

Notes

*John Lewis: philosopher, ex-ILP and presently a CP member, organiser of the Left Book Club groups. Appears in the title of Louis Althusser's pamphlet *A Reply to John Lewis*, where Althusser criticises the idealist humanism and Stalinism of some Communist parties.

**March Against Starvation* (FPL 1936) was a collaboratively made film about the 'national protest' of 1936 against the Unemployment Assistance Board. The protest was organised by the National Unemployment Workers' Movement led by Wal Hannington. The NUWM paid £10 towards the cost of making the film, which was shown in conjunction with Hannington's tours of the Left Book Club groups. Those involved in making the film included Helen Biggar (Glasgow School of Art), Michael Burke, Rudolph Messel (Socialist Film Council), Ivan and Sime Seruya.

***Possibly a reference to FPL secretary Hugh Cuthbertson's *The Merry Month of May*, which was shot on 16 mm Kodachrome stock.

May 1937 was the month of George VI's coronation and of the busmen's strike, which is recorded in the film *Busmen's Holiday* (1937).

WORKERS' FILM ASSOCIATION

Editorial note: *In January 1938 the National Joint Film Committee of the Labour Party and the TUC had met to inaugurate the Workers' Film Association, which was eventually formed in November of that year. The Association started production of its own films in mid-1939 and continued through the war until 1947, producing educational and propaganda films. During this period before the war the Film and Photo League was fast disintegrating. All its work was in the hands of two or three people, and its network of contacts was gradually taken over by Kino.*

TUC Congress 1939: Report on the Workers' Film Association

In the first few months of its existence some thousands of film hirings have been arranged, a certain amount of equipment has been sold, and already the Association has commissions for the production of documentary films on behalf of Trade Unions and other organisations. It is particularly hoped to develop this latest branch of activity and through that the means to provide a supply of first-class documentary films vividly conveying the message which the Movement has to give to its members and to those who are not yet members.

SPAIN AND ANTI-FASCISM

Editorial note: *The move towards a Popular Front was accompanied in Britain, as elsewhere, by the increased emphasis placed on the unity of international struggle against fascism rather than on the domestic class divisions over such issues as unemployment. As the Spanish Civil War became the focal point of this struggle, teams were dispatched from Britain to make films which could then be distributed via the circuit of Left Book Club groups and political meetings. In October 1936, Ivor Montagu went to Spain with Norman McLaren as his cameraman and made* Defence of Madrid. *This was released in January 1937 and brought in an estimated £6,000 in collections and donations to the various committees organising medical aid and relief for Spain. In 1938 another team including Thorold Dickinson and Sidney Cole shot footage which was made into two films—* Spanish ABC (*directed by Dickinson*) *and* Behind the Spanish Lines (*directed by Cole*). *Both these films were financed by a grant of £3,000 from the Republican government in Spain. In addition, Montagu took two films of German and Italian prisoners of war (*Prisoners Prove Intervention in Spain, *and* Testimony of Non-Intervention) *to the Emergency Conference for Spain in April 1938, and to the League of Nations in Geneva (as recounted by Montagu in an interview in* Screen, *Autumn 1972). The PFI film* Britain Expects! *was also used by the 'Red Duchess' of Atholl in her election campaign in December 1938. The footage shot by these British crews in Spain was used in several other films both in Britain and abroad. Compilations of this footage, and from Spanish or Soviet sources, made up films such as* News from Spain (*released by PFI in April 1937*), A Call to Arms (*released by Kino in June 1937*), *and* Crime Against Madrid (*released by Kino in July 1937*).*

These films on Spain were perhaps the most widely seen of the oppositional films produced in Britain in the Thirties, and were used by left groups in a manner which had become the classical model for the use of 'political films'; that is to say, they were used first as 'star attractions' to assist in fund-raising campaigns, and secondly to present a visual illustration of political struggles abroad to support the traditional methods of verbal or literary propaganda. Their success in raising funds for groups such as the National Joint Committee for Spanish Relief, the British Committee for the Relief of the Victims of Fascism, the British Medical Aid Committee, and the Co-operative movement's 'Milk for Spain' campaign, is shown by the increased audiences at meetings reported in Left News, *the monthly bulletin of the Left Book Club (see below). Their political role, however, was that of pressurising 'public opinion' against the British government's policy of 'non-intervention' in Spain. The government and the British Labour Party's view of non-intervention was that they would not supply* arms to either the Republican forces or to Franco's fascist rebel forces in the full knowledge that Franco was amply supplied by the German and Italian fascist governments. The Republican interpretation of non-intervention was that there should be no legislation in any country which should prevent them from buying arms.

In keeping with the Popular Front spirit, the films on Spain are notable for emphasising the legality of the Spanish Republican cause and concentrating on its popular education and literacy programmes, and the need for medical relief and food supplies.

Note
by Paul Willemen

In relation to the widespread campaign for solidarity with the Republican cause, it must be pointed out that the Popular Front strategy adopted in the late Thirties by the International Communist Movement (Comintern) had dubious not to say disastrous effects, particularly in Spain itself. The fight for the Republican cause was presented as a fight against fascism, and many militants fought and died in this struggle. However, none of the reports from Spain, nor any of the film documents brought back by intrepid film makers such as Ivor Montagu, Thorold Dickinson, Sidney Cole and others, mentioned that the Spanish Communist Party was waging a ruthless and at times bloody sectarian war against the anarcho-syndicalist movement on its left as well as against the Falange and Franco's army on the right. Moreover, the entire mythology of the civil war suggested that it was part of an international war against fascism. In fact, the applicability of notions such as fascism or anti-fascism in relation to the Spanish Civil War is more than questionable. Indeed, the fact that this struggle was defined and presented as an anti-fascist war rather than as a revolutionary struggle can be seen as one of the major errors of the international communist movement which significantly contributed to Franco's victory. As Ronald Fraser put it at the Ruskin History Workshop, 1979: 'The implementation of the Popular Front policies ... precluded social revolution. Even more, it precluded revolutionary methods of fighting the war.

Working class alliance with anti-fascist sectors of the bourgeoisie was conflated into bourgeois (in mentality and politics, if not sociological) *leadership* of the struggle ... In leaning towards the reformist sectors of the socialists and liberal republicans, in seeking to "contain" the revolution, it rejected an alliance with those sectors of the anarcho-syndicalist movement and left socialists who understood (or were open to understanding) the needs of the revolution in terms of the war (and thus isolating the ultra-left sectors unable to assimilate this). In neglecting this revolutionary potential, the PCE reinforced the historical divisions of the Spanish working class... instead of securing the unity of purpose so necessary to winning the war. This, I would argue, was the major error ascribable to the policy of an "Anti-Fascist" war.'

Spanish A.B.C.

A film dealing with the state of education in a country at war seemed a curious subject to be faced with—and perhaps a trifle dull. Little did we know!

We got out to Barcelona on January 14th this year, and from 11 a.m. on the 15th until nearly noon on the 16th we had no less than six air raids. We were in a hotel in the new part of the town and not all of the raids came right over us, but it was a warming experience after London all the same. At 11.30 at night they dropped twenty bombs down by the port. Watching from our bedroom window it was a fascinating sight, but daylight revealed scenes of devastation which increased with appalling frequency during our ten weeks in the country.

We filmed under difficulties, visiting children's colonies, schools, factories and mines in and around Madrid, Valencia, Barcelona and some front line trenches. We could not make a scenario but worked from statistics and local information arranged as best we could. You see, we only had a couple of hours in any given spot—just time to look around, concoct a plan of action in a couple of minutes and then shoot. It seemed strange to be making a film on education under fire—the sounds were very distracting! A film on the war itself would have been much easier; we sometimes found it hard to concentrate on so detached a subject.

Many of the facts we discovered are amazing. For example, during 1937 they opened no less than 10,000 new schools in Republican Spain. The keenness of the people to learn is astonishing. At the front, 300 yards from the insurgent lines, we entered a little shell-pocked cottage and found twenty to thirty soldiers learning trigonometry. An hour before and an hour later they were firing rifles...

And again, at a munitions factory we found the whole staff attending a physics class. The idea behind it all is the conviction that a man or a woman is no good as a citizen or fighter unless he has some grasp of the wider issues involved in the life around them, an opportunity denied to a vast proportion of the Spanish nation in former times.

In Madrid, when we arrived, shells were dropping. Passers-by appeared to show very little concern: they just moved over *en masse* to the side of the street nearest the shelling as one moves to the lee of a wall to get shelter from slanting rain. There was a shell-hole in our bedroom corridor, but nobody seemed to mind.

My most vivid memories? A beaming little Professor in Barcelona surveying the shattered University and saying: 'The drugs in my laboratory are all right, so I can carry on'; the floodlights at night in Barcelona after air raids and the gangs of men working feverishly in the glare extracting bodies from the wreckage...

THOROLD DICKINSON
Sight and Sound, Spring 1938

Shooting in Spain

...Shots of this destruction figure in the two films—*Spanish A.B.C.* and *Behind the Spanish Lines*—which the units I was with went to Spain to make. The units comprised Ivor Montagu, producer; Thorold Dickinson and myself, directors; Arthur Graham and Alan Lawson, cameramen; Ray Pitt and Phillip Leacock, cutters. But our main object was not to stress such horrors as these, but rather the every-day life of a country fighting a war on its own soil, an angle that gets rather overlooked when people have become accustomed to journalistic exaggeration. When I got back I saw the English papers of that period, with such headlines as 'Barcelona In Flames'. That was wildly far from the truth. Unless you happen to wander down the particular streets that have been hit the town presents a quite normal appearance...

...We visited the front line to take shots for *Spanish A.B.C.,* because perhaps the most remarkable thing is the attention being paid to education. Spain had the highest illiteracy rate in Europe, namely 52%, and the government faced a tremendous task trying to get rid of this state of affairs. Then the war started and by the middle of the last year most of the men they had to teach were fighting in the army. They consequently formed a special department of the Ministry of Education, called the Militias of Culture, whose job it was to give classes to the soldiers. This they did, right up to and including the front line. In the Casa de Campo we visited a school where some two dozen soldiers were being taught their A.B.C. This, like the observation post, was 300 yards from the enemy trenches, and needless to say, there were no windows on the outside wall. In the nine months since the Militias of Culture started it has taught their letters to about 10,000 soldiers each month.

Madrid is no longer bombed from the air. Apparently it had proved too expensive because of the efficacy of anti-aircraft guns and fighter planes. But one lunch time we heard a factory siren, which is the usual method of air-raid warning, and dashing out into the street, we looked up and saw eight or nine black shapes in perfect formation. Everybody in the street was looking up at them. Suddenly, as we watched, the formation wavered and with a roar of laughter the Madrid crowd realised that it was a flock of wild geese, followed immediately by an enormous mass formation of about 100 more.

We had naturally to work rather quickly because it could very rarely be the case that we would have an opportunity to revisit any location. At the same time, we equally could not know exactly what material would be found at any location. Consequently after a rapid preliminary survey we had to make up our minds very quickly. It was doubtless very good training to have to justify every shot, but cypress trees and mountains kept tempting us with their possibilities.

We had with us two Newman Sinclair cameras and two Eyemos. We at times found it necessary, in shooting interiors, to use lighting which we supplied by means of photo-floods purchased in Barcelona, and run off the local power. In photographing some coalmines at a village called Meqinenza, where there was no electric supply, we had to use the miners' carbide lamps as a source of illumination and to move the miners holding them around as if they were spots on the studio floor. (The miners, by the way, gave us a grand time. The village has since been captured and most of them, I suppose, have fled or been shot.) On another occasion, in the trenches in Madrid, we very successfully used the reflectors from our lamps as sun reflectors to project light from outside the door on to the faces of the men we were photographing.

All our processing was done in Spanish laboratories, the bulk of it in Barcelona but some of it in Madrid. Owing to the shortage of stock we had to take with us our own positive stock for this purpose. In Madrid the laboratory showed us with great pride a newsreel, the picture of which had been shot on sound stock, which apart from a slight softness, was of very good quality.

A fascinating and instructive experience.

SIDNEY COLE
The Cine-Technician, May–June 1938

May 19 Film Meeting on Spain. This was a great success. The hall was packed and the audience most attentive and enthusiastic. Both middle class and working class were well represented. David Davies made an excellent speech and the film *News from Spain* was very impressive. There were yellow leaflets on every chair, recruiting posters on the walls, and a bookstall. A member did two excellent posters for the platform, and the Spanish Embassy sent over 300 free pamphlets for distribution. The Woking Labour Party were extremely pleased about the meeting and at once offered to arrange joint activities with the Group. The Labour Party agent here was most helpful in every way, particularly with the advertising. There must have been from 250 to 280 people present. Advertising was by posters, handbills, and the local press. The sale of tickets exceeded expenses by £1 10s. and there was also a collection for the National Joint Committee for Spanish Relief...

Left News, February 1938

Building the Groups

We propose to print here the substance of reports submitted to the Conference on the development of two vigorous Groups, one in an industrial and the other in a residential area:

Woking

April 6 Inaugural Meeting. Ten members were present. It was decided amongst other things to hold meetings fortnightly, alternatively, for business and discussion.

April 20 Discussion Meeting on *The Road to Wigan Pier*. Opened by members of Group. Ten members were present.

May 4 Business Meeting. Twelve members present. Circular letter to be sent to T.U.'s and other progressive organisations in the district was read and approved. Press Representative was appointed. Delegate appointed to attend L.B.C. Theatre Guild Conference. Subscription of 6d. a month from each member decided on.

May 18 Discussion Meeting. Nine members present. Member of Group read a paper proposing 'that Trade Unionism should take political action to hasten the decline of capitalism'.

PART IV

Avant-garde/Art/Criticism

Introduction

Before 1966, except for the isolated examples of Len Lye and Norman McLaren, Britain is usually represented as marked by an 'absence of avant-garde activity' in cinema; also, it is generally taken for granted that by 1930 the flourishing European avant-gardes of the 1920s had all but ceased to exist. Neither Britain nor the Thirties therefore have tended to appear in the historiography of the 'avant-garde'. However, rather than talking in terms of 'absences' it seems necessary, first, to examine the cinematic activity taking place in Britain during the Thirties, and secondly, to question some of the assumptions underlying the construction of avant-garde histories from which that activity has been excluded.

The different historical phases of the European avant-gardes met in Britain either with outright repression (e.g. Oscar Wilde) or with a gradual absorption into an already established natural culture (e.g. the Bloomsbury tradition). The lack of any articulation between vanguard artistic practices and vanguard politics in Britain was particularly noticeable throughout the Thirties: British Communist intellectuals reacted hostilely to all manifestations of 'avant-gardism', which was permanently branded as a reflection of the last phases of bourgeois decadence, and by its nature counter-revolutionary. The 'subjective stress on fantasy' in the 1936 Surrealist Exhibition, for example, was severely criticised by critics in *Left Review* despite the fact that the relationship between the theories of Marx and Freud was soon to be a topic of discussion among such enlightened circles as the Left Book Club. An alternative to this artistic/political marginality or commercial work in the advertising industry, however, was presented by the policy of the state-funded GPO Film Unit, which was represented as the location for 'experimental' work in the spirit of scientific and technical research for the progress and enlightenment of humanity. The unit was able to offer avant-garde film-makers such as Lye and McLaren a much larger public for their work than could possibly have been obtained in any 'oppositional' institution.

The relationship between Norman McLaren's 'independent' work and his GPO-sponsored work, is, however, emblematic of a tension between concerns with politics and avant-garde aesthetics during the Thirties. McLaren's work as a student at the Glasgow School of Art (1933–36) brought together the representational strategies of Eisentein and Pudovkin as well as influences from contemporary animators in the European avant-garde such as Alexandre Alexeieff and Oskar Fischinger, and the pioneering animation films of Emile Cohl. As an art student he was also a member of the Communist Party in a particularly militant region, which was able to support a thriving Workers' Film Society showing Soviet and European films to audiences of workers and intellectuals. His early work, *7 till 5* (1933) and *Camera Makes Whoopee* (1935), experimented with animation and movement, particularly in the compression of time and the movement of inanimate objects obtained through stop-frame photography reminiscent of Vertov's *Man With a Movie Camera*. During this work he also filmed newsreels of demonstrations, which were shown by the local Kino group. These concerns came together in *Hell Unltd.* (1936), made with sculptress and film-maker Helen Biggar, in which rapid montage, animation, models, stop-frame photography were used in a film designed to agitate against speculation in profits from armaments. Between Grierson seeing McLaren's films at a Scottish Amateur Film Festival and his arrival at the GPO, McLaren went to Spain as a cameraman with Ivor Montagu to produce a newsreel on the *Defence of Madrid*, which was subsequently distributed throughout Britain at political meetings and via the Left Book Club circuit. While at the GPO and the Film Centre, however, McLaren's work fell into two parts: (i) the making of a series of nondescript documentaries on, for example, the printing of the London Telephone Directory (for which attempts at a synthetic soundtrack were allegedly rejected by Calvacanti), and the advantages of cooking by gas; and (ii) animation work, including *Love on the Wing* (1938), which was banned by the Minister of Posts for being too erotic and too 'Freudian'. *Hell. Unltd.* represents an integration of political and avant-garde practices which McLaren was never able to achieve again.

The texts in this section, however, have not been selected to represent a coherent movement, to fill the 'absence' of avant-garde activities in Britain, but rather in order to allow a number of related questions to be posed: firstly, the relationship between discourses of 'film' and 'art' in the ideology of 'film as art' and 'film-maker as artist', and the contemporary connection between film and other traditionally accepted arts, such as painting; secondly, the relationship between a theoretical/critical discourse with film as its object, and a self-reflective artistic practice; thirdly, the reactions by film-makers and critics to developments in film technology such as the advent of sound and colour; fourthly, the problem of sponsorship for an art form which was still relatively expensive and generally uncommercial; fifthly, the relationship of these concerns to contemporary attitudes about politics and its relation to art; sixthly, the 'exile' sensed by those working within the terms of an 'avant-garde attitude' in England. As a final note, it should be added that it is not a question of emphasising the intrinsic importance of these diverse practices; rather it is in terms of their very historical marginality, and the gradual disintegration of the potentially subversive position afforded by such marginality, that they should be taken for consideration.

As Is

. . . And all this is very roughly, where we have arrived; a fifty fifty pull of good and bad, the time has come to know what it is all about and where it is leading and what one is to expect. Perplexities, debates, arguments. Cinematography has stuck itself in front of the artist, and the artist wants to work his medium straight. His conflict is with the business manager. He also wants HIS medium straight. The thing one sees in consequence is compromise, and the beginning of a problem. As usual there are ways and means, which we will talk about later. I want first of all to cavil a bit in a general way and work in a bit of analysis and criticism.

All this big talk, for instance about an English film revival. It is no good pretending one has any feeling of hope about it. At best it may, IF anything does eventually come of it, as one rather doubts, achieve a sort of penny in the slot success for those who are venturesome enough to back it. And I don't want particularly to be hard on England. Simply as one sees it, the sort of thing England is about to begin trying is the sort of thing Hollywood will have to be about to discard if the popularity of the cinema is to remain. England is going to start, not with any new angle, not with any experiment, to go on trundling in wake, not deplorably perhaps, one hopes efficiently, but with a complete acceptance of the film convention as is. The truth is that the average attitude of England and the English to art is so wholly nonchalant and clownish that it is quite useless to expect any art to indigenously flower there. Isolated instances may here and there crop up, but REALLY the Englishman can only be roused to enthusiasm on the football field. A cup final will evoke tens of thousands of whooping maniacs. One doesn't mind that, but in the face of it one does ask WHY attempt art? The preference between the two is so undisputable. One can see that the English revival will be exactly along old lines. They are going to imitate. And unhappily the English thing has neither the *weltgeist* quality of the German nor the exactness of the American, both of which are fundamentally national. I haven't found out quite what the English quality is, but having seen all its principal films I hesitate to try to name it.

After all, what CAN you expect? England cannot even turn out a pepful magazine. Take any weekly, and you get the sort of thing I mean, that hugely sterile flimflam decorously and expensively printed on best quality art paper, and an attitude of really awfully indecent arrogance, especially towards anything new or progressive or intelligent.

None the less, England IS going ahead on this revival, and that its sole purpose is the revival of the film INDUSTRY, and not film ART, is no sin at all, because really good art IS commercial, and the mob has a curious nose for what is good—that is, what is *real*. We know that an announcement 'British Film' outside a movie theatre will chill the hardiest away from its door, and what a pity. Why?

After all, here is England with certain excellent, not to say unsurpassed qualifications for commercial adroitness, in some of its phases, admirable achievement. Turn to films and you get muck. The reason is clear. Where England is efficient you will find there SPECIALISTS. A hard technical training, and long experience back of it. I don't say you won't find specialists in the film industry, at least one expects to now in the face of things, but I do happen to know that any specialists there may have been have probably been living on the dole while the butcher and baker and candlestick maker solemnly were taking matters into their own hands, and making sort of town hall tableaux in a local church bazaar, borrowing sometimes London's worst and ugliest actors to draw the crowd.

And, oh hell, haven't you heard enough of that wretched alms-begging attitude, 'Poor little England, how can it be expected to stand up to America where there is so much money?' What rot. One hundred pounds will make a film as noble as anything you can wish to see. Money is no excuse. Nothing is any excuse for trying to put over rotten work on the public. The public isn't a pack of fools. Narrow and illiterate very often, but there are distinct limits beyond which one cannot descend, just as, there are distinct limits beyond which one cannot ascend if one is out to grab its attention. You cannot trick and cheat your way into its favour. That is what the various butchers, bakers, etc would not learn, and what one feels, more in sorrow than in anger, the industry as a whole has

167

yet to learn before it has a dog's chance. Actually, as things are, no new country can expect to build up an industry on old lines. Mediocrity has been so utterly perfected, in Hollywood mediocrity even flashed across, now and then, with greatness, that it is rather silly to butt in there. Germany has its quality, so has France, Russia might have too, only the Soviet administration has clapped a dog-collar on its chances, and tagged it 'Slave to Soviet approval'. The point is HAS England a quality? I am rather afraid the English thing is barren, mind and super-mind and the dimensions (the only things which make for greatness) being so taboo. Oh, it's a mess. And yet one so sincerely wishes them well, but there just doesn't seem anything to say. Making their films compulsory* would be alright if they had something to show for them, but unless they scour and ransack and snap right up in every branch, it will mean only a needless loss for theatres that after all, are usually sufficiently discerning to chose what they feel will bring in money. Anyhow va bene...

KENNETH MACPHERSON
Close Up, No. 1, July 1927

Note
*A reference to the 1927 Cinematograph Films Act which established a quota of British films to be shown in cinemas each year.

The Independent Cinema Congress

An international congress of the independent cinema was held from the second to the seventh of September at the chateau of Madame de Mandrot at La Sarraz.

S. M. Eisenstein was present as delegate from Russia. He came at the last moment (the other two delegates not having been able to obtain the Swiss visa) accompanied by his assistant G. Alexandroff and his cameraman E. Tisse. Alberto Cavalcanti, Leon Moussinac, Janine Boussounouse, J. G. Auriol and Robert Aron (who was president of the congress) represented France, Walter Ruttmann, Hans Richter and Bela Balazs came from Germany (Pabst was prevented from being present), J. Isaacs* and Ivor Montagu from England, Montgomery-Evans from the United States, F. Rosenfeld from Austria, Prampolini and Sartoris from Italy, M. Franken from Holland, Moituro Tsuytja and Hijo from Japan, Caballero from Spain, and from Switzerland Guye, Schmitt, Kohler and Masset.

There were several difficulties at the beginning. The nature of the independent film (formerly *avant-garde* film) was not understood in the same way by the different members of the Congress. For example, Hans Richter was rather perturbed that Pabst had been invited, for, said he, Pabst made 'spielfilms', i.e. films with plot and action, with professional actors. It was clear that only absolute and abstract films could be denominated independent films.

It has often enough been pointed out that the absolute film is definitely a genre of cinema interesting in itself, but at once an error if it is considered as the only possible manifestation of cinema, that is to say as soon as cause and effect are confused. It seems to me negligible and of secondary importance whether a film is made with living or inanimate objects if it has its own integrity.

At last a basis was found. A practical discussion became possible. The results of this discussion are the creation of an International League of Independent Cinema and of a co-operative of production. The League will have for its principal aim distribution among the already existing clubs (such as the Film Society or Film Liga)** and the creation of films of note. Naturally the films produced by the co-operative will be contained in the programmes of these clubs. The League will also distribute current films which for one reason or another could not be released in the commercial theatres, on the condition, of course, that their cinegraphic value justifies the idea.

Most important, though not always of the most practical value, is the contact of various groups all over the world whose aim is the furtherance of good films.

It was decided also to send a petition to the Institut International Intellectuel at Rome, asking for favourable conditions in respect of censorship and quota for films of the co-operative and those which the League will distribute; a justifiable demand, since these productions will be confined to a public already educated and intelligent, and able to furnish sufficient guarantee of moral responsibility.

The big event was the arrival of S. M. Eisenstein, who the next day made a little film, in which all members of the congress played a rôle, a short comedy which will incidentally be the first production of the co-operative.

The enthusiasm of Eisenstein was so infectious that all the serious minded were tempted to forget their dignity and do as he instructed.

I shall not speak here of Eisenstein himself, who so greatly changed the aspects of the congress, but I should in any event like to proclaim my admiration for this splendidly youthful man who has to his credit *Potemkin, Ten Days* and *The General Line*.

We must now wait for the results of the congress. But in spite of a vivid scepticism which I maintain always toward any sort of congress, very little was said (which is well enough, since it at least prevents the usual *bêtises*) and it is to be hoped that the goodwill of all these different beings, who all more or less pursue the same ends, will lance itself strongly enough to be a real creative force.***

JEAN LENAUER
Close Up, Vol. 5, No. 4, October 1929

Notes
*Professor Jack Isaacs, a founder member of the London Film Society.

**Film Liga/Filmliga: a Dutch organisation similar to the London Film Society, formed in 1927 to show Soviet films to audiences under club conditions and 'artistic' auspices.

***For further information on this Congress, see I. Montagu, *With Eisenstein in Hollywood*, Berlin 1968.

Moreover, as Peter Wollen remarked in *The Two Avant-Gardes* (*Edinburgh Magazine* '76) the meeting at La Sarraz 'turned out to mark the end rather than the beginning of an epoch'. When after the war the French and Swiss film society movements set up a series of conferences explicitly referring back to La Sarraz as their point of departure, they called it the CICI—Congresses, thus tactfully masking the fundamental policy-shift they had introduced.

Instead of a Congrès International du Cinéma Indépendant, we now have, every year, a Congrès Indépendant du Cinéma International. It is obviously much simpler to label a Congress independent (of what?) than to have to face the difficult problem of independence in cinema. By this sleight of hand, the organisers are now able to exploit the prestigious aura of La Sarraz while aiming their conferences directly against the very cinema Eisenstein, Richter, etc were calling for, replacing it with a blatant celebration of the most dubious aspects of cinephiliac gratification.

Scrutiny
By the Editor

With the exception of two London cinemas there is not in England, as far as we know, a single cinema which has a record for showing consistently films which are not primarily made with an eye on the box-office. If, by chance, a cinema happens to show *Kameradschaft* or *Mädchen in Uniform* one week, it shows *Blonde Venus* or *Rockabye* the next. The film public is treated as one, as if two book lovers who read Ethel M. Dell and James Joyce, respectively, were of the same mental capacity. To attempt to force intelligent films on a sensation seeking public would be ridiculous. There will always be a public for crime novels; similarly will there always be one for Glamorous All-Star movies.

Rather than attempt to destroy a sensation seeking public, we wish to create a new one. This second public has, in the past, remained silent; now it is hoped it will speak.

Only the narrow commercialised minds of the big entrepreneurs of cinema entertainment, confine good cinema going to such organisations as film societies.

The commercialisation of any art is its downfall, for commercialism disregards any aesthetic significance, and judges a product by its popularity in the field it caters for. The present day universally shown film is a totally unimaginative performance. A film is not to be despised because it makes money. The film to despise (and it forms the bulk of present day cinema) is that in which characters and incidents are given a vulgar glamour which is unlike life, and which is an insult to any standard of intelligence.

The public which is potentially interested in good films and which, furthermore, does not want to see inferior films at all, requires a certain amount of organisation and a guide. This, we feel, is part of our job. *Film* is not going to devote a certain amount of incidental space to good cinema, but is going to be entirely devoted to the film as an art. We shall seek a film-form, and attempt to solve problems which prevent a realisation of that film-form.

In our criticism we shall remain unbiased, and shall only consider the films which have a definite significance to film art. Although the film, or films, may, on the whole, be bad, we shall consider them if we think they will help our readers to understanding those things which constitute cinema in its purest form.

The publication of this quarterly is an entirely independent one. It has no outside financial backing whatsoever. We have issued this publication at a price that will just pay for its production, and we ask our readers to introduce it to anyone to whom they think its contents and purpose might be of interest.

B. BRAUN
Film, No. 1, Spring 1933

The Principles of the Film

Although artistic beliefs demand that knowledge of theory should be unconscious, it is a pity that both practical and theoretical workers should demonstrate this faith in print. The practical man of the film world has the same contempt for film theory as the village blacksmith has for theoretical metallurgy. Both know they can turn out better work than the theorists, and both prove the uselessness of theories by brandishing their own.

Some conflict between practical and theoretical tendencies is essential for sound achievement, but in the cinema the conflict is partly due to the fact that neither theorist nor applicant seem to know what a theory is, and what it can, or cannot do. Another cause of trouble is the general belief that film theory began and ended with Kuleshoff's attack on the principles of construction. To prevent better brains wasting time by upsetting the already unstable Kuleshoffian Aunt Sally, this article attempts to sum up the development of film theory to the present day.

There is a qualitative difference between the film of to-day, and the film of, say, twelve years ago, quite apart from the presence of sound. This is not due to any change in the themes, which remain one or other of the immortal three, nor to technical advances affecting technique. The only two technical developments worthy of notice, apart from the invention of photographic cinematography, are the camera truck (first used in Swedish films in about 1918, but too generally adopted after the success of Dupont's *Vaudeville*), and the addition of sound. The former had the more profound influence on the nature of films, for it helped to distinguish a film from the stage and the lantern lecture.

The film of to-day differs from the film of yesterday in the theoretical principles of its construction, and this difference is greater than that caused by the coming of sound. The film of the past was a photographed stage play. It would have remained so— the public found it adequate—but for the fact that films have to be made. The actual making of a film, as opposed to its inception, demands intelligence and technical ability, which implies, in spite of contemporary social mythology, some artistic qualifications. Thus it comes about that, though mostly the film industry exists by doing well what is not worth doing at all, the theory of film construction possesses a certain narrow and thumby thoroughness.

The number of formulated theories is in excess of the number of theorists, but the principles affecting general practice have been evolved from them and from experiment—or fashion. In practice they work fairly adequately but, owing to their fundamental unsoundness, they can only be applied to immediate problems. Like all machine-shop theories, they are almost useless for prediction or for other than routine problems. Their effect is natural, for the problem of film construction has been attacked before investigating the formal properties of the material. In fact the material has never even been described.

Until recently a film was made by placing

the camera in the front row of the stalls, and then presenting to the audience a potted version of the camera's evening out. The film was a two-dimensional monochromatic version of the stage, sometimes enlivened by camera tricks. Well done it was terribly boring, but at its worst was excellent entertainment, till shackled by dialogue.

Dramatic episodes, linked by redundant and sometimes explanatory lettering, were the basis of the film till well after the War. They would be still, frozen stiffer by acoustic technique, if the technicians had not unconsciously evolved a new conception. It is worth noting that progress comes first in the short film, generally the 'comic', where experiments are looked at as legitimate eccentricity. This is particularly noticeable at the moment.

The credit for the new conception cannot be given to any one man. It was actually articulated by Kuleshoff, in 1920. The principle was simple and obvious, but ran athwart the idea of the film as a theatrical record with elaborate settings. In it the strips of film, or rather, the visual impressions resulting therefrom were the material only. They had only visual significance. The image of an elephant walking down the street was an image of an elephant walking down the street, nothing more. Intellectual significance, ever the most direct, was formed by the relations of an image to the other images forming the film; like the letters of a word, they had significance in combination not deducible from their separate meanings. The making of a film was supposed to begin, after the photography, with the cutting and editing. It was the subjection of the camera by the Sickle. Eisenstein added the Hammer later.

In Kuleshoff's view the recording of incident was a preliminary, the film incident being synthetized from the records as sentences are from words. Some of his demonstrations were crude but amusing, and may be unfamiliar to the uninitiated. In one he created the impression of a moving woman by consecutive presentation of close-ups of the arms, legs, head, and body of different women, photographed at different times and in different places. In another, a shot was made of an actor looking at something off the screen. This was placed in three parts of the film where it was followed by shots of a plate of food, a dead man, and a woman respectively. Although the actor had the same neutral expression on his face in all three shots, the audience was impressed by his acting, or so the story goes. Thus 'stars' are made.

The virtue of this theory of construction was that it recognized the film as depending more on the interaction of its parts than on the content of the parts themselves. This merit was, and is still, obscured by lack of clear thought in its exposition. As usual, the implicit assumption was made that the film consists of strips of celluloid. It was also implied that a visual event was altered only in duration by shortening its celluloid equivalent, as if a man were only altered in height by having his head cut off.

None of these errors alter the truth of the importance of ordinal relations, and the lack of importance of the camera as such, but these were the errors which were hailed as the basis of the theory. Their cruder manifestations, unlike those of the theatrical film, were not amusing. In the more esoteric circle appeared films so crammed with irrelevant shots, giving alleged significance by contrast or comparison, that there was some suspicion that they were put in to make it more difficult. Though there is no *a priori* objection to shots in negative or upside down, they require some justification.

In Dziga Vertov's *The Man with the Movie Camera* the cameraman himself is shown at work, a scene as factitious as anything in a *spielfilm*. This part of the theory, the Kino-Eye, can never be carried into practice, for 'real' material is inevitably manipulated by the very process of obtaining it. Which side of the lens the manipulation takes place is a matter of indifference.

Because of the increasing importance of the documentary film, it is as well to clear up the error in Vertov's dichotomy. The clue lies in the fact that a 'real photograph' has no more significance than an artist's picture to an audience *having no previous acquaintance with the photographic process*. 'Actuality' is not a fundamental property, but a relation between film and audience of precisely the same order as slow motion, which demands previous knowledge of natural motion to give its peculiar effect.

The value of Vertov's work does not lie in his theory of the Kino-Eye, but in his theory of the assembly of film. Having no control over the secondary visual characteristics of the material he collected, he was forced to make the interaction of the content of the film events more powerful than their appearance. This was done by impressing a more or less temporal metric on the film, to echo, emphasize, or run contrapuntal to the intellectual relations. The principle was used by Eisenstein in *Ten Days that Shook the World*, and for the first time with sound, to which the method is peculiarly applicable, in Milestone's *All Quiet on the Western Front*.

When the metrical construction was over-applied it destroyed itself. It is possible to inflict on the film temporal relations so complicated that they can only be ascertained by measuring up the celluloid with a footrule, but they are not necessarily rhythms. Also the visual content must be considered. Film rhythm is spatial as well as temporal, and the duration of a shot and its visual content interact on each other. In fact, the duration of the film events can only be controlled before they are made. Understanding would be helped by some term implying both *pattern* and *rhythm*.

From such considerations Eisenstein arrived at his idea of Overtonal Montage. The theory, as stated by the originator, is somewhat complex. So complex, indeed, that one suspects it of being an explanation rather than a tool. This may be so, but does not affect the value of the theory, which is considerable, or its truth, which is at least partial.

Briefly, Eisenstein recognizes a hierarchy of methods of assembly. These will be referred to as montage methods, with the understanding that the montage is not to be confused with film splicing. Each montage operates on the results of the last in such a way as to co-ordinate the significances of the action with the visual qualities of the images. Going up the series the significances concerned become more diffuse, and the co-ordinated visual qualities intrinsic rather than predominant. It is worth noting that the visual, not the pictorial qualities, are those considered. The film image cannot possess pictorial qualities as commonly understood, for it has both duration and direction in time. It is a visual event, not a picture—not even a moving picture.

Kuleshoff's synthesis of a woman is an example of the lowest order of montage. The order and predominant characteristics of the events were combined to achieve the immediate purpose of the film, the representation of a woman. The next step is to combine the result of the last so as to fit the durations into the dramatic action. *This is Metric Montage*. Above this is formed the metric of the metric, or rhythm, which combines the significance of the action with the motions in the ordered film images. Above the rhythmic lies the tonal montage, of which a purely spatial example is the deliberate use of 'camera angle'. We are now free of any superstition that the film can be made at the cutting desk. The final stage is what Eisenstein calls Overtonal Montage, the analogy being with the musical theories of Scriabin and Debussy. In it the screen images are treated as psychical stimuli having no individual significance, only their integrated effect being subjected to the process of montage. The direct action of the film is carried by the dominant qualities of the images, while the significance and appeal are conveyed by the summation of diffuse qualities below the level of awareness. In much the same way a printer uses different type faces, whose distinctive appearance is due to the summation of minute differences separately unnoticed by the reader. There is a verbal parallel in the methods of James Joyce.

Concentration on the more diffuse qualities of film components, rather than on the still fundamental primary qualities of action and duration, has led to a very great apparent simplification of the rhythmic structure. At its best, the rhythmic construction could give a flavour of Bach to the film, at its worst it produced a kinetic patchwork. Only in an abstract film should the structure overshadow the content.

Though the pragmatic correctness of overtonal montage is a matter of experience, and though it seems to be a necessary consequence of the properties of film material, the greatest objection to it, as used by Eisenstein, is that it is frankly hypnotic. If the hypnosis is unsuccessful there is an emotional dislike to the film. Thus *The General Line*, which dealt with the unemotional and almost politically neutral subject of collective farming, caused greater commotion in this country than frankly revolutionary films like *The End of St. Petersburg*. Possibly this is only a defect of present day Soviet mentality, or is intrinsic in the nature of the purpose for which such films are made. The method certainly seems to attract propagandists of all countries and creeds.

Since the statement of Overtonal Montage, theory has remained inarticulate, though there is evidence of the growth of a purely practical and implicit understanding of film material. The coming of sound led to a number of wild statements, by courtesy, theoretical. They are not worth comment, or the trouble of looking them up, as they made no attempt to analyse the nature of the visual-acoustic. Although a visual event combined with an acoustic event is something more than the sum of the two, the formal qualities of the combination can be understood from study of the formal properties of the components and the nature of the cross relations between them. The mildly mathematical will see the analogy with complex numbers. The comparative structural simplicity of acoustic events makes them most suitable for controlled use in the higher orders of the Eisenstein montage hierarchy.

On the constructive side film theory of to-day is useful without being theoretical. The few feeble attempts at fundamental analysis are too ludicrous for criticism. The absurdity of 'motion composition' implies that there is no distinction between the beginning and end of a film event, and theories that cannot see anything odd in a film run backwards, should be rejected at sight.

A worse fault in practice, is the lack of research into available material. The range of the film is all visual and acoustic experience. Even visual experience is by no means confined to the representational. This article is visual experience, if nothing else, but it is not representational. Possible visual material ranges from the abstract pattern event (a somewhat ideal conception) having sharp visual and diffuse intellectual significances, to the verbal typographic events, having sharp intellectual and diffuse visual significances. The classification of visual and acoustic material can be left, in the manner of text books, as an exercise for the reader. No distinction can be made between 'documentary' and 'studio' shots in a fundamental classification, for the distinction depends on a relation between film and audience.

The only film theorist to use non-representational methods was *Felix the Cat*. His habit of interchanging typographical symbols with reality was probably a manifestation of the scientific and the economic spirit of the age.

In conclusion, a prediction. In about eight years stereoscopy, variable screen openings, colour, and the like, will have ruined film achievement by finding the practical men of the cinema influenced by *fashion* instead of *understanding*. A small, but dreadful, example is the current fashion in scene changing. There are two conventions —the Sternbergian sleepy sickness mix, and the British geometrical wipe of the duster. Apparently the employers of these methods are so blind to the basic principles of the cinema film that they fail to realise the transition from one scene to another to be a separate scene in itself.

ROBERT FAIRTHORNE
Film, No. 1, Spring 1933

Manifesto on the Documentary Film

Years ago the documentary film had value because it presented us with facts: from the documents of four or five years ago it was possible to learn.

We believed, then, that the document film had a vigorous and rigorous future: the clearer presentation of valuable information seemed to define the development of the filmic documentary.

Alas! A camorra of folk on the fringe of moviedom discovered, when talkies came in, that they could no longer afford to finance their own movies: but how desperately they wanted to go on telling their friends that they were in the movies, how pathetically they wanted to horde up a few more lines of print from the trade papers. So, they turned to the film document, realising that this less expensive genre of movie, which can be shot silent and post-synched, offered them their last chance to remain 'directors'.

All the same, these hangers-on did not intend, and were not capable of adhering to the logical and excellent formula of the document. Their shoddy minds were too muddled and doped with meretricious theatricalities to work with the purity of the real film document. They brought to the document outmoded montage belonging to a certain type of emotional drama, and their yards of theatre tinsel, in the form of joking commentaries, together with the rest of their aged properties. The result is that we now have documents about the making of a gramophone which are filled with trick angles and ultra rapid sections of montage, and which teach us nothing at all about the actual process of gramophone manufacture. We have travel documents which string together all the arty 'nookies', the against-the-sky shots of prognathous natives and tree-top silhouettes, while not the slightest attempt is made to catalogue scientifically the customs, flora, mineralogical structure, etcetera, of the country.

Probably, someone will try to twist our manifesto into a statement that a film without artistes cannot be dramatic: but we hold that a film without actors can be intensely dramatic, and also that the document has nothing to do with drama. We want back film documents with real cultural significance. We are infuriated with pseudo-documents which exploit the prestige of the worthwhile documentaries of yesterday: their obscene dramatic over-layer abolishes their worth for the scholar, the lack of imagination of their directors guarantees their failure as drama.

It would be easy to make a dramatic film without artistes—easy for a Francis Bruguière.* In his stills, Bruguière has shown how he can send the horses from an Italian painting thudding across the head of a Grecian statue, or how the spire of an English Cathedral can come to life and penetrate the shadow of a Florentine doorway. Inanimate objects or landscapes can be given, by the camera of a Bruguière, fibres, nerves, arteries, personalities, can be made to take part in a truly magic drama. Such a film would have no need to pose as a document—it would have its own possession.

To repeat: we are incensed because films are shown to the public, who are always about five years behind and have just dimly associated 'document' with 'culture', under false prestige and false pretences: were these films to be presented to the public as drama, the exhibitors would be lynched.

To repeat: we want documents which will show, with the clarity and logic of a scholar's thesis, the subjects they are supposed to tackle: we want no more filtered skies, 'Russian' montage and other vulgarities in our 'educational' productions.

OSWELL BLAKESTON
Close Up, Vol. 10, No. 4, December 1933

Note:
*A Belgian photographer with whom Blakeston made the abstract film *Light Rhythms* in 1930.

Film: Definition

The real film is a visual poem.

The real film is the representation of incidents and emotions by moving masses of light variations.

It is the expression *through cinematic form* of the matters or emotions to be expressed.

Poetry is only seldom a subjection of everything to verbal abstraction. Poems can, and do, represent a series of incidents or a story. That the ideal film is a poem in visualness does not mean an incidentless or a storyless film. Film is the cinematic representation of a certain emotion, theme or story. The principles of all may be found in a representation of one. A story film often contains abstract sequences. The abstract film is the emotion-film. It does not rely in any way on its subject matter which is merely a medium through which is expressed the desired emotion. Children laughing, rain on water, corn waving, and a saw cutting wood may all be one logical sequence, perhaps representing joy or exhilaration.

Montage is film editing done constructively. Exactly *when* and *where* each single shot is begun and ended. In a film a scene is meaningless by itself. When mounted, when put with other scenes, it has meaning.

Film is not a representation of reality. If it

174

was it would not be art. Nor does this infer that to make a film an art film it must be distorted and made as unreal as possible. If that was so, show everything out of focus! It is the unavoidable (but advantageous) principles of the film which separate it from nature, and make it art. For instance, time and space in cinema know no limitations. In reality time and space are impossible to manipulate. In film they are always being manipulated. That's why we everlastingly talk about montage and say montage montage montage and montage again. Because it is montage (constructive film editing) that is, (in the words of Robert Fairthorne), *the manipulation of (this) sequence and duration to create the desired effect.*

Finally, film is a visual medium. And the visual is the most powerful of all our senses. Through the visual sense may be expressed any other sense. This must be done in film; all our senses must be expressed through the visual one.

B. VIVIAN BRAUN

Film Art, No. 2, Winter 1933

Half a Year of Film Art

... This—*Film Art*—was the outcome of a two hour talk in a Chelsea café on the seventeenth of March 1933.

We were discussing (strange as it seems) films.

In particular the hopelessness of the film position from an artistic point of view. The present day film.

Commercialism gone mad.

And then we talked of the glories of independent cinema.

When the director is a creator, a poet building up his material, and manifesting his ideals, and making a film that was— whatever else it might be—a creative effort.

And we realised (probably a little late) that there was such a thing as a second film public. That there were people in England, continental Europe and America who were

interested in film as art. A minority, certainly, but a minority of millions.

And then we decided (far too late) to do something about it.

All very nice—but what?

And very suddenly we thought—a magazine.

Not just 'a magazine' but something more.

Something that would do more than talk.

Something that stood for ACTION.

AN INTERNATIONAL REVIEW THAT WOULD ACT AS A MANIFESTO TO THE ADVANCE-GUARD FILM MOVEMENTS OF THE WORLD.

Vital in its very aspect.

Always in contact with its readers. CONTACT. And co-operation. Two essentials.

And a review that could, if necessary, damn all commercialism and thus raise higher its own pedantic ideals.

We choose the name *film art* (*film* first), and that alone was a definite title. The 'art' probably frightened some people, but only those of the wrong kind.

We immediately laid down rules.

As non-political as possible, for example, but also that articles would be printed as received, except when space demanded cutting.

Another thing we made definite:

OUR DESIRE WOULD NOT BE TO DESTROY THE ORDINARY (SENSATION-LOVING) PUBLIC BUT TO CREATE A NEW ONE ...

... We began planning.

An advance-guard cinema must be opened and advance-guard films must be made.

These are still in existence (I mean the plans).

But we meant to carry theory into practice. We will, D.V. ...

First let us take the film situation.

The things the (what we will call for want of a better name) artistic cinema are going to need are stimulance, encouragement and support.

Except on substandard (i.e. film smaller than that used in cinemas), films are too expensive to be made and never shown or shown at only one or two cinemas only. And even substandard is very expensive.

The new cinema public (for it is a *new* public; there will always be a large audience for sensational theatre-on-celluloid presentations of sex, murder, war, comedy, etc. just as in the book world the blood-and-thunder novel will always have its readers), must be collected, informed and guided in order that the genuinely good film may be supported. But good films (i.e. modern ones; one cannot re-issue for ever) are very scarce and therefore those making them need all possible encouragement and support. All this, and a lot more, we feel, is part of our job...

Film Art exists
TO ANALYSE THE POTENTIALITIES AND SOLVE THE AESTHETIC PROBLEMS OF CINEMA ART.

TO SUPPORT ANY ARTISTIC FILM MOVEMENT, SOCIETY, GROUP, CLUB, CINEMA, OR INDIVIDUAL WHOSE AIMS ARE SIMILAR TO OUR OWN.

TO PRESENT THE WRITINGS, THEORIES, REVIEWS, AND OPINIONS OF BOTH WORLD-FAMOUS AND UNKNOWN PERSONS, AND TO PRESENT THEM EXACTLY AS STATED HOWEVER OUTSPOKEN OR REVOLUTIONARY.

TO ENCOURAGE THE USE OF THE CINEMA AS A SOCIAL REFORMER, AS A MEANS FOR INTERNATIONAL UNDERSTANDING AND FOR GENERAL EDUCATION.

These, briefly, are our aims and desires.

If we ever make a fortune we shall organise groups for making artistic films and organise cinemas for showing them.

Already our contributors include some of the greatest film directors in the world, and we soon hope to print articles by such directors as Dovzhenko, Turin, Vertov, etc.

We also propose to increase the number of pages and print many more illustrations as time goes on.

But to acquire influence we must increase our circulation.

And so may we ask our readers to join us in making *film art* known throughout the world, and known not only for what it is but also for what it hopes to accomplish, by introducing it to any and everyone who they think will be interested in this—'review of the advance-guard cinema'.

B. VIVIAN BRAUN

Film Art, No. 3, Spring 1934

OPEN LETTER from Moholy-Nagy*

To the Film Industry and to all who are interested in the evolution of the good film

Shall we look on while the film, this wonderful instrument, is being destroyed before our eyes by stupidity and a dull-witted amateurism?

The unbiased observer cannot fail to see, to his great distress, that the film production of the world is growing more and more trivial every year. To the trained eye and mind the present-day film can give no pleasure.

This criticism is not confined to the artistic side of film-making. The whole film industry is in danger. This is shown by its increasing incapacity to produce a financial return. Gigantic sums are swallowed up by desperate experiments, extravagance in superficial matters not strictly proper to the film; monster decorations, piling up of stars, paying huge salaries to secure performers who turn out unsuitable for filming. This expenditure will never bring in its return, so that the film is slipping back with increasing certainty into the hands of the adventurers, from whom it had been rescued after its initial period of being a purely speculative business.

II.

The root of all evil is the exclusion of the experimental film creator, of the free independent producer.

III.

Yesterday there were still crowds of pioneers in all countries; to-day the whole field is made a desert, mown bare. But art can know no further development without the artist, and art requires full sovereignty over the means to be employed. Every work of art attains its achievement only through the responsible activity of the artist, driven to his objective by his vision of the whole. This is true of architecture, of painting, of drama. It is equally true of the film, and cannot be otherwise.

IV.

From the nature of the film arises the difficulty of experimentation, the nursery garden of good film work; for to the film there is attached a machinery of production and distribution, the organisation of which

176

stretches from the scenario through acting, photography, sound recording, direction, and film-cutting up to press propaganda, leasing and cinema halls. Only thus could what was once a side-show at a fair be converted into a world-wide business. Amongst the economic complications of this enormous machine the artistic aspect is treated so incidentally, judged so entirely from the mercantile standpoint, that the significance of the creative artist of the film is completely eliminated. One might almost say the director is forced through fear of penalisation to do without the cinematograph art. By becoming part of the prevailing system of production, even the best pioneers have, to the bitter disappointment of all those interested in films, sunk to the level of the average director. The independent producers were an embarrassment to the industry. The existence of the pioneers implied a destructive criticism of official production. The vitality of the small works, their faith in the cinematographic art, while hardly removing mountains, did box the ears of the industry soundly. They swung out for a counter-blow without realising the soundness of these pioneer movements, their effort to press forward on the artistic side. So the industry carefully stamped out anything which was even suggestive of pioneer effort. Their crowning victory was found in the necessity of specially constructed buildings for sound-film production and showing, and consequently the final business monopolisation of the 'art of the film'.

V.

The way was freed once more for mechanised business. The industry was victorious all along the line.

Everything contributed to help them; legislation regulations concerning quotas and import restrictions, censorship, leasing, cinema owners and short-sighted critics. But the victory of the industry has been a costly one. Art was to be destroyed in the interests of business, but the boomerang has whizzed back and struck the business side. People do not go to boring films, in spite of the calculation of returns made by the film magnate on the theory that every adult *must* visit the cinema twice weekly at an average price of so many cents, pennies, pfennigs or sous, per ticket.

VI.

Shall the artist now, after all the kicks he has received, turn round and help the business side to think? Shall he take a hand again, and beg with economic arguments for the weapons of the spirit that were struck from his hands?

VII.

Good, we will do so.
Now *we* start estimating profits.

VIII.

The culture of the film grew with the onlooker. History records no similar process of general passive participation, extending to all nations and continents, in an applied art and its development to that relating to the cinema. By the numerically enormous part played in human life generally by attendance at cinemas, even the most primitive member of an audience is in a position to exercise criticism of the film and register any slackening of creative interest. This means the necessity of straining every nerve in creative work. But where is that work to come from, if the artist is to be excluded from the creative process?

IX.

A pioneer group is thus not only an artistic but an economic necessity.

X.

All barriers against pioneer effort must therefore be removed. Encouragement, private, industrial and official, must therefore be extended to the independent cinematograph artist.

XI.

This means that we demand for him:—
(1) From the State
    (a) Removal of censorship restrictions.
    (b) No taxation on his creations.
    (c) Payment of allowances.
(2) From the industry, in accordance with output
    (a) Studio
    (b) Sound
    (c) Material
    (d) Obligatory performances by leasing agents and theatres.
(3) Education in artistic film work must be begun long before the practical side. The antiquated art school curriculum must be replaced by the establishment of
    (a) Studios for lighting (artificial light)
    (b) Photo and film studios (camera technique)

(c) Dramatic classes

(d) Theoretical, physical and experimental departments.

XII.

To formulate and fight for these demands is terribly necessary at the present time, for our generation is beginning to exploit without initiative or talent the magnificent technical heritage of the previous century. It remains to be hoped that these statements of opinion will remind a few, at least, of the intellectual problems which the conscience of the thinking man bids him solve.

Sight and Sound, Vol. 3, No. 10, Summer 1934

Note

*Moholy-Nagy was one of several artists who arrived in England in the mid to late Thirties. He had shown his film *ABC of Sound* to the London Film Society in 1934 and moved to London the next year where he stayed until 1937 when the new Bauhaus was founded in Chicago. An exhibition of his work was held in London which was extensively discussed in *Film Art*, and he also published an article called *Problems of the Modern Film* in B. Vivian Braun's magazine *New Cinema* in 1936.

Manifesto: Dialogue on Sound*
Its proper use in film

Wright: First we must realise that films have always been sound-films, even in the silent days. The bigger the orchestra the better the film appeared.

Vivian Braun: Quite. And now that talk has been made possible, do you consider it as good an adjunct as music?

W: No, because a good 'talkie' is a stage-play possibly improved by the mechanical advantages of the camera, e.g. pans, close-ups, cutting, etc.

V.B: You mean that 'talkies' are not films?

W: 'Talkies' are technically film, but cinematically they are not.

V.B: Then the only thing to do is to separate 'talkies' and sound-films into different categories from the start.

W: Yes, and so we need not discuss 'talkies' any further, let's go on to sound-film proper. To begin with, what do the aesthetes say about sound-film?

V.B: A great deal. Firstly they crack up contrapuntal sound and sound imagery as grand artistic effects.

I believe this was originally due to a typical aesthetic reaction when the talking film first came; they refused to recognise them, quite rightly, and then when a year had passed and talking films had not wilted under their disapproval they went to the other extreme.

W: Yes, I remember the hanging scene in *The Virginian*** came in for a lot of praise.

V.B: Still the aesthetes (I am never quite clear as to who these folk are) have a good deal on their side.

W: Of course they have; most of the opinions are good solid cinema theory, but the difficulty is that they are unaware of this. It doesn't harm the theory, but it vitiates the practice.

V.B: Well perhaps we had better analyse the advantages of sound and in particular the advantages of sound imagery, if any, and counterpoint.

W: But we must not forget that the film is visual, so much so that the perfect film should be satisfactory from every point of view without sound and, therefore, shown in complete silence.

V.B: BUT THIS IS NOT TO SAY THAT THE PERFECT FILM COULD NOT BE SUPER-PERFECTED BY THE USE OF SOUND AS AN ADJUNCT.

W: The use of sound imagistically, the cross-cutting of sound and visuals (counterpoint) can undoubtedly be effective, but this does not mean to say that good visuals could not get the same effect more legitimately—in fact I begin to wonder if sound has any advantage at all.

V.B: Yes it has. It can and does undoubtedly intensify the effect of visuals. But it does not necessarily create that effect. The wrong sound (so powerful is sound) can kill the image.

W: Yes, and I happen to have seen my pet sequence killed stone dead by the addition of Bach's music which happens to be better than any film yet made. It killed my visuals because it was too powerful.

V.B: Which reminds us that one of the most potent arts is sound.

W: What do we mean by sound in connection with film?

178

V.B: Before you start your film you have available every sound in the world from the lark's song to Mae West's voice, to the Jupiter symphony to the internal combustion engine.

W: And the human voice is no greater in value than any other sound.

V.B: When synchronising your film you select, from all the sounds, those you require.

If you put natural sound corresponding to visual image, and in particular concentrate on the human voice, you make a 'talkie'.

W: If you put any natural sound which doesn't correspond with the visual action, you make a dull highbrow film!

V.B: If you make a good visual film which is self-contained without any sound, you will find that the only sound which will really intensify your visuals is abstract sound.

W: Music is abstract.

V.B: But music confines itself, very rightly, to noises produced by a limited number of special instruments. You are at liberty to orchestrate any sound in the world.

W: Once orchestrated they will become as abstract as music. Orchestrated abstract sound is the true accompliment to film.

It can intensify the value of, say, an aeroplane in flight in a way which natural aeroplane sound could not achieve—

V.B: Because natural sound is uncontrolled. No art is uncontrolled. Abstract sound is completely controlled by the artist, in this case the director of the film.

The director must create his sound as well as his visuals, and as he cannot create natural sound he must orchestrate it for his own purpose.

W: When he can do this as well as Cézanne orchestrated nature onto canvas, the first film will have been made.

BASIL WRIGHT—B. VIVIAN BRAUN

Film Art, No. 3, Spring 1934

Note
*The 'dialogue' was published while Wright was working on his GPO film *Song of Ceylon* (1934) for which the sound synchronisation was to be 'a problem calling for very solid experimentation in sound technique' (*Cinema Quarterly*, Summer 1934). The film was eventually accorded the status of an 'art' film, playing only certain art-houses and the non-theatrical circuit.

**The Virginian* was directed by Victor Fleming, USA 1929, starring Gary Cooper.

Reply to letter by
H. P. J. Marshall*

The direct mixing of politics and art is fatal. Politics is one thing, art another. But this is not to pretend that art is not influenced (BUT NOT DICTATED BY) by current affairs and goings-on. But to Marshall only the thing that is said matters. How it is said matters not. But the Soviet cinema, that terrific, dynamic and (at its best) aesthetically superb affair is a great cinema not merely because it glorifies a political issue, but because it gives to its subject matter FORM. CINEMATIC FORM. If Eisenstein were a fascist his films would be just as magnificent as are his present (communist) ones.

It is the one thing the American cinema lacks—this application of form. Cinema—different speeds of cutting, camera angles, tones of photography, panning, trolleying, SOUND, and all the other components of film are used without thought and without reason.

Marshall says 'so at the rock-bottom we come to *purpose*—one must choose that and everything follows'. Therefore a stage play-on-celluloid which propagates the clearance of slums is, of necessity, a great film? (and an aesthetic work—since we are discussing film, an art form).

Film Art is not, and never will be, a political paper so we will not discuss the advantages or disadvantages of communism, but Marshall's letter should have been labelled 'The underlying purpose and conception of the Soviet film'.

Film can be the cinematic presentation of a certain theme. That theme may be communist, fascist or (and heaven knows how often it is) capitalist. The political trend of the film does not interfere with its merits or demerits, although we would be the last to deny its significance in its relation to everyday life. But is a painting which serves as propaganda for an 'anti-litter'

179

campaign necessarily greater than one which depicts, say, a dockyard scene, because the former happens to have a deliberate social value?

The American film (hardly art, I know) is, and this is quite obvious, the outcome of a social system *in its meaning*, but if America suddenly became a communist country, would every Hollywood film automatically become a great work of cinema just because the whole meaning behind the films would be changed?

B. VIVIAN BRAUN

Film Art, No. 3, Spring 1934

Note
*Braun replies to a letter published in *Film Art* No. 2, Winter 1933 by Herbert Marshall, who was then a senior foreign student at the State Film School (GIK) in the Soviet Union studying under Eisenstein. Marshall was also the Russian 'correspondent' for *Film Art*.

The Future of Documentary*

The recent successes of Documentary Films in the ordinary cinemas have made a great difference in the approach to the subject of the sponsor, the financier and the producer. There is a growing feeling that there is something in the documentary racket after all. The development of organisations such as Strand Films and Associated Realist Film Producers, coordinating all the directors of Documentary Films under one banner, is an important step forward.** It ensures that the quality of Documentary Films, in this country at any rate, will keep to reasonably high level.

For the future there are two problems. First—what will be the main lines of production? Second—where exactly is Documentary going to find its permanent public?

Production
The primary interest of the true Documentary Director is sociological. But the finance for a sociological subject is in general only to be found from either a Government Department or a big Corporation, which have begun to realise the

value of 'Public Relations' as opposed to direct advertisement or propaganda. Indeed even in smaller firms which cannot claim to be public service corporations, the same sociological opportunities may be found.

This means that the plan of a Documentary tends to have a double edge. On the side of the sponsors, the main interest is naturally how far public opinion can be interested (however indirectly). On the side of the director, the interest is both that of the sociological problem and that of making the best film expression possible out of the subject in hand (in ideal cases these two aspects will coincide).

The influence on technique of this situation may be defined as follows:— There is in nature bound to be a split in the fundamental approach to the Documentary Film. Not merely differences of subjects, but differences of psychological approach are bound to enter in. Thus we find the Documentary of direct reporting, e.g. *Housing Problems* (Elton), *Stand by for Work* (Anstey); expressionist Documentary (expressionist in the best sense) as exemplified by *Shipyard* and *Face of Britain* (Rotha); the dialectic-instructional *The Mine* (Holmes), and the dialectic-lyric (as in certain GPO films). The interesting point is that all these aspects can exist comfortably under one banner and in one unquarrelsome group

In any case the classifications indicated above (the pure interest and scientific film being deliberately omitted) are in a way a grand guarantee to potential sponsors, not merely of the integrity, but also of the efficiency (if necessary, in box office terms) of the purposed production.

Distribution
But there still remains the problem of the audience. For it should not be supposed that any and every Documentary is a box-office proposition. It would indeed be regrettable if that were so; Documentary has other fish to fry.

There will always be a public for Documentaries of the type of *Shipyard*, *Weather Forecast* and *Night Mail*—a public, that is, who will enjoy such films as part of their evening's programme.

But what must not be forgotten is that there is a growing public represented by uplift societies, film groups, study circles, adult education schools, universities and last but not least the schools, whether local

180

council, grammar or public. The value of this audience cannot be underestimated. At the moment Documentary is sowing in this field at least five million people a year. This figure may be expected to increase with considerable rapidity. Note too that many of the films seen by this audience are sponsored by commercial firms or public corporations.

In fact, we are reaching a point in which the teaching of civics and the go-getting interests of big concerns coincide. This means that Documentary can do itself service and serve the state (however constituted) at the same time.

With the increasing importance of the use of film to the B.B.C., now intensified by the imminence of practical television, the fields indicated above seem susceptible to an infinite expansion. For while it seems improbable that existing film-technique will be suitable for television purposes, it is equally certain that sooner or later television will be compelled to use the material of film, and especially of Documentary Film, to develop the form of expression most necessary to its artistic and sociological existence.

BASIL WRIGHT, M.A.
Film Art, Vol. 3, No. 8, Spring 1936

Notes
*Wright's far-reaching article came at a time when 'documentary' was at its peak, and different types of sponsorship were being sought. The question of alliance to 'either a Government Department or a big Corporation' was therefore of contemporary relevance. The idea of building a mass audience via television (officially opened for limited services in November 1936) is indicative of the future alliance sought with a state-sponsored mass medium, after the early successes of the Empire Marketing Board and the GPO Film Units.
**Strand Film Company: the first private, independent firm devoted to documentary production, founded in 1935 by Donald Taylor and Ralph Keene with heads of production Paul Rotha (1935-7) and Stuart Legg (1937-9).

Associated Realist Film Producers: set up in 1935 to liaise between the 'leading documentary film-makers' and potential sponsors as part of the developing 'art of sponsorship' in the late Thirties. Its members included Edgar Anstey, William Coldstream, Arthur Elton, Marion Grierson, J. B. Holmes, Stuart Legg, Paul Rotha, Alex Shaw, Evelyn Spice, Donald Taylor, Harry Watt and Basil Wright. Its 'consultants' included Grierson, Andrew Buchanan, Cavalcanti, Professor J. B. S. Haldane, Julian Huxley, E. McKnight Kauffer and others.

Notes on Art and Movie

One of the chief things which mitigate [*sic*] against the camera, as it is generally used, is the time factor. The painter, who is working with a brush, is able to let his work exist with him. Good painting occurs when both the painter and the painting exist. Each day the painter is able to add to his canvas— one day the paints themselves may force the direction of expression, while at another time thought manipulates technique. Finally, the painting stands as a totality of experience and not as a fragmentary impression. Such painting remains for ever a useful storehouse of values.

The photographer, with the roving camera, who goes directly to life for his material, records the passing minute. Now, surely, the passing minute is a record rather than a storehouse of values; it is a document and it remains to discuss the taste or science with which it is executed.

The artist paints what he thinks about reality, or he paints directly from his head; but the man who uses the camera, as it is generally used, cannot integrate what the lens sees with his philosophy. Even if ectoplasmatic film-stock were invented, the fundamental problem would remain unsolved: the thought, on the ectoplasmatic stock, would be of the passing moment and not an expression of the complete man.

One does not wish to belittle the documentary as document, but one does wish to protest against the lavish use of the word ART in connection with this type of work. Humphrey Jennings, one of the ablest of the young cineastes, has shown, by the production of his admirable documents devoid of all art flummery, how much his competitors are missing by their muddled thinking.

181

An artist, as a human, is biologically limited to a certain amount of energy for a given work. If he persists, after he has exhausted his quota of energy for a given undertaking, the work will lose its freshness and vigour and finally fall down dead on the canvas. Sometimes an unfinished picture is so refreshing because the artist had the good sense to take his hands from his brushes with the departure of the impulse. On the other side, the approach of 'Oh! this would be a good idea for a picture', is rapidly making painting bankrupt.

Painters (it's all right, cineastes, we're working round to movies, but I must put this down as Humphrey Jennings explained it to me) used not to start with ideas but sensations. The idea is the sensation at a final stage. The idea-painter has dangerously little energy left to make a work of art. That is why Picasso has to finish his pictures in such a hurry, using commercial poster-paints which dry almost before application. Were he to delay in his legerdemain of production, the energy which he can command for the task might evaporate.

The idea-picture is, of its essence, made for exhibition and publicity: it has dominated for about as long as the art papers have ruled. (Ah! Movies! there is some moral here, but . . .).

In painting the idea is the bounding line of the objects and the canvas. Put down the bounding line, keep enough energy to fill in with flat colours and you have the *mental photo* as contrasted with the work of art which is made with the complex patterns of experience. The mental photo is journalism, and supplies no reference for the values of existence.

When ideas are taken as starting points for pictures, the only changes which can be made are in the bounding lines which have to move through abstractions, to secure variety, till they spin like an eccentric wheel. So with the idea-painter, like Picasso, recent work is little better than early work. (How quickly is exhausted the human interest of still photography! But we are not there yet . . .).

But the painter who makes use of all available energy to integrate sensations has a life of artistic growth. (How many directors make their first movie their best? . . .).

NOW, how may the film director avoid mental snapshots, journalism and the rest? Will it be by some extension of the puppet film, in which the time factor is controllable? Or by some extension of the painting directly on film method which has been so successfully exploited by Len Lye?

When we have solved the problem of how the film director, as artist and human, can have a life of artistic growth—then we may begin talking about the films and art!

The young men who are reacting from the dominance of ideas in painting are, by the very nature of their cause, not surrounded by spotlights. They are what Humphrey Jennings calls 'moral' artists. This does not mean that they have anything in common with those Victorian brush-pushers whose compositions had 'MORAL' smirked all over them: it means that these young men consider the technique of the medium *together with its implications*.

Perhaps what the cinema needs is fewer cameramen who think themselves artists and more who consider themselves 'moral' . . .

Bruguière hints that quite special things might be done through the invention of new emulsions that would be sensitive only to certain tones and lights—the modern emulsion aims to record every detail, while art lies in selection.

OSWELL BLAKESTON
New Cinema, No. 1, 1936
(Extract)

'Colour won't stand dignity' says Humphrey Jennings

(*The Trail of the Lonesome Pine** definitely establishes the following points, which are presented not as highbrow speculation, but as part of the urgent problem of how to use colour.)

Colour is hopelessly revealing. It reveals not only new physical aspects and properties of objects, but becomes a devastatingly accurate index of the mentality of the film-maker, and of his approach to his material in the smallest details; and anything faked—faked sets or faked situations—shriek in colour where they could be got away with in black-and-white. This is because *Colour* and *Ideas* are fundamentally opposed; the black-and-white film has always lived on ideas; but colour depends upon *sensations*. It is an instinct for this that has sent people out of doors to make colour films. In *The Lonesome Pine* horses, rifles and trees look grand—the small-part players look pretty good—the 'stars' look definitely not so hot.

Far greater care has been taken in shooting Sylvia Sidney and MacMurray than with the extras and log cabins. But that's just it; all that care shows—little touches of blue back-lighting and dabs of powder look terrible, because you can feel 'the experts' putting them there. Again, on people the definition *seems* less good than on machines and dogs. It isn't. But one is satisfied with a sensation of dog; one is not so satisfied with a sensation in place of a *star*; and colour is a sensation. Hence by far the best parts of this film are scenes of a camp on fire, stampeding horses and roughhouse scenes, where the action has got out of the Director's and Art Director's control. And unutterably awful are the smart hotel interiors with Sylvia Sidney telephoning in her negligée: they smell of arcs and plaster, simply because they are in colour and because the colour has been put there on purpose to look good. Of course, real interior locations should have been chosen.

There is one exception. When Sylvia Sidney has mud all over her face, and MacMurray has a swollen jaw, they look good. They have been knocked off their dignity and have become human beings. And this, in fact, is the secret of the business. Colour won't stand dignity. And the scenes of fire and rapid action do show what a whopping film will be made in Technicolor when everybody has come off the high horse. In the meantime, it should be said that the colour printing and Technicolor lab. work are as good as ever.

World Film News, June 1936

Note

*The Trail of the Lonesome Pine, directed by Henry Hathaway, USA 1936. The first three-colour 'outdoors' picture, starring Sylvia Sidney, Fred MacMurray and Henry Fonda in a story of a young engineer who walks into the middle of a long-standing family feud. With some sequences filmed for their 'colour effect' the film received much attention in the press.

Avant-garde to the Rescue
Revolution in Advertising Films

The growing ambition of British cinema is reflected in the new attitude to publicity or advertising films.

Until recently, when excellent advertising films in colour suddenly appeared from the Continent, these films were confined for the most part to second line houses. With colour and improved techniques there is every prospect that even high-class houses will welcome them. In the upper fields novelty is an advantage, and entertainment value imperative.

In spite of steady work in cartoon by Publicity Films, Revelation Films, and others, British technique has, on the whole, lagged behind foreign. The brilliant advertising movement which took the poster to the aesthetic heights of McKnight Kauffer* and established the present high levels of presentation in Press lay-out and public exhibition has had no counterpart in film publicity. The French advertising films done by Aurenche have been funnier than ours; French, German and American animation work has shown a level of technical skill far beyond anything attempted locally.

German Influence Strong

Recent events which are likely to mark a turning point are the winning of the fantasy prize at Brussels by an English advertising film and the circulation in this country of advertising films done in Germany by the great Fischinger. The fantasy film was made in colour by Len Lye without the use of a camera. Colour rhythm, synchronised to music, were painted direct on to the celluloid. The Fischinger films were made in Gasparcolour and advertised, in animated ballet, cigarettes and the radio products of Philips, Holland.**

One of the Philips films, *Ship of The Ether*, has been run extensively, without payment, so great are the charm and novelty of its technique. *Colour Box*, the Lye film, has had similar success. Recent films for Carreras and Churchman show that the lesson has been taken.

Novelties Promised

The GPO film unit reports further experiment, but on different lines. Len Lye

183

is to do a ballet film with real dance against changing colour backgrounds for the Savings Bank. A further effort is being discussed exploiting Lotte Reiniger silhouettes. A film on slapstick comedy lines is being worked out by Coldstream for the Gas people.

The magnificent trick work of Ned Mann in *Things to Come**** and an improving grip on cartoon technique are expected to have considerable influence on publicity films. These much abused films may presently come into their own if great technicians of the order of Cavalcanti, Kauffer, Fischinger, Reiniger, Ubiwerks and Lye continue to be interested. The experimental work until recently associated with *avant-gardes* and film societies appears to be the key to development.

World Film News, April 1936

Notes

*Designer, on the council of the London Film Society and consultant to the ARFP.

**George Pal, a popular English puppet animator who made several advertisement films in the Thirties, became a resident artist for Philips in Holland and later directed fantasy features for M.G.M.

***Ned Mann, American special effects director associated with the work of Alexander Korda, including *Things to Come* (G.B. 1935).

Experiment in Colour

Rainbow Dance, Len Lye's new colour film, represents an important step forward in the control of colour. The complex laboratory processes have not yet been completely mastered and *Rainbow Dance* seems less finished than *Colour Box*, but it indicates far greater possibilities in design and fantasy. Lye's theoretical notes are difficult but they will be evidence to students of experimental cinema, of the deep considerations which are involved in this artist's work.

SYNOPSIS. A rainbow forms behind a man standing in a rainy City street. The rainbow changes him into a colour silhouette and his city clothes into a hiker's outfit. He sets off on holiday activities and dances in a fantasy

of colour. The end slogan is 'The P.O.S.B.* puts a pot of gold at the end of the Rainbow.' Tangible rainbows symbolise the general idea.

In this film the technical purpose was to use only the colours of the Gasparcolor film stock. **These are pink, yellow, and blue dyes which exist in three layers on the film celluloid itself. (The pink, yellow, and blue of any image is protected by three black and white photographic records from the printing light.) The printing light 'knocks out' the unprotected pink, yellow and blue dyes which are eventually dissolved or fixed in the laboratory tanks, according to which portions were exposed or unexposed to it.

The difference in colour technique for this film as compared with the shooting of a straight colour film is that all colour records were taken as separate films. No colour was used on the sets, where every object was painted in terms of black and white. For instance, a green hill (a 'prop' hill) was painted white and photographed continuously for the red record, painted dark grey and photographed for the yellow record, painted a light grey, and finally photographed for the blue record. This meant the hill was split into three records for the required densities of the pink, yellow and blue dyes of the Gasparcolor film stock. A silhouette of a man was superimposed over each colour record in densities according to the dye required for his colour.

This method of colour control meant that our colour would be clean and not suffer from any opacity of photographic colour light. In other words, an artist separated the colours instead of leaving it to the colour filters. So that all colours for the objects were pure colours achieved without the necessity of reproducing colours of different pigmentation by the colour dyes of the film stock.

Although a strong sensation of colour-flow was attempted in both the films *Colour Box* and *Rainbow Dance* there are differences in technical and pictorial treatment between the two. *Colour Box* was painted straight on to the film celluloid and printed in the Dufay colour system*** direct from this 'master'; *Rainbow Dance* is a combination of black and white photographic records equalling densities of colour which are printed on Gasparcolor film stock. In pictorial treatment, the differences lie in the use of colour. Colour was used in *Colour Box* in an objective way, and in *Rainbow Dance* in a subjective way.

In *Colour Box* the colour was 'on the surface' in a arabesque of colour design (apparently motivated by the light arabesque quality of the simple dance music it accompanied). Whatever movement occurred was colour movement alone.

In *Rainbow Dance* the colour is used in a 'spatial' way so that it comes up to the eye or recedes from it or vanishes and re-appears in definite colour rhythms. In fact, colour is made to turn inside out in movement regardless of the movement of the object or objects on which it is seen. Here the colour movement is a form of counterpoint to the movement of the object carrying the colour —often this counterpoint of colour-flow dominates the movement of the object to such an extent that the object becomes merely an element of the colour movement, instead of the usual circumstance of colour being merely an element in an object enacting a strong literary role. In other words, the colour movement dominates all other movement, *both* pictorial and cinematic.

This new form of colour planning necessitates a new approach to criticism, which cannot be based on standards already established in relation to black and white film tempo.

A tabulation of the aspects of colour treatment established in RAINBOW DANCE:

1. Three dimensional colour-flow between the colour of moving objects and their background—
   e.g., a hiker changes colour in a natural colour setting of a hilly countryside until the colour is abruptly drained out of the hills, a marbled map appearing in the sky, and the man altering colour to accent the background change—
2. The investing of straight black and white film shots with unnatural colour to emphasise any fantasy element it was desired to associate with those shots—
   e.g., successive sea shots were invested with colour so that greens, purples and blues changed the sea into intense sunny, twilight and underwater scenes in which hand-painted fish and yachts appear. The shots of seas were used to convey colour form—
3. The colour in a moving object changing in spatial depths of intensity without the moving object in which it is contained shifting in its dimensional plane—
   e.g., a man in movement, contained in a few square yards, undergoes changes of colour densities that indicate changes of depth from foreground to infinity. The colour focus, although remaining sharp in definition, is at one moment ranged at 'nearness', in the next is ranged on 'infinity' with the man and the background remaining on a steady spatial plane.
4. Coloured objects splitting up into parts of themselves so that they become echoes of their movement and dominant colour—
   e.g., a man jumping through the air leaves successive images of himself behind, which retain elements of his colour and when the images disappear he assumes a different colour.
5. Pure colour sensation—
   e.g., rainbow shapes float upwards in movement while the divisions of colour alternate exactly in time to strong rhythmic music. Vibrant colour spots are then fluttered over the rainbows to create further sensational stimuli.
6. 'Sour' colour is used as an offset to bright 'saturation' of colour—
   e.g., natural black and white shots of a girl's head were falsified by using negative densities of the photo which were then invested with muddy browns and neutral colours to intensify the brightness of the rainbows which succeed this scene.

LEN LYE

World Film News, December 1936

Notes
*Post Office Savings Bank.

**Gasparcolor: a printing process in which for the first time a triple-layer coloured emulsion positive material was made which could be printed and processed with quite minor modification of contemporary laboratory technique. With this a full three-colour continuous tone image could be obtained without the use of dyes or chemical toning, or any extraneous colouring matter in processing. It was based on the separate application of the three light-primary dyes (cyan, magenta and yellow) from which all colours could be obtained by mixing. Malcolm Le Grice has noted that 'The synthesis of "natural" colour was achieved by a camera which recorded a prismatically split image on three roles of monochrome film. Len Lye, like Oskar Fischinger, had different ideas about it. They saw at once that the synthetic process need not be used simply to reconstruct a previous colour analysis, but could form the basis of any kind of colour manipulation.' (*Abstract Film and Beyond*, London 1977.)

***Dufay Colour: the only successful three colour 'additive' process. Introduced in 1934 as a 16mm reversal process, a panchromatic emulsion was exposed through a filter layer made up of patches of red, green and blue dye arranged in a grid. A negative-positive process in 35mm was not commercially available until 1938. Barry Salt writes that 'the process had the drawback of all additive colour processes in that it passed only a quarter of the light on to the screen when compared with a subtractive process such as Technicolor, Agfacolor or Kodachrome'. (*Film Style and Technology in the Thirties* in *Film Quarterly*, Fall 1976.)

Len Lye reviews
Major Klein's 'Coloured Light'

All technicians take a bow: all technicians advancing their work take a double bow. If you read this book you'll know why. It's 'Why' makes the wheels of thought go round. Particularly the wheels connected with colour pleasures. Mainly treating colour as colour in its own rights as a medium of art for both creative and receptive sensory stimulation. In other words, Sir—beauty, loveliness, or any other word you have for aesthetic kick. And the technical advancements that give a greater means for its expression.

The subject matter is put down in a clear, concise statement of theory, practice, and technical outline of colour manipulations which sharpen your own thoughts about colour or create new ones. And your new thoughts may sharpen the appreciation of the work listed and done by the pioneers in creative colour and its mechanics.

We're lucky to have research workers who can not only give lucid details of their views and experiments, but also those of other workers in the same or analogous fields.

A. B. Klein has marshalled the theories and reference data of seemingly every known worker in the field of colour thought in its scientific and aesthetic aspects. He presents mature theories and puts forward interesting viewpoints on the social values and standards of painting, music, and the colour research in which he has taken a large share.

I myself am no technician and designate myself as a colour playboy intent on my contact with reality to supply it with a mental aphrodisiac just for the sake of what happens.

The author is versed in the Western European art traditions and has kept alive his own thoughts in relation to them which is also evidence to me that the technical knowledge outlined in the book is as advanced in content.

This is a relief to find nowadays when the external forces of reality absorb so much of our mind's virility on problems of economics, social organisation, human annihilation, liberties, and so on; so that we have hardly any mind left for creating or approaching mind gems in any aesthetic medium.

Film people who feel that eventually they will be dealing with the more subtle of the aesthetic problems in colour films will find many oblique lines of thought bearing on film presentation, such as back-projected colour in sensory movement for sets presenting dance, drama, music, and the placing of characters in colour controlled movement backgrounds.

If the book is too expensive in these days of incessant economic demands and upsets, at least it is worth having access to in the studio or general reference library, to read in between jobs, and as a preparation for a self-confident contribution to the only thing that matters finally apart from behaviour and bread and butter, namely, the subtleties of mind content invested in beauty.

The Cine-Technician, Dec-Jan. 1937-38

Appendix

Television and Radio

The following manifestos appeared in Grierson's magazine World Film News *during the spring of 1936, in the context of a debate on the kind of institutions required by the nation to develop the public broadcasting service, which was to include television.*

Regular BBC television broadcasts, the first of their kind in the world, started on 2 November 1936. In the years preceding this, however, the problems of sponsorship and funding, as well as editorial and financial control, had been the subject of several government inquiries.

In 1935 the Selsdon Committee had made decisions in two main areas: firstly, that the cost of technical development should be shared by the Treasury and the BBC out of their respective shares of the public licence fee; and secondly, that although the Postmaster General was to participate on a special advisory committee, the BBC was to be the authority involved both technically and editorially.

In 1936 the BBC monopoly was preserved by the Ullswater Committee's report on the grounds of the protection of the 'intellectual and ethical integrity' of the nation's broadcasting system. 'Discrete sponsorship' of television was to be allowed, but advertising was ruled out. In the light of the experience of the General Strike the committee suggested that a right of direct government control in the case of a 'national emergency' should be stated, and it wanted the responsibility for broadcasting to be assumed by a cabinet minister instead of the Postmaster General.

In return for this monopoly, the BBC was urged to quell the fears of some members of Parliament that it was usurping the functions of political patronage, in order to consult 'major political parties', i.e. Conservative, Labour and Liberal, on major issues. In addition it was urged to express 'minority' and 'unpopular' views. The BBC's reputation as a commendable example of public enterprise was largely accepted by the Labour Party, despite Attlee's reservations that the BBC should at all times reflect the views of 'opposition'.

The BBC's monopoly of authority was preserved in the face of groups already interested in the lucrative commercial possibilities of a 'mass public'. The manifestos' fundamental aims to 'exploit the BBC's monopoly of authority' in the interests of expanding the 'limitations' of a new art form, remain tied to the idea of allying a strong state-controlled authority to progressive cultural forms, in the presumed interest of educating the masses. Sir Stephen Tallents, who had moved from the Empire Marketing Board to the GPO, and then to the key post of the BBC's controller of public relations, commented on the popular appeal of television, particularly among the 'less educated', who were thought to derive special advantage from the double support of sight and sound impressions.

The manifestos continue the tradition of broadcasting in Britain described by Anthony Smith as 'an instrument of parliament, as a kind of embassy of the national culture within the nation', setting the basis for the organisations which exist today. Television did not, however, become a 'mass medium' until it re-emerged after the Second World War. By the end of 1937 only 2,000 sets had been sold, and the total of twenty programme hours per week (the assumed minimum basis for a television service) had only been achieved by 1939, when it was forced to close. The pre-war history of television is not, however, without its emblematic aspects. The coronation of May 1937 was the first public outside broadcast, watched by an estimated 50,000 people; the highlight of the show, given headline treatment by the press, was a special smile by the King into the television camera.

187

Manifesto on Television

We appreciate the fact that television must develop slowly. We appreciate the need for a preliminary period of test and experiment. We realise that from the television qualities and BBC monies at first available we can only expect the simplest results. But we remember with concern that the tradition of radio is to REPRODUCE. We ask an assurance from the BBC that the new medium—at least in part—will be used to CREATE.

The Use of Film

TELEVISION MUST BE KEPT WITHIN THE LIMITS OF EFFECTIVE VISUAL PRESENTATION.

Magic lantern levels and direct demonstration from maps, etc., should not be despised if they give a higher quality of definition. Better good magic lantern than bad film. Better good information than crude aesthetic.

CONSIDER FIRST THE FIELDS WHICH ARE NOT NOW EFFECTIVELY COVERED BY THE MOVIE THEATRES.

The announced programme—with its emphasis on news-reel and ciné-magazine—suggests an imitation of the trifles now satisfactorily supplied to the public in its weekly film programmes.

A repetition of film news-reels is superfluous and beneath the level of news announcement we expect from the BBC.

Far better to have the BBC's own news service, with simple illustrations. This need not be dramatised like *The March of Time*, but might be presented with a straightforward use of maps and stills. It might incorporate different points of view and different levels of appreciation.

Let the BBC in these matters create standards for the film trade, and not vice-versa.

CONSIDER THE MORE PRIVATE ATMOSPHERE IN WHICH TELEVISION WILL DEVELOP.

Television represents showmanship to the same people who go to the theatres, but to the same people in a different mood. The atmosphere of the home and the smallness of the screen emphasise the privacy of television.

It should not be taken for granted, therefore, that film sequence can satisfactorily be transferred to the television screen.

The BBC should consider the possibility of television sequence being a new craft which must be discovered and built up by the BBC itself. A training in *existing* film technique may be less useful than is now supposed.

With these qualifications, film may be regarded as a principal factor in the television scheme.

FILM PROVIDES A STORE AND LIBRARY FOR IMAGES. IT GIVES RANGE TO TELEVISION.

FILM PERMITS EFFECTIVE AND RICH EDITORIAL WORK. IT ALLOWS TELEVISION A CREATIVE AS DISTINCT FROM A REPRODUCTIVE ROLE: TELEVISION AS AN ART MEDIUM DEPENDS ON THE USE OF FILM.

FILM ELIMINATES CLUMSY METHODS OF TIMING.

Present BBC methods of production, while preserving—and over a large part of the field rightly preserving—direct contact with broadcasters, appear to the film mind naïve. The organisation of production through many microphones and many cubicles allows of only the simplest forms. Where mechanical means can ensure the consideration and reconsideration of sequence and *tempo*, and determine beforehand the technical perfection of a broadcast, it is foolish not to take advantage of mechanical means.

FILM PERMITS EXPERIMENT.

Most important criticisms of BBC working are as follows: the administrative and executive staffs are too detached from each other; consequently, the creative staff lacks the incentive of real responsibility. The fear of mistakes tends, in both staffs, to create inhibition, diminish energy, cynicise ambition and weaken results.

The preparation of programmes on film will enable the creative staff to experiment, and the administrative staff to consider experiment, before broadcast.

FILM ESTABLISHES TECHNICAL STANDARDS.

A film basis for television will give to the BBC what it has long lacked: a body of established technical standards which personnel may consider and absorb and develop. It will give the BBC an effective body of criticism. It has been difficult to build a body of criticism among the evanescent impressions of direct broadcast.

ALBERTO CAVALCANTI
CEDRIC BELFRAGE
THOROLD DICKINSON
JOHN GRIERSON
GRAHAM GREENE
World Film News, April 1936

Manifesto:
Television must contact the individual

Consider the radio services and the radio audiences now served. To the general audience the BBC gives:

1. Respite from labour and a substitute for cinema.
2. Information on the events of the day.
3. A contact with London and a sense of being in the know.

To more specialised audiences the BBC gives:

4. Education for the purposes of self-improvement.
5. Education for purposes of civic improvement (often called propaganda).
6. Sectional services in music, education and information.

Where Radio beats Films

On this analysis radio performs a much wider and, in fact, a greater community service than film. Film does (1) brilliantly; fails dismally on (2) and (3); shuns (4); but is already, in documentary and instructional films, highly equipped for the performance of (5) and (6). The difference is interesting. On news and public affairs, and even on metropolitan gossip for the general audience, radio scores heavily, but it has authority. It really is in the know, and the people trust its knowledge.

Film Technique no Guide

If television follows BBC tradition and practice, it is clear that only in services (1), (5) and (6) will it find a guide in cinema (i.e., in entertainment, documentary and instructional films). For the other services of authoritative news, intimate interview and public improvement, it will have to create its own technique.

The Rational Appeal

In close conjunction with these various services there is a difference in mood between film audiences and radio audiences.

The film audience is large, subject to crowd psychology, imposed upon, i.e., disciplined, by every trick of mass presentation. Publicity and showmanship create a glamour around stars and romances. *The atmosphere of the film theatre is one of escape.*

The radio audience is small, informal, intimate and essentially undisciplined. The radio has to win its way through a hundred distractions. *The radio audience must be talked over and won on the merits of the material if it is to be held.*

The radio appeal is, therefore, more rational; it is to the individual and his good sense. It is more informal and, except on exceptional occasions like the King's death, cannot build on a ready-made tenseness of atmosphere. Its art will, therefore, incline to the more ordinary and experiment may not pass too far from conversational level. It depends on a quick interest in the subject matter—unless the full forces of publicity be used to create a special interest. Here again the radio must depend on ready-made interest. *It thrives, therefore, on the traditional, on the news of the day; it follows up rather than originates.*

News-value later

This suggests the need for a conservative policy in television. On the other hand the BBC's monopoly of authority and the belief that it really is in the know can be exploited further. Intimate interview and authoritative comment might be made the basic factor in the creation of a new style of reporting.

Against the film's glamour of showmanship the radio has the glamour of immediacy. This the newspapers had occasion to note when the King's death was announced. Television will, no doubt, in this matter seek the same immediacy as the microphone to-day, but not for some time. There is interest and not art in immediate things. The hotter the news-reels, the more foolish they are. No doubt it will be the same with television but the hot news will serve its evanescent purpose.

Moral as usual

But whatever the limitations of the medium in terms of informality, intimacy, etc, the usual aesthetic rules will obtain. *All arts are built by exploiting their limitations.*

World Film News, June 1936

Radio—The Problem of the Audience

The promoter leads with his eye on the audience; the artist follows. It was always the custom of kings to take clerks on their travels; and the method still obtains. But it is not the clerks who dictate the line of march; they merely make the best of a compulsory journey. So they took slapstick out of cinema vaudeville, epic out of wild western, documentary out of the limited film finance of propaganda, and montage out of (*a*) Russia's desire to shout international messages, and (*b*) Russia's shortage of film stock.

Much the same thing has happened in broadcasting, except that the clerks have not been so quick to exploit their opportunities. The exercise of radio has been determined exclusively by the desire to fulfil audience services. Music, public information, education, light entertainment have been given because large masses of the people wanted them. But they have been given straight, without any historic attempt on the part of the artist to convert or enliven them on their mechanised journey to the audience.

Two facts emerge. The first is that it is useless for the artist to attempt a discovery of television without reference to audience demands. He will quite definitely not be permitted across the frontier. The second fact is that the tradition of radio suggests a more slavish service of the audience than the tradition of cinema—and a minimum of discovery, unless a real effort is made to wake the creative conscience of the BBC.

To any such criticism the BBC replies that it must be simple: it must think of its millions. We can answer that, and shortly. The necessary simplicity and the necessary millions of cinema have not prevented Chaplin, Cruze, Griffith and Pudovkin. More radically we answer: who are these millions the BBC people are always talking about? There is vanity, and nonsense, in the conception.

The BBC has a monopoly of air time, and this it distributes sensibly to a hundred different audiences: some directly educational, some informational, some entertaining, some in the highest sense aesthetic. It has also services which are either minority or sectional: to farmers, seamen, schoolchildren, specialists in music, etc. Not every BBC audience is a majority audience; not every listening mood is a majority mood.

No consideration of radio psychology—and of television psychology to come—can avoid these issues. There will be consideration of minority appeals as well as majority ones. Creative achievement as well as simple report will be expected of it. Too many people are now instructed in visual image to allow the art of television—like the art of microphone—to be trifled with.

These things granted, there must continue to be vast differences between the attitude to radio and the attitude to film. Television will reflect them.

World Film News, May 1936

PART V
Amateur Films

Introduction

TECHNOLOGY: THE IDEOLOGIES OF
'AMATEURISM'/'PROFESSIONALISM'

Little work has been done on the 'amateur' movement and its industry. What follows is a schematic account of the development of the 'sub-standard' gauge (16mm) and the technological constraints this imposed on independent work in the 1930s, together with some notes on their implications for the development of 'independent cinema'. In attempting such work it is not a question of promoting 'amateur' films as essentially different from, or subversive to, 'dominant cinema', but of discovering the constraints which allow that conception of cinema to exist.

The expectations of 'cinema' are governed by a dual notion of 'professionalism': (i) *socially*: cinema is a process of industrial production by skilled paid personnel; (ii) *ideologically*: a film will possess the attributes of 'quality', 'perfection', a technical mastery of certain codes of operation. Allowing for a certain non-correspondence between these social and ideological functions, i.e. that 'professionals' will not always produce 'professional' work and that 'professional work' can also be produced by 'amateurs', these ethics of 'professionalism' produce the technological, organisational, ideological constraints within which 'cinema' is produced. It should be noted, of course, that the definition of 'professionalism' is itself variable and historically coded. A shaky camera movement in a Thirties film may signify an unintentional message of 'amateurism', whereas in a 'ciné vérité' film it will have a completely different, 'motivated' connotation. What is known as 'mainstream' or 'entertainment' cinema is therefore a specific conjuncture of audience and practice, and within it specific modes of regulation (technological and others) are produced which differentiate it from others. The fact of its economic and ideological dominance gives it an obvious importance but it has always to be thought of in terms of other audiences, different practices. For such practices to become productive it is necessary to recognise the constraints and boundaries, the tendencies of dominant cinema, and most importantly to recognise its constant redefinition of those boundaries. If cinema is the achievement of a unity of presentation between film and subject, it is also the fragmentation of that unity. This is not only true within the specific operation of each film, but for different types of cinema. It is important to stress that 'cinema' is always multiple, never a unity; the term 'dominant cinema' only indicates the unity in separation of an alliance of diverse practices, articulated conjuncturally around a strategy of political

191

opposition. The term's basis can therefore only be historical and political, and does not identify a constant real grouping of forces.

THE HISTORY OF 16mm

Proposals for a new and separate standard gauge for films used outside cinema theatres were first made in 1918 in the USA. Several attempts had previously been made to save in raw material, all based on the mistaken assumption that each manufacturer could monopolise the film supply, which therefore had deliberately been made incompatible with the products of competing manufacturers.

The advocacy of a common separate standard for 'amateurs, schools and industries' was made for two reasons: firstly, that as long as standard 35mm was offered to the non-theatrical user, there could never be an industry since no insurance company would write insurance on any building in which this film was used, owing to its high inflammability, unless fireproof booths were installed; secondly, that no individual manufacturer had the necessary finances to produce a sufficient supply of film if using an arbitrary and individual style of film.

A number of gauges had previously been considered. 28mm had initially been decided upon, but since the raw material was more expensive, this was abandoned; $17\frac{1}{2}$mm was feared to provide too many chances for 'bootlegging' simply by cutting 35mm in two. In 1923, Eastman Kodak made the first 16mm film after having perfected the reversal process (by which original film is developed directly into a positive image suitable for projection), and the first 16mm cameras and projectors came on the market in that year.

The reversal process was not new—it had been employed in colour photography—but its application to 'motion pictures' was an innovation. The process had two main advantages: (i) it was finer in grain structure so that a film having a smaller area gave the same result as one of a larger area made with the old process, allowing great savings on the cost of stock; (ii) if only one picture was wanted, it did away with the need for a negative, again greatly saving in cost.

The gauge was originally marketed in black and white, but sound stocks were added in 1933 and colour in 1934, by which time 8mm had been introduced in the USA. In France, however, the 9.5mm gauge produced by Pathé proved a strong competitor with 16mm for the amateur market and was imported into Britain. For a time it was further developed in terms of the speed of camera lenses and the availability of film stocks, but it could not compete with the scale of production on 16mm equipment and declined with the fall of France in 1940. An additional factor in the popularity of 16mm was the availability of commercial entertainment pictures in that gauge, and during the Second World War the American armed forces opted for 16mm in the circulation of their feature films in Europe, thus ensuring its dominance in a market vastly expanded by the war.

The period 1929–39 saw a tremendous expansion in the amateur market in Britain. It was, however, rigidly separated from the professional market;

screenings were confined to non-theatrical use, and sound-stocks were delayed so as to assure a larger market for the producers of film equipment; facilities for making several prints from the 16mm original were limited in Britain until a new printing process was started at Denham in 1942.

Other technical difficulties added to the sharp distinction between 'professionalism' and 'amateurism'. There were no facilities for complicated wipes or similar optical effects on 16mm. It was, for example, not until the late Thirties that the first Bolex cameras had an accurate frame counter and a variable shutter which would work while the camera was running, thus enabling fades and dissolves to be performed in the camera. 'Amateur' cameras did not possess a 'through the lens' viewfinder. The viewfinder could only be used for focusing, but not for framing since the whole frame could not be seen. On some only a circular image could be obtained, and problems of precision were encountered with subjects close to the lens. No 16mm camera had an electric motor, and so the length of a shot was effectively restricted to the amount of film taken at one winding. The camera could be wound up while shooting, but would obviously be liable to shake (whereas the very freedom from a tripod was an important factor in the success of 16mm cameras), and this therefore tended towards breaking up shots into shorter units of film, and a concentration on the editing process. The portable nature of 16mm equipment did, however, make it possible to seek out new locations, places of work, meetings, demonstrations, and other exteriors, and the camera could be operated by one person. The linking together of different locations without voice-over could be done by explanatory titles which were frequently featured as cut-outs in amateur magazines, with ready-made titles for such popular topics as 'Our Holiday', 'The King's Jubilee', 'Baby Grows Up' and so forth. Differing standards of shooting and projection therefore confirmed a crucial factor of the amateur/sub-standard sector in which a relation now existed between the price paid for the equipment and the 'quality' of the image, so that the notion of 'quality' became a much more variable and fragile one.

Several tentative points can be drawn from the expansion of the amateur market during the period. The strict separation of professional and amateur markets ensured a separation of their ideological effects on conceptions of 'the cinema'. Each was initially protected from the other, and attempts to organise 'amateur' groups into forming their own distinct social and aesthetic strategies met with little success. The aesthetic conditions of development were severely limited vis-à-vis 'professional' standards, producing a situation where emulation of Hollywood-style fiction and narrative was impeded by technical shortcomings. More fundamentally, the direct relationship between technical quality and the equipment's commodity status opened up a range of 'quality' which sharpened the superiority of 'professional' over 'amateur' strategies.

The amateur market channelled off the energies desiring to 'play' with different permutations of screen images, to produce incoherent forms of address, images which were fragmented and spatially and temporally discontinuous. A massive investment in magazines detailing 'technical tips' for amateurs promoted the ideal of learning to structure a 'well ordered narrative', by eliminating endless repetition, excessive redundancy of images and so forth. In this way the amateur market provided Hollywood with its mirror image: an aspiration to 'professionalism', a learning of 'film grammar' with limited technical means, a way of making films whose mistakes, incoherences and inconsistencies served to highlight the perfection of the commercial product.

Fundamentally in the amateur films there is the re-entry of codes previously restricted to the so-called 'primitive' cinema in which the dominant strategies of representation had not yet been settled: the lack of a coherent point of view or system of address, the incoherence of the fiction, its failure to engage the spectator in its fiction, these potentially 'disruptive' devices were subsumed within a 'rethinking' of 'cinema' and its parameters. Far from unavoidably fragmenting the unity of the dominant cinema, a *different* conception of that cinema was produced which was able to contain such interruptions. The space opened up by these interruptions, however, provided a niche for independent practices *between* 'amateur' and 'professional' boundaries, in which the contradictions produced by those oppositions became productive.

HOME MOVIES

As a rule, the phenomenon of the 'home movie' has been relegated to areas outside the cinema, a move facilitated by the historians' and critics' insistence on specific, narrowly defined criteria of 'artistic', technological and thematic development. As if it were self-evident or accidental, the model of cinema thus produced covered only the products (films) that could be accommodated within the exhibition sector of a highly specialised, capital and labour intensive economic machine. One serious consequence of this has been the repression of cinematic practices functioning primarily in terms of memory and fiction, or memory as fiction, exactly the areas of most concern to home movies. As Stephen Heath put it: 'It is easy enough to see the home movie as fulfilling much the same role as the photographs in the family album (record, memory) and in many respects this is clearly correct. Yet there is equally a fundamental and significant difference. The photograph has a massive investment in *identity*, "the stupefying evidence of *this is how it was*" [Roland Barthes, *Image-Music-Text,* London 1977, p. 44], held and fixed, a currency of reality, transportable, exchangeable, referable; present, of course, but mutely, irreparably the past, "the photograph is never experienced as illusion, is in no way a *presence*" [Barthes]. Composed of photographic images, the investment of film is nevertheless different, much less simply an identity than an identification; film, that is, is irreparably present, its inevitable past subsumed in a present *event*, movement, narration, enunciation, a whole play of relations. A photograph is looked at, a film is watched (to look at a film is rather doubtful actually, the stance of a study, against the flow, the prerogative of professionals or students—or the police, converting a film back into a series of identity photos). The home movies in [George Cukor's] *Adam's Rib* are typical: little incidents outdoors, in a garden, funny moments (what

194

Louis Lumière pioneered was not cinema but the home movie—feeding baby, mishaps with hosepipes); for Adam and Amanda, for their friends, the movies are an action, a process, a refiguring (and not a mere recognition). In *Adam's Rib*, the home movies are not "the real film". What distinguishes them and the home movie in general quite as much as technical limitations, is the lack of a "fiction", and a fiction for and of the spectator; the pattern of identification is unsure, disorganised, too "short" (still dependent on certain identities; hence the circumscribed audience, the absence of interest "for *me*"), the look is incoherent, *unsolicited*. Cinema, on the contrary, is the sure exploitation of the fiction of film, where the terms of the sureness are not those of any fiction but those particularly of *family romance'*. (*'Contexts'* in *Edinburgh '77 Magazine*).

The specific historical terms of this relation between cinema and the history of the subject were based in the dual achievement of the family as both a dominant consumer unit, and as an object for active rememoration. The latter is the explicit concern of several articles in the early amateur magazines: *Home Movies and Home Talkies,* June 1932, p. 10: '. . . for a moving picture is, after all, the way of *recording and remembering the performance* [Ed.'s emphasis] of your husband or son, your horse, your yacht, your dog, your car, or whatever it may be. It is completely true to say that once you have made a movie of any event you have it in your power literally to "see it all over again" at any time'. And further on in the same magazine: 'Grave or gay, the memories we can obtain with our cine-camera are unique. Think of those scenes of holiday-times you would give anything to recall. *Think how every member of the family can share in the leisure of the hobby'* [Ed.'s emphasis].

This then coincides with the magazines' aspects of marketing equipment, their concern to 'popularise film-making'. 'We seek, then, to popularise the hobby and widen its field. We want to see the projector as much as a feature of the home as a wireless set or a gramophone. We want to see the cine-camera as popular as the snapshot camera.'

This 'popularisation' was, however, restricted by its expense, so that purchase was effectively limited to those with a high income and sufficient leisure time to spend filming. Film-making for most people came therefore via organised local amateur cine-societies which combined their film-making activities with 'the promotion of social intercourse', in the manner objected to by early critics (see Leslie Duckworth's article, p. 199), with dances, Sunday rambles and 'soirées'. Film-making thus became a *recreational* activity, in which home life was transformed into both home entertainment and social spectacle. The use of the word 'play' in connection with these activities is therefore important in two contexts: firstly, as producing 'fictions' ('acted' as opposed to 'unacted' films in the distinction made by Soviet film-makers and critics in the late 1920s); secondly, as a 'leisure' practice or pastime. For the first time a family was able to reproduce moving images of itself as a spectacle/process both for private and social consumption: families were now able to act out stories about a family, made by the family, and viewed in a family situation. The same opportunity was potentially there for other types of leisure group. However, as is stated in the *Home Movies Competition of*

1934: 'Four out of five cameras are purchased to make a record of the children.' There was a certain magic in recording/reactivating 'other positions' held in the family: a child or a baby (or on occasions a dog or cat) was no longer transfixed as in a photograph, as evidence of 'this is how it was'. Film afforded an 'inevitable past subsumed in a present event'; the succession of images provided not so much a recognition but a refiguring of those positions.

The popularity of these activities can be gauged to some extent by the provision of ready-made titles for amateur films in magazines. An invitation to 'Meet the Family', for example, is represented by the shadows of four family figures with a dog in the foreground, while future delights are summoned up by such titles as 'Holiday Happiness', and 'Week-End'. However, one major problem persisted: the endless repetition of the same familial subjects resulted in the elimination of interest for the spectator and inevitable frustration with the films and their inadequacies in producing coherent fictions. The amateur magazine *Movie Makers* had the answer: 'Simple variations will improve the amateur film'. The magazines of the period, then as now, are therefore packed with technical tips for 'trick devices' to regain the viewers' fascination with the process, and their continued interest in the expanding range of equipment at the consumer's disposal.

It is therefore important to stress how the early hopes for the 'amateur movement' were confounded by the intellectual underestimation of the seemingly endless possibilities for investment in memory and fiction by the amateur cinema, as opposed to the 'serious' documentary approach. Basil Wright, writing as late as 1938, repeated these unrealised hopes in 'It began like this' (*Amateur Cine World*, April 1938): 'A final word, if I may, to the amateurs. To most of us in the documentary movement they represent a potential force of social and civic value. They have in their power the economic forces; they have also the possibilities of technique denied to workers on standard film, who are bound by bulky apparatus and who are to some extent denied the intimacies which go with a light and easily worked hand-camera. I often think with envy of the possibilities awaiting the go-ahead amateur groups, possibilities of starting a service of analysis, dramatic presentation and even propaganda, on behalf of the community in which the group exists.'

The 'potential . . . social and civic value' was, however, subverted by precisely those interests which the so-called documentary movement attacked: the play on memory and fiction by the Hollywood/entertainment cinema. The 'amateur movement' in the Thirties can therefore be seen to have developed as the underside of the Hollywood industry, dealing with those areas of memory and fiction which mainstream independent cinema, founded on a rigid oppositional stance vis-à-vis 'Hollywood', had neglected except, to some extent at least, in the form of newsreels which provided a record of 'the people's memory', popular memory as opposed to familial memories. There are, of course, still traces of the family romance in left newsreels, as in the various exemplary paternal figures promoted in them and in the narration of acts performed by 'heroes'. But on the whole, newsreels attempted to

196

reintegrate these heroes as members, even if exemplary members, of the workers' 'movement', as embodiments of 'the people', that is to say, as symbols for a collective movement.

INDEPENDENT/AMATEUR/EXPERIMENTAL

From these remarks, some tentative conclusions can be drawn in relation to the 1930s. The advent of the new 'sub-standard' 16mm technology for the non-professional market had produced a variety of expectations for 'amateur production'. Notably in the late 1920s and early 1930s, several attempts were made to set up an organisation which would embrace all aspects of the amateur film; had these been successful, there would undoubtedly have been internal conflict as to the tendency such a movement would inevitably have to adopt. Such an organisation, however, never came into being, partly because of the deep political, ideological and aesthetic differences which already existed between the various groups. In this sense 'amateur film' never developed as a 'movement' outside the context of the 'home movies' and 'amateur film-making' as we know it today. The main tendencies in the conflicts during the late Twenties and early Thirties can be summarised as follows:

(i) *Agit-Prop:* a tendency desiring a link between amateur film and the labour movement, to develop film as a political force under the economic and ideological control of the workers, as suggested by Benn's articles in the Independent Labour Party newspaper *The New Leader*;

(ii) *Social and Civic Purpose:* a tendency associated with such magazines as *Cinema Quarterly* and the ideology of the 'documentary movement' which saw the 'amateur movement' as a potential extension of the documentary ideology, that is to say, as an artistic tool in civic and community life, as education and propaganda, to be organised by local groups but co-ordinated nationally;

(iii) *Experiment:* a tendency which saw amateur film-making as a means of the aesthetic potential of film denied by the commercial industry, with its anti-commercial ideology broadly associated with a 'progressive' politics, but in the end granting autonomy to the aesthetic function of art;

(iv) *Home Movies:* the dominant and prevailing tendency which incorporated amateur film as a hobby for the leisured classes, in conjunction with other leisure pursuits, and whose 'amateurishness' and 'playful' aspects was the counterpart of the 'professionalism' of work.

The first agit-prop groups developed among the organisationally autonomous propaganda groups aligned with political parties. However, the debate over alignment/non-alignment with a political party, the Communist Party particularly, caused many factional splits, as can be seen in the development of the original Kino group from the Communist Workers' Theatre Movement. The transition into the Workers' Film and Photo League, an autonomous organisation, was followed by a split which involved the omission of the word 'Workers' from their title—perhaps a decision based on the new Comintern line of a Popular Front, or equally reflecting the less markedly 'political' motivation of the film-makers involved. The tendency towards establishing groups as an extension of the documentary movement's ideology of 'social and civic purpose' found expression in the Independent Film Makers' Association, which, however, disintegrated soon after its foundation.

The following texts illustrate some of the major problems faced in organising amateur film-makers, and some of the conflicting social and aesthetic tendencies involved. These can be crudely summarised as follows: (i) the danger noted by Ralph Bond of 'experimentation' in technique, typified by the expression 'this montage business', testifying both to the contemporary influence of 'montage' and its status as a mere 'technique' divorced from any theoretical or political context; (ii) the tendency, expressed by Leslie Duckworth, to believe the 'amateur movement' to be already an anachronism, both in the absence of sound equipment, and in the failure to develop the potentiality of the silent film past the work of the Soviet film-makers; (iii) the tendency, again noted by Duckworth, for amateur film-making to become merely a social recreation, confined to the status of a hobby or leisure time activity; (iv) the absence of any serious alternative schemes of film education and/or analysis noted by Erik Chisholm, to ensure a familiarity with 'film grammar' (this, however, is seen by Chisholm as a process of acquiring the skills to eliminate unnecessary or confusing images in order to achieve a 'normality in story film technique'); (v) an interest, later developed by Vivian Braun as Editor of *Film Art* and *New Cinema*, in 'pure cinema'—here the 'amateur documentary' is seen as a potential source of a pure document of reality, in an interpretation of the Soviet films as supposedly recording visual facts on celluloid; (vi) a marked tendency, exemplified by an American writer, Eric M. Knight, which identified Hollywood with 'film plays' and the concern of any oppositional/experimental cinema (bearing in mind the 'broken hopes' of Eisenstein, Murnau and Flaherty) as outside such commercial ranks; (vii) the need felt for a central amateur organisation expressed in the several national conventions of amateur leagues, and typified by the early demise of the IFMA.

These texts and notes sketch in the shifting relations which existed between such terms as 'independence', 'amateur', 'experimental', 'educational' and 'documentary' during the period. Institutions such as the GPO Film Unit later laid claim to several of such terms. However, the fact of the dispersal of such terms around several institutions (ranging from the commercial magazines to the film groups attached to the Communist Party) gives some indication of the contradictory status of these terms in the discourses of the period.

'This Montage Business'

The Film Guild of London, an amateur organisation, is suffering from a bad attack of 'this montage business'. The phrase in quotes is not mine; one of the members of the Guild aptly but thoughtlessly employed it at their meeting last month when several recent productions of the Guild were screened.

Chief among these was *Waitress*, produced on 9mm stock by Mr. Orlton West. *Waitress* is a bad film, very bad. Originally it was made as a one-reeler, but after he had made it Mr. West went to the Continent and saw the work of Vertov. He was so impressed with Vertov's montage that he came back, added another reel to his film, and endeavoured to cut the whole production in the Vertov manner.

Now cutting, or montage as some people prefer to call it, is something more than clipping every possible shot to a couple of frames. Cutting should be composed, and Mr. West has neither composed his film nor his cutting. The result is a striving after effect purely. If the director had paid a little more attention to his lighting and photography (which were terribly poor), and to his story construction, and less to stunts, *Waitress* might have been a better film. The very long and almost unintelligible double exposure sequence which attempts to express the mental collapse of the girl in the cafe could well have been dispensed with, or, at least, shortened considerably.

This desperate endeavour to be clever in order to be different also spoilt *Fade Out*, a first effort by Miss Norah Cutting. (The name is quite genuine, I believe!) This short has possibilities, but again is almost ruined by 'this montage business'. Its climax, when the man who is helping an amateur company on location falls from the tree and dies, is killed by a rapid succession of closely cut shots which the mind positively refuses to follow. The weather conditions under which the film was made were obviously bad, and this should have been taken into consideration when *Fade Out* was edited. If Vertov had been working under similar conditions, he would never have attempted to do what the director of *Fade Out* has done. Film Guilders, please note!

In case I be misunderstood, let me say that the members of the Film Guild are honestly endeavouring to do good work, but they are afflicted with an attitude which can best be described as posing. Everybody recognises the difficult conditions under which the British amateurs have to work to-day. But these difficulties cannot always be used as an excuse for careless work. Carelessness is impermissible in amateur production.

The Guild is certainly working towards something, and most of its work is experimental, but in doing so it is wasting a terrible amount of time and energy. *Gaiety of Nations,* an amateur film reviewed by me in *Close Up* last month, took over six

months to make, and it was worth it. I am not suggesting that every amateur film should take a similar length of time, but the lesson to be learned from *Gaiety of Nations* is that adequate care, thought and attention must be given to all amateur production if the British amateur film movement is to compete successfully with similar movements on the Continent and in the U.S.A.

Hastily conceived and shoddily constructed work will only bring discredit.

R. Bond
Close Up, November 1929

The Future of the Amateur Film Movement

What is to become of the amateur film movement?

Sound has brought it to the crossroads and there is no leader to point the way.

Obviously to produce sound films—even if they were intelligent and God forbid it if they weren't—is beyond the resources of most amateur societies. Is it, then, any use going on? If it is, and I doubt it, which road will they take— The hard way of experiment and originality or the easy descent of imitation, lingering in the pleasant valley of 'let's-photograph-dear-grandmamma-on-the-lawn'?

Is it any use making films on substandard stock any longer? Have Eisenstein Pudovkin, Metzner and the others really left us anything to do in silence? Apart, of course, from photographing drains upside down or getting new angles on kitchen sinks, which is no longer done even in the most advanced circles. (All Hollywood left us to do in silence, of course, is suffer. In talkies, even more so.)

It is a great pity that the Amateur Film League of Great Britain and Ireland died almost before it was born. Incidentally, I have never seen any reference in any film journal to its demise, which caused much heart burning in the breasts of the members of at least one society I know. Here, I think, is an appropriate place to mention it. I have been wanting to get it off my chest for a long time.

Club delegates to the first (and the last?) National Cine Convention held in London in October, 1929, unanimously decided to form the League with the object of unifying and co-ordinating the movement in the British Isles. What happened to the

199

unanimity when they reached home is a mystery.

It was hoped, we were told in a circular, to place services at the disposal of clubs which would include a library for the interchange of films, a library of film books, an annual production competition, a technical bureau and other facilities.

Each society was asked to send a minimum donation of £2—'anything in excess would be gladly received and indeed welcome'—to set up a fund for working expenses.

I was very enthusiastic about the scheme and persuaded the society with which I was then connected to send two pounds. Some of the members were against it because the Society had only just been formed and we were very short of funds.

The receipt of the two pounds was acknowledged and then for a long time we heard nothing. *Amateur Films* had been chosen as the official organ of the Central Body (and how it became a body!) and the first sign that all was not well came when that ceased publication.

We went on hoping, but heard nothing and finally, on the instructions of my society, I wrote the provisional secretary asking for information. He replied that he was afraid the League had died a sudden death, that the response to the appeal for donations had been very disappointing and that (he believed) the few pounds which were subscribed had been swallowed up in expenses.

He also gave me the address of the gentleman who had been elected chairman and I wrote twice to him asking for information, but I have never received any reply.

I do not know whether any other societies were similarly treated. If they were they have my sympathy. I was very sorry that the scheme had fallen through, but mingled with that sorrow was indignation at the way in which my society had been treated after responding to the limit of its resources.

In view of this failure it is doubtful if any further steps will be taken in the near future to co-ordinate the activities of the many societies scattered throughout the British Isles.

The result is that they are leaderless, working independently of each other and more or less in the dark. In those circumstances how can they know whether they are progressing or marking time?

I wonder if these societies have solved the problem of social activities? Is their chief object seriously to make films in the hope of achieving something really worth while, or are they doing it just for the fun of the thing, so that the members can have a good time?

In my view nothing should be allowed to interfere with the serious business of a society. After all if one wants social recreation one does not join a film society, but a club.

Surely members should be enthusiastic enough about their work—and it should be looked on as work—without the aid of social intercourse. Or do they want dominoes and darts to absorb their superfluous energies?

I do not suggest of course, that things have reached such a pass, but no doubt many societies have had this problem to tackle and it seems to me that they are merely wasting their time, if they do not concentrate on what should be their main function—to make films which contain the best that is in them all.

These two questions—sound and social—have put the movement in a peculiar position and between the two it seems unlikely that any work of real value will be done. I hope, however, that I am wrong.

LESLIE B. DUCKWORTH
Close Up, March 1931

The Amateur Film Maker
Work or play?
A plan for amateur cine societies

In film-making one is undertaking a creative adventure, using a relatively unfamiliar idiom for expression.

If most of us find it necessary to spend ten or twelve years at school to gain some mastery over English Grammar and English Literature in order to express ourselves intelligibly in good English prose, it is unreasonable to expect that we can use a moving pictorial language expressively and create a good piece of film work if we have made little attempt to learn the A.B.C. of this language. The creative musician thinks it advisable to study the grammar of music and other social matters concerned with his Art over a period of from six to ten years before venturing on the composition of a large creative work such as a Symphony. If the amateur film-maker essays to create the cinematic equivalent of a Symphony

200

without first having undergone as strict a training as the composer and author find necessary, it is little to be wondered at if the finished product is incompetent and worthless.

Instead of engaging in grandiose attempts at production the first thing an amateur Society should do is to form its members into a class for the study of the fundamental elements involved in film-making. I know of no text-book on the Cinema written with the same objective as are written Prout's 'Harmony' and the 'Standard English Grammar', but this is obviously what we require. Pudovkin's excellent 'Film Technique' is the nearest approach to a text-book of this kind known to me. The second half of Rotha's 'The Film till Now', and Elliot's rather pretentious 'Anatomy of Motion Picture Art' would help to supplement the Pudovkin book.

The Analytical Method needs no commendation, and is as useful a mode of instruction for film students as it has proved to be for medical and art students. Sequences from film 'Classics' in the Pathé and Kodak sub-standard libraries, chosen to illustrate a particular point in film technique, should be selected for study. Those dealing with the simplest type of action should, of course, be dealt with first. The Kuleshov experimental sequence, given on pages 85-86 of Pudovkin's book, might serve as an introduction. This little example contains illustrations of most of the fundamentals of the story-telling film. From it can be demonstrated that (a) the camera represents the eye of the spectator; (b) that the camera represents the eye of a spectator gifted with the power of altering his point of observation, and hence able to vary the distance between himself and the object observed (this is, of course, the cardinal difference between the techniques of stage and cinema); (c) that dramatic continuity is established on the basis of shots 3 and 4 of this example, i.e., shot 3—the young man points, shot 4—that at which he points is shown; (d) that the relative lengths of the various shots to one another is important.

The sequence to be studied should be shown in a half-darkened room, only the unlit screen being in complete darkness, and the members should sit with writing material in front of them. The sequence should be shown once through (the dura-

tion of its screening being duly noted), and then it should be screened shot by shot. After a shot has been shown, the members (whom we now may call students, in the best sense of that word) should be asked to write a line or two describing what they have just seen. The shots should be numbered, and whether adjacent shots are dissolved or cut should be noted. The distance of the observer (i.e., the camera) from the scene should also be recorded—close up, mid-shot, or long-shot. When finished, each student will have before him a shooting script of the sequence, taken down by his observations, from which, in conjunction with the film itself, he may learn much. A comparison of the various descriptions of one and the same shot is often instructive, and is invaluable for deducting how much actual movement in a shot 'gets across'.

Having broken the flowing sequence up into separate shots (a procedure essential before an analysis can be begun), we can now study it in detail. Each time the observer's viewpoint changes, the *reason* for this change should be clearly understood. . .

The Fritz Lang films are excellent examples of a *normal* story-telling technique, and students should aim at acquiring just such a sane normality before attempting experiments in technique.

In an analysis of a film sequence we should endeavour to understand the reason for every change in the *distance* of the observer's viewpoint: why, for example, the mid-shot of Siegfried and the Dragon where *Siegfried is about to strike the dragon's eye* is followed up by a close-up of *the eye itself and the sword plunging into it* . . . to emphasise the importance of a detail which might otherwise escape our notice.

The time for which each shot holds the screen should be noted, and the general 'tempo' of the sequence determined. The significance of 'tempo' would be realised by working out the first five minutes of Dupont's *Vaudeville* and contrasting the relatively long shots in the opening Prison scene with their effect of ponderous solemnity—speaking of a world where normal reckonings of time are displaced by a wearisome infinity of time—with the succeeding Fair scene in which the quick succession of short lively scenes create an impression of light-hearted gaiety.

Analysis continued into a second year of study could concern itself with the balance of the various sequences in relation to one another and to the film as a whole, and to detailed analysis within the single frame (a subject made particularly complex by the acceptance of camera mobility as a part of the cinema's regular technique) and with other aspects of cinematic art.

Exercises which aim at training the imagination (a faculty which, like every other human faculty, is capable of development) should be frequently indulged in. That of giving out a short incident in narrative form suitable for cinematic treatment which the student has to cast as a shooting script is excellent for this purpose, and one which is valuable in training the student in cinema to visualise his images and select from those visualised the ones most suitable to his particular treatment of the subject. Exercises should be compiled in finished scenario (shooting-script) form, and submitted for correction either to the individual member who has been acting as 'teacher' or to a professional film expert, for criticism. The incident chosen should not exceed 50 or 60 single shots, to allow for detailed criticism, and it should be selected with the object of setting a definite problem to the student for solution . . .

A grounding in such a course of study as I have suggested would eventually give the student of cinema a sub-conscious background of film grammar. He would then no longer be inclined to take topical pictures merely for their photographic value. He would take little pride in any individual shot, however good by itself, unless he could mentally 'place it' and link it up with other shots into an ordered and logical sequence.

I doubt very much if the amateur ciné societies in this country as they are at present constituted are disposed to put in the necessary year or two of really hard study necessary to give them a foundation on which to build. With the exception of a solitary individual here and there, societies for the most part are quite content to amuse themselves playing at film making, expending an enormous amount of energy and misguided enthusiasm but producing films which, as films, are so much wasted celluloid. When the means of expression becomes second nature to a creative artist only then can he fully concern himself with the matter to be expressed; which is equivalent to saying that only then can he create Art.

ERIK CHISHOLM
Cinema Quarterly, Vol. 1, no. 1, Winter 1932-33 (Extract)

The Independent Film-maker
No More Film Plays!

After many years of writing on cinema I have begun to despair of revolt against screen-pap coming from within the industry itself. I consider Hollywood and recall the broken hopes of Eisenstein, Stiller, Murnau, Flaherty, Dudley Murphy, and the other able men who were battered by the system there.

The crystallization of the film method must come from outside commercial ranks. More and more I am convinced that the 16mm film is the avenue to progress.

The tremendous cost of modern tone-film production raises an insurmountable barrier before the young would-be creator in celluloid. But the sub-calibre film offers him an inexpensive field in which to work.

The amazing lack of good sub-calibre film work is not due, as is commonly supposed, to the machines now available. I find it due almost solely to lack of imagination on the part of the workmen in the narrow-film field. Give a cinema group a supply of film stock and usually it will try to produce a 'play' in imitation of Hollywood. If the world didn't produce another film-play for five years we'd still be over-supplied. Shoot sonatas of leaves and grass, tone-poems of clouds and water, gavottes in abstract shape, documentaries of the machines you toil at and the land you live in! But don't shoot a play!

The greatest need, as I see it, for progress in the narrow-film field, is for greater technical knowledge on the part of the creator. Generally the artist detests anything that smacks of figures and tables; yet cinema is art-through-machine and it must be studied. You may have the finely sensitive eye that can see a camera-angle, frame a composition, see the delight of splashed sunlight and half-lit shadows; but that's only the beginning. If you won't learn to use a photometer, to set the right stop, to handle your filters, you'd better go back to pencil-sketching.

In fact, the best workman will go beyond his needs and will start at once to do his own laboratory work. For the one great drawback of the sub-calibre film at this time is the use of reversal stock—*i.e.*, stock that is developed by the film maker into a positive. You send the exposed film back to the maker. In some factories your film is machine-developed—by a machine that automatically labours to iron out all the fades that you slaved to get.

To record on negative stock, to develop and print it yourself, immediately makes your medium flexible; the grace of dissolves, superimpositions, the entire possibilities of montage, are then available. Under these conditions the rank amateurishness of the sub-calibre film disappears, and in truth you can attain all the technical perfection of the standard film of commercial cinema—and even more.

The sub-calibre film as a field for the film-artist is now being enriched by the 16mm sound-cameras.

Two years ago the American Society of Motion Picture Engineers declared publicly that 16 mm. sound-on-film was impossible. Recently I made a film with the 'impossible' camera created by RCA-Victor. Still in the experimental stage at that time, still full of many 'bugs,' the camera could fulfil its major destiny: it could record sound with all the fidelity of any ten thousand dollar Hollywood apparatus. Speech recorded perfectly; music recordings were surpassed only by the lately developed 'High Fidelity' and 'Wide Range' systems now used in Hollywood, which record overtones in the extremely high and extremely low cycles.

The only drawback to the coming sound cameras in the narrow-film field is lack of flexibility. They are produced for the amateur who wants to take a picture of little Nancy singing 'Oats, peas, beans, and barley grows.' Recording again is on the rigid reversal film stock, and there is no means of post-synchronization of sound. In other words, it is a talkie-camera—and what the film-creator needs is a tone-film camera; one that records on negative stock and which will thus allow all conceivable variations of sight-images and sound-images that are corelated at the desire of the artist in the printing.

Possibly the construction of such cameras must be worked out by ingenious amateurs who will guide the mass-production men much as radio amateurs were always far ahead of the industrial radio-builders in the earlier days of development.

But whether in sound or in silence, the narrow-film field offers a chance to those young men who groan at the vulgarity and artistic sterility of the movie industry's product.

There are clubs, schools, and homes, all with 16 mm. projectors. The present supply of 16 mm. films is pretty poor, and I see no great reason for making those projectors grind merrily. There are reissues of Hollywood films in stock at movie camera stores—if that cheers you up. But, apart from the remarkable *Fall of the House of Usher*, I know of no sub-calibre film that is worth showing twice.

The would-be film creator on both sides of the Atlantic would do well to bottle up the energy now expended on impotent hate of Hollywood and its screen lollipops. That energy could be better expended upon production of good sub-calibre films; in formation of a central bureau to distribute such pictures to the clubs, schools, and homes that need them. Thus the public, fed for years on the dope of sex-stories, could be made to realise that the screen can give us something far more stirring and vital than *Cocktail Hour* or *Gold Diggers of 1933*.

ERIC M. KNIGHT
Cinema Quarterly, Autumn 1933

Independent Film Makers Association

Hon. Secy., G. A. SHAW
Hon. Treas., J. C. H. DUNLOP
32 SHAFTESBURY AVENUE, LONDON,
*W.*1.

Advisers:
ANTHONY ASQUITH
ANDREW BUCHANAN
JOHN GRIERSON
STUART LEGG
PAUL ROTHA
BASIL WRIGHT
ALAN HARPER (*Sub-Standard Apparatus*)

The Independent Film-Makers Association has been formed to bring together and assist those who are interested in the production of Documentary, Experimental, and Educational films.

CO-OPERATIVE EFFORT
The Association will put members in touch with each other and where practicable will

arrange that several members, though living in different parts of the country, may work together as a unit on one film. In suitable centres autonomous groups will be formed so that by pooling their resources members may be able to widen the scope of their activities and even set up collective studios.

PROFESSIONAL ADVICE
The Advisers of the Association are at all times prepared to place their expert knowledge at the disposal of members. Advice on production, on the preparation of scenarios, on treatment, photography, editing and every aspect of film-making is available on application, in the first instance, to the Hon. Secretary.

REVIEWS OF FILMS
Certain of the Advisers have agreed to review members' films and to give constructive criticism either privately or in the official organ of the Association.

FILM EXCHANGE
A catalogue of films made by members will be prepared and circulated. A suitable rental will be charged to non-members. Where possible the Association will endeavour to find a market for the production of its members.

Scenarios which meet the requirements of the objects of the Association may be entered in the Scenario Service. Manuscripts will be available for production by members free of charge, but suitable fees will be asked from non-members. A list of themes and subjects required by commercial firms and educational organizations will be circulated to members.

INFORMATION BULLETIN
A private Bulletin will be issued to members periodically. This will contain the names and addresses of all members as enrolled and confidential information regarding the various activities of the Association.

SUMMER SCHOOL
It is proposed to hold each year at least one Summer Production School at which prominent directors and experts will give practical instruction in different branches of film-making. From time to time it is also intended to arrange demonstrations of apparatus and exhibitions of films.

OFFICIAL ORGAN
The official organ of the Association is *Cinema Quarterly* which will contain in each issue a special section devoted to the activities of the Independent Film-Makers. *Cinema Quarterly* will be posted free to members on publication.

SUBSCRIPTION
The Annual Subscription is 10/6, which includes all services, Bulletin, and official organ.

Cinema Quarterly, Autumn 1933

'HOME MOVIES' 1934 COMPETITIONS
Editorial note:
Competitions were one means by which amateur production was stimulated quantitatively in the commercial interests of the equipment and stock manufacturers. However, competitions also occasionally functioned as talent contests, giving a chance to the 'independent' film-maker to 'turn professional'. Judges for competitions held by the Institute of Amateur Cinematographers, for example, included such well known figures as Alexander Korda, Victor Saville and C. A. Lejeune (film critic of the Observer). Similarly, Norman McLaren was 'discovered' by John Grierson and asked to join the GPO Film Unit after Grierson saw McLaren's films at the Scottish Amateur Film Festival in 1936.

More important, however, is the ideology implicit in the competition's division into categories: the amateur film-maker became a type of local anthropologist who recorded and examined 'family', 'nature' and 'community', three contexts in which the film-maker/subject could be placed (cf. the reference to Flaherty's more exotic Man of Aran). *In the case of the 'child films', however, this gave rise to what the judges called 'insufficient originality in most child pictures, charming as they are in the main.'*

While the 'child film' remained a popular genre, a variety of other amateur genres were proposed. The following year's choices, for example, included the topic of 'The Red Cross' and 'They Have Passed This Way', a category devoted to films dealing with the place or places associated with some famous character in history or fiction.

For the Encouragement of Amateur Cinematography

A Gold Medal and Five Pounds Cash for:
The Best Nature Film on 9½mm.
The Best Nature Film on 16mm.

Under the heading of 'Nature Films' may be included life stories of flowers, plants, animals, birds and insects, stop-motion studies, the story of the seasons, and so forth. The winners in this section will stand a good chance of selling their films to the libraries, as was the case with Mr. Le Grice's film The Swan, which won our Gold Medal last year. See that your titles are clearly explanatory and accurate, but not too long.

A Gold Medal and Five Pounds Cash for:
The Best Child Film on 9½mm.
The Best Child Film on 16mm.

The 'Child' film is perhaps the most popular of all cine subjects, for it has been said with much truth that four out of five cine cameras are purchased to make a record of the children. Maybe you have a series of pictures of your child taken over a number of years which can be edited into a most fascinating series. Perhaps you have thought of a picture showing 'Baby's Day', from the first ray of sunshine falling on the cot in the morning up to the final shot of a tired but contented little head resting on the pillow at night. Maybe a 'Child Adventure' picture appeals to you—There is unlimited scope, and we anticipate many novel entries.

A Gold Medal and Five Pounds Cash for:
The Best 'Local Life' Film on 9½mm.
The Best 'Local Life' Film on 16mm.

Here is a new subject for competition, but one of great importance. Tell the story of your town, your village, your district; film some little known local industry in an understanding way; show British rural life as it really is, seek out something missed by the professional—opportunities are to be found everywhere. Remember what Flaherty did in Man of Aran, and let this film inspire you. But avoid at all costs the slavish imitation of professional 'travel' pictures, with their often false values and wrong emphasis on non-essentials.
Home Movies and Home Talkies, Aug. 1934

THE EDITOR'S NEWSREEL

Editorial note:
Amid the usual gamut of technical tips, the editor of Home Movies and Home Talkies *here defends in an editorial the right of the amateur to use film as a 'measure of memory' as opposed to what he calls documentary and other serious pictures beloved by the sneering highbrows.*

Winter may be the proper time for titling, editing and projection, but the current custom of putting the camera on the shelf so far as general shooting is concerned seems one to be regretted. That the habit is widespread is plain from correspondence received from our readers, and the fact moves me to offer a suggestion; I will put it in the form of a question: Have you ever worked out just what it would cost to make an indoor picture by artificial light?

To many movie makers the answer would probably be surprising. Let us see how it works out: For a film consisting of close-ups and semi-close shots showing head and shoulders of not more than two persons, three photoflood bulbs will suffice with a lens of only fair speed, and that means seven shillings and sixpence. Some flex and three simple reflectors and holders might cost another twelve shillings, and a few shillings-worth of wood will build the necessary supports to carry the lights.

There is your lighting equipment for a little over a sovereign, and for the rest you want enough film to run perhaps five minutes, and you can work out the cost of that for yourself. For this very modest total you can taste the fascination of artificial light work, wherein all your effects are under exact control, you never have to wait for the conditions you want, and your results have the added touch of intimacy that comes from working in your own home.

There is indeed a very special interest and attraction about filming by artificial light, for even with quite simple equipment there is great scope for the production of artistic and attractive effects, and whenever you achieve something striking you have the satisfaction of feeling that you really did it yourself without having to share the credit with King Sol!

Not Really Difficult

A very little experimenting will suffice to put you on the track of correct lighting and exposure conditions, and then you can tackle your film. The idea is scarcely new, but the family portrait gallery still has much to commend it if a little thought is given to its planning. Suppose, for example, that you arrange the film to show how various members of the family set about spending a quiet evening at home; there is abundant scope for simple close-up treatment there, and the resulting film can be quite a pleasant little affair to possess.

May I at this point put in a plea for the simple and unpretentious little picture of just ourselves in characteristic activities and surroundings? We amateurs are often urged to make 'documentary' and other 'serious' pictures, and no doubt that is all very excellent, but we should not feel embarrassed about exploiting also what is really one of the greatest charms of the cine camera—its power to make vivid personal records.

As Time Passes

We should remember that even the simplest film of this sort can become a treasured possession in only a few years' time—the increase of interest that comes with the passing of time is a phenomenon familiar enough to those who have been at the game for a while, but the newcomer should be warned that he ought to make a certain amount of footage of the personal type every year simply as an investment for the future.

Let me give you an instance of the way films can in time become measures of memory. Some four years ago I happened to be near a certain bungalow on the Yorkshire coast at which I stayed for many happy holidays as a boy, and I took the trouble to carry a confoundedly heavy camera some three miles across rough country paths and shoot the place up with some thoroughness.

At the time I did not perhaps understand quite why I did it, but I have just heard that the present owner has pulled the old place down to build something more modern in its place, and you can imagine how I value those few feet of film now! I only wish that I could have shot them on colour stock, for much of the charm of the place was in its colour.

Go Your Own Way!

That is but one example of the way the cine camera can make records which will become priceless possessions in years to come, but it will serve to explain why I feel that it is doing the newcomer a service to urge him to exploit this capability of the instrument to the full. Do not be afflicted with any sense of false shame—shoot the baby on the lawn if you want to, and turn a deaf ear to the sneers of the highbrows! Your projector will be the magician's wand to bring back the happy times of the present in years to come.

Does all this sound rather unbecoming in a magazine wherein the amateur is often exhorted to make 'worth-while' pictures? Maybe it does, but of that I am no more ashamed than *you* should be of making films for frankly sentimental reasons! It would be a dull world if we spent all our time improving ourselves.

Home Movies and Home Talkies, October 1936

DOCUMENTARIES AND PROFESSIONALISM

Editorial note: *The distinction between professional/non-professional and sponsored commercial film became a growing point of contention, voiced here at the end of the Thirties in the journal of the Association of Cinematograph Technicians, later to develop into the film and TV workers' union, the ACTT.*

Cinema Log
Documentary Films should be the Professional's Province

Met John Grierson, much publicised documentary chief, and enquired why he encourages amateurs to take up the making of documentary 16 mm. films in competition with the professional who has been so hard hit by the trade slump. His reply was that a number of concerns had only £50 to spend on film propaganda and so he recommended these clients to hand their filming over to amateur cine societies as he didn't think the money worth a professional film technician's consideration.

I undertook to show he was wrong. And here are a few rough figures to prove it. Many technicians who are out of work could do these jobs and profit could be obtained by any firm backing such a project.

(All figures are for 16 mm. film).

	£	s.	d.
Hire of camera (1 week)	2	2	0
400ft. neg. stock (equivalent to 1,000ft. 35 mm.)	4	4	0
Printing 400 ft. (1 copy)	2	10	0
Developing Neg.		12	0
Cameraman	15	0	0
Lights (if required)	5	0	0
Travelling and general expenses	6	0	0
Editing	2	2	0
Making and Printing Titles ..	2	2	0
	£39	12	0

leaving us £10 8s. 0d. for incidentals, or £15 8s. 0d. if lights are not needed.

I personally have a great respect for our amateur friends, and have seen some very good work turned out by them. But hospitals, churches and other institutions requiring the greatest appeal in the 16 mm. field with limited funds should know that they can obtain a professional job at these figures. Music and commentary can be added if a little more cash is available.

Says Andrew Buchanan

As guest speaker at the London Film Institute Society's showing of sub-standard films, Mr. Buchanan spoke in challenging vein. Quotes *The Cinema*:

'He stressed the importance of keeping the amateur movement alive, saying it was an example to the professional industry and that he had seen a film costing £5 which had shown more ingenuity and appreciation of film values than some mammoth picture. Mr. Buchanan pointed out that the non-professional has freedom to do what he likes—the amateur, too, does not think of film making in terms of money'.

You're telling us, Mr. Buchanan!

After some more deprecatory remarks concerning the British industry, the effect thereon of Bills, and the high wages thought by some technicians to be their due: 'If', said Mr. Buchanan, 'we have succeeded in making better documentaries than any other country, we should extend this field. Amateurs were keeping alive this spirit and were more liable to create a true revival than any Bill'.

There were a lot more documentary garnishings in his speech which space prevents my reporting. What I want to point out to Mr. Buchanan is that his name has been built on the loyal co-operation of professional technicians. Many documentary people learned their job in a Government department, where time was no object. Professional film folk have had to contend with commercial supervision. I welcome the documentary, but dislike this continual depreciation of the professional technician. My own work and that of my colleagues in this field is turned out in a day or part of a day, and the resulting films are highly commercial and not entirely inartistic. They have had a market in all parts of the world and many times have been used as cut-ins and backgrounds for major productions both at home and in America. The screen magazines to which they are a contribution hold the record for the longest continuous run in the motion picture world.

Buchanan made his name by his linked commentary in Gaumont Cine-Magazine—Grierson by 'Drifters'. Each were backed by a first-class professional technical crew. 'Drifters' received very wide praise and is regarded as a landmark in documentary. But it is not the only possible story to be found in the herring fleets. The drama of the thousand or more boats, fishing in hundreds of miles of stormy waters, catching millions of herrings, and the thousands of families dependent on the vicissitudes of the shoals and markets, has never yet been told in motion pictures.

Why not stop riding the professional film technician, documentary chiefs?

KENNETH GORDON
The Cine Technician, May-June 1938

Filmography

Trevor Ryan

Introduction

This filmography is intended to fulfil two functions: firstly, to provide essential information concerning the films produced, distributed and screened by the various 'independent' film groups active in Britain in the 1930s; secondly, to give some indication of the extent and nature of this activity. The principal criterion for inclusion was whether or not the film had been made or used by an 'independent' film group on a non-commercial basis. The brief was to compile a list of films made outside the commercial cinema industry, with a political-educational rather than a commercial purpose, offered as 'alternative' or 'oppositional' to the ideology of the commercial cinema. Films are therefore included which were not made by independent film groups, but were clearly produced and used as alternatives to the dominant 'entertainment' cinema, as in the case of the Soviet films. On this basis it is hoped that the bulk of films handled by Atlas Films, Kino Films, the Film and Photo League, and the Progressive Film Institute have been included. However, this is not the case with the social-democratic film organisations such as the Workers' Film Association, the National Association of Co-operative Education Committees' Film Department, and the London and Royal Arsenal Co-operative Societies' Film Departments. The majority of films handled by these organisations were entertainment, interest or travel films produced by commercial organisations, and Co-operative Wholesale Society publicity films. The WFA acted largely as agents for the commercial distributors in offering programmes of their films to labour organisations for social and political meetings. Only a small number of films handled by the WFA and the Co-operative film bodies were political-educational in content and purpose. On the other hand, only a small number of films handled by the independent film groups were of a social or purely educational character, and even these were produced by independent, non-commercial film groups, such as the films of the Dartington Film Unit, and *Vitamins*, produced by Cambridge Film Productions. These have been included to suggest the full range of films distributed by such groups as Kino and PFI. Other independently made films have been included where it was evident that they had been used in social-political campaigns or were themselves direct political interventions in particular situations, even though they were probably not distributed by the main independent film groups under consideration. The individual productions of J. W. Harris (*Hunger Marchers*) and G. Sewell (*Gaiety of Nations*) fall within this category. Films by 'documentary' film units

208

have not been included except where they were commissioned to make films specifically for labour organisations. The WFA and the various Co-operative film groups envisaged using films as part of the political and educational campaigns of the Labour Party and the Trades Union Congress. In this respect, they viewed films as an 'alternative' to the dominant uses of the cinema, and as a definite alternative or 'counter measure' to the content of the newsreels, and the work of the Conservative Party's film unit. It is with these considerations in mind that those films of the Realist Film Unit commissioned by the social democratic organisations are included in the filmography.

Of the titles listed, about half had foreign origins. Just over fifty per cent of the foreign films came from the Soviet Union and were distributed, with very few exceptions, by Atlas, Kino and/or the PFI. As suggested elsewhere in this book, the building of such a large library of Soviet films for commercial and non-commercial distribution must be seen in the context of the policies of the Comintern and of the CPGB. Exclusion of these foreign films generally, and the Soviet films in particular, from the filmography would give a totally erroneous impression of the character of the work of these independent film groups. The primary task which Kino had set itself was the importation and distribution of Soviet films. With the closing of Mezhrabpomfilm in 1936 and the outbreak of war in Spain the same year, Kino lost its main source for such films, but gained a new focal point for its activity, as did the Progressive Film Institute which had originally been established to import and distribute 35mm Soviet and other foreign films which would otherwise have not become available in Britain. The PFI began production in 1936 in response to the Spanish situation. Both groups went on to produce films on events in Britain, but these were, as far as can be determined, secondary tasks until the Munich crisis of September 1938. Yet even though changes in emphasis appear to have taken place in the aftermath of Munich, Kino introduced eight new Soviet films to Britain in February 1939.

The paucity of internal documents has proved a major problem in the compilation of this filmography. There are, above all, no single sources to which reference can be made for a full list of the films which any particular group handled. Consequently this list cannot be regarded as in any way 'complete'. Foreign 'independent' films are very difficult to trace, often being known by more than one title; there are probably many more which need to be included, yet for which there is no clear evidence that they were distributed by a particular group. On the other hand, several titles have been discovered in association with an independent distributor, yet little further information has surfaced to pinpoint either their origins, their date of release in Britain, or their format: e.g., *Chinese Soviet Army*. (An indispensable source has been a small folder of photostats of Kino publicity slips and library catalogues, kindly given to the author by Herbert Marshall.) Lack of information on this initial level is compounded by a general lack of information for non-standard films: they neither received much attention from the film press, nor were they usually submitted to the British Board of Film Censors. Recourse to the pages of the *Daily Worker* or the various film journals is only partially rewarding and reliance on these sources raises further problems. Some films were advertised well in advance of the proposed release date, and never completed—or, if finished, there are occasionally no indications that they were released. The FPL gave wide publicity to their proposed series of films designed to promote the popular front; yet, as far as can be determined, only one of the seven (*People's Front Newsreel*) was ever made. A principal source of information within these papers and journals is advertisements for political and social meetings. Necessarily brief, these items regularly refer to film shows, but often name the films to be shown with little regard for accuracy in relation to the titles. Subsequently particular films were shown by several titles, and several films had the same title, which in the absence of further information about them leads to much confusion. It is for this reason, among others, that wherever possible the date of release has been pinpointed to a particular month in any one year. In the large majority of cases this is reasonably accurate, the date being derived from the first screening of the finished film (there were often previews of the rough-cut films of the FPL). In a few cases, namely the cluster of Soviet new films made available in 1935 and 1936, the months given can only be taken as a rough guide. In most cases the date of release indicates when a particular film was first available in Britain. There are exceptions, however. *Alone,* for example, was made available by the Film Society in 1932. Several Soviet and German films were briefly available through Atlas before Kino and PFI released them. In such cases two release dates are provided. Where there was a considerable delay between the 16mm and 35mm release of a film, release dates for both gauges have been given; otherwise the date given applies to all groups listed for any one film. To indicate, in such cases, the agency to which each date refers, the distributors are read 'chronologically'.

Running times have similarly proved difficult to determine with any real accuracy, and it must be stressed that those given should be taken only as a guide. Individual films were advertised within the space of one year with up to two or three different running times. *Soap Bubbles* was advertised as being both 60 and 45 minutes; *Crime Against Madrid*, 30 and 45 minutes; *Peace and Plenty*, 20 and 30 minutes. This problem has been complicated by the considerable discrepancies between contemporary advertised running times and the footage surviving today. Perhaps the most obvious case is that of *Free Thaelmann*: advertised in *Kino News* as 25 minutes long, and in a Kino leaflet as 30 minutes, the existing copies are no more than 15 minutes. Moreover, it was customary to increase the length of a film in publicity in order to attract more people to the show, which doesn't simplify the task of checking against contemporary sources. As a general rule, therefore, the running times given are those which are to be found in the contemporary sources, even where they clearly do not coincide with those of the surviving films.

Another persistent difficulty has been the placing of extant 'films' which are without titles or incomplete. Some of these are perhaps pieces of footage which were never made into completed films. A more likely explanation is that they were items in newsreel films, which on losing their topicality were cut up

210

again for future use in compilations as stock shots, or shown separately. This appears to be the case, for example, with *Busmen's Holiday* which was never intended to be 'released' on its own, but as a part of *News Review 1937*. Similarly *ILP Summer School, May Day 1935, Tom Mann at Pioneers' Camp* and *Soviet Folk Dancers* were items in *Workers' Newsreel No. 4*.

It is doubtful whether today a listing of this kind can be arranged fully satisfactorily. Since several films were distributed by two or more of the independent film groups, and there are many whose production origins are uncertain, the arrangement of the filmography by either distributor or producer would lead to much confusion. The list has therefore been arranged alphabetically by the English title. Despite obvious drawbacks, it is hoped that such an arrangement provides easier access to the available information. For reasons of space the individuals involved in the production of particular films are omitted. Print location has only been given for films produced or partly produced by film groups in Britain. Lastly—and inherent in any arrangement of films without a commentary for each entry—such a list gives the impression that these films were of comparable or equal significance in the pre-war period. This is far from the case, now or then. It can only be pointed out that the films vary considerably in their technical, aesthetic and political orientation, being produced for a variety of social and political purposes: for specific political campaigns or broad cultural movements; for cadre audiences or more heterogeneous or popular audiences; as newsreels or as fiction.

It is of course significant that several of the films are no longer extant, and are known only by written references or verbal descriptions. As Claire Johnston points out in her article in this book, the repression of 'alternative' discourses within history is one of the means by which a 'system of enunciability' is maintained and stabilised in the interests of the *status quo*. In addition, and perhaps more resistant to analysis, it is interesting to note how the films have also been 'forgotten' by the very movement for which they were made. The present filmography aims to provide some raw material to begin examining that process*.

---

*As this book is being printed, further information has come to light about a number of these films. Additions and corrections to the filmography will be included in any subsequent edition.— T.R.

Sources

Published: The papers and journals *The Board of Trade Journal, Close Up, Co-operative News, The Daily Worker, Kino News, Left News, The Monthly Film Bulletin, The New Leader, Russia Today, The Sunday Worker, The Times.*

A Directory of British Film and Television Libraries, ed. F. Thorpe, London, 1975.

Films for Historians, BUFC, London, 1974.

Kino, by Jay Leyda, London, 1973.

Some British and Foreign Documentary and other Short Films, BFI, London, 1938.

Workers' Film Association, first and second Annual Reports, 1939, 1940.

WFA Bulletin of Films, 1942.

WFA Catalogue of Films, (circa 1943).

WFA Catalogue of 16mm Sound Films, 1942.

Unpublished: Catalogue of 'Film and Photo League' Films, compiled by Victoria Wegg-Prosser; ETV and PFI Acquisition Files (NFA); Slade Film History Register; National Film Archive Catalogues.

Many titles in this collection are available for study at the National Film Archive. A substantial number of British titles will shortly be available for hire from the BFI's Distribution Library.

Symbol: † May not have been completed/released.

Abbreviations

ACT	Association of Cinematograph Technicians
BFU	British Film Unit
CGT	Confédération Générale du Travail
CNT	Confédération National des Travailleurs
CPGB	Communist Party of Great Britain
CWS	Co-operative Wholesale Society
ETV	Educational and Television Films
FAI	Iberian Anarchist Federation
FPL	Film and Photo League
FSU	Friends of the Soviet Union
IPC	International Peace Campaign
ISF	International Sound Films
KLPG	Kino London Production Group
LCS	London Co-operative Society
LDCP	London District Communist Party
LWFS	London Workers' Film Society
M	Metropolis Pictures
MWFS	Merseyside Workers Film Society
NACEC	National Association of Co-operative Educational Committees
NFA	National Film Archive
NJCSR	National Joint Committee for Spanish Relief
PFI	Progressive Film Institute
PN	People's Newsreel
PPU	Peace Pledge Union
RACS	Royal Arsenal Co-operative Society
RFU	Realist Film Unit
RCVGF	Relief Committee for the Victims of German Fascism
SCFL	Scottish Central Film Library
SFC	Socialist Film Council
SPFA	Scottish People's Film Association
WFA	Workers' Film Association
WFPL	Workers' Film and Photo League

Title	Country	Production	Distribution	Gauge silent/sound running time	Date (first available through these organisations)	Print location
ABYSSINIA	Germany	Praesens	PFI	35/sd./50	1936	
ABYSSINIA	USSR	Soyuzkinochronika	PFI/ISF	16 & 35/sd./45	Dec. 1937	
ACHIEVEMENT	GB	RFU	WFA	16 & 35/sd./20	?Oct. 1939	ETV, NFA
ACTION AGAINST THE MEANS TEST	GB	FPL	?Kino	16/sil./10	1935	NFA
ADVANCE DEMOCRACY	GB	RFU	WFA	16 & 35/sd./18	Oct. 1938	
AGAINST IMPERIALIST WAR MAY DAY 1932	GB	?Atlas	?Atlas/?FSU	16/sil./?15	?July 1932	M
AIR BOMBING OF MADRID	Spain		PFI/Kino	16 & 35/sil./9	1937	NFA
ALONE	USSR	Soyuzkino	?Atlas/?FSU	35/sd./82	?Sept. 1932	
ALQUEZAR	Spain		Kino	16/sil./15	?1937	
ANIMAL, VEGETABLE, MINERAL	USSR		Kino	16/sd./10	Feb. 1939	ETV
ANTI-FASCIST DEMONSTRATIONS, 1937	GB	Kino	Kino	16/sil./2	Nov. 1937	
A.R.P.†	GB	British Film Unit	Kino	16/sd./?	1939	
THE AWAKENING OF MR COLE	GB	LCS	CWS/WFA	16/sd./20	May 1939	
BANANAS	GB	Dartington Film Unit	Kino	16/sil./10	?1936	
BARCELONA NEWSREEL	Spain	?Laya Films	Kino/PFI	16 & 35/sd./10	Feb. 1937	
BATTLESHIP POTEMKIN	USSR	Goskino	Kino/PFI	9.5 & 16 & 35/sil./72	Dec. 1933/ Mar. 1936	
BEHIND THE SPANISH LINES	GB	PFI	Kino/PFI	16 & 35/sd./20	June 1938	NFA, SCFL
BIRTH OF AN EMPIRE	USSR		PFI/WFA	35/?sd./?	?1936	
BLOW BUGLES BLOW!	GB	R. Messel	PFI	35/sd./75	Apr. 1936	
THE BOMBING OF CANTON	China	China Motion Picture Corporation	PFI	35/sd./9	1938	
BREAD (Alt. title: STUFF OF LIFE)	GB	Kino London Production Group	Kino	16/sil./12	May 1934	NFA

213

Title	Country	Production	Distribution	Gauge silent/ sound running time	Date (first available through these organisations)	Print location
BRITAIN EXPECTS (Alt. title: ENGLAND EXPECTS)	GB	PFI	Kino/PFI	16 & 35/sd./20	Dec. 1938 Jan. 1939	
THE BUILDERS	GB	WFA	WFA	16/sd./35	1940	
BUILDING THE WHITE SEA CANAL (Alt. title: PORT OF FIVE SEAS)	USSR	Vostok–Kino	Kino/PFI	16 & 35/sil./30	Sept. 1935	
BUSMEN'S HOLIDAY	GB	Kino	Kino	16/sil./7	1937	ETV, NFA
A CALL TO ARMS	France/ Spain	CNT/FAI	Kino	16/sd./20	Mar. 1937	
CAMBERWELL IS PREPARED	GB	WFA	WFA	16/sd./30	June 1939	
CANON STUART MORRIS OF BIRMINGHAM	GB	PPU	PPU	35/sd./2	1937	NFA
THE CHALLENGE OF YOUTH (Alt. title: YOUTH MARCHES ON)	GB	FPL	FPL	16/sil./?20	Dec. 1937	NFA
CHALLENGE TO FASCISM: GLASGOW'S MAY DAY 1938	GB	Glasgow Kino	Glasgow Kino	16/sil./17	June 1938	NFA
CHINA FIGHTS FOR FREEDOM	USA	?Frontier Films	Kino	16/sd./40	Dec. 1937	NFA
CHINA STRIKES BACK	USA	Frontier Films	Kino/PFI/ WFA	16 & 35/sd./25	Jan. 1938	NFA
CHINESE SOVIET ARMY	USA	?Frontier Films	Kino	16/?sd./30	?Oct. 1937	
CONSTRUCTION	GB	WFPL	Kino/FPL	16/sil./10	Dec. 1935	M
CORONATION MAY DAY (Alt. title: MERRY MONTH OF MAY)	GB	FPL	FPL	16/sil./?20	June 1937	M
CP DEMONSTRATIONS MAY DAY 1937	GB	Kino	Kino	16/sil./9	1937	ETV
CP 15th CONGRESS (Alt. title: CP CONGRESS-BIRMINGHAM 1938)	GB	PFI	Kino	16/sil./10	Nov. 1938	ETV, NFA
CRIME AGAINST MADRID	Spain	CNT/PFI	Kino	16/sd./30	July 1937	ETV

214

Title	Country	Production	Distributor	Format	Date	Archive
CRIMEA	USSR	Intourist	Kino	16/sil./12	1936	
CZECHOSLOVAKIA (Alt. title: PRELUDE TO CONQUEST)	USA	March of Time	Kino/ISF	16 & 35/sd./15	Sept. 1938	
THE DAILY WORKER FILM	GB	Kino/?LDCP	Kino/People's Newsreel	9.5 & 16/sil./3	Dec. 1937	NFA
THE DAWN	Eire	Hibernia	ISF/Kino	16 & 35/sd.,/80	Feb. 1937 Oct. 1937	NFA
DEFENCE OF BRITAIN	GB	WFPL	Kino/FPL	16/sil./10	Dec. 1935	
DEFENCE OF MADRID	GB	PFI	Kino	16/sil./45	Nov. 1936	
THE DESERTER	USSR	Mezhrabpomfilm	Kino	16/sd./75	Oct. 1937	
DICK SHEPHERD, FOUNDER OF PPU	GB	PPU	PPU	35/sd./8	1937	NFA
DOCKWORKERS	GB	FPL	FPL	16/sil./10	Nov. 1937	M
EARTH	USSR	VUFKU	Atlas Films	35/sil./85	?1931	
THE END OF ST PETERSBURG	USSR	Mezhrabpomfilm	PFI/Kino	16 & 35/sil./122	1935/1936	
FACES OF FRANCE	France	?Ciné-Liberté	Kino	16/sd./30	Jan. 1938	
FIGHT	GB	WFPL	FPL	16/sil./?	Dec. 1935	
FOR THE YOUNG	USSR	Soyuzkinochronika	Kino	16/sd./10	Oct. 1938	
FREE THAELMANN! (U.S. title: ERNST THAELMANN: FIGHTER AGAINST FASCISM)	USA/ Germany	RCVGF/FPL— New York	PFI/Kino	16 & 35/sil./20	July 1935	ETV, NFA
GAIETY OF NATIONS	GB	G. H. Sewell	?WFPL	16/sil./?	Oct. 1935	
THE GENERAL LINE (Alt. title: OLD AND NEW)	USSR	Sovkino	Atlas Films/ Kino	9.5 & 16 & 35/ sil./95	1931/Jan. 1934	
GENEROUS SOIL†	GB	FPL	FPL	16/sil./10	?Oct. 1937	
THE GHOST THAT NEVER RETURNS	USSR	Sovkino	Kino	9.5 & 16/sil./ 114	Sept. 1935	BFI
GIBRALTAR (Alt. title: THREAT TO GIBRALTAR)	USA	March of Time	PFI	35/sd./?	1938	
GLIMPSES OF MODERN RUSSIA (Alt. title: SNAPSHOTS OF MODERN RUSSIA)	GB	Atlas Films	Atlas Films	35/sil./10	Oct. 1930	NFA
GROWING UP	USSR		Kino	16/sd./10	Feb. 1939	

Title	Country	Production	Distribution	Gauge silent/sound running time	Date (first available through these organisations)	Print location
HARVEST FESTIVAL	USSR	Film Popular	PFI/Kino	16 & 35/sd./40	Oct. 1937	NFA
THE HEALTH OF SPAIN	Spain		PFI	35/sd./15	July 1938	NFA
HELL UNLIMITED (Alt. title: HELL UNLTD.)	GB	Glasgow School of Art Group	Kino	16/sil./20	1936	
HELP SPAIN	GB	NJCSR	NJCSR/Kino	16/sd./40	?Sept. 1938	NFA
HEROES OF THE ARCTIC	USSR	Soyuzkino	Kino	16/sil./90	April 1935	
HOLIDAY FROM UNEMPLOYMENT	GB	?WFPL/?Oxford Trades Council	WFPL/Kino	16/sil./15	Sept. 1935	
HUNGER MARCH 1934 (Alt. title: NATIONAL HUNGER MARCH 1934)	GB	Kino London Production	Kino/WFPL	16/sil./15	April 1934	M
HUNGER MARCH 1936 (Alt. title: MARCH AGAINST STARVATION)	GB	FPL	FPL	16/sil./10 20	April 1937	M
HUNGER MARCHERS	GB	J. Harris	?FPL/?Cambridge Film Productions	16/sil./10	Oct. 1934	
IF WAR SHOULD COME (Alt. title: IF WAR COMES)	USSR	Mosfilm	Kino/PFI	16 & 35/sd./50	Nov. 1938	NFA
ILP SUMMER SCHOOL, 1935	GB	Kino	Kino	16/sil./3	1935	ETV, NFA
IN THE LAND OF THE SOVIETS	USSR	?FSU	PFI/Kino/FSU	16/sil. 35/sd./60	Feb. 1936	ETV
INSIDE NAZI GERMANY	USA	March of Time	Kino	16/sd./15	Mar. 1939	
INTERNATIONAL BRIGADE	GB	PFI	Kino	16/sd./10	May 1938	ETV, NFA
INTERNATIONAL BRIGADE EMPRESS HALL (Alt. title: RETURN OF THE INTERNATIONAL BRIGADE)	GB	Association of Cinematograph Technicians		16/sil./?	1939	
INTERNATIONAL COLUMN	GB	PFI	Kino	16/sil./30	April 1937	

Title	Country	Production	Distributor	Format	Date	Archive
ISOTOV THE BOLSHEVIK	USSR	Soyuzkinochronika	Kino	16/sil./15	Jan. 1935	
INVASION OF SHANGHAI	Switzerland	?Prometheus	?Atlas Films	35/sil./?	?1932	
JUBILANT MARCH						
JUBILEE (Alt. title: BRITAIN 1935: JUBILEE YEAR)	USSR	North London Film Society/WFPL	Kino/PFI WFPL/ Kino	16 & 35/sd./15 16/sil./8	Nov. 1937 Oct. 1935	ETV, M, NFA
JUVENILE CRIME	USA	March of Time	Kino	16/sd./10	Feb. 1939	
LANCASHIRE PEACE DEMONSTRATION	GB	WFPL (Manchester)	WFPL	16/sil./?	1936	
LAND WITHOUT BREAD (Orig. title: LAS HURDES)	Spain	L. Buñuel	PFI/Kino	16 & 35/sd./30	1936	NFA
LENIN IN OCTOBER	USSR	Mosfilm	PFI	35/sd./97	1938	ETV
LENINGRAD	USSR	Intourist	Kino	16/sil./12	1936	
LIMESTONE	GB	Dartington Film Unit	Kino	16/sil./10	Mar. 1936	
THE LITTLE SCREW	USSR	Sovkino	Kino	16/sil./10	?Sept. 1934	
LIVERPOOL	GB	Merseyside Workers Film Society	MWFS/ Kino	16/sil./12	April 1934; 1936	
LONDON MAY DAY 1933†	GB	Kino London Production Group	Kino	16/sil./7	1936	M
LONDON WORKERS' OUTING EASTER 1935	GB	?Kino	Kino	16/sil./2		ETV, NFA
LONDON'S LABOUR DAY 1938	GB	Kino	Kino	16/?sd./?	1938	
MADRID 1936	Spain	L. Buñuel/Spanish Min. of Public Instruction	ISF	16 & 35/sd./35	Mar. 1938	
MADRID NOW	GB	PFI	Kino	16/sd./?20	1937	NFA, SCFL
MADRID TODAY	Spain	PFI/Spanish Min. of Public Instruction	PFI/Kino	16 & 35/sd./8	May 1937	
MANCHESTER AT WORK	GB	FPL (Manchester)	FPL	16/sil./?	Oct. 1937	

Title	Country	Production	Distribution	Gauge silent/ sound running time	Date (first available through these organisations)	Print location
MARIONETTES (Alt. title: A KING IS MADE)	USSR		Kino/PFI	16 & 35/sd./80	Oct. 1937	
MARTYRED TOWNS	GB	International Peace Campaign	Kino	16/sd./10	Sept. 1938	
MAY DAY 1935	GB	WFPL	Kino/WFPL	16/sil./2	Sept. 1938	ETV, NFA
MAY DAY 1937 (Alt. title: MAY 1st 1937)	GB	FPL	FPL	16/sil./10	?Dec. 1937	M
MEN AND JOBS	USSR	Soyuzkino	Kino/?FSU	16 & 35/sd./70	April/May 1936	NFA
MILLIONS OF US	USA	FPL	Kino/PFI	16 & 35/sd./15	1936	NFA
MR ATTLEE IN SPAIN	Spain		PFI	35/sil./5	?Mar. 1938	NFA
MODERN ORPHANS OF THE STORM (16mm title: BASQUE CHILDREN)	GB	NJCSR/V. Saville/ RFU	Kino/ NJCSR/ WFA	16 & 35/sd./10	1937	
MODERN RUSSIA	USSR		Kino	16/sil./15	?1936	
MOSCOW (Alt. title: MOSCOW TODAY)	USSR	Intourist	PFI/Kino	16 & 35/sil./15	?1936	
MOTHER	USSR	Mezhrabpom—Russ	Atlas Films/ Kino	35 & 16/sil./ 80	1930/Mar. 1935	
NANKING CAPTURED	China	?Frontier Films	Kino	16/sil./10, 20	1938	
NAZI CONQUEST NO. 1.	USA	March of Time	Kino	16/sd./10	Feb. 1939	
NEW BABYLON	USSR	Sovkino	Atlas Films/ PFI/ Kino/IF Kino	35 & 16/sil./ 111	1930/Jan. 1935	
A NEW RECRUIT	GB	London Co-operative Society	CWS/WFA	16/sd./40	May 1939	
NEW SCHOOLS FOR OLD	USA	March of Time	Kino	16/sd./10	Feb. 1939	
NEW SPAIN	Spain	L. Buñuel	ISF	35/sd./35	1938	

NEWS FROM SPAIN	GB	PFI	PFI/Kino/NACEC Film Dept.	16 & 35/sd./40	Apr. 1937	ETV, NFA
NEWS FROM SPAIN NO. 1.	Spain	Laya Films	?PFI	35/sd./13	1937	NFA
NEWS FROM SPAIN NO. 2.	Spain	Laya Films	?PFI	35/sd./10	1937	NFA
NEWS FROM SPAIN NO. 3.	Spain	Laya Films	?PFI	35/sd./10	1937	NFA
NEWS FROM SPAIN NO. 4.	Spain	Laya Films	?PFI	35/sd./10	1937	NFA
NEWS PARADE—HITLER OVER AUSTRIA	USA	Castle Films	Kino/FPL	16/sil./sd./10	Apr. 1938	M
NEWS PARADE NO. 1. (Alt. title: WAR IN CHINA)	USA	Castle Films	Kino/FPL	16/sil./sd./10	Oct. 1937	M
NEWS PARADE OF THE YEAR	USA	Castle Films	Kino/FPL	16/sil./sd./10	Jan. 1938	M
NEWS REVIEW 1937	GB	Kino	Kino	16/sil./30	Dec. 1937	
1931 (Alt. title: THE CHARTER FILM)	GB	Atlas Films	Atlas Films	35/sil./20	May 1931	
NON-INTERVENTION	GB	PFI	PFI	35/sd./10	July 1938	NFA
OCTOBER (Alt. title: TEN DAYS THAT SHOOK THE WORLD)	USSR	Sovkino	Kino	9.5 & 16/sil./150	Oct. 1935	
OIL SYMPHONY	USSR	Azerbaidjan Films	Kino	9.5 & 16/sil./15	Apr. 1935	
PALACE OF WONDERS	USSR	Mezhrabpomfilm	Kino	16/sd./12	Feb. 1939	
PATRIOTS (Alt. title: OUTSKIRTS)	USSR	I. Montagu/ B. Megarry	Kino	16/sd./80	?Nov. 1937	
PEACE AND PLENTY	GB		Kino	16/sd./20	Mar. 1939	ETV, NFA
PEACE OF BRITAIN	GB	Freenat Films	Dofil/Kino	16 & 35/sd./3	Apr. 1936	NFA
THE PEACE PARADE	GB	Pelly and Healey	CWS/LCS	16/sd./12	Oct. 1937	
A PENNY TO SPEND†	GB	FPL	FPL	16/sil./?10	?Oct. 1937	
PEOPLE WHO COUNT	GB	Pelly and Healey	LCS/CWS	16/sd./20	Oct. 1937	NFA
PEOPLE WITH A PURPOSE	G3	RFU	RACS/WFA	16 & 35/sd./26	Oct. 1939	
PEOPLE'S FRONT NEWSREEL	GB	FPL	FPL	9.5/sil./?10	Dec. 1937	NFA
PEOPLE'S SCRAPBOOK 1938	GB	People's Newsreel	People's Newsreel	9.5/sil./6	Jan. 1939	
PEOPLE'S SCRAPBOOK 1939 (Alt. title: SUSSEX 1939)	GB	People's Newsreel	People's Newsreel	9.5/sil./10	Sept. 1939	NFA
PIANO PRODIGIES	USSR	PFI	PFI	35/sd./8	Dec. 1937	NFA

Title	Country	Production	Distribution	Gauge silent/ sound running time	Date (first available through these organisations)	Print location
PLACES AND PEOPLE	USSR		Kino	16/sd./10	Feb. 1939	
POPULAR FRONT FILM NO. 3	GB	?British Film Unit	?Kino	16/sd./40	?Feb. 1939	
POTTER'S CLAY	GB	LCS	CWS/WFA	16/sd./20	May 1939	
PRISONERS	USSR	Mosfilm	Kino	16/sd./?	Apr. 1937	
PRISONERS PROVE INTERVENTION IN SPAIN	GB	PFI	PFI	35/sd./5	May 1938	NFA
RED, RIGHT AND BLOO	GB	Left Book Club/ FPL	FPL/LBC	16/sil./30	Nov. 1937	M
RETURN OF THE NORTH POLE HEROES	USSR		PFI	35/sd./55	1937	
REVOLT OF THE FISHERMEN	GB	WFPL	FPL	16/sil./10	Dec. 1935	M
REVOLT OF THE FISHERMEN	USSR	Mezhrabpomfilm	Kino	16/sd./90	?Oct. 1937	
RHONDDA (Alt. title: RHONDDA DEPRESSION YEARS)	GB	?Kino	Kino	16/sil./12	1936	ETV, NFA
THE RICH BRIDE	USSR	Ukrainfilm	PFI	35/sd./80	1939	
THE RIGHT HONOURABLE GEORGE LANSBURY	GB	PPU	PPU	35/sd./4	1937	NFA, SCFL
THE ROAD TO HELL	GB	Socialist Film Council	SFC	16/sil./?	Aug. 1933	M
THE ROAD TO LIFE	USSR	Mezhrabpomfilm	?Atlas Films/ PFI/ Kino/ ISF	16 & 35/sd./95	1932/1935/ 1936	ETV
RUSSIA 1935	?GB	?FSU	Kino/FSU/ ?PFI	16 & 35/sil./?	Dec. 1935	
RUSSIA 1936	USSR	?FSU	Kino/FSU/ ?PFI	16 & 35/sil./15	1936	
RUSSIA TODAY (Alt. title: ?RUSSIAN NEWSREEL NO. 1)	USSR		?PFI/FSU	35/sil./?	?Jan. 1935	

Title	Country	Production	Distribution	Gauge/sound/length	Date	Archive
RUSSIAN JOURNEY†	GB	FPL	FPL	9.5/sil./?	?1938	
RUSSIAN NEWSREEL NO. 2.	USSR		FSU/Kino	16 & 35/sil./?	Mar. 1936	
SCOTLAND SPEAKS	GB	Scottish Peoples Film Assoc.	SPFA/?Kino	16/sil./?	?Sept. 1938	
SHADOW OF THE MACHINE	Germany	Prometheus	Atlas Films/PFI	35/sil./?	Jan. 1930/1936	
SHADOW OF THE MINE (Alt. title: HUNGER IN WALDENBURG)	Germany	Weltfilm	Atlas Films/Kino/IF	35 & 16/sil./40	1930/Jan., 1935	
SHANGHAI DOCUMENT	USSR/Germany	Soyuzkino/Prometheus	Atlas Films/Kino	35 & 16/sil./30	1930?/Jan. 1936	
SHEEP DIP	GB	Dartington Film Unit	Kino	16/sil./10	?1936	
SHOTS OF THE CLASS WAR	?GB	?Atlas	Atlas	35/sil./?	?1930	
SOAP BUBBLES (Orig. title: SEIFENBLASEN)	France/Germany	S. Dudow	Kino	16/sd./45	Oct. 1937	NFA
SON OF A SOLDIER	USSR	Scyuzfilm	Kino	16/sd./80	?Nov. 1934	
SOVIET FOLK DANCERS	?GB	?Kino/FSU	?Kino	16/sil./?5	Oct. 1935	
SOVIET PARLIAMENT	USSR		Kino	16/sd./30	Feb. 1939	
SOVIET RUSSIA PAST AND PRESENT (Alt. title: FIVE YEAR PLAN)	?GB	?Atlas	?Atlas/?FSU	9.5 & 16 & 35/sil./75	?May 1932	NFA
SOVIET SPORTS	USSR		Kino	16/sd./15	Feb. 1939	
SOVIET SPORTS PARADE	USSR		PFI	35/sd./?	Sept. 1937	
SOVIETS CONQUER THE STRATOSPHERE	USSR	Soyuzkinochronika	Kino/FSU	16/sil./15	?Jan. 1935	
SPAIN 1936–37	GB	FFL	FPL	16/sil./?20	?Oct. 1937	ETV, NFA
SPANISH A.B.C.	GB	PFI	PFI/Kino	16 & 35/sd./20	?June 1938	NFA
SPANISH EARTH	USA	Contemporary Historians	Unity Films/Kino	35 & 16/sd./50	Dec. 1937; July 1938	
SPANISH TRAVAIL (Alt. title: THE SPANISH DANCE)†	GB	FPL	FPL	16/sil./?20	?Jan. 1938	
SPIRIT OF MAY DAY	GB	FPL	FPL	9.5/sil./?10	?July 1937	M
STALIN'S REPORT	USSR		?FSU	35/sd./?	Apr. 1937	
STAY IN STRIKES (Alt. title: THE STRIKES OF JUNE)	France	Ciné-Liberté/CGT	Kino/PFI	16/sil./10	1937	
STOP FASCISM	GB	Kino	Kino	16/sd./3	Apr. 1938	ETV

221

Title	Country	Production	Distribution	Gauge silent/ sound running time	Date (first available through these organisations)	Print location
STOP JAPAN	USA	?Nykino/China Campaign Cttee.	Kino	16/sd./?	?Sept. 1938	
STORM OVER ASIA	USSR	Mezhrabpom-Russ	Atlas Films/ PFI/Kino	9.5 & 16 & 35 /sil./110	1930	
THE STORY OF CZECHOSLOVAKIA	GB	LCS	LCS/WFA	16/sd./?	Apr. 1935	
STRIFE	GB	FPL	FPL	16/sil./?20	Oct. 1939	
SUNSHINE IN SHADOW	Spain	Film Popular	PFI	35/sd./12	?Aug. 1937 / ?July 1938	M / NFA
TENANTS IN REVOLT	GB	British Film Unit	Kino	16/sd./20	?Mar. 1939	
TENANTS ON STRIKE (Alt. title: TENANTS RENT STRIKE)	USA		Kino	16/?sd./?	Jan. 1939	
TESTIMONY ON NON-INTERVENTION	GB	PFI	PFI/?Kino	16 & 35/sd./33	?June 1938	NFA
THEY SHALL NOT PASS	Spain	Spanish Ministry of Public Instruction	PFI/ISF	16 & 35/sd./32	Jan. 1937	
THE THIRTEEN	USSR	Mosfilm	PFI	35/sd./85	1938	
THREE SONGS OF LENIN	USSR	Mezhrabpomfilm	Kino	16/sd./55	Jan. 1936	ETV
TOM MANN AT PIONEERS' CAMP	GB	Kino	Kino/WFPL	16/sil./?10	Dec. 1935	
TORN SHOES	USSR	Mezhrabpom	Kino	16/sd./75	Feb. 1937	
TRANSPORT	GB	WFPL	Kino/WFPL	16/sil./?15	May 1935	
A TRIP TO RUSSIA	GB	WFPL	WFPL/Kino /FSU	16/sil./10, 25	?Aug. 1934	
A TRIP TO RUSSIA	GB	FSU	Kino/?FSU	16/sil./30	?1936	
TURKSIB	USSR	Vostok-Kino	Atlas Films/ Kino	35 & 16/sil./88	1935/?1936	BFI
TWO DAYS	USSR	VUFKU	LWFS (Atlas Films)	35/sil./?70	Nov. 1929	
USSR	USSR	?Intourist	Kino	16/sil./25	1936	
USSR ON THE SCREEN	USSR		Kino/PFI	16 & 35/sd./30	Dec. 1937	

Title	Country	Production	Distribution	Format	Date	Archive
UTOPIA? (Alt. title: TROUBLE IN UTOPIA)	GB	LCS	LCS/CWS	16/sd./22	Mar. 1938	
VITAMINS	GB	Cambridge Film Prods. (Jim Harris/G. Innes)	PFI/Kino	16 & 35/sd./20	1937	NFA
VOICE OF THE PEOPLE	GB	RFU	WFA	16 & 35/sd./20	Oct. 1939	NFA
VOLGA	USSR	?Intourist	Kino	16/sil./15	1936	NFA
WAR IS HELL (Alt. title: NO MAN'S LAND Orig. title: NIEMANNSLAND)	Germany	Brescoe	Kino/Nacec Film Dept.	16/sd./93	Apr. 1936	NFA
THE WAY TO PROSPERITY	USSR	Sovuzkinochronika	Kino	16/sil./30	Jan. 1935	
WE ARE THE ENGLISH	GB	?Kino/London District Communist Party	?FPL/?LDCP	16/sil./8	?Nov. 1936	M
WEMBLEY PAGEANT (Alt. title: TOWARDS TOMORROW)	GB	LCS	LCS/CWS	16/sd./42	Sept. 1938	NFA
WHAT THE NEWSREEL DOES NOT SHOW	GB	Socialist Film Council	SFC	16/sil./?	Aug. 1933	M
WINTER	GB	FPL	FPL/Kino	16/sil./10	?Jan. 1936	M
WORKERS' EDUCATION (Alt. title: EDUCATE AND LIBERATE)	GB	RACS	RACS/WFA	16/sd./15	1939	
WORKERS' EXCERPTS FROM METROPOLIS	GB	(FPL)	FPL	9.5/sil./?10	?Dec. 1937	
WORKERS' FILM ASSOCIATION NEWSREEL NO. 1	GB	WFA	WFA	16/sil./10	1939	
WORKERS' NEWSREEL NO. 1	GB	Kino London Production Group	Kino/WFPL	16/sil./10	Aug. 1934	
WORKERS' NEWSREEL NO. 2	GR	Kino London Production Group	Kino/WFPL	16/sil./15	Oct. 1934	M
WORKERS' NEWSREEL NO. 3 (Alt. title: U.A.B./MASS ACTION BEATS THE U.A.B./FEBRUARY 24)	GB	WFPL	WFPL/Kino	16/sil./15	Mar. 1935	M
WORKERS' NEWSREEL NO. 4	GB	WFPL/Kino	WFPL/Kino	16/sil./15	?Sept. 1935	

Title	Country	Production	Distribution	Gauge silent/ sound running time	Date (first available through these organisations)	Print location
WORKERS' TOPICAL NEWS NO. 1	GB	Atlas Films	Atlas Films	35/sil./5	Mar. 1930	NFA, SCFL
WORKERS' TOPICAL NEWS NO. 2	GB	Atlas Films	Atlas Films	35/sil./12	May 1930	NFA, SCFL
WORKERS' TOPICAL NEWS NO. 3	GB	Atlas Films	Atlas Films	35/sil./?15	Mar. 1931	NFA
THE WORLD TODAY (Alt. title: THE BLACK LEGION)	USA	NYKINO	PFI	35/sd./6	?1937	
YOUTH	USSR		PFI/Kino	16 & 35/sd./25	Apr. 1937	
YOUTH PEACE PILGRIMAGE 1939	GB	?British Film Unit	?Kino	16/sil./9	?Mar. 1939	ETV, NFA

Selective Bibliography

Anthony Aldgate, *Cinema and History: British Newsreels and the Spanish Civil War*, London 1979.

Ralph Bond, *Monopoly: The Future of British Films*, London 1946.

Huntly Carter, *New Spirit in the Cinema*, London 1930.

Forsyth Hardy, *Grierson on Documentary*, rev. ed., London 1979.

Bert Hogenkamp, 'Film and the Workers' Movement in Britain, 1929–39' in *Sight and Sound*, vol. 45, no. 2, Spring 1976.

——'Workers' Newsreels in the 1920s and 1930s' in *Our History*, no. 68, 1978.

Neville Hunnings, *Film Censors and the Law*, London 1967.

F. D. Klingender and Stuart Legg, *Money Behind the Screen*, London 1937.

Alan Lovell and Jim Hillier, *Studies in Documentary*, London 1972.

Rachael Low, *The History of the British Film 1918–1929*, London 1971.

——*The History of the British Film 1929–39—Documentary and Educational Films of the 1930s*, London 1979.

——*The History of the British Film 1929–1939—Films of Comment and Persuasion of the 1930s*, London 1979.

Ivor Montagu, *The Political Censorship of Film*, London 1929.

——*With Eisenstein in Hollywood*, Berlin 1968.

—— *The Youngest Son*, London 1970.

Francis Mulhern, *The Moment of Scrutiny*, London 1979.

Eva Orbanz, *Journey to a Legend and Back: The British Realistic Film*, Berlin 1977.

Paul Rotha, *Documentary Film*, London 1936 (3rd edition, 1952).

——*Documentary Diary*, London 1973.

Ralph Samuel, 'The Workers' Theatre Movement' in *History Workshop*, no. 4, Autumn 1977.

Elizabeth Sussex, *The Rise and Fall of the British Documentary*, London 1975.

Victoria Wegg-Prosser, 'The Archive of the Film and Photo League' in *Sight and Sound*, vol. 46, no. 4, Autumn 1977.

Newspapers   *The New Leader, The Daily Worker, Co-operative News.*

Periodicals   *Kino News, Left News, Left Review, Close Up, Film Art, New Cinema, Cinema Quarterly, World Film News, New Red Stage, The Plebs, Sight and Sound, Today's Cinema, Daily Film Renter, The Cine-Technician, Home Movies and Home Talkies.*

Libraries   British Film Institute, Marx Memorial Library, TUC Library, NCCL Archives, Brynmor Jones Library, University of Hull, Film and Photo League Archive (Metropolis Films), Public Records Office.

Submission to the Parliamentary Under-Secretary of State for Trade on *The Future Of The British Film Industry*, by the Independent Film-makers Association (IFA, July 1978).

Nigel Andrews, 'Soft Landings' in the *Financial Times*, 21 July 1978 (Review of above IFA report).

Seeing in the Dark, a pamphlet on a season of films presented by The Other Cinema at the Institute of Contemporary Arts, January 1979.

Independent Film Workshops in Britain, 1979, edited by Rod Stoneman, IFA 1979.

'The Other Cinema—Screen Memory' by Jane Clarke and Rosie Elliot in *Wedge*, no. 2, Spring 1978.

TV Programme

The Other Cinema, 30 mins., *Open Door* programme for BBC2, first screened December 1977.